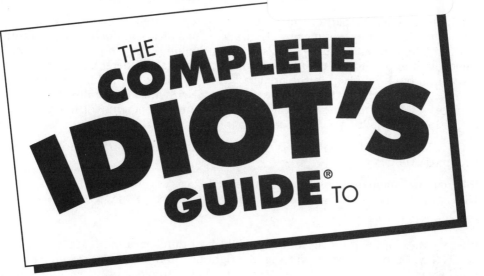

THE COMPLETE IDIOT'S GUIDE® TO

Making Money with Your Hobby

by Barbara Arena of the National Craft Association

alpha books

A member of Penguin Group (USA) Inc.

Publisher
Marie Butler-Knight

Product Manager
Phil Kitchel

Managing Editor
Jennifer Chisholm

Acquisitions Editor
Amy Zavatto

Development Editor
Doris Cross

Senior Production Editor
Christy Wagner

Copy Editor
Krista Hansing

Illustrator
Brian Moyer

Cover Designers
Mike Freeland
Kevin Spear

Book Designers
Scott Cook and Amy Adams of DesignLab

Indexer
Amy Lawrance

Layout/Proofreading
Svetlana Dominguez
Heather Hiatt Miller
Ayanna Lacey
Stacey Richwine-DeRome

Contents at a Glance

Part 1: **So You're Thinking About Making Money with Your Hobby**   **1**

  1 Making Your Secret Dream Come True   3
Encouragement from friends and loved ones is a start. Now you can learn how to turn your dream of starting a business into a reality.

  2 Brave New World: Know What You Do Best and Do It   13
Here's where you assess your skills and experience, and make the best choices for your transition from hobbyist to business owner.

  3 Going for the Goal   23
When you've decided to meet the challenge of starting a new business, learn how to prepare for it.

Part 2: **What Is Your Plan?**   **35**

  4 Make Contact: Doing Your Market Research   37
Finding and defining your potential market niche.

  5 The Real Deal: Setting Yourself Up as a Legitimate Business   49
When it's time to take the plunge and structure your company, you'll find an array of possibilities in this chapter, and ideas on where to get free help.

  6 The Basics of Running Your Ongoing Business   61
Learn what a business plan is, and how to develop one to start and run your business, and allow for its continued growth.

  7 Using a Computer to Lighten Your Business Load   73
Discover just how much time and work a computer will save you in starting and maintaining your business.

  8 Placing Value on Your Intellectual Property   85
What you need to know about copyrights, trademarks, patents, and trade names, and how to avoid the pitfalls of using commercial designs.

Part 3: **Legal and Financial Stuff You Need to Know**   **99**

  9 How It Works: Can I Run My Business from Home?   101
Getting a handle on the basics of starting a home-based business.

  10 Uncle Sam and You   113
Why, when, and how to get a sales tax number, and what you can deduct when the IRS sees your hobby as a legitimate business.

  11 Protect Thyself: Insurance   125
Why you need insurance, what kinds of insurance are available, and what coverage your particular business needs.

12 Keeping Financial Records 135
How to keep financial records that will help you keep track of how your business is doing.

13 Money Matters 147
Figuring start-up costs, and exploring financing, banking, and getting a merchant credit card account.

14 Control Issues: Government Regulation of What You Produce 159
Consumer safety laws, tag and label laws, mail order regulations, and other legislation that may affect the way you do business.

15 Bringing in the Pros 171
Choosing an attorney, accountant, and other professionals who can help you in your business, and determining when to consult them.

Part 4: Gearing Up for Profit **181**

16 Tricks of the Wholesale Buying Trade 183
What you need to know about purchasing wholesale for your business.

17 Setting Up Shop: The World of Manufacturing 195
Getting prepared to produce your products in volume, and learning when you may need outside help.

18 Time Is Money: Understanding the Value of Your Time 203
Find out how to determine what your time is worth in dollars and cents, and how to be paid fairly for your work.

19 Playing the Pricing Game 211
Learn how to set prices for your products and services so that you can make a profit.

Part 5: Where Do I Start Selling My Product Line? **225**

20 Selling at Art and Craft Shows and Fairs 227
Finding the good art and craft shows, and picking the right shows for your products or services.

21 Batteries Not Included: Preparing to Sell at Professionally Promoted Shows 239
Get the inside scoop on how to display and sell your products at shows.

22 Other Sales Outlets 253
Successfully selling through consignment shops, art galleries, and craft malls.

23 Selling Through Private Venues 263
More ways to make money selling your handmade products at studios, workshops, and home parties.

24 Am I Ready for Selling Wholesale? 271
Getting prepared to enter the world of selling wholesale.

25 More Ways to Make Money with Your Hobby   281
    Products are not the only way to make money. Learn about how
    to sell your original designs and patterns, and how to add to
    your income by teaching, and writing articles and how-to book-
    lets.

26 Should I Open a Retail Store?   293
    This chapter brings you face to face with the realities of what it
    takes to open a retail store for consumers.

Part 6: Marketing Strategies That Will Help You Build
Your Business   305

27 The Big Marketing Secret   307
    Learn the key to developing marketing techniques that work for
    your specific type of business.

28 Effective Local Marketing on a Shoestring   315
    Plain, down-to-earth "marketing on a shoestring" tactics that
    you can take to the bank.

29 Put the Internet to Work for You   325
    Now is the time to put the Internet on your sales team. Why you
    can't afford to ignore this exploding market, and how easy it is
    to get started.

30 Staying Ahead of Your Competition   335
    Ways to avoid letting the competition eat up the sales that you
    should have had by keeping on top of what your target cus-
    tomers are thinking and knowing what the experts say about fu-
    ture market trends.

Appendixes

A Resources   347

B Glossary of Art and Craft Industry Terms   385

   Index   393

Contents

**Part 1: So You're Thinking About Making
Money with Your Hobby**   **1**

1 Making Your Secret Dream Come True   **3**

Today's Artisans and Craftspeople 4
  Room at the Top 5
  Handmade Goes Trendy 5
From Hobby to Home Business...6
So You're Making Money—Now What? 8
  Choosing the Right Business 9
  Good Reasons to Start a Business 10
Traits of Successful Entrepreneurs..11
How to Succeed in Your Own Business 12

**2 Brave New World: Know What You Do Best
and Do It**   **13**

Define Your Dream 14
It's *Your* Life 14
  Decisions, Decisions 14
  Be Wise, Don't Compromise 15
  Choose It or Lose It 15
Discover Your Passion 15
One Crafter's Story 16
Tips for Choosing a Business 19
Refining Your Business Focus 20
What's Your Mission? 21

3 Going for the Goal   **23**

Hats, Hats, Hats 24
Do You Have What It Takes?..26
  Strengths and Weaknesses Checklist..26
  Are You Cut Out for Entrepreneurship?..................................28
Focus on What You Want 28
  Tips for Goal-Setting 29
  Your Goals Are on Paper—Now What? 30
  Quantify Your Goals 30
  Short-Term Goal-Setting..31
Be the Master of Your Fate 32
Keep Goals Flexible 33

Part 2: What Is Your Plan? 35

4 Make Contact: Doing Your Market Research 37

What Is Market Research? 37
How Market Research Helps *38*
What Market Research Can Tell You *39*
Market Research Types, Methods, and Techniques 40
Secondary Research *40*
Primary Research *42*
Getting Started on Market Research 45

5 The Real Deal: Setting Yourself Up as a Legitimate Business 49

Choosing the Legal Form of Your Business 50
Sole Proprietorship 50
Partnership *51*
Corporation 52
Corporation vs. Limited Liability Company (LLC) *52*
Why Go the Corporation or LLC Route? *53*
Forming a Corporation 53
Deciding Where to Incorporate *54*
Choosing Your Corporate Tax Structure *54*
Selecting a Corporate Name 55
Trademark Implications *55*
Getting a U.S. Employer Identification
Number (EIN) 56
Do I Need a Corporate Kit? *56*
IRS Information 57
State Regulations and Fees 57
Registered Agents *57*
State Corporation Fees *57*
What's an Offshore Company? 58

6 The Basics of Running Your Ongoing Business 61

A Typical Business Plan Outline 62
How Do I *Do* This? 63
The Beginning *63*
The Middle *64*
The End *68*
More Suggestions and Strategies 70
Determining How Much Start-Up Capital You'll Need *70*
Pricing and Sales *70*
Advertising and Public Relations *71*

**7 Using a Computer to Lighten Your
   Business Load**   **73**

If You're Buying a Computer 74
Computer Software 75
   Business Software Suites *75*
   Selecting Accounting Software Packages *76*
   Image-Editing and Design Software *77*
Use Your Computer for Improving Communications 78
Use Your Computer for Business Research 80
   How Search Engines Work *80*
   Some Popular Search Engines *81*
Use Your Computer for Market Research 81
Use Your Computer for Marketing 82
Use Your Computer to Make Money with
   Your Hobby 82

8 Placing Value on Your Intellectual Property   **85**

What Intellectual Property Means for You 86
Trade Name Registration 87
   Corporate Names *87*
   Trade Names *87*
Copyrights 88
   What's Covered by Copyright Law? *88*
   Proof of Ownership *89*
   Owners' Rights *89*
   Registering Your Work *89*
   Notice of Copyright *90*
Trademarks...91
   Trademark Criteria *91*
   Trademark Searches *91*
   Registration *91*
Patents 92
Industrial Design Registration...92
Plant Breeders' Rights 93
   Obtaining Protection *93*
   Specific Protections *93*
How Important Is Registering Intellectual Property? 94
Protecting Your Rights and the Rights of Others 94
Tips on Infringement 95
Making Competitive Products and Product Lines 96

Part 3: Legal and Financial Stuff You Need to Know   **99**

9 How It Works: Can I Run My Business from Home?   **101**

The Zoning Laws 102
  Dealing with Local Building and Zoning Officials *102*
  The Decision Is Not Necessarily Final *103*
  Certificate of Occupancy *104*
  Be Prepared for Obstacles *104*
Building Codes 105
Permits and Licenses 105
Government Regulations and Your Business 107
  What's the Worst That Could Happen? *107*
  Check Your State Business Licenses *108*
Protect Your Safety 108
  Occupational Safety and Health Act Rules and
    Regulations *109*
  OSHA's Small Business Safety Management Series *110*
Home Business Boom! 110

10 Uncle Sam and You   **113**

The Sales Tax Number Plays a Dual Role 114
Sales Tax Tips 115
The Deal on Business Deductions 116
  Hobby or Business?—the IRS View *116*
  Avoiding Restrictions on Your Hobby's
    Deductible Expenses *117*
  What Is Deductible? *117*
  The Cost of Goods Sold *118*
  Capital Expenses *118*
  Personal Expenses *119*
Business Use of Your Home 119
  Home-Office Storage Areas *119*
Business Deductions 120
  Business Use of a Vehicle *120*
  Business Equipment *121*
  Entertainment Expenses *121*
  Membership Dues *122*
  Write-Offs for Home Phones *122*
  Business Trip Meals *123*
Keeping Records 124

11   Protect Thyself: Insurance   125

Why You Need Insurance 126
Cause-of-Loss Insurance 126
Business Income Insurance 127
Workers' Compensation and Employers' Liability 128
Liability Insurance..128
   Comprehensive General Liability *129*
   Products Liability..*130*
Business Owner's Policy (BOP) 131
Health Insurance: Key Decision Factors
   for Small Business 132
   Managed Care *132*
   Fee-for-Service Plans, or Indemnity Plans *132*
   Special Provisions for Small Business *133*

12   Keeping Financial Records   135

Accounting 101 136
Setting Up an Accounting System 136
Inventory 138
   Tracking Your Inventory *138*
   The Importance of Inventory Control *138*
Payroll Accounting 139
Income and Expenses: Profit and Loss 139
Monitoring Three Key Financial Statements 140
Banking Concerns 141
   Shopping for a Checking Account *142*
   The Ins and Outs of Business Banking *143*
   When a Customer's Check Bounces *144*
Accepting Credit Card Payment 145

13   Money Matters   147

Researching Start-Up Costs 148
Start-Up and Operating Budgets 149
   Start-Up Budget *149*
   Operating Budget...*150*
Tips on Reducing Your Business Costs 151
Where to Find the Money You Need 151
Your Guide to E-Commerce 152
   E-Commerce Definitions *153*
   Merchant Accounts *154*
   Facts About Accepting Credit Cards *155*
   Understanding Merchant Account Costs *156*
   Other Associated Expenses *157*

**14 Control Issues: Government Regulation
of What You Produce**   **159**

The Consumer Product Safety Act 160
   Suggested Safety Guidelines for Making Toys *160*
   Paints and Surface Coatings *161*
   Lead Testing for Food or Drink Containers *161*
Labels for Textiles, Fabrics, Fibers, and Yarn
   or Wool Products..161
   Content Labeling Law *162*
   Care Labeling Law..*162*
   Wool Content Label Law *162*
   State Bedding and Upholstered Furniture Laws *163*
   The Flammable Fabrics Act *163*
   Other Products That May Require Labeling *164*
   Making the Required Labels *164*
Food and the Gift Basket Industry 165
Commercial Use Issues 165
   Commercial Use of Designer Fabrics and Logos *166*
   Celebrity Rights Act *166*
Personal Care Products and Herbal Remedies
   (or Aromatherapy)...167
   Sanitary Production of Cosmetics *167*
   Soap Labeling *167*
   Herbal Remedies: Aromatherapy *168*
Food Products for Resale or Catering 168
The Federal Trade Commission and Mail Orders 169
The Value of Disclaimers...170

15 Bringing in the Pros   **171**

Finding the Professionals You Need 171
Selecting an Attorney 172
   Finding Attorneys to Consider *172*
   Questions to Ask Attorneys You're Considering............................*173*
   Factors to Consider *173*
   When to Call in an Attorney *174*
   How Much Will It Cost? *175*
Working with Your Attorney..176
   Attorney-Client Privilege *176*
   Tips on Cutting Attorneys' Fees *177*
Selecting the Right Accounting Services..................................177
   What Accounting Services Are Available?.....................................*178*
   Cutting Accounting Costs...*179*

Part 4: Gearing Up for Profit   181

16 Tricks of the Wholesale Buying Trade   183

Wholesale Buying 184
  Qualifying to Buy Wholesale *184*
  Ordering Catalogs *184*
  Buying Supplies *185*
Wholesale Suppliers 186
  Supplier Preference Checklist *187*
  Finding Wholesale Sources *188*
  Getting Help from Trade Associations *191*
Shopping a Trade Show...192

17 Setting Up Shop: The World of Manufacturing   195

Your Work Area: Focus on Efficiency 195
Planning Your Work Space 196
Manufacturing Tips 198
Open-to-Buy: A Business Buying Plan 200
  Structuring Your Open-to-Buy Plan....................................*201*
  The Bottom Line of Buying *201*

18 Time Is Money: Understanding the Value of
Your Time   203

How Much Are You Worth Per Hour?.....................................203
Your Product's *Real* Cost and Pricing 205
What to Charge for Freelance Work 206
  Research Tips...*207*
  Online Resources *207*
Maximizing Your Time 207
Service Businesses: The Need to Please 209

19 Playing the Pricing Game   211

Pricing Strategies 211
Pricing Policy...213
Unit Cost Per Item..214
Costing Terms 215
  Direct Costs..*215*
  Indirect Costs = Overhead *215*
Determining Costs...216
Market-Based Pricing..217
Product Pricing Formulas 218
Retail Pricing 220
Deceptive Pricing..221
  Price Comparisons *221*
  Free Offers *222*

Part 5: Where Do I Start Selling My Product Line?   **225**

20 Selling at Art and Craft Shows and Fairs   **227**

Choosing the Right Art and Craft Show...................................227
   Bazaars/Flea Markets...228
   Festivals and Fairs..229
   Art and Craft Shows 229
Selling at Art and Craft Shows 230
Dealing with Show Applications...231
   Deadlines 233
   Photos and Slides..233
   The Application 234
   Show Fees 234
   Show Calendar 234
Getting Started Selling at Shows..234
How Do I Find Art and Craft Shows? 235

21 Batteries Not Included: Preparing to Sell at Professionally Promoted Shows   **239**

Display with Pizzazz 239
   Visual Appeal 240
   Lighting..240
   Sound 240
   Color Basics 240
   Layout Concepts 241
   Signs 241
   Motion 242
   Aroma..242
   Table Covers 243
   Promotion 243
   Plan Your Booth 243
   Basics to Bear in Mind..244
   Where to Get Display Stuff 244
Getting Organized: Craft Show Checklist...............................245
Surviving the Show 247
   Canopies for Outdoor Show Survival 248
   Show Travel Safety..248
   Safety in Your Vehicle 249
The Exhibitors' Golden Rule...250

22 Other Sales Outlets   **253**

Selling in Craft Malls...253
   Craft Mall Benefits 255
   Choosing a Craft Mall 255

The Contracts *256*
How to Be Successful in a Craft Mall *256*
Monitoring Your Booth Space *257*
Keep Good Records..*257*
Plan Properly *258*
Be Optimistic..*258*
Craft Mall Research *259*
Selling on Consignment *260*

23 Selling Through Private Venues   263

Home Shows and Seasonal Boutiques *263*
Artisans' Open House or Studio Tour *264*
Planning a Group Event *265*
Make-It/Take-It Craft Parties or Classes *268*
Follow-Up Pays *269*

24 Am I Ready for Selling Wholesale?   271

Timing Is Everything..*271*
Trade Show Marketing..*272*
Wholesale Biz Tips...*273*
Selling Terms *274*
Minimum Order Amounts *275*
Shipping Charges *275*
Scheduling Order Shipments.............................*276*
Using a Rep *276*
Selling Direct *277*
The Mail Approach *278*

25 More Ways to Make Money with Your Hobby   281

Publishing Your Designs....................................*281*
Licensing a New Line..*283*
Freelance Designing for the Consumer Craft Market *283*
The All Rights/Electronic Rights Issue................*286*
Making Money Selling How-To Information *288*
A Dozen Mistakes That You Don't Want to Make *288*

26 Should I Open a Retail Store?   293

The Store *293*
The Margin *294*
Inventory Turns *294*
Technology Is the Answer..................................*295*
Location, Location, Location *296*
The Sales Team *296*

Why Retail Arts and Crafts Products?..297
  Can Retail Be Profitable? 298
Researching the Product Mix 299
Store Layout and Design 300
  How Color Affects Your Displays 300
  Arranging Merchandise 301
  Store Traffic Flow 301
Advertising and Promotion 301
  Offer Classes and Training...302
  Targeted Promotions 302
  Staying on Top...302
  Attend Trade Shows 302
Retail Resources 303

**Part 6: Marketing Strategies That Will Help
         You Build Your Business   305**

27 The Big Marketing Secret   307
Getting Attention 308
Your Silent Sales Partners 308
How to Reach Your Target Market 311
Believe in Yourself 313

28 Effective Local Marketing on a Shoestring   315
Don't Overlook Opportunities 315
The Business-Builder Marketing Approach...............................317
  Product Originality 318
  Increased Perceived Value..319
  Reach Out 320
  Ad Copy and Sales Brochures...322
The Four Marketing Keywords 322
  The Plan 322
  The Content 323
  The Patience 323
  The Perseverance 323

29 Put the Internet to Work for You   325
Web Site Start-Up...325
Web Site Marketing 328
  Keeping Visitors at Your Site 329
  Why People Don't Buy...330
Domain Name Game..331
E-Mail Rules 332

30 Staying Ahead of Your Competition   **335**

Is Your Comfort Zone a Rut?......................................335
Keep Creative Thinking Alive 336
  Brainstorming 337
  Your Competitive Edge 338
  The Customer Service Edge................................339
Plan for Profits...340
What Are Fads and Trends?....................................341
  What's the Difference Between a Fad and a Trend? 341
  The Color Story and Social Trends 342
  Designing Trends Forecast 343
Product Life Cycle 343
The Challenge of Change 344
  Expect Change..344
  Take Defensive Action in Advance: Diversify 345
  Look for Opportunity Hidden in Change..................345

Appendixes

  A Resources   **347**

  B Glossary of Art and Craft Industry Terms   **385**

  Index   **393**

Foreword

One advantage of working for a large company is that you have the support of a wide variety of professionals in everything from accounting, insurance, sales, marketing, and research and development to contracts and other legal matters. You also have access to resources such as training and motivational seminars. But when you venture out on your own, *you* are the whole company; you must do all these jobs. When you start your own business, you'll work harder than you have ever done before, but when you're doing something you love, that hard work seems easier, and it's so much more rewarding.

The great thing about a business in the art and craft industry is the opportunity to start small—and with very limited resources. Instead of renting a store, you can rent space in a craft mall or set up a booth for the weekend at an art and craft show. You probably already have many of the tools and supplies you need to get started and plenty of opportunities to test your products and fine-tune your business ideas before you quit your "paying job" or invest large amounts of money.

Having jumped from successful careers with very large companies directly into starting our own businesses, my wife, Mary, and I can speak firsthand about the value of this book. Barbara Arena has managed to combine a wealth of information and resources with advice from a vast array of industry professionals—an extremely valuable combination for any small business owner. I know we'll be using *The Complete Idiot's Guide to Making Money with Your Hobby* extensively to strengthen some of our own weak areas—even after nearly 10 years in business!

Keep investing in yourself and your business by continuing your quest for knowledge. The time you invest in learning how to set up your business properly will reward you many times over. But don't try to learn everything that you might ever need to know at once: Get started. Start small, and keep it simple. Get an overview of how to make money with your hobby from the sections at the end of each chapter in this book called "The Least You Need to Know." You can go back for more information later!

When we started our business almost 10 years ago, our plan was to produce a bi-monthly magazine that would tell the general public about craft fairs in the Appalachian area (we defined this as a 150-mile radius around Knoxville, Tennessee). After six months, we had learned that the people buying our magazine were the artists, crafters, and food vendors who exhibited at shows, rather than the general public who might like to visit them. We changed our focus and went to producing a quarterly, and then a semi-annual publication that covered 12 months of shows in 10 southeastern states. We continued to build and refine our directory until, five years after our initial publication, we were producing just one book for the whole year that covered over 3,000 shows across the entire country. This greatly enhanced our retail sales and advertising revenue. We continue to refine and improve each annual edition. Our plans have been continually updated, and our product has changed drastically, but we are still journeying toward the same goals.

Set goals for your business and make a plan for accomplishing them. Then expect to continually revise your goals and adjust your plans as you gain experience. Your plans will be a roadmap that will keep you from getting lost when you encounter road-blocks and are forced to take detours. Believe me, you *will* encounter many obstacles during your journey!

Follow your dreams and make them a reality! Reading this book is a great first step. It offers you the advice of countless professionals and access to the many resources available to help turn your dreams into a profitable business.

Phillip L. Reed
Publisher, *The ABC Art & Craft Event Directory,* www.TheABCDirectory.com

Phillip Reed and his wife, Mary, left careers with large companies with the goal of starting their own business. Their pastime of attending local art and craft events led them to start what has become the fastest-growing national art and craft event direc-tory on the market. Phillip and Mary both had extensive experience in sales and mar-keting work for large companies. They wanted to start a business that would allow them to use their talents and experience to help other people who were self-employed or who were interested in starting their own business. They also wanted their business to give them the opportunity to work from home and to travel with their son Evans. And finally, they wanted to have the time and freedom to homeschool their son. Their current publication represents an evolution of ideas and work that began nearly 10 years ago. Their experiences are a testimony to the many joys and rewards of turn-ing your talents and passions into a business.

Introduction

Because you're reading this, I feel that I already know a little about you. First, you're wondering whether it's possible to make money with your hobby. Second, you probably feel that you can develop a product or service that's different from what's out there, and you probably believe that you can do it more creatively. Third, you probably want something better out of life than what you already have, so you're looking for some experienced advice to help you succeed in achieving your dream of making money at something that you enjoy doing. How do I know all this? Because I work with people just like you every day at the National Craft Association. The signs are easy to recognize; we see them in most of the small business owners that we have the pleasure of dealing with regularly.

Most of the artisans that we know based the businesses they started on skills that they developed while enjoying their art or craft as a hobby. Like you, when they decided to take the next step of really trying to make money with their hobby, they immediately sought out some professional business start-up advice. Congratulations—now that you have this book in your hands, you've taken the first big step toward turning your dream into a reality.

New entrepreneurs often have no idea how to launch a new business. We at the National Craft Association (NCA) are familiar with the potential pitfalls of this industry, and in this book, we identify the issues and challenges that you can expect to face and show you how to deal with them. Not everyone succeeds in their own business, but those who do are the ones who have taken the time to discover what they need to know to make their new ventures a success. In this book, we guide you step by step through all the phases of starting and running your own business. Plus, you'll benefit from the real-world experiences of other small business owners who have moved forward into making money with their hobbies.

We've learned a lot of lessons along the way that we hope to pass on to you. Business is usually a lot more complicated than any of us initially realizes. It helps to know you're not alone in your fears, desires, and dreams, and that people who have worked in the industry for years will share with you their inside information about how it works. Their tips, resources, and information will get you pointed in the right direction.

I know there's nothing more exciting than seeing your idea become a thriving reality, so let's get started on discovering how you can make money with your hobby.

How to Use This Book

This book is divided into six parts. The sequence is designed to guide you step by step along the path to turning your hobby into a into a successful ongoing business venture.

In **Part 1, "So, You're Thinking About Making Money with Your Hobby,"** you're asked to examine your motivations and decide if you're ready to make your dream of opening a business a reality. What skills do you already have that you can use in your business? What skills will you need to acquire, if any? What product or service do you want to offer? This part helps you answer these questions and decide if you're ready to go forward with your plans. It prepares you for meeting the challenge of starting a business, and helps you create a plan so you take the next step.

Part 2, "What Is Your Plan?" presents the guidelines that will help you create a structure for your business. You can learn about the legal business structures you can choose from, how to develop a business plan that ensures your ongoing success, and the ways that a computer can help you in both starting and running your business. Finally, it guides you through ways to protect your intellectual property rights and avoid infringements on the rights of other artisans.

Part 3, "Legal and Financial Stuff You Need to Know," gives you the legal and financial aspects of starting and running a business in user-friendly terms to help you make the transition from enjoying a hobby to starting a home-based business. You can learn what financial records you should keep, how to calculate start-up costs, and how to go about choosing financing, the right banking institutions and accounts, and appropriate business insurance and levels of coverage. Also explored are laws that may affect your business and the decisions for which you may need the advice of professionals.

Part 4, "Gearing Up for Profit," is the part you've been waiting for—how to make some money! Profits don't just happen; they take planning and business know-how. Making a profit starts with knowing how to buy your supplies wholesale and being prepared to produce your products in volume. We show you how to value your time so that you can make the money you deserve for your work. Then, we cover the various ways to price your products or services. After all, just covering your expenses isn't enough; the goal is to make a profit and build in a plan for increasing future profits. This part show you what steps to take to make it all possible.

Part 5, "Where Do I Start Selling My Product Line?": To make a profit, you need to know where and how to sell your product or service. You need a plan of action. In this part we introduce you to the many ways available to sell and market your work, such as art and craft shows, consignment shops, art galleries, craft malls, private venues, boutiques, and wholesaling. You also get an overview of what it takes to open a retail store, how to market service businesses, and ways to extend your craft to make money selling your designs, writing how-to booklets, and so on. This part is exciting to read because it's full of advice from entrepreneurs like you who share tips and experiences that will help you along your path to business success.

Part 6, "Marketing Strategies That Will Help You Build Your Business," fine-tunes what you need to know to keep your business growing. Building a business happens one step at a time. Marketing works that way; the more you expand your efforts, the more opportunities you'll have to build your profits. In this part we prepare you for running a growth-structured business using marketing tactics that you can take to the bank. There's also a chapter on how to put the Internet to work for you, and a final chapter that's full of advice on how you can remain competitive by selling the right product or service at the right time and remaining flexible and responding to future trends.

Extras

As part of our guidance in helping you achieve your dream of making money with your hobby, we provide extra information, advice, and resources in the special sidebar boxes. These valuable additions to the text will alert you to useful tips, resources, cautions, and words of wisdom to speed you on your way.

Trade Terms

Industry and business terms that you'll encounter along the way are defined in these boxes.

Crafter Alert

Here's where to look for warnings about potential problems and useful tips on avoiding mistakes.

Pointers

These boxes give you shortcuts to useful information and helpful advice on making business decisions.

Artisan's Corner

In these boxes, you'll find perspectives, concepts, and overviews that you'll want to consider as you follow your path to making money with your hobby.

How to Use Our Resources Appendix

But did we stop with "Extras"? No way. We have more in store for you—all the business resources that you want—in Appendix A, "Resources," which is full of inside information on resources that you'll need to keep you ahead of the competition. You'll find trade associations, books, trade magazines, and Web sites that will provide you with a wealth of key contacts and information. Then, to top it off, we give you the wholesale sources that you need to locate supplies, equipment, tools or fixtures, and display materials for running your business. Yes—more sources on top of what we provided in so many of the chapters. This appendix will save you the time and money of countless hours of research.

In Appendix B, "Glossary of Art and Craft Industry Terms," you'll find a handy reference tool. So, don't waste any more time—get comfortable and start reading up on how to make money with your hobby. Remember, nothing will happen until you take some action.

Acknowledgments

We would like to acknowledge and thank the numerous people who contributed to this book. Their contributions have made this book more than it would have been without their expertise, vision, experiences, and encouragement to help you discover how to make money with your hobby:

Barbara Brabec, of Barbara Brabec Productions, an author and nationally known authority on home-based business (www.BarbaraBrabec.com); Betty Chypre, metalsmith, and editor of the periodical *Choices for Craftsmen and Artists* (www.smartfrogs.com); Cindy Testerink, of Testerink Studio, a polymer clay artisan (www.testerinkstudio.com) and (www.fairydomes.net); Connie Calloway, a Society of Craft Designers (SCD) designer; author and instructor; Frank Chandler, director and professor at the Faculty of Pharmacy at Dalhousie University; Sharion Cox; Christine Dickey, Crafters Gateway licensed pattern designer; Sue Hannah, of the Color Marketing Group, and co-chair of the Consumer Color Directions Committee in Alexandria, Virginia; Penny Durnim, of Penelope's Quilt Closet, a quilt artisan and painter (www.quiltcloset.com); Alicia Ellis, a professional artisan; Mark Fitzgerald, President of Sales Training Institute, Inc., a professional speaker and trainer (www.saleskills.com); Susan Grant, of Internet Fraud Watch (www.fraud.org); Debbie Gragg, of Gragg Enterprises, a wholesaler of handcrafted giftware and decorative accents (www.homebizprofits.com); Cristiana Kinzle, owner of Cristiana Crafts, a professional crafter (www.ajoytosew.com); Linnea J. Kilgren, of California, a professional artisan; Angela M. Leisner, of Home Office Connection, which provides professional office support services for businesses and individuals; Arles Mitchell, of N2 Crafts, a ceramics artisan and decorative painter (www.intocrafts.com); Diane Morgan, of Morgan Mailboxes & More, a decorative painter and machine knit designer (www.dianemorgan.com); Kevin O'Connor, Director of Craft Operations at Peddler's Village Craft Mall (www.peddlersmall.com);

Nancy Olson, contract in-house designer for Delta Technical Coatings in Whittier, California; Beverly Petty, of Design by PettyKash, an embroidery designer (www.craftassoc.com/pettyk.html); Mary Reed, editor of *The ABC Art & Craft Event Directory* (www.TheABCDirectory.com); Phil Reed, publisher of *The ABC Art & Craft Event Directory,* author and speaker in the arts and crafts industry; Torrie Richards, of Gifts of Nature, a professional crafter; Pat Sorbini, of Simplesong Studio, a professional crafter; Michael Smith, of Rubric Co. Director of Product Marketing (www.rubic.co.uk/about.htm); Carolyn Spray, of CSpray & Associates, a professional sales rep for handcrafted work; Evelyn Villegas, owner of Crystal Star*Works, featuring MagicGems "Intentional Jewelry," a professional crafter; Michael Vertolli, a member of the federal task force Advisory Panel on Herbal Remedies; Susan West, of SunShine Glass Works, a stained glass artisan (www.sunshineglassworks.com); Beverly Williams, of Beverly Ann Pottery Works, a potter and design artist.

I want to thank my family for their patience and support during the time it took me to complete my work on this book. And I especially want to thank you, the reader, for allowing me the opportunity to share with you the enthusiasm and satisfaction I've had the privilege of experiencing during the many years that I've worked in the arts and crafts field. My wish for you is that you have in your new venture as rewarding an experience and as much personal growth as I have had.

Special Thanks to the National Craft Association Staff

The Complete Idiot's Guide to Making Money with Your Hobby was a collective effort in which I was engaged with the NCA staff. Ann Barber worked tirelessly to research, compile, edit, and provide the support documentation necessary to ensure that this book gives you everything you need to know about making money with your hobby. Angie Leisner worked along with us to provide the technical support and editing required to present you with all of the concepts, resources, and know-how you'll need to start and run a successful business.

Trademarks

Part 1

So You're Thinking About Making Money with Your Hobby

We start off by asking you to thoroughly examine yourself, your motivations, and your personal situation. Are you ready to make your dream of opening a business a reality? What should you consider? What skills do you already have that will benefit you? What skills will you need to acquire, if any? What product or service do you want to offer? This part helps you answer these questions and determine whether you're ready to go forward with your plans to make money with your hobby. It will prepare you for meeting the challenge of starting a business and tell you just what it takes to be ready to do it.

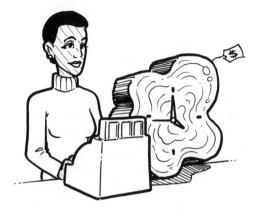

Chapter 1

Making Your Secret Dream Come True

In This Chapter

➤ Deciding if your hobby can be turned into a moneymaker

➤ Making your dream a reality

➤ Identifying your entrepreneurial traits

➤ Learning the keys to success in your own business

We may enjoy many hobbies immensely, but would they earn money? If your favorite pastime is putting together complex puzzles; building model cars, planes, or ships from kits; reading; or playing computer or video games, then you may not have a tangible product to sell. You do, however, have acquired knowledge. This could be used to write how-to booklets, produce how-to videos or CDs, teach a class, develop a newsletter, start a users' club, or be a consultant. Most people immediately think of tangible products to sell, but the possibility of making money exists with almost every hobby. The trick is to find a target market that needs and wants what you have to offer.

So, you want to start a business—but what kind, and how? One of the most common questions potential business owners ask is, "What business should I start?"

The answer is always the same:

Start a business that you already know intimately.

The business that you choose should have a solid chance of making a profit, but be sure that it also suits your particular skills and strengths.

Most people know a great deal about their favorite hobby, but turning it into a for-profit business is a special skill that they have to learn. This is perhaps the most critical part of starting and running a new business.

Fortunately, making money with your hobby is more realistic than you may realize. That's right—the most successful new businesses are those started by people who know all about—and enjoy—the craft or hobby that their business is based on.

A hobby is a favorite pursuit or pastime. Couple this with the possibility of earning money at it, and, admit it: Deep down, isn't that your secret dream? In this chapter, we take a look at how starting with what you know gives you the best chance at success.

Today's Artisans and Craftspeople

Artisans are as diverse as the range of handcrafted work they represent, from fine art, to fine crafts, to traditional crafts. Artisans range from hobbyists, or beginners, to seasoned professionals. While many are already in the business of selling their work, others are just discovering how to turn their *hobby* into their own small moneymaking business.

Trade Terms

Artisan is a term used widely to describe a craftsperson or artist skilled in designing, and possibly producing, objects that reflect his or her unique creativity. *Webster's New World Dictionary* (Macmillan USA) defines **hobby** as "something that one likes to do in one's spare time." Almost anything that you like to do in your spare time is considered a hobby.

The artisan or craftsperson of today is a reflection of our heritage. Arts and crafts have been at the very roots of our way of life from colonial times to the present day. Today's artisans, in fact, are carrying on our cultural traditions through the quality craftsmanship passed on to them from generation to generation. Artisans stimulate our creativity and keep alive traditional styles and techniques that would otherwise have disappeared with the advent of mass production. We celebrate and honor artisans for their valuable contribution to our heritage, just as we recognize all of our presidents and first ladies for their contributions to history.

What is important to realize is that in this high-tech, fast-paced world of mass-produced and imported products, appreciation for handcrafted work is alive and well. Consumers tired of seeing identical items in store after store are motivated and excited by discovering the diversity and uniqueness of handcrafted designs. This is evidenced by the growing number of craft shows held nationwide. Baby boomers, now middle-aged, are a growing market for handmade products, and today's youth are discovering the value of handcrafted work as a uniquely personal form of self-expression. The twenty-first-century consumer is supporting the idea that handmade products are at the very core of our nation's culture and way of life.

Room at the Top

The craft movement was propelled into mainstream American acceptance in 1993 when, under the leadership of First Lady Hillary Rodham Clinton, the White House Crafts Collection was established and housed at the National Museum of American Art. "We've tried to elevate the role and visibility of American artisans because there is some very fine work being done," Clinton said in the September 1994 issue of *ARTnews*. "We look at some of the [decorative arts] that were given to the White House as gifts or which were purchased during the nineteenth century—and they were crafts of their time, so I think it's important that we appreciate the artistry of crafts of our time."

Handmade Goes Trendy

Handmade products are not only in demand, they are helping to define popular cultural trends across the country. The following is a brief look at today's trends and lifestyles, and how, in each area, creative artisans have developed hot-selling products to meet consumer demand:

➤ **Preserving our environment.** The back-to-nature movement has enhanced both indoor and outdoor gardening themes for our homes and places of work. Decorative painters, metal crafters, glass designers, ceramic artisans, and woodworkers are selling garden stakes, yard signs, stepping stones, deck and patio decorations, and lawn and garden furniture.

➤ **Using natural personal products.** Makers of soap and toiletries are cashing in with products made of all-natural ingredients.

➤ **Displaying multicultural color and design influences.** Fiber artisans and jewelry makers are branching out into multicultural designs.

➤ **Pursuing leisure activities such as travel, sports, recreation, and hobbies.** Mixed-media artisans are cleverly taking advantage of creating products compatible with the vast range of leisure activities.

➤ **Strengthening the family, relationships, beliefs, sensitivity, and feelings.** Paper artisans are developing stationery lines and greeting cards to feed our sensitivity. Inspirational speakers, teachers, and writers are responding to our thirst for knowledge. This also includes the areas of self-awareness, self-help, and self-improvement.

➤ **Reflecting the nesting, or cocooning, phase.** Americans are seeking relief from their high-pressure, high-tech existence by spending more time at home, and they're personalizing their homes to reflect their individual tastes and choices of comfort. People want what reflects their taste and lifestyle regardless of what the "in fashion" trends are at the time. As a result, producers of home decor and gifts are designing products to decorate or add convenience and functionality to our homes.

➤ **Reflecting the information age, seeking more knowledge.** The powerful home computer has changed the way we do things, from basic schoolwork and home chores to the way we run our businesses. With the growth of the Internet and wireless communications, fads and trends that once took months or years to travel from region to region can now be communicated worldwide in a matter of seconds. The ease and convenience of computers adds to the speed of today's communication of product lines and helps make it possible for artisans to keep in touch with current trends and to respond accordingly.

As you can see, artisans help define trends in popular culture. They are also quick to take advantage of current trends and lifestyles by using their creativity to design and produce products and services that meet consumer demand.

Pointers

One key to business success is: Find a need and fill it. Always be on the lookout for new ways to design or adapt your products to meet the needs and wants of your customer.

From Hobby to Home Business

The advantage that small business has over big business is the ability to react faster to change, fads, and trends. An artisan who spots a trend or style change can immediately design a product to fill the demand. This unique ability to find a need and fill it allows the artisan to get new products to the consumer market and reap the profits quickly.

The art and craft industry is huge, and your possibilities are limited only by the limitations that you place on yourself! Your hobby can become your business. Did you check out the tear card at the front of the book? It gives you some examples of the types of businesses that started as hobbies. Quite an eye opener, isn't it? And I'll bet that you thought of a few more to add when you read the list. The potential for profit has been proven over and over again by artisans who had the vision to put their dreams into action.

If you're like most hobby enthusiasts, you started out in one small corner of a room and gradually spread out until your gear took over the entire room, or even several rooms. See if this doesn't sound familiar.

A crafter, Angela Ross, once told me how she started sewing as a hobby. At first she was using just a portion of the spare bedroom. The sewing machine was in one corner, and the bed became a place to lay out her projects as they progressed to various stages. Then she took over the dining room. The table was a perfect place to cut and modify her patterns, and the chairs worked out great for holding the uncut material. She then used the laundry room wash tub to dye trim material to match her fabrics. The family room had sewing projects that required some hand sewing piled up next to her favorite chair.

Artisan's Corner

"Attitude determines your altitude" (attributed to Harry F. Banks). To pursue your dream, you must have a positive attitude and the willingness to commit to what it takes to make it happen.

Little by little, her hobby was taking over her house. She enjoyed sewing so much that she kept finding more and more projects to work on. Everyone around her encouraged her and told her that her work was really good. They even persuaded her to sell it. Soon she wasn't just making things for her own use; her family, friends, and neighbors were asking her to make things for them, and they wanted to pay her. At first, she thought of the money that she was making as extra cash to buy more sewing materials and equipment, but it soon became pretty clear to her that she had gone past the hobby stage and had the beginnings of a small business.

Sound familiar? We hear this story over and over again, no matter what the particular hobby is. A man who started out making wooden toys for his grandchildren ended up doing it as a business. A mother-daughter team decided to make candles as Christmas gifts and ended up with a full-time home-based candle-making business.

Once you start to sell your work casually to people you know and gain their positive feedback, you're usually hooked. Most people never really appreciate the work that they do until they realize that other people not only admire it, but are willing to pay real cash for it.

Many crafters have told me that they weren't in business, that they were selling only to acquaintances and taking their work to a couple of church or school functions a year. They said they were using the cash they made to purchase more materials, or that they had to sell some of what they produced so that it didn't take over their entire living space. It's been no surprise to me that some of the same crafters made the transition from being enthusiastic hobbyists to running successful small businesses.

So You're Making Money—Now What?

Once you start getting paid for your finished projects, your hobby isn't just a hobby anymore; it's a business, and it's time to wake up and start thinking like a businessperson.

➤ Are you buying your materials and still paying retail prices?

➤ Could you sell more if you kept track of trends, styles, and popular colors?

➤ Could you make more items if your work area was organized or you streamlined your production?

In most cases, the answer is yes!

Crafter Alert

Once you start receiving money for your work, it is no longer a hobby. It is a business. The IRS's definition is fairly broad. Basically, any activity engaged in to make a profit counts as a business. Not surprisingly, you're not allowed to deduct the expenses of your favorite activities; you *are* allowed to deduct the expenses of a legitimate, profit-motivated business. If you're audited, you'll have to prove to the IRS that your hobby is in fact a legitimate business.

As you progress through this book, you'll discover just how to start and operate your own business. You probably already have the skills to produce your products. Now you need to discover the business side of selling your work. It's the key to your success in making money with your hobby.

More than 5,000 professionally promoted craft shows nationwide, each with about 200 to 300 or more vendors per show, equals about 1,250,000 artisans selling their work—just at craft shows! This does not even account for the thousands of craft shows put on by churches, schools, organizations, clubs, and civic groups. Nor does it cover any of many other ways that artisans sell their arts and crafts.

Before we explore all of these options and give you a step-by-step guide on how to make money with your hobby, let's look at what selling the things that you make really means: It means that you can learn how to set yourself up as a small business, joining forces with the more than 30 million Americans now operating small or home-based businesses.

Most small or home-based businesses were started by people who turned an acquired skill and/or knowledge of a particular field into a profit-making enterprise. A majority of the artisans I know operate their businesses with one to four people. Often, it's a husband-wife team (some with their children also participating) or a group effort made up of individuals working together, each providing their talents to ensure that the business runs smoothly. Whether you start alone or with several people, the first item on the agenda is a clear understanding of what you need to do to set your idea in motion.

Choosing the Right Business

No business exists that is so foolproof that any-one can make a sure profit from it. A skilled, dedicated owner, however, can often make a venture successful when others have failed. Remember, your potential customers will exchange their money for your product only when they're convinced that you're giving them their money's worth; that means you have to know what you're doing. While this point should be obvious, sadly, it isn't. Many people enter businesses that they know little or nothing about.

Artisan's Corner

The *Sunshine Artist Audit Book* has the latest art and craft five-year show reviews, trends, contact data, and short summaries of more than 5,000 events nationwide. Check it out at www.sunshineartist.com/.

Crafter Alert

No business guarantees a profit, but a skilled, dedicated owner can often succeed when others have failed.

Let's say that you've heard that homemade pasta makes lots of money, and you want to start a homemade pasta business. First, you have to learn everything you can about every aspect of pasta-making. If you don't know anything about it, get a job working for a pasta producer, even if you have to work for free. After a few months, you should be an expert in every aspect of pasta making, from mixing eggs and flour to rolling the dough and cutting it into shapes. Ask yourself whether you enjoy the work and whether you're good at it. If your answer is yes, go on to the second important question: Is the business a potential moneymaker? You should have a pretty good answer to that question after working in the field for a few months.

If you're unable to find employment in the pasta business, make a tour of delicatessens and shops that make their own pasta. Interview the owners. To get reliable answers, talk to owners outside the area where you're thinking of locating your business. Small business owners are often quite willing to share their knowledge once they're sure that you won't be competing with them.

There's a management philosophy that says that a good manager doesn't have to know every job—that manager just needs to know how to get other people to do it. That approach may work well in a large corporation, but for a small business, it's dangerously naive. In short, don't start your small venture until you know it from the ground up. Take this literally! If you're opening a wood shop, you should be able to run the saw to cut your own designs and finish the wood—*and* keep a coherent set of books. If you have elegant apparel line and the styles or colors are not on target, you're the one who either improves it in a hurry or goes broke.

If you don't want to or can't pitch in and be willing to wear all the hats necessary to run your business of choice, then you should think twice about going into it. Find a business that you'll enjoy working in, no matter what has to be done to make it run smoothly.

Good Reasons to Start a Business

Examine your goals and expectations before you decide to become your own boss.

"Hope springs eternal in the human breast," English poet and essayist Alexander Pope said several centuries ago. He wasn't describing people expanding or starting a business, but he may as well have been. People who go into business for themselves hope to meet or surpass their goals.

While your particular business idea is sure to be unique, you probably share these aspirations with other budding entrepreneurs:

➤ **Independence.** A search for freedom and independence is the driving force behind many businesspeople. Wasn't it Johnny Paycheck who wrote the song "Take This Job and Shove It"?

➤ **Personal fulfillment.** For many people, owning a business is a genuinely fulfilling experience, one that lifetime employees never know.

➤ **Lifestyle change.** Many people find that while they can make a good income working for other people, they are missing some of life's precious moments. With the flexibility of small business ownership, you can take time to stop and smell the roses.

➤ **Respect.** Successful small business owners are respected, both by themselves and by their peers.

➤ **Money.** You can get rich in a small business, or at least do very well financially. Most entrepreneurs don't get wealthy, but some do. If money is your motivator, admit it.

➤ **Power.** When it's *your* business, you can have your employees do it *your* way. There's a little Ghengis Khan in us all, so don't be surprised if power is one of your goals. If it is, think about how to use this goal in a constructive way.

➤ **Right livelihood.** From natural foods to environmentally safe items to many types of service businesses, a great many *cause-driven* small businesses have done very well by doing good.

Choosing the right business and having the aspirations of an entrepreneur are fundamental for success. Now let's consider the importance of the entrepreneurial spirit.

Traits of Successful Entrepreneurs

The traits associated with entrepreneurial success are found in most of us. The traits I believe most often characterize the successful *entrepreneur* are these:

➤ **The visionary.** The person with the ability to look at the overall picture, to put everything into perspective. These people have the passion, the fuel, and the drive to keep going.

➤ **The planner.** The person who does the organizing, figures out the "how" of doing things, and makes sure that all the steps are in place to accomplish the job.

➤ **The craftsperson.** The person who actually does the details of the job. These are the specialists who are often in love with the creative detail and the process of doing the work.

Each of us has these three traits within us, to varying degrees. A successful business needs a visionary to keep the others motivated and on track, or the planner and the craftsperson will either get lost in the details or lose sight of the overall objective. The visionary often has a hard time coming up with the plan and an even tougher time dealing with minute details. All three of these traits are needed to get the job done, though. Most of us have a tendency to pass in and out of the three traits in phases. You may call them something different, but basically, the phases are these:

Trade Terms

An **entrepreneur** is someone who organizes a business undertaking, assuming the risk for the sake of profit.

➤ **The creative phase.** A time when you want to imagine, create design concepts, and come up with new ideas. You are driven and motivated (the visionary).

➤ **The productive phase.** When you just want to get the job done, to do tasks that don't take a lot of creative thought but that require work and time (the craftsperson).

➤ **The organizational phase.** A time for cleaning up after the solid production phase: organizing files, planning a new strategy, and organizing your time and your life (the planner).

Most of us go through each of these three phases repeatedly for a few weeks at a time. *It's very helpful to recognize which phase you're in so that you can take the best advantage of it.* Don't become frustrated when, for example, you can't be creative during your productive phase.

How to Succeed in Your Own Business

The rest of this book deals with the details of how to make money with your hobby, but it's important to remember that the foundation of running a successful business is to recognize what you do best and focus your work around your talents—that is, what you are truly suited to do best, regardless of your particular entrepreneurial traits. This will make you happy, feed your ability to be motivated, and give you the passion to stay driven. Delegate, or even eliminate, some of the aspects of the work that are outside the realm of what you're best at doing. Doing what you do best gives you the best chance of success.

The Least You Need to Know

➤ Start a business that you already basically know something about and enjoy doing.

➤ Handmade products are in demand because artisans take advantage of current trends and lifestyles.

➤ Almost any hobby can be a moneymaker; first find a need and fill it, and then operate as a for-profit business.

➤ Focusing on your talents is the soundest basis for a successful business venture.

Chapter 2

Brave New World: Know What You Do Best and Do It

In This Chapter

➤ Defining who you are and where you want to go

➤ Understanding the good and the bad aspects of compromise

➤ Choosing your approach to the marketplace

➤ Framing your mission and formulating a plan to achieve it

We all need to know what path we plan to take when we want to get from point A to point B. If you're making a life-changing decision such as going from being a hobbyist to a part- or full-time businessperson, you'll need to take many factors into consideration. In this chapter, we help you explore what you know about yourself and learn how that translates into how you attain your goals.

Every action we take at every moment of every day, and even our inaction, involves making choices. Compromises are inevitable and can be beneficial—a growth experience. But compromising your soul or someone else's happiness to achieve your objective is too great a sacrifice. This chapter helps you define what your passion is, determine how to match your skills to that passion, and learn how to position yourself to accomplish your mission.

Define Your Dream

Of course we're happiest when we work at what we enjoy doing; it's most people's dream. But sometimes it's difficult to define exactly what work we want to do or to evaluate the skills we have and figure out how they can help us turn our dream into a new kind of life. Okay, so you've been thinking for a while about how to make money with your hobby. Well, trust me on this: Until you formulate a plan and start putting that plan into action, nothing is going to happen!

Pointers

To achieve your goals you need to ...

➤ Be clear about your purpose or mission in life.

➤ Live true to that purpose.

➤ Develop a purposeful compatibility in all areas of your life.

If you're thinking of making the move from hobbyist to businessperson, make sure you're ready. Evaluate every factor: your interests, skills, time, money, family situation, and reason for wanting to do it. Once you decide to start a business, it takes personal commitment and dedication to carry out the plan you've set in motion. If you think through all of your options before you act, you'll have a much greater chance of success.

It's *Your* Life

Try to think of life as a journey leading you to your purpose. This journey is all about *you!* What will help you live more passionately every day and achieve your goals? Beneath the degrees, titles, or accomplishments, what is inside you to be discovered? What is your unique and special spark? Is it buried deep? Is it neglected? Or have you just chosen to ignore it? Have you been seeking to please whomever, drowning out the pure longings of *your* heart? Listen to the whispers from your spirit, the voice from deep within. *You* can claim it! It is *your* life! Set your goals, map out your plan, and then you can begin!

Your plan to make the transition from hobbyist to businessperson has to be an extension of you, with your traits and your skills carefully applied to achieve your ultimate goals. Business success doesn't happen overnight, but each small step you take will move you closer to your goal.

Decisions, Decisions

Think for a moment about how many decisions you make every day. Isn't everything a decision? Do you get up as soon as the alarm goes off in the morning, or do you hit the snooze button? Do you wear your blue outfit today, or your green one? Will your day start with a purpose, or will you just go through the motions that are expected of you?

Every action or inaction we take, every moment of every day, involves making choices. What decisions are you making today? What will the combined impact of today's choices be on your tomorrow, your next month, or your next year? Regardless of how insignificant a decision may seem, think about it.

Be Wise, Don't Compromise

True freedom means breaking the codes of convention. Habitual compromise, as a lifestyle, adds nourishment to continued complacency. It lulls people into a catatonic state of passivity.

This is not to say that all compromise is inherently bad. Not at all. In fact, mutual compromise can be very heartening, and even inspiring.

What about your life? If you want to live *your* life, living with a purpose is the bridge that can carry you from inaction to action.

Crafter Alert

It's your choice: Either live the life you were meant to live, or survive in a life based on compromise. What do you really want?

Choose It or Lose It

Starting today, when you're faced with a choice, consider it for an extra second and then take action—action to bring you closer to realizing your ideal life. Theodore Roosevelt said, "In any moment of decision, the best thing you can do is the right thing. The worst thing you can do is nothing." Deciding *not* to take action is like deciding to keep the door locked to your self-created prison. If your heart is racing, if you feel restless, if the feeling stirs you deep inside, the message to you is to make powerful choices. *Take action! Live your life as you were meant to live it!*

Discover Your Passion

The following quiz can help you discover your passion *only* if you take it, so please either take a moment now to grab a pad or notebook and something to write with or bookmark this page and promise yourself that you'll complete this exercise later. It's a look at your whole life history, so it may take you some thinking time to get it done.

Find Your Joy Factor

1. When did you experience the most sustained period of joy? What were you doing then? Where were you? Who were you with? How did it feel?

2. What are your three most favorite things to do? If you had a free day with *no* commitments, where would you be found? What would you be doing, and who would you be doing it with?

3. In what area do you excel? (No modesty allowed here!) Truly, what are you complimented on a lot? It could be anything.

4. What do you most want to be remembered for? If you were designing your epitaph, what would *you* want it to say?

5. If you had a magic wand, what would you change about your life today? How would it look compared to how it looks now? Which aspects of your life are changeable, both short-term and long-term?

Artisan's Corner

Once you discover your true passion and have taken time to understand who you are and where you want to go, you'll be focused on what will work for you. That's when you'll be able to set out in new directions, such as turning your hobby into a business.

6. How does your joy factor overlap with your favorite activities and the areas you excel in? Does doing the things you do well bring *you* joy, or are they really for someone else? Do you see which activities are obvious joy matches and which aren't?

7. What is the first small step you can take to living out your passion as you defined it in question 6? Take some time to really think this one through. Concentrate and focus before you respond.

In your response to question 6, the activities that you thought of as overlapping with your joy factor, those that bring you the most joy are likely to be the things that will bring you into passionate purposeful living.

Now you'll be able to start the next step: building your overall business road map.

One Crafter's Story

Working with the National Craft Association has given me the luxury of being able to interact with many artisans across the country who are involved in building their businesses. The amount of enthusiasm and commitment that they display is incredible. This is the driving force that propels them to achieve the goals they've set. Torrie Richards, owner of Gifts of Nature in Vancouver, Washington, is one of those crafters. She shared with me the thoughts and experiences that went into building her business, and I pass them on to you.

"My entrepreneurial urge began when I was about 14 years old. My mother gave me a candy-making kit that I was just thrilled to try out. Six years later, I was running my own baking company. Being young and inexperienced, I decided that I needed to go back to school because I wasn't sure what I was doing or if it was really what I wanted to do for the rest of my life. What I did know was that I liked the prospect of running my own business. Where I fell short was that I lacked the skills that I needed to proceed to the next step.

"Over the following years, I tried to pay attention to everything going on around me. This skill I attribute to my mother, who was the most observant person I have ever known. She would notice the slightest change in anything. What does this have to do with crafts and starting your own business, you ask? Everything! I learned to watch others' mistakes and devise ways to avoid making similar ones myself. By being observant, I had accumulated a bank of life experience that I applied to starting and running my business. It got me where I am now.

"I started to get involved in crafts during my mid-20s. I found that I enjoyed seeing the results of my work. A few years later I discovered Home and Garden Television (HGTV), and it was all over! I became fixated in front of the television screen, absorbing every craft idea I could find. While most of my friends were spending their money going out on the weekends, I was spending it on crafts. I was amazed at all the unique things people could make. 'I could do that,' I thought. Sometimes I would have trouble falling asleep at night because I would have so many ideas swirling around in my head that I couldn't relax.

"Then one day I pressed some pansies in a book, and I was thrilled with the results. I had no idea what I wanted to do with them, but I knew that they were too pretty to waste. From then on my passion for gardening and crafting grew even stronger. If only I could make something that had to do with both my passions, wouldn't that be an accomplishment! This is where my skills of paying attention to everything came in handy. I remembered an idea I had seen at a craft store, and thought, 'What if I took that idea one step further?' The result was my creation of Gifts of Nature: glass candleholders decorated with pressed pansies from the garden and fall leaves collected during the autumn season. They were so fun to make. Each one was unique in its own way, and I found the results of my work thrilling.

"Looking back, there were definite improvements that my product needed to go through. How could I make them look better? After some experimenting, I finally felt that I was on the right path. I gave some to friends to see what they thought, and the compliments were warm and encouraging. From that point on, I decided to try selling them on consignment at a craft store. The results were mediocre, and soon the store closed down, so I tried another store, and the results were even worse. I still wasn't going to give up. There was another store around the corner from the last one, and within a couple of days I had my products in there. The sales weren't great, but so far it was the best I had done. When the store moved down the street, I was pleased that they asked me to keep supplying them. From that point on, my sales slowly began to grow.

"I wanted to take things one step further, so I decided to do a bazaar, and that's where I really got a boost. The response was tremendous. I sold out of my products before the day was through. Some people would spend up to 20 minutes looking at the candleholders because they couldn't decide which ones to buy. The second year, my sales almost doubled! I opted to do another bazaar, and my sales were equally strong. Now people were beginning to recognize my product. Not too bad for a part-time venture.

Crafter Alert

"You will always face negative challenges, and when you do, the best thing you can do for yourself is to roll with the punches and adapt yourself accordingly. Take the negative energy thrown at you, and turn it into something good."

—Torrie Richards

"I did have many people discourage me along the way, mind you. Sometimes I think people snickered behind my back, thinking I was foolish for believing that I could make my craft a business. But that just made me more determined to make it work and prove them wrong.

"I believe one of the reasons that my sales have been so good is that my enthusiasm for what I do shows in the quality of my work. You can see that I truly enjoy what I'm doing. I feel fortunate to be able to create what I do. Not too many people get to spend their days working at their passions. Though I'm just at the beginning stages of my business, I look forward to continual growth. Some days are hard, but I keep reminding myself of where I want to be, and that seems to get me through the tough times."

The following strategies helped Richards in her business venture and could help anyone wanting to start a business:

➤ **Pay attention to everything!** Do so even if it has nothing to do with anything you think you'd be interested in. This skill will enable you to know the right questions to ask and where to get the information. You'd be surprised how some of that information might help you in the future. Past employment experiences, conversations with people, and so forth are invaluable keys to the success of your future. You'd be amazed at the things you can learn throughout the years just through simple conversations with people, things that you would have never known to ask and that you may have never come across if you had not been paying attention. If you can continually collect and store information in your brain, it can be beneficial in helping you run a business.

➤ **Never be afraid to ask people questions!** No question is dumb—really!

➤ **Be willing to fail.** Recognize your failures and be able to learn from them. Failure is as good as success. It is a stepping-stone toward your goals. It can be a process that will enrich the outcome of your business.

Richards is a shining example of how you can make money with your hobby. She has combined her passion for nature, gardening, and crafting to produce a viable product line. Because she's tuned in to everything around her, she's focused on two of the hottest retail categories—the "back to nature" trend and candles—with her line of candleholders and candle lamps. But most of all, she clung to her passion; she did not let discouragement or adversity cause her to lose her focus. Richards was persistent and true to her mission. This is really what success is all about.

Pointers

Torrie Richards has gone through many of the steps we've explored so far, taking each phase of building her business one step at a time. But most of all, as she says, she believes that one of the reasons for her rising sales is her enthusiasm, which shows in the quality of her work.

Tips for Choosing a Business

You've probably already identified some need in the market that's not being met, or you have a particular product line or service that you feel is right on target for the current marketplace. If so, you're ready to match your skills with those ideas.

You should begin by listing what you enjoy doing, what your hobbies are, which skills you've acquired, what your work experiences have been, and what your plans are for your business. Making such a list right now may seem a little simplistic, but you'll be surprised at how much writing down your ideas will help you crystallize what you want from a small business. This exercise is just a starting point; nothing is carved in stone. As you learn more about the process of making the transition from a hobbyist to a businessperson, you'll evaluate and redefine your thinking until you have a plan that you're comfortable with and confident about.

Compare the list you've just made with your list of what the market wants. Do any obvious matches leap out at you? If not, don't give up.

Eliminate any of the businesses that you don't believe you'll really enjoy owning. As a small business owner, you'll be living, sleeping, and breathing your business—if you don't enjoy it, your chances for success are slim.

On the other hand, be wary of relying too heavily on your list of interests when making your choice. Don't forget that a lot of small business owners also spend time on tasks such as managing, marketing, haggling with suppliers, meeting with a lawyer or accountant, and so on. As a small business owner, you'll have to wear many hats in addition to being responsible for the design and production of your products or services.

Suppose that photography is your passion. If you open a store that sells photographic equipment, you'll have to pay rent, buy inventory, buy fixtures for the store, budget for all the other overhead, and possibly even have to consider hiring support staff. That'll cost you a lot up front, and you won't see any return on investment until you've made sufficient profits to recover your initial investment.

Crafter Alert

Don't get in over your head. If you don't have a lot of money to start with, look for a business in which you get paid up front and don't have a lot of start-up costs. Or, consider starting on a part-time basis until you feel comfortable with taking it to a full-time business. Stay-at-home moms or people getting ready to retire in a few years often elect to start on a part-time basis. The goal is to get the business up and running and then build it into something that you can expand into a full-time operation when you're ready to make that commitment.

On the other hand, if you hire yourself out as a photographer, or if you sell your photography as prints, or perhaps if you use your photos as decoupage for wall decor or to create a stationery line, you can probably operate from home with few up-front costs. So, your return on investment is a lot quicker.

Refining Your Business Focus

You'll have many alternatives to consider and choices to make before you're ready to launch your business. Use the following list to be sure you cover all the bases:

➤ Consider businesses in which you'll have a lot of repeat customers, or create a product line or service that ensures that customers will continue to buy from you.

➤ Be realistic about your time and commitment to the venture, and whether it should be full-time or part-time.

➤ Although you may be thinking about designing decorative or gift-type products, consider functional use as well. Consumers tend to spend more money on products that serve a "useful" purpose while also being decorative so they can justify spending the money on them.

➤ Be realistic about your abilities and the time it will take to secure your market niche. Are you planning to work in *fine arts or crafts,* or *traditional arts and crafts?* Fine arts and crafts often take more time to make and require more training and skill to perfect. Yes, they usually command a higher price. This also means that they require a high-end or specialty market, which means more limited sales. Traditional arts and crafts tend to be more mainstream in price and attract a wider target market.

➤ Avoid competing with discounters, mass merchandisers, or well-established local businesses—it will be just about impossible to rival their prices or range of merchandising. Instead, you'll want to compete in service and differentiate your business.

Trade Terms

Fine arts and crafts are usually defined as completely hand-made, such as pottery, blown glass, paintings, and sculpture. **Traditional crafts** may include some manufactured products to create the finished item.

➤ Service businesses are obviously the easiest and cheapest to start because you don't have to buy a lot of equipment or produce and maintain a tangible inventory. If your goal, however, is to someday sell the business and retire, you should be aware that service businesses are also often the hardest to find buyers for because their primary asset is often you, the owner (unless you've developed the business enough to have a trained staff).

➤ Look at the total picture—not just costs and potential income, but how your decision fits with your lifestyle and family situation. Discuss your plans with those who will also be affected by the decision you make. Enlist their support and input so that as you set out to accomplish your plan, you have their understanding and willingness to see you through the process.

➤ Will this be a family affair or a partnership? If so, then you all have to participate equally in developing your plan together so that everyone is focused and in agreement on the objectives.

What's Your Mission?

Before you can progress in business, you have to have some idea of where you're headed and how you plan to get there. It's called a mission statement, and you need to have one. This is a crucial step in planning your journey.

For instance, if you leave your house determined to find a new outfit for an important upcoming business function, your mission will be to make sure that you find just the right one before you return home. You must also develop a passion for your mission and be willing to stop short of nothing to accomplish what you've determined to do. That means that, not only will you buy that new outfit before you go home, but you'll drive a hundred miles to find just the right one!

You must decide what you hope to accomplish through your business. If you want to be known for providing the best-quality handmade wood products, then that is your mission statement, plain and simple. By making it your mission, you obligate yourself to do exactly that: make every effort to provide the best-quality handmade wood products. Your mission statement also gives you a place to start on a list, if you choose to, of how you plan to accomplish your mission.

Pointers

Develop a product or service unique in design and creativity, something that others can't or don't offer. Create your own market position or niche to serve your target customers.

Write down your mission statement. When you do, you'll be more apt to live by it. Think of it as key to your business success! Find an environment that is right for you to sit down and think. Put together notes and phrases as you capture your thoughts. Then combine your notes into a mission statement that adequately sums up what you want to accomplish.

After you decide what you want to accomplish through your business, determine what you must do to carry it out, propose what you're willing to do, and do it. Keep your mission statement close by, where you'll readily be able to see it when you need to remember why you're doing what you do. Think of it as more than a group of words written on a piece of paper—make it your passion, the driving force that becomes a pathway to your success!

The Least You Need to Know

➤ Before you decide on a business, you must define who you are and what you want to accomplish.

➤ Either live the life you were meant to live or survive in a life based on compromise—the choice is yours.

➤ Your enthusiasm for what you produce or provide makes it more attractive to the consumer.

➤ Before you launch your business, consider every way possible to refine your business focus.

➤ Write a mission statement, keep it nearby, and refer to it whenever you wonder what you're doing and why.

Chapter 3

Going for the Goal

> ### In This Chapter
>
> ➤ Being responsible for a small business
>
> ➤ Identifying your strengths and weaknesses
>
> ➤ Understanding goals and why they're important
>
> ➤ Learning how to set your goals to get results
>
> ➤ Using the power of positive thinking to be a winner

In this chapter, we want you to examine some of the unknowns or variables that you may want to consider in deciding what the direction should be for your new business. Many of us hear the call to ownership of a small business—complete freedom, unlimited opportunity, dreams realized—but of those who answer it, most do not succeed. Why? What separates those who succeed from those who fail? Knowledge of the business, sufficient capital, experience, and a unique idea at the right time are just some of the characteristics of a successful business owner. Although there isn't any way to guarantee that you'll become a successful business owner, you can greatly improve your odds by becoming well prepared for the task.

In the United States, it's estimated that only about 30 percent of all start-ups are still in business after 5 years. The better you prepare yourself and understand the challenges ahead of you, the more likely it is that you'll be one of the survivors.

If all the objections and risks had to be completely removed before we decided to embark on every new project, I doubt if any of us would ever accomplish very much in our lifetime. So, what is the alternative? Research, learn, weigh the results, and then make a calculated, informed decision on how to proceed with your goals.

Hats, Hats, Hats

We've all heard the stories of the corporate executive who moans about being overworked because he or she has to wear two or three hats. Well, most small business owners would give anything if they had to wear *only* two or three hats. If you're going to own a small business, some of the hats you'll be wearing are these:

➤ **Accountant/bookkeeper.** Even if you have an accountant, you'll need to know a little about accounting: which records to keep and how to keep them. See Chapter 12, "Keeping Financial Records."

➤ **Advertising executive.** In addition to having to plan your advertising campaign, you may also write the advertising copy and design your brochures and related sales materials. See Chapter 27, "The Big Marketing Secret."

➤ **Business planner.** As the business owner, you'll inevitably want to make changes, perhaps to expand the business or add a new service or product line. If you want to make a change, it will be your responsibility to do it; you have to plan it and execute it. In making your decisions, you have to consider the outcomes that could result from them. See Chapter 6, "The Basics of Running Your Ongoing Business."

➤ **Buyer.** It will be your responsibility to locate wholesale suppliers for the equipment, supplies, and materials that you'll need to produce your products, offer your services, and run your business. See Chapter 16, "Tricks of the Wholesale Buying Trade."

➤ **Clerk/receptionist/typist/secretary.** Even if you have some clerical help, you will inevitably do some filing, typing, and mailing, as well as some of your telephone answering. At a minimum, you'll have to know how to do it so you can teach your staff how you want it done. See Chapter 12.

➤ **Collector.** If you offer open account terms, when customers don't pay, it will be up to you to collect from them. You'll have to know what you can and can't do when collecting. See Chapter 13, "Money Matters."

➤ **Human resources administrator.** If you have employees, you will be responsible for all human resources functions, including recruiting, hiring, firing, and keeping track of benefits information. You'll be the one filling out all the insurance forms, answering employee questions and complaints, and making the decisions that affect your employees. See Chapter 12.

➤ **Lawyer.** Even if you retain or hire a lawyer, you will have to know a little about the law. If you don't use a lawyer, you'll have to prepare all of your own forms, contracts, and agreements. See Chapter 15, "Bringing in the Pros."

➤ **Manager/supervisor.** The decisions are all yours, and along with that comes the responsibility of dealing with the effects that your decisions have on the success of your business. See Chapter 6.

➤ **Market researcher.** Before you start your business, you'll have to find out who your target customers are and where they're located. You may also have to conduct market research at various times during the course of your business, such as when you're considering introducing a new product or service. See Chapter 4, "Make Contact: Doing Your Market Research."

Pointers

Operating a small business requires pitching in and doing whatever is necessary to get the job done, even if it means that the CEO has to sweep the floor and take out the trash.

➤ **Policymaker.** It will be up to you to establish the policies and procedures for operating your business. See Chapter 13.

➤ **PR person.** Depending upon the type of business you own, you may have to join business groups; attend various breakfasts, lunches, and dinners; and just generally network with anyone who could help your business prosper. See Chapter 28, "Effective Local Marketing on a Shoestring."

➤ **Product developer.** It will be up to you to design your product line and packaging. See Chapter 8, "Placing Value on Your Intellectual Property."

➤ **Product producer.** If you're producing products, you are responsible for the manufacture of your product line or, if you provide a service, the delivery of your service. See Chapter 8.

➤ **Sales/marketing executive.** In addition to having to plan your marketing or advertising campaign, you will have to carry it out. You may have do some preliminary market research, contact potential customers, and make sure that existing customers stay happy. You'll also have to sell your product or service directly. See Chapter 27.

➤ **Tax collector.** If you sell goods at the retail level, you're responsible for collecting and paying the sales tax. If you have employees, you're responsible for payroll taxes. See Chapter 10, "Uncle Sam and You."

➤ **Technology expert.** As a small business owner, you will probably come to depend upon your computer. Unless you have a service contract with a computer technician, you'll have to solve problems, install upgrades, and load software. You'll also have to keep up-to-date on new software and hardware, and the latest changes in computer technology. See Chapter 7, "Using a Computer to Lighten Your Business Load."

➤ **Trade show coordinator.** If you sell at art and craft or trade shows, you'll need to prepare for and attend these events. See Chapter 21, "Batteries Not Included: Preparing to Sell at Professionally Promoted Shows."

Crafter Alert

Not everyone is cut out to be an entrepreneur. It takes a special talent. Before you invest time, energy, money, and a piece of your heart, it's important to do some serious self-analysis.

You may not plan to start a business that will require employees or the subcontracting of any of the preceding responsibilities, but consider that, as your business grows and expands, you may eventually have to wear most of the described hats. You can reduce your business risk by recognizing that you may face many of these responsibilities at some time.

Do You Have What It Takes?

Starting a business is risky, at best, but your chances of making it will be better if you understand the problems that you may encounter and have those problems worked out before you start up. The first question that you need to answer is about you: Do you have what it takes?

Strengths and Weaknesses Checklist

The following are some questions to help you evaluate if you have what it takes to run a small business:

1. Are you a self-starter?
   - ❏ I do things on my own. Nobody has to tell me to get going.
   - ❏ If someone gets me started, I can keep going all right.
   - ❏ Easy does it. I don't put myself out until I have to.

2. How do you feel about other people?
   - ❏ I like people. I can get along with just about anyone.
   - ❏ I have plenty of friends; I don't need anyone else.
   - ❏ Most people irritate me.

3. Can you lead others?

   ❏ When I start something, I can get most people to go along.

   ❏ If someone tells me what we should do, I can give the orders.

   ❏ I let someone else get things moving; then I go along if I feel like it.

4. Can you take responsibility?

   ❏ I like to take charge of things and see them through.

   ❏ I'll take over if I have to, but I'd rather let someone else be responsible.

   ❏ There's always some eager beaver around wanting to show how smart he or she is. I say, go for it.

5. How good an organizer are you?

   ❏ I like to have a plan before I start. I'm usually the one to get things lined up when the group wants to do something.

   ❏ I do all right unless things get too confused; then I quit.

   ❏ I get all set, and then something comes along and presents too many problems, so I just take things as they come.

6. How good a worker are you?

   ❏ I can keep going as long as I need to. I don't mind working hard for something I want.

   ❏ I'll work hard for a while, but when I've had enough, that's it.

   ❏ I can't see that hard work gets you anywhere.

7. Are you comfortable making decisions?

   ❏ I can make up my mind in a hurry if I have to. It usually turns out okay, too.

   ❏ I can if I have plenty of time. If I have to make up my mind fast, later I think that I should have decided the other way.

   ❏ I don't like to be the one to decide things.

8. Can people trust what you say?

   ❏ You bet they can. I don't say things that I don't mean.

   ❏ I try to be on the level most of the time, but sometimes I just say what's easiest.

   ❏ Why bother if the other person doesn't know the difference?

9. Can you stick with it?

   ❏ If I make up my mind to do something, I don't let anything stop me.

   ❏ I usually finish what I start ... if it goes well.

   ❏ If it doesn't go right immediately, I quit. Why beat my brains out?

10. How good is your health?

❑ I never run down!

❑ I have enough energy for most things that I want to do.

❑ I run out of energy sooner than most of my friends.

Now total the checks that you made next to the first answer to each question, then the second answer, and then the third. If most of your checks were next to the first answers, you probably have what it takes to run a business. If not, you're likely to have more trouble than you can handle by yourself. Better find a partner who is strong in areas where you're weak. If many of your checks are next to the third answers, even a good partner may not be able to shore you up.

Are You Cut Out for Entrepreneurship?

Being an entrepreneur takes a special talent. Some owners of small businesses have it, and some don't. The following are some more serious self-analysis questions that will help you assess your entrepreneurial abilities:

➤ Am I prepared to work hard and make sacrifices?

➤ Am I self-disciplined?

➤ Do I have management ability?

➤ Am I experienced enough in this field?

➤ What do I want out of life?

➤ Are my goals realistic and attainable?

Many studies have shown that entrepreneurs are persevering and not easily defeated. They thrive in a challenging environment and have a tremendous need to be in control. They turn diversity into opportunity. They are risk-takers. They welcome responsibility and are willing and able to make decisions.

Moreover, successful entrepreneurs are patient and able to wait out the sometimes-slow beginnings of a business. They are also able to learn from their mistakes, trust their own judgment, and maintain an optimistic outlook. It's obvious: You have to love your work. The key is to identify what you enjoy doing the most and then find a business opportunity that makes use of your skills and interests.

Focus on What You Want

Goals are important because they will affect just about everything you do, from start-up to daily operations, to long-range planning. What do you want from your business? What does "succeeding" mean to you—and if you want to succeed, how will you know it when you get there?

Knowing what you want from your business, your goal, directs all of the other decisions that you'll have to make when you launch it. It will affect which business you choose, how you evaluate your chances for success, and how you determine whether you have the right skills.

How do your goals fit with your reasons for wanting to start a business? Your reasons are often the underlying guides to your goals. Your goals are not just the destinations you're headed toward—they're also the signposts along the way that will keep you on the right road. If you're still a little uncertain about goals and what they could mean to you, think of it this way: Goals won't just determine whether you start a small business; they'll also play a major role in just about every decision you make along the way, from how you structure your business to whether you hire employees, to how you plan to sell and market your products or services. It's not enough just to say, for example, that you want a change from working for someone else. You'll need to develop specific targets by quantifying your goals.

Trade Terms

A **goal** is an end that one strives to attain. Short-term goals can help you achieve those small but important victories. Your short-term goals should be realistic and quickly achievable.

Tips for Goal-Setting

Keep the following tips in mind as you go through the process of defining your goals:

➤ Make sure that the goal you're working for is something that you really want, not just something that sounds good. The important thing to remember here is that your goals must be consistent with your values.

➤ One goal should not contradict any of your other goals. For example, you can't buy a million-dollar house if your income goal is $50,000 per year.

➤ If you need help from someone in achieving your goal, will you have that person's cooperation? If you plan to open a business with a partner, but that person doesn't share your goal, then you both need to evaluate your goals to make sure they are compatible.

➤ Write down your goal in positive, not negative, language. Work for what you want, not for what you plan to leave behind.

➤ Write out your goal in complete detail. Instead of writing, "Open a new business," write "Start a part-time woodworking business out of my home making high-quality wood shelves and curio cabinets that I design and produce to sell at craft shows on weekends." The more detail, the better. It will help you picture your goal as real, which helps make it attainable.

➤ Make sure that your goal is high enough. Shoot for the moon! If you miss, you'll still be in the company of stars.

➤ Write out your goal as if you've already achieved it; this is vitally important. For example, "I own the state's largest graphic design company specializing in business logo designs."

Your Goals Are on Paper—Now What?

First of all, unless someone is critical to helping you achieve your goal(s), keep them to yourself. A negative attitude from friends, family, and neighbors can quickly drag you down. It can give you the negative, false belief that you're not capable of achieving your goals.

If you have a false belief that you're not artistic, create your own brand of artistry. You may not be a portrait painter, but you'll be able to craft something unique. Create your world as you would prefer it to be, instead of reacting to a world of someone else's creation.

It's very important that your self-talk (the thoughts in your head) remain positive. I call this *PMI*, for *positive mental image*. This is the process of seeing or visualizing yourself as having accomplished a goal.

Reviewing your goals daily is a crucial part of your success and must become part of your routine:

Each morning when you wake up, read your goal list aloud. Visualize your goals as they appear on the list—achieved.

Each night, right before you go to bed, repeat the process.

Every time you make a decision during the day, ask yourself this question, "Does it take me closer to or farther from my goal?" If the answer is "closer to," then you've made the right decision. If the answer is "farther from," well, you know what to do.

This process will begin to replace any negative self-talk that you may have been carrying on with positive images of accomplished goals, and you will get started working toward them.

Quantify Your Goals

Quantifying your goals can be a long process. You'll have to gather a lot more information before you're ready to set specific targets. Eventually, you'll probably want to shape your quantified goals into a business plan. Before we move on to the process of gathering information needed to quantify goals, here are some guidelines for quantifying them:

➤ **Be realistic.** Having high expectations is great, but make sure that you establish targets that are reasonable and potentially achievable. If you're opening a fast-food restaurant, saying that you want to be bigger than McDonald's or Burger King within six months is not realistic.

➤ **Be aggressive.** Don't set goals that are too easily achieved; set both short-term and long-term goals that are realistic and that still aim high. If after six months in business you accomplish all of your goals, then what? Don't sell yourself short: If you want to be bigger than McDonald's or Burger King within 20 years, go for it.

➤ **Set priorities and be consistent.** Beware of inadvertently setting inconsistent goals. For example, a goal of growing fast enough to have two or three employees within three years might be inconsistent with your net earnings goal if adding employees will lead to failing to meet your short-term net earnings target. There's nothing wrong with having both goals. Just be aware that the potential conflict exists; establish priorities among your goals, and have some flexibility in sorting out any conflicts.

➤ **Be specific.** Establish targets that can actually be measured, and use figures as targets whenever possible. For example, you may set a goal of selling your products or services via craft or trade shows, of having a certain number of products or services to offer when you open, or of reaching a certain dollar amount of sales. Tie those figures to specific time frames (within six months, within two years, within five years, and so on).

Some people have a hard time setting goals because they just don't know where or how to start. One way to get started is with an easily quantifiable goal. For example, start with the amount of money that you'll need to earn to cover your actual living expenses during the start-up phase of your business; no matter what, you'll need to make enough to make ends meet.

Crafter Alert

Owning a small business is not just another job. It's a totally different lifestyle. You need to make sure that everyone's goals are compatible. You have to ask yourself whether you're ready for a complete commitment to the success of your business.

Short-Term Goal-Setting

It'll be important psychologically in those first chaotic start-up months to be able to feel that you're making some progress. Short-term goals can help you achieve those small but important victories while you're working on long-term goals, such as getting the business running and helping it grow. Your short-term goals should be realistic and quickly achievable. Some short-term goals may be to …

➤ Select and file a name for the business that reflects its nature and style.

➤ Obtain any business licenses required, or get your sales tax number.

➤ Set up the business bank account.

➤ Establish a merchant credit card account.

➤ Find a savvy small-business lawyer, accountant, and other professionals that you may need.

Be the Master of Your Fate

The Great Houdini's contracts always specified that before he disappeared into the trunk or cell from which he planned to break out, he could kiss his wife. What no one knew was that, as their lips met, his wife secretly passed a small piece of wire from her mouth to his which he used to pick the locks.

At one of his most highly publicized performances, the wire didn't seem to be doing the trick. Houdini later wrote of the experience: "After one solid minute, I didn't hear any of the familiar clicking sounds. I thought, my gosh, this could ruin my career; I'm at the pinnacle of fame, and the press is all here. After two minutes, I was beginning to sweat profusely because I was not getting this lock picked. After three minutes of failure, with thirty seconds left I reached into my pocket to get a handkerchief and dry my hands and forehead, and when I did, I leaned against the vault door and it creaked open." And there you have it. The door was never locked!

Pointers

As entrepreneurs, we can *all* be master magicians, the masters of our fate. All we have to do is face whatever barrier seems to be looming before us and then take the first step—give the door a shove. The biggest obstacles are the ones we create for ourselves in our own minds.

Harry Houdini believed the door was locked, so it may as well have been. It's the same way with all of us. The only lock is in our minds. Not only is the door not locked to us, but there may be no door at all—just the illusion of one. Give yourself permission to take a little risk. Take positive action, and unlock your mind to discover what possibilities could await you. What better road to follow as you start out on your path to making money with your hobby?

Keep Goals Flexible

If one important statement applied to all of us, it would be, "During the course of your life, the most constant thing you will experience is change." So, your goals may have to shift. If they don't, perhaps you're not working on them, or they lack focus. Or, perhaps you're *so* focused on a goal that you don't see other possibilities that can shift its original form. You may still hit the bull's eye, but it'll be on a different target.

Understand that a shift in your goal may not necessarily be negative, but a word of caution: I don't advocate changing your goals every other week or month. I merely point out that life circumstances and intense focus can attract possibilities not apparent at the time the original goal was defined.

Be flexible! And don't forget to celebrate achieving a goal with a *big* pat on the back for yourself.

The Least You Need to Know

➤ The skills and experience that you bring to your business are a deciding factor in your success.

➤ As a business owner, you may have to deal with wearing many hats.

➤ Set your goals so that they are realistic and attainable, and that they can be actually measured so you can see the results.

➤ A positive attitude is crucial to achieving success.

Part 2

What Is Your Plan?

This part presents the framework that will help you structure your business. We walk you through developing a business plan that will ensure your ongoing success, and you'll find out just how much work a computer will save you in starting—and maintaining—your business. Finally, we give our best advice on what it takes to be truly competitive in the marketplace.

Chapter 4

Make Contact: Doing Your Market Research

In This Chapter

➤ Learning what market research is

➤ Interpreting market research findings

➤ Exploring market research types, methods, and techniques

➤ Obtaining your market research findings and using them to benefit your business

---

If you've assessed your strengths and weaknesses and then defined your mission and goals, you now need to find out whether your hobby is as suitable for the marketplace as you think it is. You also need to concentrate on finding your specific target or niche market and sorting who, what, when, where, and why information to design and market your products or services down the line. The way to gain perspective and insight in all these areas is by collecting data, information that will enable you to make informed decisions based on your findings—in other words, market research.

What Is Market Research?

Market research is the collection and analysis of data about your target market, competition, and/or *environment*, with the objective of gaining an increased understanding of your potential market. Through the market research process, you can take *data*, a

variety of related or unrelated facts, and create useful *information* to guide your business decisions. Market research is not an activity that you conduct only once; it is an ongoing process to help you build a successful business.

How Market Research Helps

Information gained through market research isn't just "neat stuff" to know. It is a collection of basic, solid facts that can guide your most important strategic business decisions.

Market research is effective when the findings or conclusions you reach have a value that exceeds the cost of the research itself. For example, if you spend $500 on market research activities that yield information leading to a revenue increase of $5,000, the research was well worth it!

Market research is a good thing to do because it ...

> **Trade Terms**
>
> Your **environment** includes the economic and political circumstances that can influence your productivity and operations. Through the market research process, you can take **data,** a variety of related or unrelated facts, and create useful **information** to guide your business decisions.

➤ **Minimizes the risk of doing business.** The results of some market research may do more than identify opportunities—it may indicate a planned course of action that you should *not* pursue. For example, marketing information may indicate that a specific marketplace is saturated with the type of product or service that you plan to offer. This may cause you to alter your product or service offering or to choose an alternative location for distribution, where your product or service may be needed.

➤ **Uncovers and identifies potential problems.** Suppose that a retail outlet is thriving at its location on the main road through town. Through research, you learn that in two years, the city is planning an alternate route to bypass the main road to ease the town's traffic congestion. You've identified a potential problem! Early detection provides you with vital time to work on a countermeasure.

➤ **Helps you track your progress.** It's important to know, for later comparisons, the condition of your business at particular moments in time. Ongoing market research allows you to make comparisons against your previous research. For example, you might establish a benchmark measurement of your target market demographics and learn that 60 percent of your customers are women between the ages of 35 and 55. One year later, you again survey your customers and learn that this age group now represents 75 percent of your customer base. You're tracking a trend in your customer demographics, and you can respond to it immediately and appropriately.

➤ **Helps you evaluate your success.** Information gathered through market research helps you determine whether you're reaching your goals. In the preceding example, if your product's target market is women between the ages of 35 and 55, then you're making progress toward your goal. If not, this information can indicate a needed change in marketing strategy!

What Market Research Can Tell You

Market research data becomes information when it can *tell* you something:

➤ **Information about your customers.** What characteristics are shared by your customers? Market research answers questions such as these: Who are my customers? What is the size of their population? What percentage is female? What are their ages, races, and income and education levels? What are their occupations, skills, interests, and hobbies? How many children do they have? Do they have pets? Where do they live and work? What is their purchasing power, and what are their buying habits? What is their current usage of my services? When do they purchase? Where do they shop? Why do they decide to buy? How often do they buy? How much do they buy at a time? Do they own or rent their homes? How do they typically spend their disposable income? What methods of payment do they use? Who in the family or company makes the decisions to buy? What are the deciding factors in making a purchase? Do they want only the best for their family? Are they looking for convenience and time-saving devices? Are they concerned with how they are perceived by others? What are their unmet needs? Do they demand intensive customer service? Are they only concerned with the lowest price? What media magazines, radio, television, newspapers, Internet providers, and so on are they exposed to?

Pointers

Doing market research on your hobby will disclose what the market trends are for your product or service. It should tell you whether the industry is growing, is at a plateau, or is declining.

➤ **Marketplace competition.** This is information about the other companies in your type of business. Research answers these questions: Who are my primary competitors in the market? How do they compete with me? In what ways do they not compete with me? What are their strengths and weaknesses? Are there profitable opportunities based upon their weaknesses? What is their market niche? What makes my business unique compared with the others? How do my competitors position themselves? How do they communicate their services to the market? Who are their customers? How are they perceived by the market? Who are the industry leaders? What is their sales volume? Where are they located? Are they profitable?

➤ **Environmental factors.** This information uncovers economic and political circumstances that can influence your productivity and operations. Questions to be answered include these: What are the current and future population trends? What are the current and future socioeconomic trends? What effects do economic and political policies have on my target market or my industry? What are the growth expectations for my market? What outside factors influence the industry's performance? What are the trends for this market and for the economy? Is the industry growing, at a plateau, or declining?

Market Research Types, Methods, and Techniques

Two types of research exist: *primary research*, or original information gathered for a specific purpose; and *secondary research*, or information that already exists somewhere. Both types of research have a range of activities and methods for conducting the research associated with them. Secondary research is usually faster and less expensive to obtain than primary research. Gathering secondary research may be as simple as browsing the Internet or making a trip to your local library; an art, craft, or trade show; or a business information center.

> **Trade Terms**
>
> Two types of market research are **primary research,** or original information gathered for a specific purpose; and **secondary research,** or information that already exists somewhere else.

Secondary Research

Because secondary research is usually the easiest and least expensive, we'll take a look at it first. Secondary research may be a study, a group of articles on a topic, or demographic or statistical data gathered by someone else. For example, if you need demographic data about homeowners in your area, your Chamber of Commerce or the local Board of Realtors has already gathered it for you! Gathering secondary research data on your target markets is basically a process of reviewing and analyzing what's been published (in magazines, books, research studies, government publications, and so forth) or reported in other media.

Simply find reliable sources such as the following, and don't forget to check out the Web sites that many of them have.

The basic sources of secondary research information are …

➤ **Libraries and other public information centers.**

➤ **Books and business publications.** Many books have been written on specific industries and markets. Check out *Urlich's Directory of Serials* to see if anyone publishes a trade journal in your specific hobby area.

➤ **Magazines and newspapers.** Each and every day, studies and survey results make news. So do environmental factors, such as the leading economic indicators, housing starts, or political elections.

➤ **Trade associations.** Most associations publish reports on the industry they serve, the standards they operate under, and the leaders in their industry. They may have industry figures that you can use as benchmarks to compare with your results. Many even conduct educational seminars on trends and other issues.

Two great ways to find the right association are *Gale's Directory of Associations* and the *National Trade and Professional Associations* directory, both available in your library.

➤ **Local college marketing departments.** What successful college marketing student hasn't conducted a research project? Ask for access to data that has been collected through special research projects. Sometimes you may even be able to have students help you with your research.

➤ **Chambers of Commerce.** Your local Chamber of Commerce is a terrific resource for area maps and information on the community that you hope to serve and its businesses. You can also learn from other members at networking events.

➤ **Banks, real estate brokers, and insurance companies.** They may have information and statistics on the communities they serve.

➤ **Wholesalers and manufacturers.** Contact manufacturers and wholesalers of your type of product or service for information on industry standards, customers, costs, distribution, and potential problems. The *Thomas Register* is a listing of manufacturers grouped by industry and product. You can find it online at www.thomasregister.com and in your public library.

➤ **Federal government resources.** The government provides extensive demographic data on population, markets, and the economy. Two resources from the U.S. Department of Commerce include the "U.S. Industrial Outlook," published annually and categorized by *SIC* code (*Standard Industrial Classification*) and U.S. Census Bureau Statistics.

➤ **Regional planning organizations.** Local governments have historical and current data on community growth trends. Many offices also have forecasted future demographic statistics for the area.

➤ **Media representatives.** Advertising salespeople at television, radio, and print media outlets compile studies and reports on their audience to target potential advertisers. If you call and ask for a media kit you'll usually get some very valuable demographic information on the area they serve.

➤ **Competitive businesses.** Ask your competitors for company brochures, lists of products and services, prices, annual reports, and so forth. Hint: It helps to disguise yourself as a potential customer!

➤ **Business Information Centers (BICs).** These are area offices of the U.S. Small Business Administration (SBA). Most BICs have collections of books, publications, videos, CDs, and other sources of information exclusively for small business owners.

Primary Research

Sometimes the information you need just doesn't exist—anywhere! You searched the Internet, and you scoured the library, the journals, and the databases—all to no avail. That's when you may need to conduct primary research, or original research conducted for a specific purpose.

Primary research activities include conducting surveys to create market data or using other research instruments, such as questionnaires, focus groups, and interviews. Each method uses some form of "sampling," which allows the researcher to reach conclusions about a population within a certain degree of accuracy without having to survey everyone. Under the direction of experienced researchers, samples as small as 1 percent of a target market can often provide reliable results.

Primary research can be either qualitative or quantitative. *Qualitative research* provides definitive market information regarding the opinions and behaviors of the subjects in the market research study. *Quantitative research* is used to achieve a variety of objectives.

Qualitative research is used for the following purposes:

➤ To obtain helpful background information on a market segment

➤ To explore concepts and positioning of a business or product

➤ To identify attitudes, opinions, and behaviors shared by a target market

➤ To prioritize variables for further study

➤ To fully define problems

➤ To provide direction for the development of questionnaires

Trade Terms

Qualitative research relates the opinions and behaviors of the subjects in a market research study to the likelihood that specific products or services can be marketed to them. **Quantitative research** creates statistically valid market information that can be used in any number of ways.

Personal interviews and focus groups are the most common methods of qualitative market research.

Generally, no more than 50 interviews are conducted on a one-on-one basis (usually recorded on audio tape), most often using an unstructured survey and open-ended probing questions. Focus groups are groups of 8 to 12 people led by a moderator who follows a script.

Quantitative research creates statistically valid market information typically used ...

➤ To substantiate a hypothesis or prove a theory.

➤ To minimize risk, or to obtain reliable samples for projecting trends.

Personal, telephone, and mail surveys are the most common quantitative techniques.

The advantages of personal surveys include ...

➤ The interviewer can observe reactions, probe, and clarify answers.

➤ The technique usually nets a high percentage of completed surveys.

➤ The interviewer has flexibility with locations and schedules.

➤ The interviewer can use visual displays.

➤ Under controlled conditions, interviewing allows good sampling.

The disadvantages include ...

➤ Interviewing is costly and time-consuming.

➤ Results may contain interviewer biases.

Artisan's Corner

You can personally conduct simple market research, such as asking customers to complete a questionnaire while visiting your booth at an art, craft, or trade show, or by posting it on your Web site.

Telephone surveys have some advantages:

➤ They are faster and lower cost than personal surveys.

➤ They have a lower response bias than personal surveys.

➤ They have a wide geographic reach compared to personal surveys.

The disadvantages are that …

➤ The survey length is limited, and it is difficult to reach busy people.

➤ It is difficult to discuss certain topics, and it can be expensive compared to mail surveys.

Mail surveys have some advantages, such as …

➤ Wide distribution and low cost.

➤ No interviewer bias is present.

➤ Respondents remain anonymous.

➤ Respondents can answer at their leisure.

The disadvantages are …

➤ Obtaining accurate mailing lists is difficult.

➤ Respondents are not necessarily representative of the target population.

➤ The survey is limited by its length.

➤ Survey questions are not timely.

➤ Probing questions and clarifying answers are not possible.

➤ A specific total sample cannot be guaranteed.

Whatever research method you select, the key thing to remember is that, first, you must define your specific objective or exact goal. Then you can select the most effective research method to accomplish the task.

Getting Started on Market Research

Like other components of marketing, such as advertising, market research can be quite simple or very complex. An example of some simple market research that you might conduct is gathering demographic information about your customers by asking those who visit your booth at an arts, craft, or trade show to complete a questionnaire. On the more complex side, you might engage a professional market research firm to conduct primary research to aid you in developing a marketing strategy for launching a new product.

Regardless of the simplicity or complexity of your marketing research project, you'll benefit by reviewing the following steps in the market research process:

1. **Define marketing problems and opportunities.** The market research process begins with identifying and defining the problems and opportunities that exist for your business—opportunities such as launching a new product or service, and problems such as low awareness of your company and its products or services, or underutilization of your company's products or services (the market is familiar with your company but is not doing business with you), a poor company image and/or reputation, or problems with distribution (your goods and services are not reaching the buying public in a timely manner).

2. **Develop objectives, budget, and timetable.**

   a. **Objectives.** With a marketing problem or opportunity defined, the next step is to set objectives for your market research. Your objective may be to explore the nature of a problem so that you may further define it. Or, perhaps it is to determine how many people will buy your product if it's packaged in a certain way and offered at a certain price.

   Crafter Alert

   Existing small business owners often establish a marketing budget by allocating about 2 percent of their most recent annual gross sales. A new business, however, may want to allocate as much as 10 percent of estimated gross sales for marketing.

   b. **Budget your research.** How much money are you willing to invest in your market research? How much can you afford? Your market research budget is a portion of your overall marketing budget. One popular method that small business owners use to establish an overall marketing budget is to allocate to it a small percentage of gross sales for the most recent year. This usually amounts to about 2 percent for an existing business. Other methods used by small businesses include analyzing and estimating the competition's budget, and calculating its cost of marketing per sale.

45

c. **Prepare a timetable.** Prepare a detailed, realistic time frame for completing all steps of the market research process. If your business operates in cycles, establish target dates that will allow the best accessibility to your market. For example, a holiday greeting card business may want to conduct research before or around the holiday buying period, when customers are most likely to be thinking about their purchases.

3. **Select research types, methods, and techniques.** Refer to the market research types, methods, and techniques in the preceding sections on primary and secondary research.

4. **Design research instruments.** The most common research instrument is the questionnaire. When you're designing a questionnaire for your market research, keep these tips in mind: First, keep it simple! Include instructions for answering all questions on the survey. Second, begin the survey with general questions, and then move toward more specific ones. Third, keep questions brief. Fourth, remember to design a questionnaire that is graphically pleasing and easy to read. Finally, before taking the survey to the printer, ask a few people for feedback on its style, its user-friendliness, and what they perceive as its purpose.

Vary the formats of the questions: Use scales, rankings, open-ended questions, and closed-ended questions for different sections of the questionnaire. The format may influence the responses. Basically, there are two question formats: *closed-ended* and *open-ended.*

a. **Closed-ended questions.** Respondents choose from possible answers included on the questionnaire. Types of closed-ended questions include multiple choice, which offer respondents the ability to answer yes or no, or to choose from a list of several answer choices. Scales refer to questions that ask respondents to rank their answers or measure their answers on a scale.

b. **Open-ended questions.** Respondents answer questions in their own words. Completely unstructured questions allow respondents to answer any way they choose. Types of open-ended questions include word association questions; and sentence, story, or picture completion questions such as, "I commute by _____ (mode of transportation)."

5. **Collect data.** Unless you conduct the research, before beginning the collection of data, it is important to train and educate staff. An untrained staff person conducting primary research will lead to interviewer bias.

Trade Terms

With **closed-ended** questions, respondents choose from possible answers included on the questionnaire. Respondents answer **open-ended** questions in their own words.

6. **Organize and analyze data.** Once your data has been collected, it needs to be "cleaned." Cleaning research data involves editing, coding, and tabulating results. To make this step easier, start with a simply designed research instrument or questionnaire. Some helpful tips for organizing and analyzing your data are listed here. Look for relevant data that focuses on your immediate market needs. Rely on subjective information only as support for more general findings of objective research.

Pointers

A questionnaire should be simple and should include instructions for answering all questions. Keep questions brief, and begin with general questions before moving toward more specific ones.

   a. **Analyze for consistency.** Compare the results of different methods of your data collection.

   b. **Quantify your results.** Look for common opinions that may be counted together. Read between the lines. For example, combine U.S. Census Bureau statistics on median income levels for a given location with the number of homeowners versus renters in the area.

7. **Present and use market research findings.** Once marketing information about your target market, competition, and environment is collected and analyzed, unless you're running a one-person operation, present it in an organized manner to everyone working with you in the business venture.

In summary, the market research information that you create is to help guide you through your business decisions, from deciding what business to start, to initiating your start-up, to evaluating the products or services that you plan to market, to gathering the continuous informational support that you'll need as you continue to build your enterprise.

Market research is something you really need to do if you're serious about making money with your hobby.

The Least You Need to Know

➤ You need market research to define your target market so that you can focus your marketing efforts in the right direction.

➤ Market research can tell you about your customers, your competition, and your potential market.

➤ Primary market research is gathering original information, and secondary research is using existing market data.

➤ Secondary market research is less expensive than primary market research, is usually easier to obtain, and is probably all that a small business needs to do.

Chapter 5

The Real Deal: Setting Yourself Up as a Legitimate Business

In This Chapter

➤ Exploring the basic legal structures of businesses

➤ Learning the many ways tax considerations affect your business decisions

➤ Selecting a name for your business

➤ Being an employer

This chapter looks at the legal structures used for business organizations, such as the sole proprietorship, the partnership, and several types of corporations.

When you organize a new business, one of the most important decisions you'll make is choosing its legal structure. Some of the factors influencing which legal structure you choose include the following:

➤ Legal restrictions

➤ Liabilities assumed

➤ Type of business operation

➤ Earnings distribution

➤ Capital needs

➤ Number of people who will own the business

➤ Tax advantages or disadvantages

We explain how each business structure is set up so that you can compare them and determine which seems best for your venture. Bear in mind that this information is for background purposes only; never make any final decisions before seeking professional legal and accounting advice.

Choosing the Legal Form of Your Business

After you make the decision to start a business, you can choose to operate as a sole proprietor (a sole proprietorship can include your spouse), a partnership, a corporation, or a limited liability company (LLC). Which is best for your business?

There are advantages and disadvantages to each type of business structure, and they are defined differently from state to state. Before you consider your options, get basic information on the business structures in your state from the state department of revenue or taxation and finance. Whether you're going into business by yourself or with partners, first decide what's more important to you: having a simple business and tax structure, having more flexibility in your management and tax structure, or being subject to less personal liability for debts and corporate judgments?

➤ If you want a simple business and tax structure, choose a sole proprietorship or a partnership.

➤ If you want to limit your personal liability for debts, choose to incorporate.

➤ If you want more flexibility in your management and taxation structure, and if you're willing to trade it for the confusion of conflicts between state and federal laws, consider an LLC (which needs to be set up by a lawyer).

Artisan's Corner

You can choose to operate your business as a sole proprietorship, a partnership, a corporation, or a limited liability company (LLC).

You can operate by yourself as a sole proprietor, with others as a partnership, or in a formal entity such as a corporation or limited liability company (LLC). Corporations and LLCs are more expensive to create than proprietorships and partnerships, but, depending on your priorities, they may be more attractive choices anyway. As a sole proprietor, there are few legal formalities; if you're operating under an assumed name, you may need to register (usually at the county level).

Sole Proprietorship

This is the easiest and least costly way of starting a business. It varies from state to state, but there will be forms and licenses to fill out (which many owners do themselves) and modest fees to pay. Then, if you're a sole proprietor, you can just select your location and open the door for business. The owner has absolute authority over all business decisions. Your business income will be reported on a Schedule C, which is included with your individual income tax forms.

Partnership

Several types of partnerships exist. The two most common types are general and limited (LLC).

A general partnership can be formed by an oral agreement between two or more persons, but a legal partnership agreement drawn up by an attorney is highly recommended. Legal fees for drawing up a partnership agreement are higher than those for a sole proprietorship, but they may be lower than incorporating. A partnership agreement could be helpful in solving any disputes, but partners are responsible for each other's business actions as well as their own.

Partnerships engaged in a trade or business must file a return on Form 1065 showing the partnership's income, deductions, and other required information. The return shows the names and addresses of each partner and each partner's distributive share of taxable income and deductions. This is an information return and must be signed by a general partner. An LLC (limited liability partnership) is discussed later in the chapter in "Corporation vs. Limited Liability Company (LLC)."

A partnership agreement should include the following:

➤ Type of business

➤ Amount of equity invested by each partner

➤ Division of profit or loss

➤ Partners' compensation

➤ Distribution of assets on dissolution

➤ Duration of partnership

➤ Provisions for changes or for dissolving the partnership

➤ Dispute settlement clause

➤ Restrictions of authority and expenditures

➤ Settlement in case of death or incapacitation

Pointers

Starting a business can be almost as easy as hanging up a shingle. If you're a sole proprietor, there are few legal formalities. Forming a partnership or corporation is more expensive and more complicated, but, depending on your situation and your state laws, these could be appropriate choices.

Partnerships are fairly easy to create. You need to draft a partnership agreement (basically, your own private law) that governs the relationship between the parties: who gets what percentage, who makes the decisions, and so on. Again, there are few legal formalities. General partnerships usually do not need to register anywhere except maybe at the county level. Limited partnerships are more like corporations and usually require registration at the state level and the services of a registered agent (RA). Later in this chapter in "State Regulations and Fees" we cover the role of an RA.

Corporation

A corporation is a legal entity with a corporate charter from a state. Corporations can own property, borrow money, sue, and be sued. A business may incorporate without an attorney, but legal advice is highly recommended.

Crafter Alert

Incorporating without an attorney is not recommended. The corporate structure is usually the most complex and most costly to organize.

Trade Terms

A **limited liability company** (**LLC**) is an unincorporated business entity that can be called a cross between a corporation and a partnership.

The corporate structure is usually the most complex and most costly to organize. Control depends on stock ownership. Persons with the largest stock ownership (not all the shareholders as a body) control the corporation. A person or group with control of 51 percent of a corporation's stock can make policy decisions. Control is exercised through regular board of directors' meetings and annual stockholders' meetings. Records must be kept to document decisions made by the board. Small, closely held corporations can operate more informally, but record-keeping cannot be eliminated entirely. Officers of a corporation can be liable to stockholders for improper actions. Liability is generally limited to stock ownership, except where fraud is involved. You may want to incorporate as a "C" or an "S" corporation. More information on C and S corporations is in the following section.

Corporation vs. Limited Liability Company (LLC)

A *limited liability company* (LLC) is an unincorporated business entity that can be called a cross between a corporation and a partnership. Like a corporation, an LLC protects its members from personal liability for the debts and obligations of the company. Like a partnership, an LLC is typically formed by filing a "Certificate of Formation" or similar certificate with the Secretary of State of the state in which it's filed. An LLC is taxed like a partnership, and, like a partnership, the members of an LLC typically enter into an operating agreement that establishes how the LLC will be managed. This agreement controls the management of the company and how the members relate to each other.

Where S corporations have limits on the number of shareholders, who also must be U.S. residents, LLCs have no restrictions in this regard. An LLC can have more flexibility in management because it is controlled by the members' agreement, not by the Business Corporation Act (BCA) of the state.

Unless the LLC elects to be taxed as a corporation, it will be taxed as a partnership; income and deductions of the LLC will be passed through to members for inclusion in their personal income tax returns.

Here's the bottom line: If one or more of the partners is a U.S. nonresident, or if the officers and directors opt for a nontraditional management structure requiring more flexibility than the particular state's Business Corporation Act provides, then an LLC may be for you. If tax considerations are a driving factor, you can achieve the same pass-through taxation by electing S Corporation status.

LLCs are taxed as if they were partnerships; no tax is due on the entity level.

Why Go the Corporation or LLC Route?

If you're wondering why anyone would go through the trouble and expense of deciding to set up a corporation or an LLC instead of a simple partnership, there are good reasons:

➤ **Personal liability.** When a corporation enters into a transaction, the corporation is responsible, not the shareholders.

➤ **Tax considerations!** See the following "Choosing Your Corporate Tax Structure" section.

➤ **Stock.** Transferring ownership and raising capital are usually easier using stock because corporations have a perpetual life, distinct from the lives of their shareholders.

Forming a Corporation

The steps in forming a corporation are …

1. Choose a name for the corporation. Most states require that you indicate that you are a corporation in the wording of your corporate name. Corporate names can be trademarked.

2. Prepare and file articles of incorporation.

3. Elect the first board of directors.

4. Adopt bylaws.

5. Develop the financing plans for the corporation.

6. Establish a corporate bank account.

7. Set up a corporate record-keeping system.

8. Hold a directors' meeting.

9. Issue stock.

10. Decide whether to file the S corporation election. (In an S corporation, owners report their share of corporate profits on their personal income tax returns.)

Deciding Where to Incorporate

Where should you incorporate? The quick answer usually is: in your own home state. Why? It's simple: cost. Incorporating in your own state is a minor expense (covered later in this chapter), generally several hundred dollars, including state fees. If you incorporate in a state other than your own and you do business in your own state, however, you must then "qualify," or file in your home state for the authority to do business there.

Every state has a valid interest in protecting its citizens. This is one of the reasons you are required to appoint a registered agent when you incorporate (more on registered agents comes later in the chapter), to ensure that there's a valid address where a state's citizens can serve process if they have a complaint against the corporation and want to take legal action.

Artisan's Corner

In addition to Delaware, some of the other jurisdictions favored for forming corporations are Florida, New York, New Jersey, and California.

If you incorporate in a state other than your home state, the extra few hundred dollars may not mean much to you, especially if you have a strategic reason for choosing to do so. For example, certain states, such as Delaware and Nevada, require less information than other states do about the founders of a corporation; the added privacy may be important to you. Delaware (more than 50 percent of the Fortune 500 are incorporated in Delaware) is attractive for other reasons as well.

Choosing Your Corporate Tax Structure

One of the disadvantages of the normal corporate form (a C corporation) is that you may be subject to double taxation. The corporation is considered a separate entity from its stockholders and is taxed on its profits. When these profits are distributed to the shareholders as dividends, they are taxed again (on the personal level).

S corporations are not taxed at the corporate level. Income, loss, deductions, and credits are passed through to its shareholders, who then compute their business income with their individual taxes.

Selecting a Corporate Name

The name for your business can be one of the most important decisions you make. Your name is not only an important marketing tool; it often sets the tone for your whole business image.

Here are some tips for selecting your business name:

1. Check for state regulations on naming a business. Many states require specific wording for corporations and LLCs. Also, many words are limited in use or prohibited in business names.

2. Make a list of names of similar businesses that might be your competitors, and decide how you would like to differentiate yourself from them.

3. Consider how you want your business to be viewed by its customers.

4. Make a list of possible names that seem to convey the image you have, yet differentiate your business from your competitors'.

5. Try to pick a name that reflects what your business is about. It will save you marketing dollars and help build an association for your products or services.

> **Pointers**
>
> The business name ABC Designs does not hint at what the product line is, whereas ABC Woodworking tells it all. Research shows that names that tell something about the product or service are more successful than those, however catchy, that are vague. Your business name should be broad enough to fit with changes in your organization, products, and strategy.

6. Test the names on friends, family, and possible customers. Don't just ask them which names they like, but ask them what each one conveys to them.

7. Research the meaning of your name finalists in other languages and cultures. This is becoming even more important as companies are selling via the Internet.

Trademark Implications

Although you may have used a certain phrase in your corporate name, it may not be enough to stop other companies from using it in commerce, and it certainly won't be if they're located outside the state in which you're incorporated or qualified.

Crafter Alert

Filing a business name in your county or state does not protect it outside that filing area. You may want to file a trademark and register it as your domain name.

Generally, your first step in trademark protection and registration is a search to discover any potential conflicts. If you want to trademark your corporate name, then you need to check before you file your corporation name to see if it's available. A trademark is generally considered to be words or symbols that distinguish your products or services from those of all others. To protect your trademark, you must register it in the United States with the Patent and Trademark Office.

One of the first places to begin your trademark research is the official Web site of the U.S. Patent and Trademark Office: www.uspto.gov, where you'll find solid information, including access to the official U.S. Trademark Database. For general questions about patents and trademarks, please contact General Information Services: telephone: 1-800-786-9199 or 703-308-4357, TTY: 703-305-7785, e-mail: usptoinfo@uspto.gov. Mail may be sent to: Undersecretary of Commerce for Intellectual Property; Washington, DC 20231.

Getting a U.S. Employer Identification Number (EIN)

If any of the following apply to your business, you may need to have an EIN: you have employees; you have a Keogh plan; you operate as a corporation or partnership; or you file tax returns for employment; excise; or alcohol, tobacco, or firearms in the United States.

An EIN is issued by the Internal Revenue Service, and there is no charge to get one. IRS Form SS-4 is needed to apply. You can obtain the form from your local IRS office by calling 1-800-829-3676, by downloading it from the IRS Web site at www.irs. ustreas.gov, by using Telnet or iris.irs.ustreas.gov, or by using File Transfer Protocol from ftp.irs.ustreas.gov.

To obtain an EIN by telephone, first complete Form SS-4, and then call the Tele-TIN number for the location of your business, listed on the form "Where to Apply."

Do I Need a Corporate Kit?

The *corporate kit* is the only physical embodiment of your corporation, and it is used to house all the important documents that your corporation will generate. All kits come complete with a corporate seal, which is used to emboss your company's name on official documents. Banks and other institutions may often require that all documents signed by a corporation bear the corporate seal.

Most attorneys include the kit in the cost quoted for setting up the corporation.

IRS Information

The U.S. Internal Revenue Service hosts a Web site where you can download all the forms and IRS publications that you need—free. Go to www.irs.ustreas.gov/prod/cover.html. To order free publications and forms, you can also call 1-800-829-3676. You can also order tax forms by mail, computer, or fax. For a list of free tax publications, order Publication 910, "Guide to Free Tax Services." This publication also contains an index of tax topics and related publications, and describes other free tax information services available from the IRS, including tax education and assistance programs.

State Regulations and Fees

Each state has adopted its own statute that regulates the formation and governing of entities such as corporations and limited liability companies. It is usually called the Business Corporation Act (BCA) or Business Corporation Law (BCL). These acts are usually based on (and are very similar to) the Revised Model Business Corporation Act (RMBCA.)

Registered Agents

Section 5.01 of the RMBCA says that "each corporation must continuously maintain … (1) a registered office (an address where all legal notices can be sent … and (2) a registered agent. For example, your attorney's office can be your official address and your attorney the Registered Agent." In general, failure to maintain a registered agent results in the loss of "good standing" of the corporation with the state. This affects your ability to do business in the state, can result in corporate contracts being deemed void or voidable, and can possibly result in personal penalties or fines imposed on the officers and directors of the corporation.

Almost every state has enacted similar provisions in its own Business Corporation Act, which requires a registered agent or office for every corporation, LLC, or limited partnership that does business in its state. The purpose of these provisions is to ensure that each company has an office where it may be found and a person at that office who can be served any notice or process in connection with litigation.

State Corporation Fees

Each state requires that, for the minimum incorporation fees, a certain minimum number of shares, par value and no par value, must be issued by the corporation.

State statutes also dictate the minimum number of directors permitted in a corporation. Most states, such as New York, require only one director; the next most common requirement is three directors.

The fees for filing for incorporation in most states (Delaware, New York, Florida, and Nevada, for example) fall within the $50 to $200 range.

What's an Offshore Company?

An *offshore* company is a company formed in any of the jurisdictions considered tax-favored or *tax havens*. For the past few years, among the most popular have been the British Virgin Islands, the Cayman Islands, Nevis, the Bahamas, and Barbados. The more traditional and longer-established havens include the Isle of Man, Jersey, Guernsey, Panama, and Liberia.

Trade Terms

An **offshore** company is a company formed in any of the so-called tax-favored jurisdictions, also known as **tax havens.**

What these countries have in common is that they generally do not impose tax (or they impose extremely low tax) on companies formed there as long as they don't do any business in that country. The structure of offshore companies differs from country to country, but they usually have most of the characteristics of a U.S. corporation or LLC.

If you file personal income tax returns in the United States, there are few tax advantages in having an offshore company. The United States has "global" taxation, which means that all income is taxed regardless of where it is earned. However, many U.S. citizens find another legitimate advantage to having offshore companies: asset protection. It's much harder for people to get at your money by filing frivolous lawsuits, and legal proceedings are much less public than they are in the United States.

If you opt to protect your company's assets from being seized through litigation it's best to plan for it as early as possible. Many courts can seek to set aside fraudulent transfers of funds to your offshore company made within a certain period (generally three years) preceding a lawsuit, or "in contemplation" of litigation.

The Least You Need to Know

➤ When starting a new business, you can choose to operate as a sole proprietor, a partnership, a corporation, or a limited liability company (LLC).

➤ A sole proprietor (which includes your spouse) is usually the choice of small businesses unless tax consequences or asset protection are a major consideration.

➤ Try to pick a business name that says what the business is actually about, and file the business name to protect it.

➤ States vary in their statutes governing corporations and LLCs, so it's essential to know the laws of the state that your business is based in.

➤ Offshore companies do not save you tax dollars if you're a U.S. taxpayer, but they do have other advantages.

Chapter 6

The Basics of Running Your Ongoing Business

> ### In This Chapter
>
> ➤ Understanding why you need a business plan
>
> ➤ Developing a basic business plan outline
>
> ➤ Creating your plan, step by step
>
> ➤ Knowing when and where to get planning assistance

What goes into a business plan? New and potential small business owners should ask this important question, but many do not. Don't make the mistake of attempting to start up your business without doing your homework—creating your basic business plan. This will be your road map to a successful business, giving you a clear direction and signposts to guide you on your path from start-up to continued growth.

The basic business plan in this chapter allows for most of the possibilities that you may need to consider. Just adapt it to suit your specific needs, and skip the items that don't apply to your business at this time. Remember: Your business plan is not carved in stone; it should be reviewed and changed on an ongoing basis as needed to meet the needs of your business as it grows.

A Typical Business Plan Outline

Your business plan is a complete and accurate picture of your business. It's what you'll take to the bank or other investor when you need capital to grow your business, or buy new equipment, or expand your product or service line. It should be written as any good report, with a beginning, a middle, and an end. But before you write it, you'll need an outline.

The following outline typifies a basic business plan. Use it as a guide, adapting it to your specific business. You'll find that working on your outline one component at a time will make putting it together a much easier task.

The beginning contains ...

A cover page.

A statement of purpose or mission statement.

An executive summary.

The table of contents.

The middle contains ...

A description of your business.

A description of your product(s) or service(s).

A description of your target market.

A description of your competition.

A summary of your current or potential personnel issues.

A description of the business' current financial state and its financial management plan.

The operating plan.

The marketing plan.

The last section contains ...

All supporting documents and financial projections.

Copies of the last three tax returns for your business (if any).

When you create your business plan, you'll develop all the basic steps and strategies you'll need to run your ongoing business. It's the road to making money with your hobby.

How Do I *Do* This?

Creating your business plan sounds complicated, but it really isn't. Why? Simply because it's being written by the world's greatest expert on your business—you! So let's begin at the beginning and talk about each part of your plan.

The Beginning

The beginning of your plan contains the following …

1. **The cover sheet.** This include the name, address, telephone number, fax number, and (if applicable) Web site of the business, and the names, addresses, and phone numbers of all the principals.

2. **The statement of purpose or mission statement.** In one or two paragraphs, describe your hopes and aspirations for your business. What type and quality of product or service do you want to offer? What will be your company's approach to the consumer? Do you have a financial goal in mind? What is it?

3. **The executive summary.** This one is an anomaly. The executive summary is just what is says—a summary. It's a concise, focused synopsis of your entire business plan. Well, we all know that summaries can't be written before the plan is complete. So, even though the executive summary is at the beginning of your business plan, it's the next to last thing you'll write. It's where it is so that anyone interested in investing with you or loaning you capital can get a quick, overall picture of the operation and health of your business.

4. **The table of contents.** This has to be prepared last. It is what it says it is, a listing of what information can be found on what page (if you number the pages in your plan).

Artisan's Corner

A business plan is an ongoing, evolving set of objectives that should be reviewed and revised as needed as your business grows and prospers.

Pointers

Your executive summary could motivate some to read your entire business plan, or it could be the only thing some read, so it must be brief, focused, and interesting.

The Middle

The middle of your plan is where you flesh out your business. It contains the following elements:

1. **The description of your business.** This should clearly identify goals and objectives, and it should clarify why you are, or why you want to be, in business. In describing your business you should explain the following:

    ➤ The legalities of the business, or the business form. Is it a sole proprietorship, a partnership, or a corporation? List the licenses or permits that you have or will need.

    ➤ What type of business is it? Is it merchandising, manufacturing, or service?

    ➤ What is your product or service?

    ➤ Is it a new, independent business, a takeover, an expansion, or a franchise?

    ➤ Why will your business be profitable? What are its growth opportunities? Will franchising impact them?

    ➤ What will be your business days or hours? How will your products reach the market: perhaps home, art and craft, or trade shows; a retail store; the Internet, and so on.

    ➤ What have you learned about your kind of business from outside sources (trade suppliers, bankers, other business owners, franchisers, trade publications, books, articles, or trade associations [include all principal participants])?

    ➤ Give a thorough description of what makes your business unique or different from the others. Describe the unique aspects, and how or why your product or service will appeal to consumers.

    ➤ Emphasize any special features that you feel will appeal to customers, and explain how and why these features are appealing.

    ➤ Include the location of your business, and tell why the location is desirable. (If you have a franchise, the chain's management may want to assist in site selection.)

2. **The description of your product or service.** Try to describe the benefits of your goods and services from your customers' perspective. Include answers to questions such as these:

    ➤ What are you selling? Discuss the products or services offered.

    ➤ How will your product or service benefit the customer?

➤ Which products or services are in demand? Will there be a steady flow of cash?

➤ What is different or unique about the product or service your business is offering?

3. **The description of your target market.** To describe your target market, address these points:

> ➤ Identify the customer demand for your product or service.
>
> ➤ Identify your market, its size, and its locations.
>
> ➤ Explain your pricing strategy.
>
> ➤ Explain how your product or service will be advertised and marketed.

Pointers

In the description of your business, point out the unique aspects of your product or service, and tell what about them will appeal to consumers. Emphasize any special features that you predict will appeal to customers, and explain how and why.

4. **The description of your competition.** Competition is a way of life. Major companies compete for the consumer in the global marketplace, as do individual business owners on a local level. Business is a highly competitive, volatile arena; consequently, it's important that you know your competitors. Discuss the advantages that you and your business have over them. Answer questions like these:

> ➤ Who are your five nearest direct competitors?
>
> ➤ Who are your indirect competitors?
>
> ➤ How are their businesses: steady, increasing? Or decreasing?
>
> ➤ What have you learned from their operations And from their advertising?
>
> ➤ What are their strengths and weaknesses?
>
> ➤ How does their product or service differ from yours?

Crafter Alert

Business is a highly competitive, volatile arena, so it's crucial that you keep track of your competitors on an ongoing basis.

Start a file on each of your competitors. Review these files periodically, determining when and how often they advertise, sponsor promotions, and offer sales. Study the copy used in the advertising and promotional materials, as well as their sales strategy. Using this technique can help you to understand your competitors better and also understand how they operate their businesses.

5. **The description of personnel issues.** Like manufacturing plants and equipment, people are resources: In fact, people are the most valuable asset that a business has. Your partners and staff will play an important role in the total operation of your business. Consequently, it's imperative that you have a full understanding of which skills you possess and which you're lacking. Then you can look for people to hire or subcontract who have the skills that you lack and who can take on the tasks which require them. It's also imperative that you know how to manage and treat your partners and employees. Covering personnel issues should mean questions such as these:

   ➤ What are your current personnel needs?

   ➤ What are your plans for hiring and training personnel?

   ➤ What salaries, benefits, vacations, and holidays will you offer?

   ➤ What benefits, if any, can you currently afford?

6. **The description of your current financial situation and financial management plan.** Sound financial management is one of the best ways for your business to remain profitable and solvent. How well the finances of a business are managed is the cornerstone of every successful business venture. Each year thousands of potentially successful businesses fail because of poor financial management. As a business owner, you'll need to identify and implement policies that will ensure that you'll meet your financial obligations.

   a. **The financial section of your business plan.** This should include any loan applications that you've filed, a capital equipment and supply list, a balance sheet, a break-even analysis, pro-forma income projections (profit and loss statement), and a pro-forma cash flow projection. Pro-forma figures are estimates that are calculated based on historical performance or known future events. Your industry research (see Chapter 4, "Make Contact: Doing Your Market Research") will help you arrive at reasonable numbers to use for projections. The income statement and cash flow projection should include three-year summaries, detailed by month for the first year and by quarter for the second and third years.

   b. **The accounting system and the inventory control system.** The systems you'll be using are generally addressed in this section of the business plan also. Whether you develop the accounting and inventory systems yourself, have an outside financial adviser develop them, or get them from the franchiser, you'll need to acquire a thorough understanding of every aspect of the accounting and inventory control systems and know how they operate. Your financial adviser can assist you in developing this section of your business plan, which will address the following points:

      ➤ Explain the source and the amount of initial equity capital you have.

➤ Develop a monthly operating budget for the first year.

➤ Develop an expected return on investment and monthly cash flow projection for the first year.

➤ Provide projected income statements and balance sheets for a two-year period.

➤ Discuss your break-even point.

➤ Explain your personal balance sheet and method of compensation.

➤ Discuss who will maintain your accounting records and how they will be kept.

➤ Provide "what if" statements that address alternative approaches to any problems that may develop.

7. **The description of your operating plan.** This answers questions such as these:

➤ How does your background/business experience help you in this business?

➤ What are your weaknesses, and how can you compensate for them?

➤ Who will be on the management team?

➤ What are their strengths/weaknesses?

➤ What are their duties?

➤ Are these duties clearly defined?

➤ If you're setting up a franchise, what type of assistance can you expect from the franchiser, and will this assistance be ongoing?

8. **The description of your marketing plan.** Identify your customers by their age, sex, income, educational level, and residence. At first,

Crafter Alert

Every year, potentially successful businesses fail in great numbers for the same reason: poor financial management. As a business owner, you must make it a major priority to create a financial plan that will ensure that you'll meet your financial obligations.

Artisan's Corner

Managing a business requires more than just the desire to be your own boss. It demands dedication, persistence, the ability to make decisions, and the ability to manage employees as well as finances. Your overall management plan, along with your marketing and financial management plan, sets the foundation for and facilitates the success of your business.

target only those customers who are most likely to purchase your product or service. As your customer base expands, you may need to consider modifying your marketing plan to include the segments you've added to your market. The marketing plan that you develop should contain answers to questions such as these:

➤ Who are your customers? What is your target market(s)?

➤ Are your markets growing, steady, or declining?

➤ Is your market share growing, steady, or declining?

➤ If you're a franchise, how is your market segmented?

➤ Are your markets large enough to expand? How will you attract, hold, or increase your market share? (If you're a franchise, answers will be based on the franchiser's strategy.)

➤ How will you promote your sales?

➤ What pricing strategy have you devised?

9. **The description of your operating plan.** In describing your operating plan, be sure to address these points:

➤ Explain how the business will be managed on a day-to-day basis.

➤ Discuss hiring and personnel procedures.

➤ Discuss insurance, lease or rental agreements, and issues pertinent to your business.

➤ Account for the equipment necessary to produce your products or services.

➤ Account for production and delivery of products and services.

The End

The last part of your plan includes these components:

1. **All supporting documentation.** This includes the following:

➤ Loan applications

➤ Capital equipment and supply list

➤ Balance sheet

➤ Break-even analysis

➤ Pro-forma income projections (profit and loss statements), including a three-year summary, projects detailed by month for the first year, projections detailed by quarters for the second and third years, and assumptions upon which projections were based

➤ Pro-forma cash flow statement, including a three-year summary, projections detailed by month for the first year, projections detailed by quarters for the second and third years, and assumptions upon which the projections were based

2. **Additional supporting documents.** Other documents that you may include are these:

➤ Tax returns of principals for the last three years

➤ Your personal financial statement (all banks have these forms)

➤ In the case of a franchised business, a copy of the franchise contract and all supporting documents provided by the franchiser

➤ A copy of the proposed lease or purchase agreement for your building space

➤ Copies of licenses and other legal documents

➤ Copies of the resumés of all principals

➤ Copies of letters of intent from suppliers and others

3. **The executive summary.** (This was fully covered in the earlier section, "The Beginning.") Remember that the executive summary is written last but is placed in the front of the business plan.

4. **The table of contents.** The table of contents is completed at the very end, but don't forget to place it in the beginning section of your business plan.

Once you've completed your business plan, review it with a friend or a business associate, or a counselor from the Service Corps of Retired Executives (SCORE) or the Small Business Development Center (SBDC).

Don't expect to have all the answers to the questions that this chapter asks you to answer in developing your business plan. Just make note of any unanswered questions, and fill in the blanks as you progress through this book and do your business start-up research.

Pointers

Remember that a business plan is a flexible document that should change as your business grows. It is never carved in stone. It is a road map, a guide, so if you discover shortcuts, or even new directions to take, simply make the changes in your plan that will map out your new route to achieving your goals.

More Suggestions and Strategies

Just as your business is (or will be) a living, thriving, ever-growing, and changing entity, so is your business plan. You will want to revisit it many times for many different reasons. You may find that what was an accurate picture of your business at start-up is not an accurate picture of your business 5, or 10, or 15 years down the line.

The following section lists some strategies and outlines some questions that you'll want to consider and reconsider as time goes by.

Determining How Much Start-Up Capital You'll Need

To effectively manage your finances it's essential that you plan a sound, realistic budget. To do it, you have to determine the actual amount of money needed to open your business (start-up costs) and the amount needed to keep it open (operating costs) over a designated period of time.

Creating your operating budget is part of determining how much start-up capital you'll need, so you'll want to have it prepared before you're ready to open for business.

Crafter Alert

Many business owners operate under the mistaken concept that the business will promote itself, and they channel money that should be used for advertising and promotions to other areas of the business. Advertising and promotions, however, are the lifeline of a business and should be treated as such.

The operating budget will reflect your priorities in terms of how you spend your money: the expenses you expect to incur within a given time period, and how you'll meet those expenses (the income that you anticipate). Your operating budget should also include money to cover the first three to six months of operation.

See the "Start-Up and Operating Budgets" section in Chapter 13, "Money Matters," for details on how to plan for initial and ongoing operating costs.

Pricing and Sales

Your pricing strategy is another marketing technique that you can use to improve your overall competitiveness. Get a feel for the pricing strategy that your competitors are using. That way you can determine if your prices are in line with those of competitors in your market area and with industry averages. Pricing strategies are covered in detail in Chapter 19, "Playing the Pricing Game."

Advertising and Public Relations

How you advertise and promote your goods and services may make or break your business. Having a good product or service but not advertising and promoting it is like not having a business at all. Remember: The more care and attention you devote to your marketing program, the more successful your business will be.

The most important thing to realize is that *you do need a business plan*. How elaborate or how simple is not an issue. It should be a reflection of the vision that you see for your business. That vision may change as you do your research and learn more about the business that you plan to open. Your goal is simply to write a plan that will be a model for how you intend to start and operate your business. Think of writing your business plan as creating a map with the directions that will lead to the ultimate success and continued growth of your new business.

The Least You Need to Know

➤ You need a business plan that details how you'll start and run your business.

➤ How detailed your plan needs to be depends on the type of business you're starting and whether you need outside financing.

➤ A business plan is ongoing and should be updated as you make changes and your business grows.

Chapter 7

Using a Computer to Lighten Your Business Load

In This Chapter

➤ Selecting the right computer

➤ Considering software suites with all-in-one programs

➤ Making bookkeeping easy with accounting software

➤ Cutting business costs by using a computer

If you don't already know it, a computer can be one of your business's most valuable assets. Think of a computer as an extra pair of hands to lighten your workload. You can use it to write letters, design all your stationery and sales literature, make labels and hang tags, and prepare your business plan. You can also order supplies, track inventory, do your bookkeeping and financial statements, monitor your cash flow and sales results, and maintain a customer data base. If that's not enough, you can use your computer to do research, prepare camera-ready advertising, market your product or service, facilitate communications and networking, and maintain a Web site—and you may also be able to use it in the production of your products or services. The possibilities are limited only by your imagination.

If You're Buying a Computer

If you're buying a computer, first do some research to determine exactly what you want it to do for you. Start with understanding the components that make up the central processing unit (CPU), or as I like to call it, the "brain." Then you can make the right choices about memory (RAM), processing speed, video, audio, communications, hard disk space, and so on. You may want to prepare a checklist of features you need, and then compare models and prices to get your best buy. To get started on the right track to understanding computers, check out the following:

➤ *Computer Shopper* at www.zdnet.com/computershopper/. Published by Ziff-Davis Publishing Company, this a monthly magazine of PC articles and mail order advertisements that is as thick as most Yellow Pages. At the Web site, *Computer Shopper* provides two months of product reviews, buying advice, shopping tools, and a complete listing of all products advertised in each issue, arranged by product category and manufacturer. This is a good place to go to become a more astute, informed buyer.

➤ ZDNET at www.zdnet.com/. This site gives you heavy-duty searches of product reviews and technology articles from 15 computer magazines that Ziff-Davis publishes. Trust this site to give you honest assessments to help cut through ad hype.

Crafter Alert

A computer can be one of your most valuable assets. What to look for when buying a computer is a question that only you can answer after you've done some research to determine exactly what you want the computer to do for you.

➤ *PC Today* at www.pctoday.com/. An alternative magazine to *Computer Shopper,* this Web site has product reviews, user case studies, and feature articles to get you smart. Its "PC Catalog Buyers' Directory," part of its PC Cyber Shop, is an online database of more than 4,000 products from over 300 manufacturers, distributors, and vendors listed in price order for identical products. It's a quick way to get up to speed.

➤ CNET at www.cnet.com/. The Computer Network is a media company that is integrating television programming with a network of sites on the Web. Perhaps you've caught its television broadcasts on the Sci-Fi Channel and USA Network. Its editorials, technology reports, and product comparisons are all first-rate.

Once you've narrowed down what you want, try the following additional sites to compare products and prices:

Computergate: www.computergate.com/cgi-bin/start

ComputeAbility: www.cc-inc.com/cability/

Egghead: www.egghead.com

Midwest Micro: www.mwmicro.com/

Surplus Direct: www.surplusdirect.com/

Tredex: www.tredex.com/Tdx/Eng/Home/home.asp

Computer Software

A computer is only as "smart" as the software
that you have in it. When it comes to computing,
we all need to do pretty much the same types of
things: compose documents, analyze numbers,
and keep track of names, addresses, and the like.
That's why the starting point for any PC is a good
"suite," a bundle of basic software such as word
processing, spreadsheet, and graphics programs,
designed to work together. Most PCs come with
simple all-in-one packages, such as Microsoft
Works or ClarisWorks. Nevertheless, even moder-
ately sophisticated users can quickly outgrow
such programs. If you're running a business, you
may want to take advantage of what a full suite
of programs offers you.

Pointers

Any software mentioned in this
chapter can be purchased at any
one of the thousands of computer or office supply stores, as
well as online.

Business Software Suites

The following are some software suites that you may want to consider:

➤ **Lotus SmartSuite Millennium Edition.** This suite prepares you for a new era in
   computing. It contains eight innovative applications: Lotus 1-2-3 spreadsheet,
   the NEW FastSite intranet publisher, Organizer time and contact manager,
   WordPro word processor, Freelance Graphics presentation graphics, Approach
   database, ScreenCam multimedia software, and SmartCenter Internet information manager, plus integrated speech recognition from IBM ViaVoice. The
   newest member of SmartSuite is Lotus FastSite intranet document publisher.
   FastSite makes Internet/intranet publishing fast and easy. Designed for desktop
   application users, it automatically converts groups of existing SmartSuite or
   Microsoft Office files to Web formats. Rather talk than type? With integrated
   IBM ViaVoice speech-recognition software, the choice is yours. Use ViaVoice to

dictate directly into a WordPro document or to enter data into a 1-2-3 spreadsheet and turn your work into fun. Then there is Lotus 1-2-3, the spreadsheet with new features such as Web Tables that let you incorporate live Web-based data into your spreadsheets. It efficiently shares data with Lotus eSuite and popular desktop applications such as Microsoft Office, and it integrates with enterprise databases and applications including Oracle, SAP, PeopleSoft, Lotus Notes, and Domino. Check out the Lotus SmartSuite features at www.lotus.com/home.nsf/welcome/store.

➤ **Office 2000 Standard: Microsoft Office.** This suite has established a position as one of the most efficient for document creation, communication, and business information analysis. For many functions, the business platform has evolved from paper to the Web. Microsoft Office 2000 extends desktop productivity to the Web, streamlining the way you work and making it easier to share, access, and analyze information so that you get better results. Office 2000 offers a multitude of new features. Of particular importance for this release are the features that affect the entire suite. These Office-wide or shared features hold the key to the new realm of functionality. Office 2000 offers a new Web-productivity work style that integrates basic productivity tools with the Web to streamline the process of sharing information and working with others. Office 2000 makes it easier to use an organization's intranet to access vital business information and provides innovative analysis tools that help users make better, more timely business decisions. Check out Office 2000 online at shop.microsoft.com/store/products/ProductOverview.asp?&gstrGroup=software&intProductIID=722.

➤ **WordPerfect Office 2000—Small Business Edition.** Corel centers on the WordPerfect word-processing program and includes the QuattroPro spreadsheet, Corel graphics, and a slew of other software. WordPerfect Office 2000—Small Business Edition includes WordPerfect 9; Peachtree First Accounting; Norton AntiVirus 2000; Online Merchant Trellix 2; Quattro Pro 9; Corel Presentations 9; CorelCENTRAL 9; Corel Print Office 2000, Special Edition; WinFax Basic Edition; Amigo 2000; Stamps.com Internet Postage; Abobe Acrobat Reader; and Microsoft Visual Basic for Applications. You can look into it more on the Web at buy.corel.com/ProductRequirements_id-CC1FYDB84AC.html.

Selecting Accounting Software Packages

Skip hiring a bookkeeper or using the shoebox method; do it on your computer and save time and money. With accounting software, you can balance your checkbook, pay your bills, track your inventory, do job costing for the products you make, compile tax information, do order processing, and produce any financial statement or report that you need with a few clicks of the mouse. What better way to have an up-to-the-minute status report on your daily income and expenses?

Even if you use an accountant, having the reports available will save you time and money in accountant's fees. The most important thing to do before you buy any accounting software is to make a list of what you want the software to do for you. Then compare the features each program offers and the skill level required to use it, and don't forget to consider how it will serve you as your business continues to grow. In an effort to help you compare some of the popular programs, we used accounting packages that include the cost for eight basic modules: general ledger, accounts receivable, accounts payable, payroll, inventory, order entry, job costing, and system manager:

> **DAC Easy:** www.daceasy.com/products/
>
> **M.Y.O.B. Premier 1.0:** www.myob.com/pages/frameset.html
>
> **Peachtree 7.0:** www.peachtree.com/html/product.cfm
>
> **QuickBooks Pro:** www.quickbooks.com/
>
> **Microsoft Money 2000 Business & Personal:** shop.microsoft.com/store/products/ProductOverview.asp?strGroup=software&intCat=957266&strCategory=Business+Software&intSubCat=957276&strSubCat=Small+Business+Tools&intProductIID=730&strOvType=pricin (This edition is designed for sole proprietors.)

Image-Editing and Design Software

With a computer, you can design for all your business or creative needs, from logos for your letterheads and envelopes to brochures, sales flyers, show schedules, business cards, newsletters, catalogs, price lists, invoices, purchase orders, hang tags, product labels, shipping labels, or any form you may want. Gone are the days when you had to take forms to a printer to have them designed and typeset. With some basic software, you are in control, and you can save some big bucks by doing it yourself. Not to mention that the original is on your computer, ready for any changes or updates: No waiting is involved—just make the change and print off the new master.

Crafter Alert

The reason for most small business failures is that the businesses do not manage their money properly. Why? They don't keep good financial records. There is no excuse to fall into that trap when there's such a wide range of accounting software available.

With a good graphics program, you can transpose any photo, graphic, drawing, clip art, or any design of your own for use on any of your projects. Many artisans are using their computers to facilitate the design and production of their products with the help of this type of software. Only your imagination and willingness to experiment limit you. The following are just a few of the popular software programs available. There are surely hundreds more!

➤ **Adobe Software Products.** Adobe is one of the leaders in the design software department, no matter whether your end product is for hard copy or for electronic use. Many professionals think of Adobe products as the standard for professional quality. If your business depends on graphics and custom-designed work, you will find that Adobe is the answer to your needs. You can view more than 30 Adobe software products at the Adobe Web site, www.adobe.com/products/main.html.

➤ **Microsoft Publisher 2000 Deluxe.** This suite includes Publisher 2000 business desktop publishing program, an additional content CD with nearly 50,000 images, and the complete version of Microsoft Picture It! photo-editing software. Combined, these tools give you everything you need to create any flyer, brochure, catalog, newsletter, or whatever ideas you come up with.

➤ **Microsoft FrontPage 2000/PhotoDraw 2000 V.2.** This Web and graphics suite gives users everything they need to create and manage Web sites without learning the HTML language code that is used to create Web pages.

➤ **Print Artist Grande Suite.** This suite includes everything you need for print or Web publishing, including easy Web publishing, a graphics database, photo-editing software, animated e-cards, and more than 200,000 quality images!

➤ **PrintMaster Platinum 10 and The Print Shop Deluxe 10, The Print Shop Photo Pro Deluxe, The Print Shop Pro Publisher 2000, and American Greetings CreataCard Platinum 4.** All are neat, affordable, creative solutions. For the individual software details, check the Web site at www.expressit.com/180_Products/.

Use Your Computer for Improving Communications

The *Internet* is a computer network. It's a bunch of computers connected together so that they can share information, a global conglomeration of internetworked computers. New findings from IDC (leading media, research, and exposition company) show a major increase in the number of home offices with Internet access in the United States. Only 26 percent of home offices were online in 1996, but 81 percent had Internet access by the end of 1999, with the number expected to rise to 92 percent by

2004. The findings come from a recent report entitled "Home Offices on the Internet: Forecast and Analysis, 1999–2004," at www.idc.com.

Today on the Internet, you can watch film clips, meet people, talk to people, use it to make phone calls and send faxes, find almost any kind of information, and, of course, develop business contacts. Naturally, you've heard about e-mail, but if you haven't actually used it, you may not totally understand the value of being able to send instant communications worldwide with just a click of a mouse button.

Compared to regular (snail) mail, e-mail is extremely efficient and flexible. You can send a message to several people at different locations across the country in seconds, without paying for or licking stamps. In addition, you can keep copies of what you send so that you have a record of your correspondence. You can send letters, memos, Web pages, notes with hyperlinks in them to direct viewers to sites on the Internet, graphics, text files, and more. The speed and convenience of e-mail has proven a vital link to building businesses and maintaining or improving customer relations. In summary, the Internet allows you to communicate worldwide right from your own computer.

➤ **The World Wide Web (WWW).** Loosely defined as the portion of the Internet whose pages are interconnected by hyperlinks. The *World Wide Web* is viewed through a program called a Web browser. The World Wide Web is probably the most popular part of the Internet. It is constantly being updated with more bells and whistles to make it user-friendly.

➤ **Hyperlinks.** Items on World Wide Web pages that take you to another location on the Web when you click on them. Another location can mean a page on a computer half a world away, or another location on the page that you happen to be on already.

Pointers

If you don't own a computer, check out your local library. Most provide computers that you can use to get onto the Internet. All you do is type in the topic that you want information on, and the search engine searches its database and then displays links to the Web sites that contain matching key words from your inquiry.

Trade Terms

The **Internet** is a computer network, a global conglomeration of internetworked computers. The **World Wide Web (WWW)** is loosely defined as the portion of the Internet whose pages are interconnected by hyperlinks. The World Wide Web is viewed through a program called a Web browser. The World Wide Web is probably the most popular part of the Internet.

➤ **E-mail.** An abbreviation for electronic mail. E-mail is mainly used to send typed messages back and forth across the Internet. E-mail is accessed through an e-mail program and is usually provided as part of your Internet service connection.

Use Your Computer for Business Research

An Internet search engine is the best tool that any business can use to find the information it needs. You save time and gas, and you have the convenience of working at your own computer whenever you want, at home or at your business. If you don't have regular access to a computer, check out your local library where you can probably get onto the Internet.

Information on the Internet can change quickly. Don't be too surprised if a page that you visited last week either has moved or is no longer in existence. It's also easy to publish information on the Internet; you don't have to be a distinguished author or an expert, so make sure to check the reliability of your sources when you do Internet research.

Trade Terms

Search engines and **directories** are not the same. Search engines use your search terms to scour the Web for matching terms. Directories match your search terms with site descriptions, which may not be current or may not be comprehensive enough to include references to information you're looking for.

How Search Engines Work

The term "search engine" is often used generically to describe both true *search engines* and *directories*. They are not the same. The difference is in how listings are compiled. All search engines have the same basic capabilities (see the following description), but there are differences in how the capabilities are tuned. That's why the same search often produces different results on different search engines.

➤ **Search engines.** Search engines, such as HotBot, create their listings automatically. Search engines crawl the Web, and then people search through what they've found. If a Web page changes, search engines eventually find these changes, and that can affect how the page is listed. Page titles, body copy, and other elements all play a role.

➤ **Directories.** A directory such as Yahoo! depends on humans for its listings. The site submits a short description of itself to the directory, or editors write one for sites they review. A search looks for matches only in the descriptions submitted. Changes in a site's Web pages have no effect on the listing unless the listing is updated. Improving a listing with a search engine and improving a listing in a directory are different processes. The only similarity is that a good site with good content is more likely to be reviewed than a poor site.

Some Popular Search Engines

Some of the most popular search engines are listed here:

www.accufind.com

www.alltheweb.com/

www.askjeeves.com

www.dogpile.com

www.go.com

www.google.com

www.infoseek.com

www.iwon.com

www.lycos.com

www.northernlight.com/

www.oneseek.com

www.savvysearch.com/

www.webcrawler.com

www.allonesearch.com

www.altavista.com

www.directhit.com/

www.excite.com

www.goto.com

www.hotbot.com

www.inktomi.com

www.looksmart.com/

www.msn.com

search.netscape.com/

www.snap.com

www.yahoo.com

Use Your Computer for Market Research

Are you ready to get started on some market research (it's covered in Chapter 4, "Make Contact: Doing Your Market Research")? Thanks to the Web, sophisticated forms of market research are affordable to small companies. You can post surveys on a Web page, send them by e-mail, set up a chat forum, or use a targeted e-mail list to obtain the information you need. Before you take the plunge, make sure that you understand just what you want to accomplish. Do you want qualitative and quantitative information? It's like the difference between art and science:

➤ In qualitative projects (also known as focus groups), a small group of consumers is probed in-depth on a specific subject, say, how your Web site functions or the effect of your advertising strategy. What you end up with could be just the information that you need about how customers will react to your product or service.

➤ Quantitative research, by contrast, is designed to gain more hard-fact information. A large group of consumers is asked an array of multiple-choice questions. The group's answers can then be compared and statistically analyzed, revealing

important demographic or psychographic characteristics in your market. In both cases, the Internet is changing things, especially for entrepreneurs.

In many cases, quantitative research follows qualitative research. Say, for example, that you learned from a focus group that you organized in a chat room that consumers are turned off by your Web site's home page. A subsequent quantitative survey would help you determine whether your entire target market shares such feelings. Depending on the size of your sample, you might also be able to find out how various perceptions break out by age, occupation, region, income, and other categories.

These do-it-yourself projects allow you to plug your questions into the survey that you make, select a sample of respondents, and submit your questions electronically. Answers come back in about two days or less, ready to analyze.

Online research is a powerful tool, as long as you take time to understand its limitations. The biggest drawback may be that Internet users tend to be younger and better educated than the population at large; therefore, if you need to get a read on a non-tech-savvy target market, you'll want to carefully select and define your sample survey market.

Use Your Computer for Marketing

Using a computer to market your products takes your small local business and projects into the national and even international market, if you desire. Typical computer marketing includes e-mail marketing, Web sites, many forms of advertising, and a great deal of interactive network marketing. We discuss these areas in detail in Part 6, "Marketing Strategies That Will Help You Build Your Business."

Use Your Computer to Make Money with Your Hobby

"When I started sewing, I had no intention of getting into the embroidery business," says Beverly Petty, NCA (National Craft Association) member and owner of Designs by PettyKash in Galveston, Texas. "I just used the computer to draw and rescale my designs. They call it digitizing in the embroidery field. Once in business, I found I could order designs via the computer, or send designs to customers for proof before I start, by using the computer fax or the e-mail."

She continues:

> "This business really all happened because of my grandson. When he was born, I went shopping for baby clothes and couldn't find anything cute for little boys. So I decided to embroider my own designs on his clothes myself. I used the computer to draw my designs. I didn't realize that what I was doing was called 'digitizing.' Neither did I realize at the time that what I was doing out of love had the potential for me to earn money."

Artisan's Corner

To Bev Petty's surprise, her business was even the subject of an article in *Embroidery Business News* in January 2000.

Petty was surprised when teenagers who saw her with her grandson began to stop her on the street and ask her if she could sew designs on their clothes.

> "Then one day while I was reading a sewing magazine, I saw an ad about leasing professional equipment, and I just knew it was time for me to go for it," says Petty. So she leased a used single-head machine, and her new home embroidery business was underway. "In the beginning, I did anything and everything anybody wanted," she says, but she adds that she is now settling into more of a routine, sewing for local organizations such as schools and the university hospital, where she found a niche market. "I do tons of lab coats for the doctors. Right now I'm doing tote bags for a cheerleading squad at a school."

Originally, Petty thought that because she lived in Texas, people would be asking for a lot of cowboy and rodeo designs. Instead, she's found herself creating the "Mardi Gras Bra" for the local Mardi Gras celebration on Galveston Island and marketing it over the Internet, along with her western designs and personalized embroidery designs.

> "When I started, I just put a sign out in front of my house," Petty says. "I've also gone to a couple of vendor shows and passed out my cards. But the truth is, most of my business still comes by word-of-mouth, or maybe I should say word-of-sight. My grandson is eight years old now, and his clothes are still my best advertisement."

Petty considers herself to be fortunate to have found a profession that suits her interests and talents. She notes that people are not always lucky enough to find what they really love to do. "Because I love embroidery, I have to make myself realize this is a business, and keep telling myself to go sit down and do the books," she says. "I'd rather sit at my machine and try out new designs. I could sew all day long." You can view Petty's designs on her Web site www.craftassoc.com/pettyk.html/.

The Least You Need to Know

➤ Before you select a computer, decide exactly what functions you want it to accomplish for you, and buy accordingly.

➤ One software suite and one accounting package should provide all the programs you need for running your business—and running it more efficiently.

➤ You can rely on a computer to save you time and money if you use it for designs, communications, research, marketing, or any of the many other business functions that it can perform.

➤ If you make full use of a computer it can ease you through the transition from hobbyist to business owner and can save you plenty of time and money once you're up and running.

Chapter 8

Placing Value on Your Intellectual Property

> ## In This Chapter
>
> ➤ Learning what intellectual property rights are and what they mean to you
>
> ➤ Determining what intellectual properties you can register
>
> ➤ Protecting your rights and the rights of others
>
> ➤ Creating more competitive products and product lines

Once you move from being just a hobbyist to selling what you make, you become part of the business world, which opens up a whole new set of considerations about the products or services you plan to sell. If you're an artisan, your first thought will probably be: How can I protect my designs from competitors? Of course, this is important, and in this chapter we discuss the options available to you for protecting your work—in other words, your intellectual property rights. Of equal importance is ensuring that what you plan to sell does not infringe on the rights of others.

The subject of intellectual property rights is sometimes misunderstood because there are many well-meaning folk providing a lot of misinformation. The term can be best understood in the context of the term *goodwill,* which, in business, refers to the value of intangible assets. Intangible assets include everything from projected earnings to the value of product or brand name recognition. In this chapter, we look at the commercial value of your own intellect and talent.

What Intellectual Property Means for You

Intellectual property is a term that does not often mean a whole lot to the business community because most people think of it as a legal term, not a business term. However, *it is and should be considered part of business terminology.*

Businesses grow and survive as a direct result of the ideas, designs, and creativity that go into the products, services, and messages that they market to consumers.

To promote creativity, governments consider certain kinds of creative endeavors intellectual property, to be protectable through registration. Legal recognition can be granted for intellectual property (goodwill) in much the same way that a title to a house can be bought or sold.

There are many types of intellectual property, including these:

➤ **Trade names.** The name you use for your business. It's the first intellectual property issue that a new business has to face.

➤ **Copyrights.** Protection for any literary, artistic, dramatic, or musical work of an author. Included as part of this group are the tools used to promote a business—specifically, computer software, promotional literature, advertising copy, instruction manuals, designs, and so on.

➤ **Trademarks.** Words, symbols, graphics, pictures, or combinations of these, used to distinguish the goods or services of one entity from those of another.

➤ **Patents.** The exclusive rights of an inventor to exclude all others from making, using, or selling an invention within the United States and its territories and possessions.

➤ **Industrial designs.** The shape, pattern, or ornamentation of an industrially produced object.

➤ **Integrated circuit topographies.** The three-dimensional configuration of the electronic circuits embodied in integrated circuit products or layout designs.

➤ **Plant breeders' rights.** Certain new plant varieties.

➤ **Trade secrets.** Not really something you would want to register because you would be giving public notice of your secret.

➤ **Company contracts, customer lists, and agreements with employees.** Contracts and agreements are also valuable assets that form part of the base of intellectual property owned by a business.

There's more about the different types of intellectual property in the following sections.

Trade Name Registration

The most common registration of intellectual property is trade name registration. Trade names fall into two classifications: incorporated companies and names given to businesses that are not incorporated. *Everyone who carries on business uses one of these two forms of trade name.*

Corporate Names

No two corporate names registered within the same jurisdiction can be identical; however, a single owner may have corporations with similar names (Kraft Cheese and Kraft Dairy Products, for example). In general, no jurisdiction will allow incorporation without first searching the record to see if the corporate name already exists. The owner of a corporate name is granted protection of the name only, however, within the jurisdiction where it is registered. Protection does not extend to any other jurisdiction.

Crafter Alert

All businesspeople—inventors, artisans, designers, electronic microchip manufacturers, plant breeders, and others—have a stake in intellectual property. Be sure to ask a qualified legal professional to tell you how laws, practices, and information resources can work to protect your intellectual property.

Trade Names

A *trade name* is registered for evidentiary purposes only. That means that you have proof of ownership of it only in the jurisdiction in which you register it. The right to the *exclusive* use of the trade name is not expressed or implied because it could be in used in a different jurisdiction.

The owner of a trade name has protection within the confines of a specific geographic area and can therefore prevent someone from using the identical trade name or a similar one in their trading area.

A trade name can also become a common usage *trademark*. For example, when you hear "McDonald's," you think burger and fries; "Kodak" makes you think of film and cameras. Of course these companies have registered the trade name and also a trademark for the name on a national and international level. The reason is that the owner

of a trade name can prevent the registration of an unregistered trademark; however, the same owner cannot prevent the owner of an unregistered trademark from using the unregistered trademark in some other geographic location. There is more detailed information about the proper use and registration of trademarks in the "Trademarks" section later in this chapter.

No jurisdiction requires searches to be filed with requests for trade name registration. Based on the existence of millions of trade names, corporate names, and trademarks, however, it would be foolish for anyone to use a trade name without first conducting a proper search. Yet amazingly, *more than 25 percent of new businesses do so.*

Copyrights

A copyright, the right to copy, means that *an owner is the only person who may copy his or her work or permit someone else to do so.* For all works created after January 1, 1978, copyright protection was for the life of the author plus 50 years following the author's death. The 1998 law lengthened copyrights for works created on or after January 1, 1978, to the life of the author plus 70 years; it also extended copyrights for works created for hire and owned by corporations from 75 to 95 years. For specific rules on works created before 1978, or how to find out if a work may have fallen into the public domain, contact the U.S. Government Copyright Office. You can get copies of the "Copyright Information Circulars and Form Letters" that will answer almost any question you may have at www.loc.gov/copyright/circs/circ1.html.

What's Covered by Copyright Law?

The types of works covered include books, maps, lyrics, musical scores, sculpture, designs, paintings, photographs, films, tapes, computer programs, and databases. Slogans, names, and mere titles are not protected by copyright. The owner has the sole right to control any publication, production, reproduction, and performance of a work or its translation. Royalty payments may be arranged through performing rights societies, collectives, or publishing houses, or by the owners directly, through contracts.

Proof of Ownership

The term "published works" is not limited to the publication of printed matter; it includes the "public display" of your work—that is, display at a trade show, at an art or craft event, on a Web site, or in a shop or gallery.

You obtain a copyright automatically when you create an original work. Copyright protection exists from the moment the work is created, but the courts recognize ownership of works of U.S. origin only when they're registered. Registration is your proof of ownership, and it allows you to defend your rights in court if you feel that someone has infringed on your original work.

Crafter Alert

Once material falls into public domain, it cannot be copyrighted again. The rule-of-thumb guideline is that any work with a copyright date from more than 95 years ago is considered public domain. Without an actual search, however, you cannot be sure.

Owners' Rights

Modern technology has made it even easier to reproduce many kinds of works subject to copyright. Those who copy designs, computer programs, books, music, videos, or other creative output infringe upon owners' rights. Penalties for such infringement can be quite costly. Bear in mind that you can copyright the design of an item or object, as long as it can be identified separately and apart from the object itself. The object itself, such as a decorated T-shirt, a tote bag, a teacup, or a picture frame, cannot be copyrighted.

As long as you register a work within three months of its publication, or at any time prior to an infringement of the work, you, the copyright owner, may collect statutory damages for infringement and any attorneys' fees that you incurred in court actions. Otherwise, only an award of actual damages and profits is available to the copyright owner.

As you can see, infringing on someone else's rights could be expensive.

Registering Your Work

Send the following three elements in the same envelope or package to the Register of Copyrights, Copyright Office, Library of Congress, Washington, DC 20559:

➤ A properly completed application form. All the forms required to register a copyright are available online at lcweb.loc.gov/copyright/forms/, or by contacting the Copyright Office.

➤ A nonrefundable filing fee of $30 (effective through June 30, 2002) for each application.

➤ Two complete copies of the work. In the case of three-dimensional sculptural works or works published only as reproduced in or on useful items such as glass, ceramics, jewelry, plaques, dolls, floor coverings, fabrics, and other items, just send two drawings or photographs of the work.

Beware! It is your responsibility to determine the originality of what you copyright. The copyright office does not compare new works submitted with similar work already copyrighted.

Select the appropriate copyright form from one of the following:

➤ **Text Form TX.** For published and unpublished nondramatic literary works: books, directories, how-to booklets, or instructions for any project or any written words that represent income potential.

➤ **Serials Form SE.** For serials, works issued or intended to be issued in successive parts bearing numerical or chronological designations and intended to be continued indefinitely: periodicals, newspapers, magazines, newsletters, annuals, journals, and so forth.

➤ **Performing Arts Form PA.** For published and unpublished works of the performing arts: musical and dramatic works, pantomimes and choreographic works, motion pictures, and other audiovisual works.

➤ **Visual Arts Form VA.** For published and unpublished works of the visual arts: pictorial, graphic, and sculptural works, including fine, graphic, and applied art; architectural works; technical drawings; charts; diagrams; models; and photographs. Works of artistic craftsmanship fall into this category as to form, but not with respect to their utilitarian or mechanical aspects.

➤ **Sound Recordings Form SR.** For published and unpublished sound recordings: spoken, musical, or other sounds, plus all forms of audio or video tapes.

Notice of Copyright

Copyright protection exists from the moment you complete your work, whether you register it or not. You should, however, add a copyright notice to all of your original creations. It costs you nothing and does not obligate you to register, but it puts others on "notice" that your work is legally protected. Be sure to use the proper format for your copyright notice, as shown in the preceding example. If you add the words "All Rights Reserved," it simply means that the copyright protection is extended to include all of the Western Hemisphere.

Place the copyright notice where it can easily be seen on your work (it can be embedded into the product, printed on the product, or added to the product by means of a label attached to the object).

Trademarks

Trademark registration gives you exclusive rights to words, symbols, and designs, or combinations of them that distinguish your wares or services from those of others.

A trademark is a monopoly. The owner of the mark is granted the right to the exclusive use of his or her mark, relative to the "specific wares or services" for which it was registered. No one can offer any competitive product that is likely to be confused in sight, sound, or idea conveyed with that of the owner of the registered mark. Identical words, however, can be registered for unrelated wares.

Trademark Criteria

To be registered, your trademark must satisfy only two criteria.

➤ It must be used to distinguish your wares or services from those of others.

➤ It must not be too similar to one that is already registered or awaiting registration. If it is too similar to another trade name, difficulties may also arise.

Trademark Searches

Finding out about trademarks is important when you're starting a company or business. Make sure that no one else has registered or is awaiting registration of a trademark or is using a trade name similar to the one that you want to use. Most experts agree that you should not attempt trademark searches without the help of a trademark attorney.

Pointers

At the U.S. Patent and Trademark Office, at www.uspto.gov/web/menu/tmebc/index.html, you can get general trademark information and guidance, do an electronic trademark search, file online, and check the status of applications and registrations.

Registration

You do not have to register a trademark to be afforded some degree of protection (except in the case of precious metals). Proper use of an unregistered trademark carries with it certain rights that could be enforced. Registration, however, gives exclusive rights. A trademark that is registered is identified by the symbol ©. The initials TM are often used by business owners to indicate their claim to a logo or some other mark. This does not guarantee full legal trademark protection, but it does serve as "public notice" that a trademark is claimed. The reason business owners use unregistered trademarks is that use of the mark over time may gain them a certain amount of common-law protection for it.

Patents

Patents offer inventors exclusive rights to their creations and thus provide incentives for research and development. Patent protection applies in the country that issues the patent and, depending on the country, extends for up to 20 years from the date the application is first filed. You can receive a patent for a product or process that is new, improved, original, workable, and ingenious, such as a machine or the manufacture or composition of matter, including the ornamental designs for a manufactured object. In this way, patents serve as rewards for ingenuity.

Crafter Alert

A patent *does not* give the owner the right to sell the object. It prevents *others* from using, selling, or duplicating it.

In general, a patent is given to the inventor who first files an application. It is wise, therefore, to file as soon as possible after completing your invention because someone else may be on the same track. What some people do not realize is that a patent *does not* give the owner the right to sell the object; it just excludes anyone else from using, selling, or making your invention.

Because patents do more than keep creative wheels spinning, they are an important means of sharing know-how. Each patent document describes a new aspect of a technology in clear and specific terms, and is available for anyone to read. Eighteen months after a patent application is filed, the document is made public. This is done specifically to promote the sharing of knowledge. Thus, patents are vital resources for businesses, researchers, inventors, academics, and others who need to keep up with developments in their fields.

There are two issues to consider before applying for a patent. First, the cost could run as high as $5,000 or more, and requires periodic maintenance. The second is that, once you have the patent, if you do not have the wherewithal to obtain the right manufacturing, distribution, and advertising to profit from your patented invention, you may have wasted at lot of your time and money. For more information, or to do a patent search, contact the U.S. Patent and Trademark Office at www.uspto.gov/ebc/index.html or www.uspto.gov/.

Industrial Design Registration

Obtaining registration for an industrial design gives you exclusive rights for an initial period of five years, renewable for another five years. *The design must be an original shape, pattern, or ornamentation applied to a manufactured article.* The shape of a table or the decoration on the handle of a spoon is an example of an industrial design. Once registered, industrial designs are available for public inspection. Keep in mind that it is best to apply for registration before you begin marketing the products.

Plant Breeders' Rights

The Plant Breeders' Rights Act gives you exclusive rights to new varieties of some plant species. To be protected, the varieties must fulfill certain conditions. First, they must be new—that is, not previously sold. Second, they must be different from all other varieties. Third, they must be uniform—that is, all plants in the variety must be the same. Fourth, they must be stable, meaning each generation is the same.

Obtaining Protection

Before you receive the rights to a plant variety, you must submit a description for publication in the *Plant Varieties Journal*. The public has six months to object to a claim. The Plant Variety Protection Office provides application forms for protection of a plant variety, with instructions on how to file applications. Before you send for an application, be sure to visit the Web site www.ams.usda.gov/science/pvp.htm. This well-organized and easy-to-read site will provide you with complete details on everything you need to know to apply.

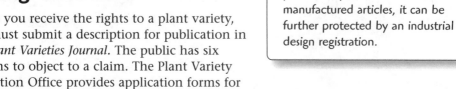

Pointers

If your design is an artistic work, it is automatically protected by copyright and can be registered as a copyrighted design. If you use the design as a model or pattern to produce 50 or more manufactured articles, it can be further protected by an industrial design registration.

To obtain an application by mail, send an inquiry via e-mail to Cheryl.Sultzer@usda.gov, or mail written inquiries to: Cheryl Sultzer, Plant Variety Protection Office, National Agricultural Library, Room 500; 10301 Baltimore Boulevard, Beltsville, MD 20705-2351; phone: 301-504-5518; fax: 301-504-5291; Web site: www.ams.usda.gov/science/pvp.htm.

Specific Protections

If your claim is granted, you are entitled to control the multiplication and sale of the seeds for up to 18 years, but others are allowed to breed, or save and grow, the varieties for their own private use without asking permission. Protection is available to citizens of countries that are members of the International Union for the Protection of New Varieties of Plants (UPOV).

How Important Is Registering Intellectual Property?

Whether or not to register depends on how strongly you feel about protecting your intellectual property rights in any of the ways outlined in this chapter.

Asking yourself questions such as the following will help you think it through:

1. Am I prepared to go to court to defend my rights?

2. What, in actual dollars and cents, is the value of the item to my business?

3. Is the value or potential value of the item worth paying the cost of protecting it?

4. How does all this fit into my long-range plans for my business, and to my feeling about the need to protect my original creativity?

Crafter Alert

This chapter is general in nature, and you should not rely on it alone to make legal decisions. Due to the changing nature of the laws and the magnitude of the area of intellectual property, you are strongly advised to seek professional advice before making any final legal decisions.

Protecting Your Rights and the Rights of Others

Now that we've explored how to protect your intellectual property rights, I think you realize how important it is to be careful to respect the rights of others who have taken the appropriate legal steps to protect theirs.

Infringement occurs whenever someone violates the exclusive rights granted to another.

Some common infringements include copying or sharing protected text or graphics on the Internet, using material from a published source in your own written work, and photocopying copyrighted materials. Before you do any of the preceding, get the owner's written permission. Remember that your use of these materials denies the rightful owner of the possibility of deriving profit from the sale of the reproduced material.

If your work is infringed upon, before you take the offender to court, consider a less expensive measure: Simply send him or her a cease and desist letter on your business stationery, with a copy to your attorney (or have your attorney send it). Ask that the offender comply immediately and respond with a written confirmation.

Tips on Infringement

You're almost sure to run into some routine infringement issues, and a few areas of infringement are frequently misunderstood. Some tips to keep in mind are these:

➤ You cannot use photocopies of someone else's patterns or designs for sale, exchange, trade, or any commercial purpose.

➤ In the area of selling products made from commercial patterns, or designs from books, magazines, how-to booklets, or instruction sheets, most of the publications give notice that the patterns or designs are for personal use only and may not be used for *commercial purposes*. *No mass production* on designs, patterns, or projects is another way of saying "may not be used for commercial purposes." That means you may not sell them wholesale or via shops. In most cases, it will probably not cause you any serious problems if you make a limited quantity of items from copyrighted patterns, designs, or how-to projects for sale in a limited quantity; even if you sell them at a craft show it's generally overlooked—as long as *only you* profit from the sales.

> **Trade Terms**
>
> **Commercial sale** usually refers to you selling the items that you make to a third party, thereby earning a profit or commission. **No mass production** is another way of referring to commercial sale.

➤ You cannot escape infringement responsibility by putting together parts of several different patterns or designs to create your own design. In fact, you just compounded the problem; you're in danger of having to deal with two or three copyright violations, all on one product. The test is, if your finished product bears even the *slightest resemblance* to what you copied and you're caught selling it commercially, you've exposed yourself to a legal headache.

➤ Most publications clearly state their policy on use of patterns or designs, including those for sewing, needlecrafts, toys, traditional crafts, decorative painting, woodworking, and so on. If a publication's policy isn't stated, call and ask what it is before you consider using anything from that publication. Definitely avoid using any likeness of licensed commercial character, such as popular cartoons or action figures. The use of these items is restricted to personal use only, and usually a licensing fee must be paid to make images of any such item for resale.

➤ Some designs are in the public domain because they were created before the copyright law existed. This is true of many Early American patterns for needlework, tinware, quilts, pottery, and woodworking, for example. All such patterns are free for use.

➤ During a discussion on the *NCA Craft Biz Connection* e-mail group, participant Alicia Ellis asked, "But why is it that people go and buy a pattern book and paint what's in it and still not get caught?" Connie Calloway, a SCD (Society of Craft Designers) designer, author, and instructor, posted this reply: "The fact that people get away with it does not mean they actually have the right to do so. It is like exceeding the legal speed limit when you are driving. If you don't get caught, you don't have to pay a fine; but that does not mean that speeding is now legal.

Artisan's Corner

An interesting aspect of public domain versus copyright is that if you were to use a quilt pattern in the public domain to design a quilt using your chosen colors, materials, textures, or stitching, this new design could qualify for copyright protection as a unique work of art. The original quilt pattern would remain in the public domain.

"The difference between the law on speeding and the law on copyright is this: The law on speeding is simple—very easy to understand; the law on copyright is complex—not so easy to understand. I think that most people who infringe on the copyrights of others do so unintentionally. They truly believe that a change of color, a different medium, or a less-than-perfect copy makes the new rendition an 'original.' How do they get away with it? The owner of the copyright may not know about it, or the owner may learn about it but decide that the financial damage is minimal and the cost of prosecution makes pursuing the issue less than practical.

"So, you may think, as long as I don't become 'rich and famous' by 'borrowing' someone else's work I don't have to worry. *Wrong!* Some folks (Walt Disney is a prime example) will pursue the smallest infringement on copyrights, regardless of the expense."

Making Competitive Products and Product Lines

Intellectual property laws have a direct effect on the products and services you plan to use in your business. As we have pointed out before, to make money with your hobby, your product or service needs to be your own unique, original design, a product that differentiates itself from others. Trying to sell products that are not original in design limits your sales and business growth potential. While such products may sell, you cannot expect the kind of income that originally designed products can provide for you. The simple fact is that original designs usually command higher prices.

Alica Ellis also told us that she took a class with a teacher who taught using patterns from a published book. The teacher then told the class that it was okay to use published patterns to make items to sell because everyone has his or her own style and color choices that change it, making it the individual's creation. That is just not so. If you *do* use someone else's design, as Connie Calloway explains, using different colors or materials does not get around the copyright restrictions.

What about a "similar design"? It depends on just how similar it is. Calloway gave this example:

> "If I do a bouquet of pink roses in oils, and you do that same bouquet of roses in watercolors; but you paint your roses red, you put them in a totally different vase and you have them on a totally different background—you are still infringing on my copyright. Even the roses have to be your own creation, not a copy of mine. You can get the inspiration to paint a bouquet of roses from seeing how I did mine, but you can't mimic mine—even if you do make all those other changes."

As you can see, there are many pitfalls when you use commercial designs rather than create original work.

Pointers

Designers are not so worried about the fact that you may make and sell a few handmade products; they are trying to protect *their right to sell their own original designs or finished products in the commercial marketplace.*

After you get through your start-up and begin making long-range plans, think in terms of defining your product line or product mix. Narrow your focus and work on developing a group of compatible products suited for your target market. Say you're a candle-maker, for example. Develop a range of price levels around a variety of candle styles, shapes, colors, and fragrances. Add compatible items such as candleholders, candle rings, or decorative items that work well with the candles. It will offer you a greater opportunity to sell more products to the same customers, build a repeat business, and attract a wider customer base. To build your company image and reputation, don't try to be a jack-of-all-trades: Become a professional in what you do best.

The Least You Need to Know

➤ Intellectual property rights are the "goodwill" of your business.

➤ You can register a copyright of your original designs, but you have some legal rights even if you don't.

➤ To file a trademark or patent, always seek the advice of an attorney.

➤ Learn about infringement issues to avoid infringing on the rights of others; it will cost you time and money.

➤ Original designs will command a higher selling price than products based on commercial patterns.

➤ Build a cohesive product line to increase your competitiveness.

Part 3

Legal and Financial Stuff You Need to Know

Don't let the title of this part scare you; basic legal and financial information is presented in simple terms that make it easy to understand and use. We explain what you need to check out if you start a home-based business, what determines whether your venture is a hobby or a real business, and when (and why) you may need business insurance. We'll also cover what financial records you will want to keep, as well as start-up costs, financing, banking, and obtaining a merchant credit card account. Then we will explore what laws you may have to comply with and the guidelines for when you may need to seek outside professional assistance. Reading this part will prepare you for running the business that you've been dreaming about.

Chapter 9

How It Works: Can I Run My Business from Home?

In This Chapter

➤ Learning how zoning laws could affect a home-based business

➤ Finding out what licenses or permits your business may need

➤ Looking at government regulations that may affect your business

➤ Considering the importance of safety measures

➤ Tracking the growth of the home-based business sector

Market research reported by Link Resources Corporation shows that more than 32 million people run either full-time or part-time businesses from their homes. Most of them require only a local business license or permit. They are easy to obtain, normally entailing a short visit to the local courthouse. Fees, if any, are minimal. If you're planning to turn your hobby into a home-based business, it's easy to determine what your local licensing requirements are; simply call or visit your city or county government offices for information.

It may be inconceivable to you that your home-based consulting service or needlework business would have to comply with any of the numerous local, state, and federal regulations, but in all likelihood, it will. A word of caution: Avoid the temptation to ignore regulatory details; you may avert some red tape in the short term, but you could encounter obstacles as your business grows. Taking the time to research the applicable regulations, which we look at in this chapter, is as important as knowing your marketing strategy.

The Zoning Laws

Zoning requirements are those laws that regulate how property can be used and, in some cases, certain activities that may not be permitted. If you intend to operate a business from your home, be sure to check local zoning requirements as well as any property covenants before you apply for any permit or license.

Zoning ordinances may be one of the biggest obstacles you'll face if you plan to operate your business from your home. Restrictive zoning in most residential areas is designed to prevent business activity that may create noise, pollution, and traffic; add commercial vehicle traffic; or bring to the residential zone other activities normally associated with commercial or industrial zones.

Many residential zones do allow professional and service businesses to operate, along with other types of business that do not interfere with a clean and quiet environment. In some residentially zoned areas that permit such businesses, however, you may be prohibited from displaying a business sign of any kind.

The purpose of zoning ordinances is to designate specific areas (zones) within municipalities and counties for specific types of activities such as residential-only, agricultural, industrial, light industrial, heavy industrial, or in some cases, a mix of residential and commercial zones. The more populated an area is, the more likely it is that you'll find stricter regulations and enforcement of the zoning laws.

Some "residential-only" zoned areas are so restricted that no business activity whatsoever is allowed, but this is very rare. In most cases, there are provisions for residential business situations. This option is becoming more prevalent with the tremendous growth in the home-based business market. Okay, worst-case scenario: You live in a residential-only area. What do you do? Ignore the zoning and go ahead anyway? Think again. What if a jealous rival or neighbor reported you? So the authorities investigate you and send you one of those dreaded "cease-and-desist" letters (people are rarely fined unless they continue operating after an official warning). Don't do it: Instead, think positively and be proactive.

Artisan's Corner

Agricultural, industrial, and commercial-residential areas should not pose a problem in setting up your new business. If you rent, even if you are in a nonrestricted area, be sure to check your lease. Some leases have clauses preventing tenants from operating a business; to do so would be in violation of your

Dealing with Local Building and Zoning Officials

There's a certain amount of administrative discretion under building codes and zoning ordinances—enough, certainly, that it can help greatly to have the administrators on your side. Here are some ideas for accomplishing this:

➤ Call or visit the zoning department. Get all the details on your zoning regulations. Treat it as one of the things you have to do to before you start your business. Make sure that you understand everything—if you don't, get answers.

➤ Find out what the procedure is for pursuing a change.

➤ Find out if a lawyer is needed to present your case to the zoning board.

➤ Find out how long the time is from petition to decision.

➤ Do some homework. Find out if other home businesses operate in your area—if so, enlist their support. Speak with the SBA, your local Chamber of Commerce, or local business organizations to enlist as much support as possible.

➤ Plan your strategy. Use the codes to your advantage. Let's say that your business will provide sales tax revenue, but you will not have retail customers coming to your house. You won't add noise or traffic congestion to the neighborhood, or cause pollution or damage, and there will be no visible changes to your property that in any way indicate that it houses a home-based business. Explain that you are doing the same thing you always did when it was just a hobby; the only difference is that now you'll be taking orders for your work, packing up your products, and taking them to the post office. If possible, get nearby neighbors to write letters supporting you, and agreeing that your business will not be a nuisance or destroy the quality of life on your block. Act now to avoid any delays in the time schedule for opening your business.

The Decision Is Not Necessarily Final

If you get an adverse decision from the local planning commission, for example, don't give up. You may be able to have a board of zoning adjustment or have a board of appeals interpret the zoning ordinance in a way that's favorable to you. Alternatively, you may be able to obtain a variance (a special exception to a zoning law) if a strict interpretation of the ordinance causes a hardship. In some cases, you can get a conditional use permit, which lets you use the property in question for your kind of business as long as you meet certain conditions set down by the administrative panel.

Pointers

There's a certain amount of administrative discretion under building codes and zoning ordinances—enough, certainly, that it can help greatly to have the administrators on your side. "No" is not always the final answer.

In dealing with administrators, and especially with appeals boards, it is important to have the support of neighbors and others in your community. A favorable petition signed by most other businesses in your immediate area, or oral expressions of support from half a dozen neighbors can make the difference between success and failure at an administrative hearing.

Certificate of Occupancy

If you're planning to occupy a building for a new business, you may have to apply for a Certificate of Occupancy (commonly called a CO or a C of O) from a city or county zoning department. For more information, contact the county or city office in your area. You may also try going to your state home page, at www.sba.gov/world/states.html. When you open the page, just select your state; then locate its search feature and type in "certificate of occupancy" or "county information."

Be Prepared for Obstacles

In some communities, you must get a zoning compliance permit before you start your business at a given location. Other communities simply wait for someone to complain before zoning compliance gets looked at.

Arles Mitchell, owner of *N2 Crafts* in Illinois, who makes handcrafted ceramics and other gift items shown at www.intocrafts.com, tells NCA about her start-up experience.

Crafter Alert

Keep in mind that by applying for a construction permit for remodeling, or by filing for a tax ID or a business license with your municipality, you may trigger an investigation of zoning compliance.

"When I applied through the state for my Illinois Retailers Tax ID license number, they automatically notified my local village of a 'new business' in the area. Of course, our village officials, being the competent individuals that they are (and I am using this term loosely), promptly sent me a very threatening letter about 'operating a business without the appropriate village license.' I talked to them over the phone and explained that I was not selling from my home, and I was not causing traffic congestion because of it. I finally wound up going over to the village offices directly. After explaining that I make the items and then ship them out of state, they 'waived' my license fee, but I still had to fill out all the forms.

"I opted to apply for a retailer's license because I felt that it would make my home business venture 'more professional' and would also allow me to buy supplies wholesale, and so on. By having this license, I get a substantial discount on my molds, glazes, and other supplies, and these businesses treat me as a business—which I am! I operate at home from our basement, which was family space until there were 600-plus molds in it. If we had more room, I'd love to have an on-site studio, but my husband just keeps insisting that we do need the garage for our car. My biggest problem is that I've even outgrown the basement. I keep reorganizing things a little at a time, but with trying to get the ceramics made and orders out, there is never enough time."

As you can see from Mitchell's story, applying for a tax number can trigger obstacles. Some artisans suggest getting a post office box in a commercially zoned area before applying for tax numbers, permits, or licenses, and then using it as your legal business address.

In addition to zoning laws that regulate traffic, environmental factors, and the placement of signs, there are historic district restrictions in some communities. They may keep you from modifying the exterior of a building or even changing the paint color without permission from a board of administrators. Years ago, people tried to argue in court that such regulation of aesthetics wasn't a proper governmental function, in that it wasn't related to the protection of the public health and safety. However, carefully drawn ordinances seeking to preserve the special appeal of historic districts have tended to survive such legal challenges.

Building Codes

For anything but the most minor renovation (such as putting in track lighting or installing shelves), you're likely to need a permit—maybe several—from the building and safety department that enforces building ordinances and codes. Often, separate permits are issued for separate parts of a construction or remodeling project, including permits for electrical, plumbing, and mechanical (heating and ventilating) work. If you don't have experience in these areas, you may need a licensed contractor to help you discover the requirements for your construction or remodeling project. Building codes are amended frequently, and each revision seems to put new restrictions and requirements on the building owners.

Permits and Licenses

There are licensing and permit requirements at all levels of government: federal, state, regional, county, and city. It is not always easy to discover exactly what licenses and permits you'll need, but it's very important. You should thoroughly research this issue before you start a new business, complete the purchase of a business, change locations, or remodel or expand your operation. If you do not, you may face expenses and hassles that you had not anticipated.

You'll probably need a basic license or permit for your business, and you may need one or more specialized licenses. This is especially likely if you serve or sell food, liquor, or firearms; work with hazardous materials; or discharge any materials into the air or water.

Each state has its own system of licensing, as does each unit of local government. Obviously, it is impossible to provide a comprehensive list of every permit and license in the United States. Fortunately, we can give you some general principles and a positive approach to help you learn about and comply with the licensing or regulation requirements that may affect your business.

Your business may be required to have one or more of the following licenses or permits:

➤ **Business license.** Check with the city and county governments to determine which business licenses are required.

➤ **Health, fire, and other special permits.** Any business that processes or sells food to the public must have a health department permit. Businesses that handle flammable materials or have large numbers of people on their premises may also be required to have a fire department permit. If you expect to discharge any substance into the air, sewer system, or local waterways, you may have to obtain a special permit from agencies controlling pollution and environmental health.

➤ **Occupational permit.** Most states require special licensing, which may entail a written or oral examination for businesses in certain categories, such as occupations that involve direct physical contact with customers (hairdressing, massage, or medical treatment are examples), or businesses that involve special technical expertise that may be related to consumer safety or health (plumbing, electrical work, auto repairs, pest control, engineering, and dry cleaning are examples). This also applies to agencies involved in real estate, insurance, and collections.

➤ **Sales tax permit.** Those who sell products directly to consumers must usually collect a sales tax (food products are exempt from a sales tax in some states). If you sell products only to wholesalers, retailers, or other middlemen, you usually do not have to collect a sales tax, but you must maintain tax exemption forms. Some states require those who sell services to collect sales taxes. Many states require that you pay a bond or an advance deposit against sales taxes to be collected when you first apply for a sales tax number.

➤ **Federal Tax ID.** Form SS-4 is the application for an employer identification number (EIN), which should be filed by every business. If you are a sole proprietor, you may use your own Social Security number rather than a separate employer identification number, but we generally recommend that even sole proprietors obtain an EIN, especially if they plan to hire employees or retain independent contractors. This is one good way to keep your business and your personal affairs separate.

➤ **Federal licensing.** This is required for gun dealers, security and investment brokers and advisers, radio and television stations, and drug manufacturers.

➤ **Licensing based on products sold.** Some licenses for businesses are based on the products sold. For example, there often are special licenses for businesses that sell liquor, food, lottery tickets, gasoline, or firearms.

Government Regulations and Your Business

Bear in mind that regulations vary by industry. If you're in the food service business, for example, you'll have to deal with the health department. If you use chemical solvents, you'll have environmental compliance to meet. Carefully investigate the regulations that affect your industry. Being out of compliance could leave you legally unprotected, may lead to expensive penalties, and could jeopardize your business.

Double-check license and permit rules. When you investigate the type of licenses and permits that you need for your business, check directly with the appropriate governmental agencies. Never rely on the fact that an existing business similar to yours did not need a license or had to meet only minimal building code requirements. Laws and ordinances are amended frequently, generally to impose more stringent requirements. Often an existing business is allowed to continue under the old rules, but new businesses must meet the higher standards.

For obvious reasons, do not rely on the advice of real estate agents, business brokers, the seller of a business, or anyone else with a financial interest in having a deal go through.

What's the Worst That Could Happen?

In a worst-case scenario, if you fail to meet government regulations, you could be prevented from operating your planned business at a particular location but still be obligated to pay rent or make mortgage payments. For example, what if you sign a five-year lease for business space and then discover that the location is not zoned properly for your type of business? What if you start a catering business and find out that you can't get a liquor license? Or suppose that you rent or buy business space thinking that you can afford to remodel or expand it, without realizing that remodeling means you must comply with all current ordinances? You may have to pay for $10,000 worth of improvements to comply with the Federal Americans with Disabilities Act, or $5,000 for a state-of-the-art waste disposal system.

Pointers

The Consumer Information Center (www.pueblo.gsa.gov) has pamphlets such as "Americans with Disabilities Act: Guide for Small Businesses," "General Information Concerning Patents," "Guide to Business Credit for Women, Minorities, and Small Businesses," "Resource Directory for Small Business Management," "Running a Small Business," "Selling a Business," and "Starting a Business."

If you lease in a plaza or a mall, in most cases, you'll be paying for all the improvements, repairs, and maintenance, so check your lease carefully before you sign.

In short, license and permit requirements can affect where you locate your business, how much you'll have to spend for remodeling, and whether you'll have to provide off-street parking. If zoning requirements are too restrictive, you may even decide to avoid the hassle and move somewhere where you don't have to fight City Hall—literally—for the right to do business. Similarly, if building codes require extensive and expensive remodeling to bring an older building up to current standards, you may want to look for newer space that already complies with building and safety laws.

Check Your State Business Licenses

Many types of licenses exist. You need one to operate legally almost everywhere. If your business is located within incorporated city limits, you must obtain a license from the city; if you're outside the city limits, you must obtain a license from the county. For more information, contact the county or city office in your area, or visit your state home page, at www.sba.gov/world/states.html, using keywords "business license" or "county information."

Protect Your Safety

To protect the safety of your employees, customers, and community, take note of the following:

➤ Beware of hazards in your industry.

➤ Implement safety procedures.

➤ Regularly and thoroughly maintain equipment and machinery.

➤ Use and maintain safety equipment.

➤ Be alert for fire hazards.

➤ Keep a first aid kit in your work area.

➤ Think safety. Train yourself to monitor safety conditions in your work areas.

Don't think you're exempt; even the most experienced people have accidents! I know a wood crafter who for 32 years worked in his shop. One day while rushing to get some orders finished, he cut off three fingers on a table saw. Why? Because he didn't take the time to engage his safety shield; after all, he just had one more board to cut. A 10-year veteran candle-maker told me of another preventable accident. She had a 12-quart kettle of hot wax that she wanted to remove from the stove, so she put on big oven mitts that had large rings sewn into them for hanging. As she picked up the kettle, one of the rings caught on the stove gas grate and caused her to spill hot wax on one of her arms and her chest. What was as painful as the burns was the fact that it had happened before (without injury). She had meant to cut those rings off the mitts, but she just hadn't stopped long enough to do it!

Occupational Safety and Health Act Rules and Regulations

As an employer, you are responsible under the Occupational Safety and Health Act (OSHA) to provide a workplace free from recognized hazards that are causing or are likely to cause death or serious physical harm to your employees. You must comply with standards, rules, and regulations issued by OSHA under the act. You must be familiar with the standards and must make copies available to employees for review upon their request.

Most employers of 11 or more employees are required to maintain records of occupational injuries and illnesses as they occur. Employers with 10 or fewer employees, and employers in certain industries, regardless of size, are exempt from keeping such records unless they are selected by the Bureau of Labor Statistics (BLS) to participate in the Annual Survey of Occupational Injuries and Illnesses.

Pointers

OSHA record-keeping is not required for employers in the retail trade or in the finance, insurance, real estate, or service industries (Standard Industrial Classification [SIC] 522–89). The exceptions are building material and garden supplies (SIC 52); general merchandise and food stores (SIC 53 and 54); hotels and other lodging places (SIC 70); repair services (SIC 75 and 76); amusement and recreation services (SIC 79); and health services (SIC 80).

OSHA's Small Business Safety Management Series

Even if you do not have employees, OSHA may be able to provide you with valuable tips to help you design a safe work environment for your business. Perhaps you work with chemicals or paints that require proper ventilation. What about safety glasses, if you use a grinder or a sander, or if you work with caustic materials? What fire safety measures do you have in place if you work with torches, hot plates, or gas burners? The flyer for small business employers "Keeping Your Workplace Safe: Q's & A's for Small Business Employers" provides an overview of OSHA services and can be downloaded from OSHA at www.osha-slc.gov/OshDoc/Additional.html.

Home Business Boom!

In J. Paul Getty's book *How to Get Rich,* his first rule for success is this: "You must be in business for yourself; you'll never get rich working for someone else." This partly explains why someone starts a new home-based business in the United States every 10 seconds. In the past 14 years alone, the number of home-based businesses has grown from 6 million to 32 million, with no slowdown in sight. In fact, an estimated 8,493 new home businesses open every day. The home-based business boom is estimated to generate around $427 billion annually.

Artisan's Corner

Right now in this country, more than 32 million Americans are making money right out of their own homes! Their average income is $50,250 per year, and one out of every five is earning more than $75,000 per year. That is twice the national average income, and half of the people who work from home are working only part-time or in their spare time!

People used to believe that their livelihood depended on living in big cities near big corporations. That is no longer true, thanks to personal computers, increased phone services, fax machines, and the Internet. Large corporations used to be necessary because they had the financial means to consolidate communication and technology. Within the last five to seven years, technology has been brought to an affordable level so that almost everyone is on a level playing field in the work-from-home industry.

Take action now! Nothing will happen until you do! Whether you decide to start a home-based business or to locate it elsewhere, the only way to figure out what is right for you is to do the research so that you can make an informed decision. Just take one step at a time and you'll soon see results. As Kay Lyons, a motivational writer, said, "Yesterday is a cancelled check; tomorrow is a promissory note; today is the only cash you have …."

The Least You Need to Know

➤ Wherever you decide to locate your business, you must first check the zoning laws to be sure that it will be allowed.

➤ Zoning regulations can be amended, so don't accept "no" without pursuing the matter further.

➤ Your business probably will need a license or a permit, and possibly several them, so be sure to find out exactly what's required before you proceed.

➤ Home-based business is a growth industry that is providing above average incomes for business owners.

Chapter 10

Uncle Sam
and You

In This Chapter

➤ Learning why and when you need a sales tax number

➤ Understanding what a resale certificate is and where to use it

➤ Knowing when the IRS really believes your hobby is a business

➤ Avoiding the hobby restriction

➤ Exploring business deductions and learning how to apply them

---

If you're serious about turning your hobby into a business, then you must comply with certain tax regulations. If you do, you'll qualify to take advantage of all the benefits you're entitled to under the law.

In this chapter, we explain the sales tax rules, detail how to qualify your hobby as a for-profit business, and cover some of the important deductions that you can take advantage of. It's really not all that complicated once you understand and apply some of the basic principles that we explain. As you'll discover, there are some real tax benefits to setting up a for-profit business. Some experts even view a small business as one of the few "tax shelters" left that anyone can take advantage of.

The Sales Tax Number Plays a Dual Role

Most products or services that you sell are taxable, so you need to obtain a sales tax number (or vendor number) from your State Department of Revenue or State Department of Taxation. The number is used for reporting the sales tax collected from your customers.

Pointers

The main office for each state tax office is listed on the U.S. Small Business Administration Web site (at www.business.gov/busadv/frame.cfm or www.sba.gov/starting/indexstartup.html&catid-55&urlplace-maincat.cmf) which offers a link to each state's home page. Just select your state, and then search your state's site for sales tax information.

Your tax number is also used when you buy supplies. You're exempt from tax when you purchase materials or supplies *that will be a component part of your product.* Tax is paid when the "end user" takes possession of the product—that is, added to the price of the final finished item when the purchaser pays for it.

To find out if your product line or service is taxable, call your state tax office. If it is, request the proper forms, and file them to be issued a tax ID number.

If you sell retail to consumers, you're responsible for collecting and paying the sales tax. Your state sales tax department will send you forms to complete and return with the total amount of taxes that you have collected for the period. If you sell wholesale, you're required to obtain and keep on file a resale certificate for each customer. This is your proof that you were not required to collect tax from that customer. If you're buying for resale, then you must supply the company you're purchasing from a completed resale certificate.

Crafter Alert

Sales tax reporting and payment is easier to do if you keep a separate bank account for the sales taxes that you collect. This way, the tax money is always on hand when it's due. If you co-mingle sales tax dollars with your general business money, it's too easy to inadvertently use some of the funds to pay other expenses. Fines and penalties are charged for late payment or late reporting of sales tax. Remember, this money is never yours to use; you're merely a collector and keeper of the funds until it's time to turn them over along with your sales tax report.

You can obtain a copy of a resale certificate from your state tax department. Most business owners fill out an original resale certificate with their company information and leave the portion blank that refers to the vendor that they are sending it to. They make copies of the form and keep them on hand to complete and send to new suppliers whenever required. Some wholesale suppliers won't even send you a catalog until they receive a copy of your resale certificate. They want to know that you're a viable business that may become a customer before they invest in you by sending a catalog.

Sales Tax Tips

Chances are, you'll run into one or more of the following situations. Here's how to handle them:

➤ If you plan to sell at retail craft or trade shows in states other than the one in which you operate your business, you're required to obtain a sales tax number for *each state* that you do business in. Most states offer temporary (if you plan to sell at only a few) or one-time sales tax permits to cover this situation.

➤ If you sell via mail order or on the Internet, you're required to collect sales tax only from residents of the states in which you have a *physical* business location. (Lawmakers are currently trying to close this loophole.) So, if you operate a home business in New York state, then only New York state residents who are buying retail products or services from you are required to pay sales tax. This includes sales via the Internet or by phone, fax, mail, or e-mail. All of these sales are considered mail orders and are covered by the laws that presently govern mail-order sales. This will probably change in the near future if the lawmakers get their way, but at present, apply this rule for collecting tax from retail customers.

Pointers

If you sell via mail order or on the Internet, you're required to collect sales tax only from residents of the states where you have a *physical* business location. The sales transaction is considered as having originated at your place of business.

➤ If you do sell wholesale, then you'll need to get a completed, signed copy of a resale certificate from your customers, with their valid tax ID number. Keep this on file as proof that you did not have to collect sales tax from this customer. This is very important documentation to have if you're ever subject to a sales tax audit. It's proof that you made a valid nontaxable sale. Without this proof, you could be subject to paying the sales tax yourself, even though you did not collect it. Keeping good records for tax purposes is very important. It can save you a lot of headaches in the future.

The Deal on Business Deductions

For many workers, particularly employees, business deductions may seem like forbidden fruit because of their strict eligibility guidelines and other restrictions. Self-employed individuals don't face the same obstacle. Expenses related to their businesses can be deducted in full on Schedule C.

Pointers

Read IRS Publication 334, "Tax Guide for Small Businesses." This publication provides overviews of the tax rules. It is a must-read guide for small businesses.

Crafter Alert

If you sell your work, whatever it may be—decorative painting, wearing apparel, florals, wood crafts, or soaps and toiletries—*any income that it generates is subject to tax.*

Hobby or Business?—the IRS View

Whether you're engaged in a hobby or a for-profit business is a critical distinction. If you have a sideline business, be it designing wearing apparel, producing wood crafts, or making soaps and toiletries, *any income that it generates is subject to tax.* The good news is that you're entitled to deduct your sideline business's expenses. How much you can deduct depends on whether your sales of products or services is deemed by the IRS to be a hobby or a profit-motivated business. If it's considered a hobby, your expenses are deductible only to the extent of income generated by the sideline during the year. For example, if you sell $500 in wooden shelves, only $500 in expenses qualify for a deduction, even if you spent three or four times that amount on advertising, craft show fees, and the like. Beyond that, you may not even be able to deduct the $500 because hobby expenses can be claimed only as a "miscellaneous" itemized deduction. Miscellaneous expenses, which include job, investment, and tax-related expenses, are deductible only to the extent that they exceed 2 percent of your adjusted gross income.

The 2 percent floor means that you may have to resign yourself to the fact that you won't receive much, if any, tax benefit from your hobby. When you spend money on your hobby, simply keep in mind that the federal government will provide little, if any, help in subsidizing the costs. Just consider your hobby a pleasurable diversion, and enjoy it.

Avoiding Restrictions on Your Hobby's Deductible Expenses

If your sideline business is more than a hobby, you may be able to avoid the tight restrictions on hobby expenses. If you can prove that your sideline is a profit-motivated business, you won't be hampered by the 2 percent floor on miscellaneous deductions. You'll be able to deduct all your expenses, even if they surpass the income generated from the business, on Schedule C, where business income and expenses are reported, and you'll be able to claim your deductions whether or not you itemize. But to do all this, you'll need to make sure that your sideline measures up to IRS standards.

As you might expect, the best way to demonstrate that your sideline is a profit-motivated business is to make the operation profitable. The IRS will automatically presume that it is if it has made a profit in at least three of the past five years (two of seven years for breeding, training, showing, or racing horses). If you can't turn a profit that often, you won't automatically lose the right to deduct expenses in excess of income. The tax law does recognize that in the real world, even the most profit-minded businesspeople sometimes have trouble turning a profit in most years—particularly in the early years of a new enterprise.

If you don't meet the three-of-five-year profit test, you can still try to convince the IRS that your sideline is more than a hobby by offering evidence that your enterprise is being run in a businesslike manner and that you're working hard to make it profitable. It's not always an easy case to make, especially if your sideline is the sort of thing that hobbyists tend to do, such as sewing, writing, stamp collecting, or breeding dogs. That's why tax advisers tell their clients to try hard to meet the three-of-five-year-profit test. If you don't meet the three-of-five-year profit test and you want to present a strong case to the IRS, make sure that you document all your business activities, save your records, and keep your business and personal finances and records separate.

What Is Deductible?

To be deductible, a business expense must be ordinary and necessary. An *ordinary expense* is one that is common and accepted in your type of business operation. A *necessary expense* is one that is helpful and appropriate for your type of business. An expense does not have to be indispensable to be considered necessary.

Trade Terms

Ordinary expenses are common to your type of business. **Necessary expenses** are appropriate and don't have to be indispensable. The rule of thumb to determine the **cost of goods sold** is to include all expenses that are required to produce your product.

117

The Cost of Goods Sold

If your business manufactures or purchases products for resale, some of your expenses include the cost of making or preparing the product that you sell. You use these expenses to figure your cost of goods sold during the year. Deduct these costs from your gross receipts to figure your gross profits for the year. You must maintain inventory records to determine your *cost of goods sold*. The same costs cannot be deducted again as business expenses. The typical expenses included in the cost of goods sold are these:

➤ The cost of products or raw materials, plus any shipping that you paid to obtain them

➤ The cost of storing your products

➤ Direct labor costs (including contributions to pension or annuity plans for workers who produce the products)

➤ The overhead to maintain your studio, workshop, or the area where production is done

➤ Product packing materials

➤ Packing and handling costs

Capital Expenses

You must capitalize some expenses rather than deduct them. These costs are considered your part of your own investment in your business. In general, there are three major capital expenses:

➤ The cost of going into business

➤ Business assets

➤ Improvements

These expenses are handled by a method of either depreciation, amortization, or depletion, all of which allow you to deduct a portion of the expense each year over a number of years. This is an area that you'll want to discuss with your accountant because various business operations may require different applications under the law.

Personal Expenses

If you have expenses that are partly business and partly personal, you must separate the personal part from the business part and keep reasonable records to support your deductions. For example, if you have a business in your home, you may qualify to deduct a percentage of your total personal household expenses (rent, utilities, insurance, water, and taxes) equal to the actual amount of designated space that your business occupies within your home. If you're able to qualify, the deductions can bring lucrative tax savings. Fortunately, more home-based workers should now be able to qualify for home-office deductions as a result of the Taxpayer Relief Act of 1997.

Business Use of Your Home

Congress has relaxed the eligibility guidelines for workers who base their businesses at home but tend to perform their services away from home (as is often the case for outside salespersons, plumbers, interior decorators, artisans who consistently sell at retail or wholesale trade shows, contractors, caterers, and so forth). Under the new law, such workers will be allowed to claim home-office deductions as long as their home office is regularly used to perform administrative or managerial tasks, and as long as there is no other fixed location where they conduct "substantial administrative or managerial activities."

If your home office is used for more than one business, each business use must qualify for home-office deductions as a separate entity. If no business use qualifies, you won't be eligible to claim any home-office deductions. IRS Publication #587, "Business Use of Your Home," is a must-read for anyone planning a home-based business. Be aware that, if you've taken the home-office deductions, there also may be tax consequences when you sell your home. Be sure to read the IRS rules on selling your home in Publications 523 and 544, which cover this topic in depth.

Home-Office Storage Areas

Home-office deductions may be claimed for a space in the home used to store product samples or inventory. People who sell products out of their homes may be able to claim some extra home-office deductions on their income tax returns, even if the storage area is sometimes used for other purposes. Storage areas are exempt from the "exclusive-use" requirement.

Crafter Alert

To make informed decisions, check out the IRS rules on selling your home in Publications 523 and 544, which cover other assets.

To qualify for storage deductions, you must be in the business of selling products, and your home must be the *only fixed location* of your business.

Business Deductions

Most of you have a pretty good idea of what *business expense* deductions are allowed. As a general rule, if the expense is a result of the operation of the business, it's a viable deduction.

Business deductions are pretty straightforward, but be careful; some deductions do have specific qualifications, as you'll see in the following sections.

Trade Terms

As a general rule, if the expense is a result of the operation of the business, it's a **business expense** and a viable deduction.

Business Use of a Vehicle

The IRS standard mileage rate is the simplest way to deduct business use, but it's not always the best option.

When writing off business use of a car, you generally have the option to deduct actual expenses or to claim the IRS standard mileage rate plus parking and tolls. The IRS mileage rate jumped from 31 cents to 32.5 cents in 1999.

The mileage rate used to be allowed only for cars that you owned, but beginning with 1998 returns, the IRS allowed the mileage rate to be used for leased cars. That should be welcome news to the growing number of drivers who lease their cars and are tired of the record-keeping burden of computing actual expenses.

If you're not going to keep the records needed to compute actual expenses, then the simpler mileage rate is the way to go. However, if you do hang on to your receipts, you'll sometimes find that, if you use your own car, adding up your actual expenses will produce a bigger deduction. (Actual expenses include not just gas and oil, but depreciation or lease payments, insurance, automobile club memberships, license fees, car washes, repairs, maintenance, and more.) Which method will produce the bigger deduction depends on how many miles you drive and how expensive your car is to maintain. If you're traveling every weekend, selling at craft or trade shows, you'll definitely want to evaluate which method gives you the best deduction. The difference between the two methods tends to be greater for leased cars. You'll probably get a larger deduction on a leased car if you use actual expenses.

To use the standard mileage rate for a car that you own, you must choose it for the first year that you use the car for business. In future years, you'll have the option to choose either method. If you want to use the standard mileage rate for a leased car, you must use it for the entire lease period.

Business Equipment

When you write off business equipment, be it a computer, a fax machine, a file cabinet, a table saw, a sewing machine, or a canopy, you'll generally find the best option to be the "first-year expensing" method. This special depreciation method, which is referred to as Section 179 on IRS tax forms, was intended to give smaller businesses a simple and fast way to write off their business equipment.

Instead of having to depreciate the equipment's cost over a period of years, the expensing method allows you to fully write off up to $20,000 of the equipment that you purchase in 2000. The following table shows future increases.

Pointers

For more information on business use of a vehicle, read IRS Publication 463, "Travel, Entertainment, Gift, and Car Expenses."

Amount of Equipment Purchases Eligible for Expensing

Year	Amount
2000	$20,000
2001	$24,000
2002	$24,000
2003 and after	$25,000

Among other restrictions, *write-offs under the expensing method are generally limited to the amount of taxable income that you have from your business.* But there is an exception if you have income from another job. The IRS allows employees with sideline businesses to count salary that they earn from their regular job as business income when figuring their limit on expensing deductions for the sideline.

Special restrictions also apply to personal computers, cellular phones, and certain other equipment that's used partly for personal purposes. To qualify for expensing, these items must be used more than 50 percent of the time for business.

For more detailed information, read IRS Publication 946, "How to Depreciate Property."

Entertainment Expenses

Taking a client or customer out to lunch or for a round of golf or a night on the town often makes good business sense. Such outings can provide the social lubrication needed to grease relationships in the business world. In many cases, not a word of

Crafter Alert

Keep in mind that business meal and entertainment expenses are only 50 percent deductible. The cost of getting to the restaurant or entertainment event, however, is 100 percent deductible.

business needs to be uttered to produce results. There is much to be said for meeting business associates in a setting away from your business base. It's more relaxed and offers a great opportunity to network, cement your business relationships, and build new ones.

So, if you take a client to lunch and hope to deduct the cost, you'll need to talk some bona-fide business and keep a written note of the nature of the discussion in case the IRS later questions the deduction.

The deductible limit on business gifts is $25 a year to any one individual. You can't circumvent the $25 limitation by making separate gifts to family members of the customer. Nor can you exceed the limit by also having your spouse make a gift to the same customer—even if your spouse has a separate business relationship with the customer.

However, you can deduct a few incidental expenses beyond the $25: the cost of engraving, wrapping, and mailing the gifts, and the cost of promotional gift items, such as pens or calendars on which your name is imprinted and which cost no more than $4 each. So, if you buy a customer a gift that costs $25, spend an extra $4 to wrap and mail it, and then give the same customer a $3 pen with your company's name on it. You'll then be eligible to deduct a total of $32 as a business expense on your tax return.

Membership Dues

Although the law itself seems to apply the ban broadly, the IRS carved out some major exceptions.

Under IRS regulations, the deduction ban is limited to country clubs, business luncheon clubs, airline lounge clubs, hotel clubs, athletic clubs, and other organizations whose principal purpose is to provide entertainment facilities or activities for members and their guests. But the IRS lists several types of membership organizations for which business deductions for dues are still generally allowed. They include professional organizations (such as bar associations and medical associations), civic or public service organizations (such as Kiwanis and Rotary), and business trade groups (such as Chambers of Commerce and your business-related trade associations).

Write-Offs for Home Phones

No matter how much a home phone may be used for business calls, the tax law doesn't permit deductions for any part of the basic monthly service charge for the first telephone line into a residence. But that prohibition does not apply to optional services on your first line. Thus, charges for such options as caller ID, call waiting, extra directory listings, and equipment rental can be deducted in proportion to your business use.

If you have a second phone line at home, both basic and optional service charges on the second line can be deducted in proportion to your business usage.

Pointers

You should obtain a separate business telephone line, rather than take business calls on your home telephone line. The phone line and all business–related charges can be deducted in full.

If you intend to present a professional business image, I strongly suggest that you have a separate business phone line. It should never be answered by anyone incapable of handling a business call in a professional, knowledgeable way. Use an answering machine or voice mail to cover the line when you're not available, and return your calls promptly. This will go a long way in helping you build strong customer relations.

For more tax deductions information, read IRS Publication 529, "Miscellaneous Deductions."

Business Trip Meals

Instead of having to total up all your receipts for meals you've had while traveling, you can take the IRS option of using a fixed-rate allowance, ranging from $30 to $46 a day, depending on the destination. (The allowance covers food and certain incidentals, including tips and dry cleaning.)

If you claim the IRS "standard meal allowance," you won't need any receipts to substantiate your meal expenses, although you still need to keep a record of the time, place, and business purpose of your travel.

Pointers

If you need any IRS forms, you can now get them online in several formats. Just go to www.business.gov/busadv/frame.cfm or www.sba.gov/starting/indexstartup.html&catid=55&urlplace=maincat.cfm. You can download or print any of the forms you select.

Be aware that if you use the IRS meal allowance for any business trip, there are, as they say in the restaurant business, no substitutions. You have to use the same method for computing meal expenses for all your business travel during the year. In other words, you can't compute actual expenses for your business trip to New York when you went on a fine-restaurant binge and then use the standard meal allowance for your business trip to South Dakota, where you dined at only fast-food restaurants or truck stops.

Keeping Records

When you start your business, set up a simple record-keeping system—or, better yet, use a computer. Try to total your financial information at least once a month, with quarterly subtotals. Then tax time will not become your worst nightmare. More important, you'll have some real information to help you gauge how your business is doing. That way, you'll be able to spot trouble right away and take steps to correct it before it becomes a major stumbling block to growth and expansion.

The financial information in this chapter should be used as only a guideline to help you understand business expense deductions. Always seek the help of a qualified professional before making any financial or tax-related business decisions.

The Least You Need to Know

➤ Most products or services that you plan to sell will be taxable.

➤ To buy wholesale the materials and supplies necessary to make your product, you'll need a tax ID number.

➤ You must be able to prove that your venture is profit-motivated to be recognized as a business by the IRS and to get the appropriate business deductions.

➤ Most ordinary business operating expenses are tax-deductible, subject to the tax rules that apply to each category.

Chapter 11

Protect Thyself: Insurance

In This Chapter

➤ Learning what business insurance does for you

➤ Exploring types of business insurance

➤ Selecting the risks that you should get coverage for

➤ Determining the kinds of insurance and the coverage levels that you need

➤ Considering health insurance options for your small business

If you operate a business out of your home, you may be surprised to learn that many homeowners' and renters' policies do not cover losses from business activities. Actually, many homeowners' and renters' policies *specifically exclude* losses from business activities. A small business cannot operate without insurance; it allows owners to minimize the risk of loss from circumstances beyond their control.

The first step in choosing types of coverage for your business is to identify the particular risks associated with the kind of business you're operating and to determine the largest amount that each loss could cost you. The amount of property or liability insurance that you need and what kind of health coverage you choose will be based on your individual circumstances. Every business has different insurance needs. After you calculate your coverage needs, the right amount of insurance for you will depend on how much the business can afford on an annual basis and what other financial reserves you could tap if you had a major loss.

Why You Need Insurance

You need insurance to cover the danger zones in your business, the areas in which a loss could be so great that it could create a serious business disruption—or, worse yet, make it impossible for you to continue to operate. Don't buy insurance for small exposures; the cost of premiums probably would outweigh the value of what you cover and would waste dollars that you'll need to buy coverage for your major exposures.

After you've determined that you do need insurance and have decided what you should cover and how much you can afford to spend on premiums, don't rush to your insurance agent's office. First see if you can do the following:

➤ Eliminate or reduce your risk by properly managing maintenance, repairs, training, and safety programs.

➤ Assume some of the risk yourself by buying policies with high deductibles and having the business pay for small losses.

Then, transfer the risk to your insurer by buying an appropriate amount of insurance tailored to your specific needs.

Pointers

Property insurance is most commonly needed to defend against fire and smoke damage. Small businesses should also consider the possibility of losses from floods, hurricanes, or other severe storms; earthquakes; building collapses; or other unusual events based on your location and the probability of such an occurrence in your particular area.

Cause-of-Loss Insurance

The Cause-of-Loss Form insures your property against all risk of direct physical loss, including fire; volcanic action; smoke; sprinkler leakage; sinkhole collapse; explosion; vandalism; riot or civil commotion; lightning; windstorm or hail; aircraft or vehicles; glass breakage; damage from falling objects on the building exterior; damage to building walls or the roof from the weight of snow, ice, or sleet; water damage caused by accidental discharge or leakage from a plumbing, heating, or air-conditioning system or domestic appliance; and the collapse of building walls or the roof.

The Cause-of-Loss Form excludes these losses: mysterious disappearance of property; damage done to property being worked upon; artificially generated electrical currents; wear, tear, marring, or scratching; insects or vermin; dampness or dryness of the atmosphere; changes in temperature; rust or corrosion; theft from an unattended or unlocked auto; fidelity of an employee or officer of the bank; damage done by rain, snow, or sleet to property in the open; earthquake; flood (surface waters or water that backs up through sewers or drains); water below the surface of the ground, including that which exerts pressure or flows, seeps, or leaks through sidewalks, driveways, foundations, walls, basement floors, or any opening; and the explosion of steam boilers and steam pipes.

Be sure you know what is and is not covered by basic insurance, and buy extra insurance that you think you need for losses not protected in the basic policy by adding special endorsements to it. Basic property insurance includes coverage for fire, sprinkler damage, and lightning, for example, but you may want to add endorsements to cover such losses from earthquakes or infestation of insects or vermin. Cost, not whether the coverage is available, is often the major factor in deciding what to include in a property insurance policy.

Coverage for loss is usually provided on the basis of full replacement costs of the items destroyed, without deduction for depreciation. Replacement costs fluctuate, so you should constantly check your insurable values to make sure that you have adequate coverage. Most insurance policies have a deductible, the amount you pay out-of-pocket off the top of the claim. So, if you had an insurance claim approved for $1,500 and your policy had a $250 deductible, the insurance company would pay you the net total due of $1,250.

Pointers

Insurance for losses covers both the property damage itself and the extra costs after the loss, such as out-of-pocket expenses for cleaning up and removing debris, unexpected storage costs, or temporary rentals and repairs. Another important kind of extra cost is business interruption loss if the business has to shut down for a period after the damage. Customers may be lost, and money may be owed to suppliers.

Business Income Insurance

The purpose of business income insurance is to replace the operating income of your business when damage to your premises or other property prevents you from earning income. If your business suffers a business interruption and has to close for several months, or if it has to operate at a reduced pace because of fire or another peril covered by this form of insurance, your operating income will remain the same.

Business income insurance covers the actual loss sustained by the insured that results directly from the necessary interruption of business caused by damage or destruction of real or personal property.

Other specific policies cover other kinds of property. Boiler and machinery policies cover a variety of business equipment, including computers, furnaces and coolers, telephone systems, and manufacturing equipment. Crime policies cover losses from vandalism or theft, by either employees or outsiders. Special insurance is also available for cash, securities, and other valuable items.

Workers' Compensation and Employers' Liability

Workers' compensation coverage pays benefits required under workers' compensation laws, and employers' liability pays employees not covered by workers' compensation laws. If you subcontract certain operations, workers' compensation laws state that the principal contractor is responsible for compensating employees of uninsured subcontractors. In determining compensation premiums, you will be charged a premium for coverage in connection with employees of subcontractors unless the subcontractors have insured this obligation and have furnished satisfactory evidence of such insurance. *You should always obtain certificates of insurance from all subcontractors working for you.*

Liability Insurance

In any small business, many unforeseen events can require *casualty,* or *liability,* insurance (the terms have the same meaning). A customer may be injured in a fall in a store and may sue for damages related to the injury. An engineer might be sued for the design of a walkway that had to be repaired at great expense to the business owner. Every small business should be covered for liabilities.

Many art and craft or trade shows now require the artisan to have liability insurance and provide proof of it before participating in the show. This is especially true of shows held in government-owned facilities, such as fairgrounds, or in parks or on public streets. When you rent a booth at a show, that booth space becomes your "store." This makes you responsible for covering your liability exposure, just as if you were operating your own retail store.

Liability insurance covers the personal injury losses involved in the liability claims, such as medical expenses after an injury, and related compensatory damages.

Another major type of liability loss is property loss, such as damage to a car resulting from the collapse of an awning in front of a retail store.

Liability insurance also covers the legal fees required to defend against lawsuits filed against a business. Often the insurance company will hire lawyers to defend the business to avoid having to pay out the loss claim.

Crafter Alert

You are just as liable for injuries to your customers in your show booth as you would be in a retail store. For example, a customer could trip over an extension cord in your booth and suffer injuries from a fall, a child could be hurt by toppling a display, or a sign could fall and hit someone. That's why it's essential to have liability insurance.

Remember that the insurance choices that you make for your business (in consultation with an insurance expert) will be based on the fundamental nature of the business, environmental factors, your state's liability legislation and typical litigation outcomes, and the amount of financial reserves that you have and could tap if you had a major loss.

In property liability, risk is always a factor, but the risks are different for each business owner. For example, a small chemical manufacturer may face higher liability losses because of the possibility of toxic chemicals escaping into the environment than would an engineering firm specializing in parking lot construction. The amount of inventory carried also plays a role; for example, a business that has $5,000 in basic inventory would pay less for property insurance than one that averages $25,000 in inventory.

Artisan's Corner

A metal sculptor working with a torch, for example, creates a greater risk of fire than would a fiber artisan who works with a sewing machine.

Many forms of liability insurance exist, and there's much to say about them. Unfortunately, space does not allow more than a brief review of the most common liability insurance types. The Insurance Information Institute provides detailed information on insuring a home-based business on its Web site at www.iii.org/inside. pl5?individuals=home=/index.html.

Comprehensive General Liability

Comprehensive general liability is a single contract policy that provides insurance needed to cover liability for injuries or property damage sustained by the public. It covers accidents occurring on your premises or away from your premises as a result of business operations. It automatically covers certain hazards that do not now exist but that may develop during the life of the policy, and it contains fewer exclusions than individual policies. Comprehensive general liability insurance is owners', landlords', and tenants' (OL&T).

OL&T insurance is intended for risks primarily confined to a specific location. Coverage is provided for the payment of all sums that the insured may become legally obligated to pay due to bodily injury or property damage caused by an incident tied to the ownership and maintenance or use of the business's premises and the operations or business activities of the insured.

Generally, the property insured by basic property insurance includes the building and its contents. An important component of contents is inventory or supplies. Furniture and interior fixtures are also protected contents. Policies cover the property of others stored in the building as well, such as customers' clothing, if you have an alterations business.

Most policies do *not* cover pieces of property outside the building, such as signs or outdoor lighting. Other assets usually excluded are cash and securities, accounting and business records, and vehicles.

Products Liability

All manufacturers, wholesalers, retailers, restaurants, bottlers, and packaging firms— or any firm that has anything to do with a product that reaches the public—should have products liability insurance. This coverage is provided by the comprehensive general liability policy unless excluded.

Crafter Alert

In most states (find out if yours is one of them), a local store is liable for products claims merely because it sells the article, even if it is impossible for the store's owner to determine whether the article is defective or contains foreign matter. If you are both the manufacturer and the seller, product liability insurance is critical to protect you and your business.

Products coverage provides protection for bodily injury and property damage claims arising from the insured's products, or the claimant's reliance upon the guarantee or warranty you may have made for your product or service. The bodily injury or property damage must occur away from the premises owned by or rented to the insured and must occur after physical possession of the product has been relinquished by the insured.

An important feature of product liability is that it covers attorney fees and court costs. This is important to a small business because products liability cases can sometimes be very costly and drawn out, so even if you win, it could still cost you a lot to defend yourself. It can be difficult to get a qualified attorney to take on your case if you can't offer the attorney the guarantee of eventual payment that a product liability policy affords. When you consider people's current tendency to sue for almost everything and the tendency of the courts to decide in their favor, product liability insurance can be well worth the investment for a small business owner. The Insurance Information Institute provides detailed information on insuring a small business. Check out its Web site at www.iii.org/inside.pl5?individuals=home=/individuals/home/index.html.

Business Owner's Policy (BOP)

Insurance companies usually offer a special combination type of policy called the business owner's policy (BOP). This policy is much like a typical homeowner's policy, covering most perils under one umbrella. Small businesses should seriously consider buying a BOP umbrella policy because it incorporates the most common types of small business coverage at a favorable price. Some kinds of small businesses, however, such as restaurants and auto shops, are not eligible for BOP policies.

Special BOP insurance programs exist for artisans. One blanket certificate can protect all your art or craft property, including finished objects, raw materials, tools, and works in progress, without the hassle of monthly inventory reporting or scheduling.

Artisan's Corner

For more information about special BOP insurance programs for artisans, contact the National Craft Association at 1-800-715-9594, or check out the Web site at www.craftassoc.com.

The plan covers your business's property at your home or studio, on exhibition, and in transit. Loss or damage from fire, theft, flood, vandalism, and similar perils can be covered anywhere in the United States and Canada. The high-limit liability plans provide up to $1 million of broad protection. This coverage defends against product liability, bodily injury, property damage, and the business owner's personal and advertising injury. Landlords and show promoters may be named as additional insureds under this coverage.

A few years ago at an arts and craft show on the sidewalks of the main streets in Canandaigua, New York, many artisans learned the sad reality of not having insurance. A powerful wind and rain storm suddenly came up, so severe that it toppled canopies and even tossed them into the store windows of the surrounding businesses. The losses were enormous. Stained glass, pottery, and ceramics were smashed. Whole displays were tossed into the streets, and what the wind didn't ruin, the heavy rain did. The worst part was that many artisans at the show admitted that they had no insurance coverage whatsoever. Those who did have insurance could quickly recover their investments. For a list of insurance agents for your state visit the National Association of Independent Insurance Adjusters Web site at www.naiia.com/members%20map%20list.htm.

Health Insurance: Key Decision Factors for Small Business

Small businesses must consider many factors in selecting health insurance. Overall, many experts recommend a four-part approach:

1. Choose the basic kind of health services that you and/or your employees want.
2. Determine the level of benefits that you need.
3. Factor in how much the alternatives cost and how much your business can afford.
4. Identify a specific insurance company and healthcare provider based on its quality and service.

Two different systems of healthcare exist. The first system is managed care. The major alternative is the fee-for-service plan, or indemnity plan.

Managed Care

This system tries to manage health services for its customers in return for a set annual fee. Generally, the insurance carrier makes long-term contracts with doctors and hospitals to provide healthcare according to a predetermined fee plan.

Managed care is regarded as more oriented toward controlling healthcare costs than are fee-for-service or indemnity plans. Because they charge a set annual fee, managed-care companies have an incentive to practice preventive healthcare, which is less expensive in the long run. However, because managed-care plans make deals with specified providers, patients cannot always use the doctor they want. In addition, the emphasis on cost control in managed care has, in a great number of cases, been shown to have compromised the quality of the care.

Fee-for-Service Plans, or Indemnity Plans

These plans pay doctors and hospitals for their services when performed, without an annual financial arrangement. Increasingly, some health insurers offer plans that combine aspects of fee-for-service and managed-care plans.

A fee-for-service (indemnity) plan is the traditional type of health insurance. It has become less common recently because it is often more expensive than managed-care plans. Many indemnity plans include some features to limit disbursements according to a schedule or to the normal amount charged for the service; however, these limitations have not been seen to be very effective in holding down costs to the business owner or the patient.

Fee-for-service plans generally do not restrict the choice of doctors to a specific list.

The payment alternatives, premium levels, benefits, and provisions of health insurance plans vary widely. As a business owner, you'll need to consider all of these factors in making your choice of a plan.

Special Provisions for Small Business

In the past, small businesses found it hard to buy health insurance because administrative costs and employees' poor health made it prohibitively expensive. Many major insurers and states have developed special programs for small business, usually defined as less than 50 employees. In some states insurers are required to offer certain benefits and are prevented from canceling policies.

Some trade associations, local Chambers of Commerce, or other types of small business groups offer group plans. You should also consider these special programs in choosing health and business insurance because the premiums and benefits offered are usually more cost-effective than other programs may be.

Pointers

For more information on health insurance check with the Health Insurance Association of America, telephone 202-824-1600, Web site at www.hiaa.org/index.html.

This overview of insurance is only to acquaint you with various types of insurance coverage available. You should always seek the advice of a qualified insurance specialist before you make any decisions about the type of business insurance you need.

The Least You Need to Know

➤ Every business has different insurance needs, so it's important to evaluate your business's risks with the help of an insurance expert before you make your coverage decisions.

➤ A business owner's policy (BOP) is an umbrella policy that is usually the best type of insurance plan for a small business.

➤ Most businesses that sell to consumers should have product liability as part of their insurance coverage.

➤ You'll have to weigh many health insurance options carefully before you choose a plan for your business.

Chapter 12

Keeping Financial Records

In This Chapter

➤ Selecting your accounting system

➤ Setting up your books

➤ Accounting for your inventory, payroll, and income and expenses

➤ Learning how the three key financial statements can guide you in running your business

➤ Understanding the banking system and merchant credit cards

This chapter will help you understand the nitty-gritty of financial records and accounting methods—the kinds of records you need to keep and why. To accomplish this, we briefly cover some basic accounting principals and related terminology that you will be working with in your business. Think of accounting as a tool that you will use to determine the financial health of your business. Even if you plan to have an accountant take care of your books, no matter how large or small your business is, you still need to have a basic working knowledge of accounting—the terms, the process, and what the figures mean. It's the only way you'll be able to manage effectively and plan for continued growth and expansion.

Accounting 101

Most businesses typically use one of two basic accounting methods in their book-keeping systems: the cash method or the accrual method. While most businesses use the accrual method, the best method for your company depends on your sales volume, whether you sell on credit, whether you have inventory, and what your business structure is. The following list summarizes the two systems and their differences:

➤ **The cash method.** This is the simplest of the two methods because the accounting is based on the actual flow of cash in and out of the business. Income is recorded when it is received, and expenses are recorded when they are actually paid. Many sole proprietors and businesses with no inventory use the cash method. From a tax standpoint, it is sometimes advantageous for a new business to use the cash method so that recording income can be put off until the next tax year, while expenses can be counted right away. That way, less income and more expenses can be reported at the end of your fiscal year, which means that your tax payment will be less.

Crafter Alert

If you have inventory, you operate as a corporation, or your annual sales exceed $5 million, you are required to use the accrual method of accounting.

➤ **The accrual method.** With the accrual method, income and expenses are recorded as transactions occur, whether or not cash has actually changed hands. An excellent example is a sale on credit. The sale is entered in the books when the invoice is generated rather than when the cash is collected. Likewise, an expense occurs when materials are ordered, not when the check is actually written. The downside of this method is that you pay income taxes on revenue before you have actually received it.

The accrual method is required if your business has inventory, if your annual sales exceed $5 million, or if you are structured as a corporation. It is also highly recommended for any business that sells on credit because it more accurately matches income and expenses during a given period.

Setting Up an Accounting System

Whether you use the cash method or the accrual method of accounting you need to set up a system for keeping your financial records. Space allows only a brief summary of the basics. For more information on setting up your accounting read *The Complete Idiot's Guide to Finance and Accounting,* by Michael Muckian and Steve Pullara (Alpha Books, 1997). Debits, credits, and double-entry bookkeeping all are demystified in this handy guide. Included in this book are the steps for setting up a company's books the right way the first time, monitoring expenditures, creating budgets, paying taxes, and managing precious cash.

➤ **Chart of accounts.** To get started, you need to set up a chart of accounts. This is simply a list of the accounts that you want to track. Whether you decide to use a manual system or a software program, you can customize the chart of accounts to your business.

➤ **General ledger.** In the general ledger, you sum up all your business transactions. Every account that is on your chart of accounts will be included in your general ledger. The system used in recording entries on a general ledger is called a system of *debits and credits*.

All general ledger entries are double entries; the amount involved in every financial transaction (whether it's cash or a commitment) goes from one place to another. When you write a check to pay for materials, for example, the money flows out of your account (cash) into the hands of your supplier (an expense). When you sell goods on account, you record a sale (income), but you must have a journal entry to make sure that you collect that account later (an account receivable).

➤ **Accounts receivable.** Money owed to you is recorded in *accounts receivable* and is tracked through an accounts receivable ledger. If you plan to sell goods or services on account, you will need a method of tracking what is owed you, by whom, how much is owed, and when it's due. This is where the accounts receivable come in. If you'll be accepting credit cards, the accounts receivable ledger is where you would record the amounts due from those credit card sales.

➤ **Accounts payable.** Money that you owe to others is tracked through the *accounts payable* ledger. Accounts payable is similar to that used to track accounts receivable. The difference is that accounts payable occur when you purchase inventory or other assets from a supplier. It's important to track accounts payable in a timely manner to ensure that you know how much you owe each supplier and when payment is due.

➤ **Fixed assets.** How much are your business's assets worth? Fixed assets are items that will be used in your business over the long term, generally five years or more. They are not bought and sold in the normal course of business operations. Fixed assets include vehicles, land, buildings, leasehold improvements, machinery, and equipment. The value of a fixed asset is based on the original purchase price minus *depreciation* (the decrease in value that occurs as the asset ages). The balance left is referred to as the *book value*.

➤ **Liquid assets.** Liquid assets include cash, stocks, bonds, inventory, or any other asset that can be converted into cash quickly.

➤ **Liabilities.** These are unpaid amounts of money that you owe. They are also referred to as *accounts payable.* Liabilities are usually broken down into either *short-term* liabilities (due within 12 months) or *long-term* liabilities (payable over several years or more).

➤ **Depreciation.** In an accrual system of accounting, fixed assets are not recorded when they're purchased; they're expensed over a period of time that coincides with the useful life of the item (the amount of time that the asset is expected to last). This process is known as *depreciation.*

In most cases, depreciation is easy to compute. The cost of the asset is divided by its useful life. For instance, a $50,000 piece of equipment with a 5-year useful life would be depreciated at a rate of $10,000 per year. This is known as straight-line depreciation.

Other more complicated methods of fixed-asset depreciation allow for accelerated depreciation on the front end, which is advantageous from a tax standpoint. You should seek the advice of your accountant before setting up depreciation schedules for fixed-asset purchases.

Inventory

Are you selling products? Then you'll need to keep track of inventory. Unless you're starting a service business, good inventory control will be a vital part of your bookkeeping system. If you are going to be producing (manufacturing) products, you must break inventory into categories.

Tracking Your Inventory

You should establish separate inventory records for each of these categories: raw materials, works-in-process, and finished goods.

Whether you're a wholesaler or a retailer, you'll be selling many different types of inventory, and you'll need an effective system to track each inventory item offered for sale.

The Importance of Inventory Control

An up-to-date inventory control system will provide you with the following vital management information:

➤ Which items sell well, and which items are slow-moving

➤ When to order more raw materials or more items

➤ Where in the warehouse the inventory is stored

➤ Length of time in the production process for each item

➤ A typical order by key customers

➤ Minimum inventory level needed to meet daily orders

➤ Cost of goods sold

A key reason to track inventory very closely is its direct relationship to the cost of goods sold. Because nearly all businesses that stock inventory are required to use the accrual method for accounting, accurate inventory records are a must for tracking the materials cost-associated with each item sold.

Payroll Accounting

If you have employees, you have to get a handle on payroll. Payroll accounting can be quite a challenge for the new business owner. Many federal and state laws regulate what you have to track related to payroll. Failure to do so could result in heavy fines, or worse. Many small business owners use outside payroll services that guarantee compliance with all applicable laws. If you choose to do your own payroll, it is highly recommended that you purchase an automated payroll system. Even if the rest of your books are done manually, an automated payroll system will help considerably with compliance. There is not a lot of margin for error when dealing with the federal government!

Income and Expenses: Profit and Loss

Monitoring your income *and* expenses is vital to the growth of your business. Obviously, if income is not sufficient to cover expenses, unless the business owner injects new cash or borrows money, the business cannot continue to operate.

➤ **Income.** Income is money received from the sale of your products or services. Income is broken down into *unearned income* and *earned income*. The money received before the customer has taken full possession of the item purchased—for example, deposits for special orders—is *unearned income*. When the product or service has been delivered to the customer, income is then called *earned income* because the sale is now completed.

➤ **Cost of sales.** Cost-of-sales expenses are the costs directly linked to the production or sale of a product or service (raw materials, labor, packaging, and any other related expenses).

➤ **Gross profit.** This is the amount of money left after you cover your cost of sales. Income – cost of sales = gross profit. Out of the gross profit, you pay your operating expenses.

➤ **Operating expenses.** These are the expenses associated with running your company (utilities, rent, telephone, office supplies, wages, and so on).

➤ **Net profit (also called net income).** This is money left after all the operating expenses have been paid out of the gross profit, but before state or federal taxes have been paid (also called net *profit before taxes*).

➤ **Net profit after taxes.** This is the "bottom line" earnings of the business. It is computed by subtracting taxes paid from net profit.

➤ **Owner's equity.** This is the amount left when you subtract your liabilities from your assets.

➤ **Other income and expenses.** Other income and expenses represent those items that do not occur during the normal course of operation. For instance, a pottery maker does not normally earn income from rental property or interest on investments, so these income sources are accounted for separately. Interest expense on debt is also included in this category. A net figure is computed by subtracting other expenses from other income.

Pointers

Accounting periods are measurements of time, such as months, quarters, or years, that allow you to compare your company's financial reports from one period to another. For example, the first quarter of last year compared to the first quarter of this year will allow you to compare your company's performance for the first quarter period.

Monitoring Three Key Financial Statements

The main financial statements that every business owner should monitor on a regular basis are the income statement, the balance sheet, and the cash flow analysis statement. These three statements will provide you with all the vital financial information you need to make good management decisions.

➤ **Income statement (or profit and loss statement [P&L]).** This statement totals all the income and then subtracts the expenses for one accounting period, which is usually one year. The result is your pre-tax profit. This financial statement tells you whether your business is profitable.

➤ **The balance sheet.** This shows your total assets and liabilities—it is a sneak peek at one particular moment in time. The balance sheet is based on a simple formula: assets = liabilities + owner's equity.

➤ **The cash flow analysis statement.** This is a record of exactly how much income you received and how much you spent on a monthly basis. This is perhaps the *most important financial statement* for a business owner because it tells you whether you have enough cash to pay your bills. Yes, tracking your assets and liabilities is important over the long term. When you are just starting a new business, however, your main objective is probably to keep enough money coming in to pay expenses and to provide for continued growth.

The cash flow statement lets you actually track cash as it flows in and out of your business, and shows you the causes of cash flow shortfalls and surpluses.

The increase or decrease in the cash figure at the bottom of the cash flow statement represents the net results of operating, investing, and financing activities. If a business runs out of cash, it cannot survive, so this is a key number to focus on.

You will be able to use the cash flow statement to analyze your sources and uses of cash not only from year to year, but also from month to month if you set up your accounting system to produce monthly statements.

Artisan's Corner

You'll find the cash flow statement to be an invaluable tool in understanding the how and why of cash flowing into and out of your business. For more information and examples of the financial statements we have mentioned, read *The Complete Idiot's Guide to Starting Your Own Business,* by Ed Paulson and Marcia Layton (Alpha Books, 1998).

Banking Concerns

While we're on the topic of financial matters, now is a good time to explore some concerns that you may have about how the banking system works. If you're starting a business, this is the time to check out banks in your area. You may want to look for a full-service bank that offers not only checking accounts, but also small business loans, merchant credit card services, and debit, or "smart" business cards for checking accounts. Even if you don't need all these services when you first open your business, at least you'll know that they're available when you do want to take advantage of them, and you'll already be an established bank customer.

Banks are competitive, so shop around before you open your business checking account. You do not have to get a fancy business checking account, but *you do have to get a separate account.* The IRS does not allow co-mingling of business and personal funds. Also, if you incorporate, a corporation is a legal entity, and checks written to a corporate name can be deposited only in an account owned by that corporation.

Crafter Alert

You *must* open a checking account for your business. It's required by the IRS, which does not allow business owners to co-mingle business and personal funds. If you file income and expenses on a Schedule C form, the lack of a separate checking account for the business could result in the IRS ruling that your operation was a hobby and not a business. That ruling could even cost you all the Schedule C deductions that you took in previous tax years, which would expose you to a very large IRS tax bill. The cost of a separate checking account is a small price to pay to protect your business deductions.

Shopping for a Checking Account

There are a lot of differences in bank services and charges, so do some shopping before you open your business account. Things that you should find out include these:

➤ What does the bank charge for imprinted checks?

➤ Is there a per-item or per-transaction charge?

➤ Is there a cost per check written?

➤ Is a fee charged for deposits?

➤ Will interest be paid on a checking account balance?

➤ How much is the bounced check charge if your check bounces? Are there bounced-check charges if your customer bounces a check?

➤ Is the bank fully automated?

➤ How long of a hold is put on out-of-state checks before the funds are made available to you?

➤ What is the fee and what are the requirements for processing an international money order or a check drawn on a foreign bank?

➤ Is there a transaction fee for wire transfers of money to your account?

➤ Is a minimum account balance required to avoid extra service charges?

➤ Does the bank offer debit cards or smart business cards for the account? (It's an advantage to have one if you want to order supplies over the phone. These work like a credit card, but the funds are deducted directly from your checking account.)

➤ What are the hours of operation? Is night deposit available?

➤ Does the bank offer lines of credit or small business loans?

➤ Does the bank offer merchant credit card services?

The Ins and Outs of Business Banking

If you've never had a business checking account, keep the following in mind when you do your banking:

➤ You must deposit a check made out to your company.

➤ To withdraw funds from a business checking account, write a check to yourself or to "Cash."

➤ Uncollected funds are funds on checks that you deposited but that the issuing bank has not paid to your bank. Until a check clears (your bank has been paid), your bank will not consider it usable funds (unless you have an account with a credit line), even though the amount of the check appears as a deposit in your account.

➤ Out-of-state checks can take 10 to 15 days or more to clear, and local checks can take 1 to 3 days.

➤ Not all banks are fully automated, which can increase the time that it takes for checks to clear between banks.

➤ If you bounce your company's check for any reason (including uncollected funds), your bank will charge a hefty service fee. Some banks charge as much as $25 to $30 per check.

➤ If a customer's check bounces, you will be charged a service fee by your bank. Some banks may automatically redeposit a bounced check, while others will return it to you with a notice explaining why it bounced.

➤ A bounced check may be deposited a second time. If it's a customer's check, it's best to call the customer to verify that there will be funds in the account before you redeposit it. If the check bounces a second time, you will be charged by your bank again.

➤ Some banks will not process a check drawn on a foreign bank unless it is for at least $101. Also, most banks charge a processing fee to collect on an international check, although Canada may be excepted. Be sure to find out what your bank's policy is if you'll be dealing with international checks and money orders.

➤ If you accept a foreign check or money order, be sure that it includes the phrase "Payable in U.S. Funds"; otherwise, it will be paid at the current foreign exchange rate for that country's currency. If you accepted a foreign check for $200 without that written notice on it, and if the exchange rate was 40 percent less than the U.S. rate, you would be paid $120, not $200, when the check cleared your bank.

➤ Customer credit card payments drawn on foreign banks will be made in U.S. funds after the credit card processor applies the exchange rate.

➤ If you receive a check on which the amounts do not agree (for example, the figures may show $15.95, but the written words say $15.00) a bank will generally pay the amount that is written out rather than the amount in figures.

➤ If you receive a check that is not made out to your correct company name, or if the name is misspelled, simply endorse the back of the check the same way that your company name was written, and then rubber stamp it underneath with the company endorsement stamp that bears all your company information.

➤ You do not have to reorder imprinted checks from your bank. You may order them from another source that may charge less. Just make sure that the check information is identical by sending a sample check marked "Void" along with your order.

Crafter Alert

If a customer's check bounces, before you redeposit it, call the customer to be sure that sufficient funds are in his or her account. Otherwise, if the check bounces a second time, your bank will charge you another fee.

When a Customer's Check Bounces

Do you want to charge a customer whose check bounces? If you do, *the law states that the customer must be notified* of this and of the amount of the fee before that person writes the check to you.

If you decide to charge customers fees for bounced checks, you must post a sign that is clearly visible to customers making payments. If you have a store, or if you sell at a booth in a show, the sign must be posted near the checkout area. If you sell by mail or on the Internet, your policy must be stated on your order form. Almost all businesses have a bounced check charge to offset bank charges that they must pay when a customer's check bounces. Bank fees usually start at around $20, and a lot of businesses simply charge the customer double their bank charge.

How will you handle a bad check from a customer who ignores your polite efforts to collect on one returned to you for nonsufficient funds (NSF)? You can ask your bank to collect it for you. You fill out a "protest check form" at the bank and pay a fee (usually around $15 to $20). Then your bank will instruct the bank that the check was drawn on to pay the check as soon as funds are available in the account. Banks will usually hold the check for payment for one month, so if funds are deposited into the customer's account during the holding period, you'll get paid; if not, you won't.

If a customer's check is returned marked "account closed" or "no account," it may be evidence of fraud. You can send a copy of the returned check, along with documentation about what efforts you made to collect the money, to the District Attorney's office. It is a crime to write a bad check, and if it's an out-of-state check for $250 or more, that makes it a felony instead of a misdemeanor. You could also consider using small claims court to collect the check.

Evaluate how much time and expense you're willing to commit to collecting on a bad check, based on the amount of the check. The number of bad checks given to vendors who sell at art and craft events seems to run way below the retail store averages. Most artisans report that they have very few problems in this area, and that if they do get an occasional bad check they can usually just resolve it with a phone call to the customer. Nevertheless, it's good to have a plan for dealing with a serious collection problem.

Accepting Credit Card Payment

If you're opening a physical retail store or will sell on the Internet or by mail order, then you need to be able to accept credit card payments. Not being able to take payments by phone, fax, e-mail, Web page forms, or regular mail will hinder your business. Even if you plan to sell at art and craft shows, or wholesale only, the value of offering your customers the opportunity and convenience of using credit cards will greatly improve your sales. Without a merchant account, businesses cannot accept credit cards, and according to what the experts say, those businesses may miss out on more than 60 percent of their sales opportunities.

You can learn more about how merchant credit cards work in Chapter 13, "Money Matters."

Pointers

The National Craft Association offers its members complete merchant credit card programs at very competitive rates for both traditional and online businesses. Call the NCA at 1–800–715–9594, or visit the Web site at www.craftassoc.com for more information.

The Least You Need to Know

➤ Two methods of accounting exist: the cash basis and the accrual method; the accrual method is required if your business has inventory, if your annual sales exceed $5 million, or if you're structured as a corporation.

➤ Even if an accountant handles your books, no matter how large or small your company is, your business will run better if you understand its accounting system.

➤ One of many good reasons to track inventory very closely is that it can tell you the cost of goods sold.

➤ For efficient management and planning, the three key financial statements that you need to review carefully are the income statement (P&L), the balance sheet, and the cash flow analysis.

➤ Check out several banks before you decide where to establish your business checking account.

Chapter 13

Money Matters

In This Chapter

➤ Researching and preparing your start-up budget

➤ Creating your operating budget

➤ Reducing operating costs

➤ Finding the financing for your business

➤ Understanding e-commerce and merchant accounts

Money matters are important to your business start-up. Unless you have lots of start-up cash available, perhaps the best way to start making money with your hobby is with a full- or part-time home-based business. Recent data shows that small businesses account for between 90 and 95 percent of the businesses in the United States (according to *Business USA,* out of 10 million businesses listed in its CD-ROM, only 1.1 million have a staff of 20 or more), and figures worldwide correspond with these.

Consider how much less your start-up costs and operating expenses will be if you are able to run your business from your home. Artisans have started a business with as little as a few hundred dollars this way. In this chapter, we explain e-commerce options and how a merchant account program works; these are viable tools that you can use to increase sales and profits. Offering your customer the convenience of paying you by credit card will help build your bottom line.

Researching Start-Up Costs

Whether your start-up costs total $500 or $50,000, the challenge is to find reliable information about what things will cost. You need to get hard data, plus valuable insight, from a variety of resources, and then compare the information that you've researched. Here are some sources to begin your research:

➤ How-to start-up guides for your business are available from publishing companies and some trade associations. Some are included in Appendix A, "Resources," for your convenience.

Make sure that they are not outdated, and keep in mind that some costs vary widely throughout the country. Always be on the lookout for tips that can help you lower your start-up costs.

➤ Suppliers are another excellent resource for researching start-up costs. Tell the supplier that you're interested in costs in a particular area because you're planning to start a business. Usually, suppliers are very cooperative because they hope to get your future business. Do some comparison shopping; it can make a big difference in your start-up costs. Ask about equipment leasing, bulk-buying discounts, credit terms, start-up inventory packages, and other options that might lower your initial costs.

Pointers

In evaluating your information, a good rule of thumb is to always try to get three points of view for each number. Then weigh the value of those three numbers, and come up with a number that you think is correct.

➤ Trade associations are like business owners and suppliers; they are an excellent source because you're dealing directly with your particular market niche. Depending on the industry, trade associations may be able to give you sample start-up cost worksheets and financial statements, names of established business owners and suppliers in the industry, market research data, and other useful information. Suppliers' associations are good resources, too.

➤ Business owners with businesses similar to the one that you intend to start are a valuable resource for start-up cost information. Your future competitors probably won't want to assist you, of course, but business owners outside your geographic area are often more than willing to help.

➤ The Service Corps of Retired Executives (SCORE), sponsored by the Small Business Administration (SBA), is a valuable resource for start-ups. In addition to the publications offered on starting a business, SCORE can pair you with an experienced retired business owner who can guide you through the entire process of launching your company. The volunteer counselor can point you in the right direction and suggest resources that you may have overlooked. In addition to in-person counseling, SCORE offers a handy Internet-based service that gives users access to more than 12,400 participating counselors nationwide. Visit SCORE's Web site at www.score.org.

➤ Business start-up articles in trade publications, newspapers, and magazines offer ballpark estimates of overall start-up costs and help you come up with itemized lists of the costs that you'll need to research. Always use credible sources.

➤ A qualified business consultant can offer excellent advice about start-ups. If you do decide to work with a consultant, find someone who is familiar with your in-dustry and who has had experience with start-ups and with established compa-nies as well. The downside to hiring an expert is the cost. Don't forget that your attorney or accountant may also be a valuable resource.

➤ If you are thinking about buying a franchise, the franchise organization will give you lots of data about start-up costs. Be careful with these projections; remem-ber that costs can vary, depending on your location. Call existing franchisees, and ask them how closely the franchiser's projections matched actual start-up costs.

A single source usually won't be able to provide you with all the facts that you need to determine the exact cost of starting your new business. Always compare three per-spectives on each number before you decide which one to use in your start-up budget. Good research can tell you whether your business idea is financially viable and can suggest ways to boost your chances of success. Once you've investigated the start-up costs and developed a sound business plan based on your numbers, you'll be ready to turn your hobby into an income-producing business.

Start-Up and Operating Budgets

To effectively manage your finances, plan a sound, realistic budget by determining the actual amount of money that you need to open your business (start-up costs) and the amount that you'll need to keep it open (operating costs).

Start-Up Budget

The start-up budget should allow for these expenses:

➤ Personnel (costs prior to opening)

➤ Legal and professional fees

➤ Occupancy

➤ Licenses and permits

➤ Equipment

➤ Insurance

➤ Supplies

➤ Advertising and promotion

➤ Salaries and wages

➤ Accounting

➤ Income

➤ Utilities

➤ Payroll expenses

Operating Budget

When you are actually ready to open for business, you prepare your operating budget. It will reflect your priorities in terms of how you spend your money, the expenses you'll incur, and how you'll meet those expenses (income). Your operating budget should also include money to cover the first three to six months of operation. It should allow for these categories:

➤ Personnel

➤ Insurance

➤ Rent

➤ Depreciation

➤ Loan payments

➤ Advertising and promotion

➤ Legal and accounting services

➤ Miscellaneous expenses

➤ Supplies

➤ Payroll expenses

➤ Salaries and wages

➤ Utilities

➤ Dues and subscriptions

➤ Taxes

➤ Repairs and maintenance

Artisan's Corner

The first step to building a sound financial plan is to devise a start-up budget. Your start-up budget usually will include such one-time costs as major equipment, utility deposits, down payments, and so forth.

Tips on Reducing Your Business Costs

You can do a lot to trim your operating budget by using some of these tips:

➤ **Barter.** If you have a business, you should be bartering goods and services with other businesses. Before you buy something, try to trade something that you have for it. Barter deals usually involve little or no money.

➤ **Network.** Try networking your business with other businesses. You could trade leads or mailing lists. This will cut down on your marketing and advertising costs.

➤ **Look for free stuff.** Before you buy your business supplies, visit the thousands of freebie sites on the Internet. You can find free software, graphics, backgrounds, online business services, e-mail service, classes, business forms, advertising and free links sources, and so on.

➤ **Borrow or rent.** Have you ever purchased business equipment that you used only once, or once in a while? You could have just borrowed it from someone else or rented it from a "rent-all" store.

➤ **Attend online/offline auctions.** You can find lower prices on business supplies and equipment at online and offline auctions. I'm not saying you'll find what you're looking for all the time, but before you pay retail prices for these items, try bidding on them first.

➤ **Buy used stuff.** If your business equipment and supplies don't need to be new, buy them used. You can find used items at yard and garage sales, used furniture and equipment stores, message boards, news groups, and classified ads in newspapers (government auctions are great for big items), trade magazines, and swap sheets.

Pointers

Make a list of business supplies or equipment that you'll need in the future. Keep an eye out for stores that have big sales, and save money by stocking up.

Where to Find the Money You Need

Consider several sources when you start looking for financing. It's important to explore all of your options before making a decision.

➤ **Personal savings.** The primary source of capital for most new businesses comes from savings and other forms of personal resources. While credit cards are often used to finance business needs, you'll pay too much interest in the long term. There may be better options available, even for very small loans.

➤ **Friends and relatives.** Many entrepreneurs look to private sources such as friends and family when starting out in a business venture. Often money is loaned interest-free or at a low interest rate, which can be helpful when you're getting started.

Crafter Alert

Using credit cards is not the best way to finance your business. Look into other funding sources before you take that route.

➤ **Banks and credit unions.** The most common source of funding, banks and credit unions, will provide a loan if you can show that your business proposal is sound. Many new business start-ups get bank loans backed by the Small Business Administration.

For complete information, contact your local SBA office, or visit the Web site at www.sba.gov/financing. To be successful in obtaining a loan, you must be prepared and organized. You must know exactly how much money you need, why you need it, and how you will pay it back. You must be able to convince the lender that you are a good credit risk.

➤ **Venture capital firms.** These firms help expanding companies grow in exchange for equity or partial ownership. Be sure to visit ACE-NET (www.sba.gov/ADVO/acenet.html), SBA's Angel Capital Electronic Network. ACE-NET gives new options to both small companies looking for investors and investors looking for promising opportunities.

Your Guide to E-Commerce

Whether you call it Internet commerce, or e-com, or e-commerce, it basically means the same thing. These terms mean buying or selling something electronically, and the time has never been better to jump in. If you have something that you'd like to sell on the Net, new technologies have opened up an array of e-com options; there's one to suit every need and requirement.

Most important, e-commerce is safe. Experts tell us that online transactions are every bit as safe as face-to-face transactions, although neither can be guaranteed to be 100 percent risk-free. You are just as likely to be mugged at an ATM as you are to run into security problems with Internet commerce!

E-commerce can be a confusing subject, and many of us need a little help sorting it all out. If some of the jargon is confusing, read on and learn some of the basic concepts. We cover three categories of information: definition of terms, facts about accepting credit cards, and e-commerce solutions compared.

E-Commerce Definitions

Some of the e-commerce terms that you're sure to come across are defined here:

➤ **Commerce service providers (CSP).** These are businesses or Web sites that provide e-commerce solutions.

➤ **Digital or electronic cash, e-cash, digital money, or immerce.** These terms are used interchangeably, and they refer to any of the various methods that allow a person to purchase goods or services by transmitting a number from one computer to another. The numbers are issued by a bank and represent sums of real money. Digital cash is anonymous and reusable. The merchant does not know the identity of the shopper, as would be the case in a credit card transaction. Cybercash (www.cybercash.com) and Digicash (www.digicash.com) are two well-known methods.

➤ **Electronic checks (or cheques).** Customers pay for merchandise by writing an electronic check that is transmitted electronically by e-mail, fax, or phone. The "check" is a message that contains all of the information that is found on an ordinary check, but it is signed (or endorsed) digitally. The digital signature is encrypted with the customer's secret electronic key. Upon receipt, the merchant, or "payee" may further endorse it using a private encryption key. When the check is processed, the resulting message is encoded with the bank's secret electronic key, thus providing proof of payment.

➤ **Electronic wallet.** Electronic wallets store your credit card numbers on your hard drive in an encrypted form. You then make purchases at Web sites that support that particular type of electronic wallet. By clicking on an OK button, customers initiate a credit card payment via a secure transaction enabled by the electronic wallet company's server.

➤ **Electronic commerce, e-com, immerce, or EC.** These terms are used interchangeably and they all mean the same thing: the paperless exchange of routine business information using electronic data interchange (EDI), e-mail, electronic bulletin boards, fax transmissions, and electronic fund transfer (EFT). They refer to Internet shopping, online stock and bond transactions, the downloading and selling of "soft merchandise" (software, documents, graphics, music, and so on), and business-to-business transactions.

➤ **Extranet.** An extranet is an extension of a corporate intranet. It connects the internal network of one company with the intranets of its customers and suppliers. This makes it possible to create e-commerce applications that link all aspects of a business relationship, from ordering to payment.

➤ **Disintermediation.** This is the process of bypassing retail channels or mail order houses and selling directly to the customer.

➤ **Hard goods vs. soft goods.** Hard goods are items that exist in the real world, as opposed to soft goods, which exist virtually or electronically. For instance, an Internet merchant selling a book that is shipped to the customer in a print version is selling hard goods; a merchant offering a book for download in electronic format is selling soft goods.

➤ **High-risk processors.** High-risk processors (or brokers) are financial institutions or companies that issue merchant status accounts to high-risk businesses. They offset their risks by charging higher transaction fees and higher rates than traditional banks do. However, the initial outlay of cash that you will be required to put up is usually much less than the large deposits required by traditional banking institutions. Some brokers may offer other added features, such as shopping cart software, Web site templates, and forms or secure lines for ordering.

➤ **Immerce.** Immerce is the new term being used for commerce that is transacted totally over the Internet.

➤ **Merchant account.** A *merchant account* is a relationship between a business (that is, a merchant) and a merchant bank that allows the retailer or merchant to accept credit card payments from customers.

Trade Terms

A **merchant account** is a special account that permits the acceptance of credit cards. Transactions are processed either online in real time, or by swiping the card in the processor. If the card is approved, the merchant gets an approval code and the sale is transacted.

Merchant Accounts

Many banks or financial institutions, especially in Canada, have stiff requirements and regulations regarding issuing a merchant account. Many small or home-based businesses report that they've had great difficulties in acquiring merchant status. If merchant status is obtained, the merchant then rents or buys special software or hardware (processing terminal) that is used to process transactions.

Online merchant accounts involve a stricter banking relationship than accounts for face-to-face transactions. The reason is that phone, fax, mail, and e-mail sale transactions do not gather signatures from purchasers, thus involving a higher risk of fraud.

Some of the terms that you'll encounter in merchant banking are defined here:

➤ **Merchant brokers.** They specialize in obtaining credit card accounts for online businesses. Brokers charge a setup fee and then lease or sell the software and hardware as needed. Expect to pay a discount rate, which is the percentage that you pay for each transaction processed, as well as various other charges that differ among services. If obtaining a merchant account through a traditional bank is a problem, merchant brokers are an alternative.

➤ **Microtransactions or micropayments.** These are transactions of tiny amounts, a few cents or a few dollars, typically made to download or access graphics, games, and information.

➤ **Phone-cash.** Still under development as this book goes to press, phone-cash allows customers who prefer not to use credit cards to buy items online by having the value of the purchase transferred from their account to another account within the Internet Banking System. For more details, visit Cybank at www.us. cybank.net/.

➤ **Telephone billing systems.** A very new approach in which telephone transactions allow the customer to purchase an item or service and have the amount billed to his or her telephone bill. To date, this is being used for soft items such as downloads, time-measured services (time spent at a Web site, for example), or for charitable donations made online. For a sample, check out e-Charge Corporation at www.echarge.com.

Facts About Accepting Credit Cards

Unless you have a merchant account, you cannot accept credit cards, so you may miss out on more than 60 percent of your sales opportunities. Accepting credit cards is a huge sales factor for online or mail order sales, but it is significant even if you plan to sell only wholesale or at art and craft shows.

Some of the factors involved in accepting credit cards are discussed here:

➤ **Real-time processing.** Some e-commerce systems offer automated transaction processing while the customer waits. Others offer manual processing, which collects payment information for later processing by hand. Real-time processing is more expensive and typically is required only in high-volume systems or for products distributed electronically, such as documents or software downloads. Here the processing is done by computer software. The costs run anywhere from $350 to $2,000 if you purchase; if you lease, the cost is much higher.

➤ **Technical compatibility.** Many MAPs (merchant account providers) offer an entire e-commerce system as part of their service (charging higher fees in return). This system may be incompatible with your current or planned hosting software or other e-commerce applications. Before you sign up for anything, check with each MAP to ensure that its software is compatible with your e-commerce system.

➤ **Swipe or point-of-sale terminal.** This is an actual processing terminal (the same as at any retail store when your card is swiped for a credit card purchase). You swipe the card—or, in the case of a phone, mail, or fax order, you just punch in the numbers, expiration date, and amount. When you hit Enter, the processor, using a phone line, transmits the information and sends back either an approval code number or a "decline" (rejection).

Understanding Merchant Account Costs

Some MAPs make quite a killing out of unexpected costs, contingency fees, and penalties. Here is a list of common MAP fees and costs:

➤ **Discount rate.** A fixed percentage taken from every credit card sale transaction. Usually, a 2½ to 4 percent discount is taken for Visa or MasterCard, and 3½ percent or more is taken for Discover or American Express cards. The Internet discount rate will generally be higher than card-swipe rates.

➤ **Transaction fee.** MAPs typically have fixed charges, usually between 25¢ and 70¢ per transaction. If you are going to sell many low-priced items through your site, high transaction costs can be devastating.

➤ **Monthly fees and minimums.** These are a variety of charges levied on a monthly basis, including statement fees starting at $10 a month, monthly minimums for total charges, and excess usage fees.

➤ **Gateway access fee.** This charge affects only online Internet merchant accounts, not those that do their processing using point-of-sale terminals. This monthly fee starts at $20.

➤ **Chargebacks or holdbacks.** Your MAP may hold back, or reserve, a percentage of your transaction receipts to cover any contested charges. The MAP may also apply chargeback fees against your account when transactions are successfully contested.

➤ **High-risk processors.** In the United States, these are merchant acquirers that specialize in high-risk businesses. They offset their risks by charging higher transaction fees and higher rates. Merchants living outside the United States will be required to find a service that works with their own banking institutions.

➤ **MAP fees.** Don't rush into any MAP service contract without gathering at least five price quotes from prospective MAPs. You can find a free, impartial listing of MAPs and their pri–mary rates and fees at Merchant Workz (www. MerchantWorkz.com). MAP rates and fees are often negotiable, so don't hesitate to push MAPs into a bidding war.

➤ **Setup and equipment fees.** Setup fees are often only a small portion of the total setup costs. Ask about required hardware or software purchases, installation fees, programming costs, and other start-up or setup expenses.

Pointers

Before you shop for a merchant account provider (MAP), take the time to determine which merchant account features and services you really need.

In addition to the greater risk of fraud they pose, online transactions are more costly for other reasons.

The major credit card companies offer their cardholders the right to contest charges on their statements that may be the result of theft, fraud, or error. A contested charge is referred to as a chargeback. When a chargeback occurs, merchants end up paying the charge to the issuing bank *and* paying a chargeback fee that can be as high as $30 or more. For example, if you sell a book for $20 through a credit card transaction, and the cardholder later contests the sale, you end up paying your bank the $30 *plus* a chargeback fee of $10 to $30 dollars. Consequently, many banks require a reserve fee when issuing merchant status. Typically, face-to-face sales have a chargeback rate of 1 percent of all sales. The potential for chargebacks is greater when it is an online sale.

Artisan's Corner

If you can't get a merchant account through your regular banking institution, check with trade associations and business groups before you take the broker option. Brokers can often arrange merchant accounts for businesses that are deemed high-risk, but the cost is usually higher for you. The National Craft Association offers its members complete merchant credit card programs at very competitive rates for both traditional and online businesses. Call the NCA at 1-800-715-9594, or visit the Web site at www.craftassoc.com for more information.

Merchant accounts should not be an obstacle to setting up shop. With a little research and planning, acquiring a merchant account can be painless and inexpensive. It can also shield you from less reputable providers seeking to profit from novice Web merchants.

Other Associated Expenses

The chargeback expense is the first and foremost concern for a merchant hoping to acquire a merchant account. However, there are other charges and expenses to factor into the budget as well. Merchants will need to investigate hidden equipment costs, setup fees, line charges, bank transaction fees, holdbacks, and discount rates, among others. These vary considerably among service providers, so compare, compare, compare!

The Least You Need to Know

➤ You need to prepare a start-up and an operating budget, but first research the costs associated with your type of business.

➤ Using some down-to-earth methods to cut start-up and operating costs will save you money.

➤ Most small businesses start out with owner financing, so a home-based business is usually the most cost-effective way to begin.

➤ A merchant credit card account is a viable way to increase the income potential of most types of business.

Chapter 14

Control Issues: Government Regulation of What You Produce

> ## In This Chapter
>
> ➤ Finding out which consumer product safety regulations may affect you
>
> ➤ Fathoming textile and other fabric-labeling requirements
>
> ➤ Learning the dangers of using designer fabrics or celebrity names
>
> ➤ Getting filled in on personal care and aromatherapy guidelines
>
> ➤ Learning about the laws that govern the manufacture of food products

As the manufacturer (producer) of products or services, some regulations or laws at one governmental level or another will probably affect you. Not shocked? I didn't think you would be. Which ones you must comply with are usually determined by the products or services that you plan to sell.

Generally, these laws relate to the safety, health, and general well-being of the consumer, and were written to ensure that manufacturers use proper labels, adhere to health or safety standards, and make disclosures to protect the consumer in all of these areas.

There are hundreds of hobbies and thousands of products you could create, many more than we can cover in the scope of this book. The information contained in this chapter is simply provided to help point you in the right direction. If you think that your product(s) may fall into any of the categories described, be sure to contact the government agency responsible for the regulation to get compliance details. If you are not quite sure about how certain laws affect your products, get some legal advice before you start selling them.

Crafter Alert

Consumer lawsuits are common these days, so make sure that you know what safety laws are associated with your product line. See to it that all your products comply with the applicable laws before you start selling them.

Pointers

If you make collectible items such as dolls, teddy bears, antique toy replicas, or other items that might look like toys but that are *not intended for children*, protect yourself by adding a label *or* a hang tag to them with the proper disclosure ("Not recommended for children under the age of three," for example).

The Consumer Product Safety Act

The Consumer Product Safety Commission (CPSC) oversees the Consumer Product Safety Act, which protects the public against unreasonable risks of injury associated with consumer products. CPSC has a toll-free hotline, 1-800-638-2772, with a menu from which you can select publications, report problems with purchased products, or connect with the Small Business Ombudsman department, which offers information to help business owners comply with CPSC regulations or solve problems related to them.

The CPSC is very active in the area of consumer products and toys designed for children. If you make any toys, be extra careful about the materials that you plan to use, and be sure to meet all the guidelines required for safety.

Suggested Safety Guidelines for Making Toys

The CPSC's guidelines for making toys are …

➤ Materials used must be nontoxic, nonflammable, and nonpoisonous.

➤ Items must be too large to be swallowed.

➤ Items must have no sharp edges or points.

➤ Items must not break easily or be apt to leave sharp or jagged edges if broken.

➤ Items must not be put together where nails, pins, or wires could be easily exposed.

➤ Use only paints, varnishes, and other finishes that are labeled *nontoxic* (lead-free).

Paints and Surface Coatings

Paints and surface coatings (varnish, lacquer, shellac, and other finishes) sold for household use must meet the Consumer Product Safety Act's (CPSA) requirements for minimum amounts of lead. The CPSA has banned paints and finishes that contain more than .06 percent lead by weight. Acrylics and other water-based paints are non-toxic. As a precaution, always check to make sure that the label shows that the product is nontoxic.

Specialty paints must have a warning on the label about the lead content. However, beware: "Artist's paints" are not required to have a warning label of any kind because they are exempt from the CPSC's lead-in-paint ban, so be sure to check all the paints, varnishes, or finishing coat materials used on your products with a lead-testing kit (available in paint stores), especially if they are intended for use in children's toys or furnishings.

The Federal Hazardous Substances Act deals with products that are toxic or corrosive, that are irritants, or that are strong sensitizers, like lye. If you're making products that may use such substances, double-check to make sure that you're in compliance with all the applicable regulations or laws.

Lead Testing for Food or Drink Containers

If you are planning to make ceramic, pottery, or porcelain items that could be used for food or drink containers, be sure that you lead-test them before you sell them. The Food and Drug Administration (FDA) regularly makes random lead tests of food container products being shipped in interstate commerce, and often works in conjunction with your state's Department of Health. The FDA is empowered to confiscate any products that fail to meet the lead release guideline of less than 0.5 parts per million.

If making your products "food safe" is a concern, start by designing a product line based on decorative ware, and label all food or drink style pieces as "to be used for decorative purposes only," or make them unusable by drilling a hole in the bottom of each piece. For your safety, do not forget that your kiln should have a hood-exhaust system that vents to the outdoors and is positioned so that it will not vent into an area where people or animals will be exposed to lead fumes.

Labels for Textiles, Fabrics, Fibers, and Yarn or Wool Products

The Federal Fair Packaging and Labeling Act requires that a label identify the product. The label must show the name of the manufacturer or distributor, and the net quantity of the contents. You can get a copy of this law from the Federal Trade Commission (FTC), Washington, DC 20580 (www.FTC.gov/).

The law requires labels if you produce products using textiles, fabrics, fibers, yarn, or wool to make wearing apparel, household furnishings, decorative accessories, or soft toys. Some state and federal government agencies require the attachment of a variety of different tags or labels to products sold in the consumer marketplace, as described in the following sections.

Content Labeling Law

The Content Labeling Law is part of the Textile Fiber Productions Identification Act, monitored by both the Bureau of Consumer Protection and the Federal Trade Commission (FTC). It covers what is in a product and who makes it.

The law requires that a special label or hang tag be attached to all textile wearing apparel and household furnishings (except wall hangings) that are made of any fabric, fiber, or yarn. This includes wearing apparel and accessories, decorative accessories, quilts, pillows, comforters, table linens, stuffed toys, floor cloths, rugs, and so forth. The tag or label must include the name of the manufacturer, and the generic name and percentages of all fibers in the product that amount to 5 percent or more, listed in order of predominance by weight content. For example: cotton 50 percent, polyester 35 percent, nylon 15 percent.

Care Labeling Law

The Care Labeling Law, also part of the Textile Fiber Productions Identification Act, covers how to care for products. Wearing apparel and household furnishings of any kind made from textiles (any fabric, yarn, or fiber), including suede and leather, must have a "permanent care" label explaining how to take care of the product. For detailed information about permanent care labeling, go to the FTC Web site at www.FTC.gov/, or write to the Consumer Response Center, Room 130, Federal Trade Commission, 600 Pennsylvania Avenue, NW; Washington, DC 20580.

If you're already aware of the details of the Care Labeling Rule (16 C.F.R. Part 423), be sure that you're up-to-date on the Amended Care Labeling Rule, which became effective September 1, 2000. The two amendments concern clarification of cleaning instructions and revision of the water temperature definitions.

For complete details on the Amended Care Labeling Rule, see www.FTC.gov/os/2000/07/carelabelingrule.html, or write to the FTC at the address in the preceding section.

Wool Content Label Law

The FTC requires products made with any wool content to have an additional label. The Wool Products Labeling Act of 1939 requires the labels of all wool or textile products to clearly indicate when imported fibers are used. For example, a sweater knitted in the United States but made from wool yarn imported from Scotland would read, "Made in the USA from imported products" (or similar wording). If the wool yarn was spun in the United States, a wool product label could be as simple as, "Made in the USA."

State Bedding and Upholstered Furniture Laws

State labeling laws affect sellers of items that have "concealed filling," such as dolls, teddy bears and critters, stuffed toys, pillows, quilts, comforters, soft picture frames, soft or padded books, and even scrapbooks or album covers. Contact your state's Consumer Protection Agency, Department of Health, or Department of Commerce and Industry Standards to find out if your state has a Bedding and Upholstered Furniture Law, and where to get information about it.

The law makes no distinction between large manufacturers and those who just make a few handmade items, so a small producer is just as liable for infractions as a large manufacturing company.

The law seems to be rarely enforced; however, NCA has heard reports that officials in Pennsylvania and New York attend regular craft shows and remove unlabeled merchandise. So, you should check with your state to see if there is such a law and how it affects what you make. The only penalty seems to be (for either state bedding or stuffed toy laws) the removal of merchandise from the vendor's shelves or the imposition of a fine on vendors who were warned to comply with the law but did not do so.

Crafter Alert

If you produce a product that contains "concealed filling" (stuffing), be sure to check with your state officials before you start to sell it.

If you plan to sell wholesale or via shops, then you must take every precaution possible to make sure you have the proper labels on all your products. You may be required to purchase a license at a cost of $25 to $100 (depending on the state), and your merchandise will have to have tags imprinted with your special registry number. NCA has learned that another possible solution is to use the fiber-fill manufacturer's information and license number (from the bulk packaging or poly bag the fill arrives in) to label products you produce using that manufacturer's fiber fill.

Before you take this alternative, however, we strongly suggest that you check with the manufacturer you purchase your fill contents from to be sure such labeling complies with this law.

The Flammable Fabrics Act

The Flammable Fabrics Act, regulated by the CPSC, pertains to manufacturers who sell products made of fabric, particularly products for children manufacturers and especially those who sell products wholesale or to shops. This act prohibits the movement in interstate commerce of articles of wearing apparel and fabrics that are so highly flammable that they are dangerous when worn or used for other purposes.

Most fabrics are in compliance with this act, but if you make children's clothes or toys, you'll want to make doubly sure that the fabrics you use are safe. Be sure your fabric supplier is in compliance with the Flammable Fabrics Act. The guarantee of compliance is often stated on the supplier's invoice; if it isn't, ask the supplier for a written guarantee, or check with the CPSC to find out if the supplier or manufacturer has filed for a continuing guarantee. For more details on this act, see www.cpsc.gov/businfo/8004.html.

Artisan's Corner

You can comply with CPSC as well as local fire safety regulations by asking the supplier or manufacturer of a product to supply compliance documentation. If, for example, you're asked as an exhibitor to provide a compliance certificate for your canopy (which you know is in compliance), ask the manufacturer for the required documentation.

Other Products That May Require Labeling

To find out if products you're producing may require labeling, check the following FTC Web pages, or write to the address in the preceding section, "Content Labeling Law."

➤ Advertising and labeling of feather and down products: www.FTC.gov/bcp/conline/pubs/buspubs/down.htm

➤ Fur Product Labeling Act: www.FTC.gov/os/statutes/textile/furact.htm

➤ Wedding gown labels: www.FTC.gov/bcp/conline/pubs/buspubs/wedgown.htm

➤ Labeling and advertising cotton products: www.FTC.gov/bcp/conline/pubs/buspubs/cotton.htm

➤ FTC/U.S. Customs Service regarding textile country of origin marking: www.FTC.gov/be/v980034.htm

Making the Required Labels

Many artisans make whatever tags or labels are required and affix them in the manner specified by the law. With a computer and the wide array of software available, making your own labels is a very practical option. Of course, you can opt to order them from companies that specialize in tags and labels. They offer stock labels and custom designs to meet specific needs.

Label supply sources include ...

➤ **Name Maker Inc.**, PO Box 43821, Atlanta, GA 30336; phone: 1-800-241-2890; fax: 404-691-7711; e-mail: cs@namemaker.com; Web site: www.namemaker.com.

➤ **Sterling Name Tape Company**, PO Box 939, Winsted, CT 06098; phone: 1-888-312-0113; fax: 860-379-0394; e-mail: postman@sterlingtape.com; Web site: www.sterlingtape.com/.

➤ **Widby Fabric Label Company**, 4321 Crestfield Road, Knoxville, TN 37921-3104; phone: 1-888-522-2458 or 865-558-6204; fax: 865-558-6135; e-mail: general information: don@widbylabel.com, design information: design@ widbylabel.com; Web site: www.widbylabel.com/.

Food and the Gift Basket Industry

A majority of gift basket makers use food as a staple in the contents of their arrangements. So, naturally, you have to find out what your state laws are for the handling and preparation of food items sold to consumers. The safest way to protect yourself and your clients is to purchase and use only prepackaged foods, snacks, and beverages. That means that items are in ready-to-use size units, packed in cellophane, boxes, or bags so that your hands have no direct contact with the food products.

When you check with your health department, find out: (1) if they restrict home-based businesses from buying prepackaged food for resale in baskets, (2) if an inspection of your premises is required, (3) if a permit or health department certification is required, and (4) what, if any, fees are involved.

In many states a health department license is required if you prepare or wrap food, but is not if you use only prepackaged food items. Be sure to check your state and local regulations governing gift baskets produced by home-based businesses.

Crafter Alert

Is including alcohol in your gift baskets worth the licensing expense, and the risk, for example, that a minor might accept delivery and drink the alcohol? There are many exciting new substitutes. Sparkling juices and ciders are very popular, and come in interesting flavors, bottle shapes, and labels to complement any special theme.

Commercial Use Issues

Many fabrics, images, and likenesses have restrictions on their commercial use. Two areas commonly related to products produced from fabrics are outlined in the following sections.

Commercial Use of Designer Fabrics and Logos

Just because you can buy designer fabrics from a wholesaler or a manufacturer does not mean that you have unlimited commercial use of it. Always ask the fabric distributor if there are any restrictions on its commercial use, or contact the copyright owner or manufacturer to be sure.

On fabrics purchased at retail shops, check the salvage edge for warnings. If there is a notice such as "This fabric is for individual consumption (or use) only," or if there's a copyright notice with a designer's name, *do not use it to make your products*. For example, you must avoid any use of designs made by Disney, copyrighted cartoon characters, or sports logos such as the NFL's.

Pointers

If you do want to use a particular team's sports logo or a famous cartoon, for example, you'll most likely have to pay a licensing fee and a percentage of your sales to the copyright holder for the right to use it. To find out the cost and details, call the company and ask for the licensing department. Of course, the larger the organization, the more you can expect to pay for the licensing rights.

Pointers

If you want to find out who handles the estate of a celebrity, you can contact the Academy of Motion Picture Arts, at www.oscar.org/, or the Screen Actor's Guild, at www.sag.org/.

Celebrity Rights Act

The Celebrity Rights Act is a special law that protects the rights of deceased personalities. You cannot produce a product, advertise a product, or provide a service that in any way utilizes the name, photograph, likeness, voice, or signature of a deceased person for a period lasting 50 years after that person's death unless you have a license or special permission. Manufacturers, distributors, and retailers caught selling unlicensed products can be sued, so forget about using Elvis in a design for your new line of wall hangings.

Personal Care Products and Herbal Remedies (or Aromatherapy)

The FDA statute defines cosmetics as "articles intended to be rubbed ... or otherwise applied to the human body ... for cleaning ... except that the term cosmetics shall *not include soap*," unless the soap claims to have certain cosmetic properties.

Sanitary Production of Cosmetics

If federal law classifies your product as a cosmetic, then you must manufacture and store it under sanitary conditions and avoid contamination with filth. This is a standard of cleanliness that home producers are hard pressed to meet. Sanitized equipment, gloves, hairnets, confirmation of weights and measures by a second person, sampling, water testing, and absence of tobacco products are just a few of the Good Manufacturing Practice Guidelines that cosmetic manufacturers are measured against.

Soap Labeling

Whether or not your soap is considered a cosmetic under FDA rules, the label must contain several things:

➤ The weight must always be expressed in ounces (you may also include metric units).

➤ The name and complete address of the manufacturer must be listed. (The street address may be omitted only if the company is listed in a current telephone directory.)

➤ If under FDA regulations your soap is classified as a cosmetic, you must list all *ingredients* in the order of their predominance. Color additives and ingredients of less than 1 percent may be listed without regard for predominance.

➤ Some ingredients are exempt from disclosure regulations and may be referred to as "and other ingredients."

➤ Listed ingredients must be identified by the names established or adopted by regulation. The list of ingredients must be conspicuously placed on the product label so that it is likely to be read by the purchaser.

Trade Terms

Ingredients as defined by the FDA means "any single chemical entity or mixture used as a component in the making of any cosmetic product." This definition clearly disputes the erroneous impression, which some soap makers have, that a chemical is not an ingredient if it reacts with other chemicals and thus is no longer present in the final product.

➤ If the safety of your materials has not been substantiated—for instance, if you used a color additive not tested and approved by the FDA (a natural colorant, for example, such as rose hips or brazilwood)—your label may have to carry a conspicuous warning: "Warning: The safety of this product has not been determined." That is why many soap makers prefer to work with soap base and commercial melt-and-pour products—to avoid having their product classified as a cosmetic.

A good book to read on this subject is *The Soapmaker's Companion* (Storey Books, 1977), by Susan Miller Cavtich.

Herbal Remedies: Aromatherapy

Currently, alternative remedies can fall under food or drug regulations, depending on their ingredients and the claims being made about them. Remedies that are governed by food regulations are not required to meet any standards in terms of efficacy or patient information. Those that are deemed to be drugs are few and far between, partly because of the expense involved (considered prohibitive by the many small producers of alternative remedies) and partly because the scientific testing applied to mainstream, single active-ingredient synthetic drugs cannot be transferred to most alternative remedies.

By law, drug labels must provide essential information, but herbal remedies are being marketed as "dietary supplements" with little of the type of information needed to enable people to use these products properly. The herbal industry blames current regulatory policies for some of these problems. The FDA is bound by law to regulate products that make medical claims as drugs. Be sure to contact the FDA and visit the Web site www.fda.gov/comments.html to get a clear understanding of the rules and regulations before selling your products.

Food Products for Resale or Catering

The state health departments under the guidance of the FDA regulations require licenses for and inspection of the facilities where food products are made. The regulations are known in the business as the "commercial kitchen laws."

In most cases, the regulations governing the preparation of food products for resale require a kitchen, utensils, a food storage area, and appliances that are separate from those for your personal or family use. The food products prepared for resale also cannot be co-mingled with the food used for your family.

Strict sanitary guidelines are enforced, even more rigidly than those required for the cosmetics industry; in many states, it is almost impossibly costly to set up a food-related home-based business. However, enterprising individuals have found that renting time-sharing space in a commercial kitchen (using a restaurant kitchen during off-hours, for example) or the facilities at churches or private clubs is a way to get around the problem.

The Federal Trade Commission and Mail Orders

FTC rules apply to all businesses and cover a broad range of categories, such as trade practices, truth in advertising, unfair methods of competition, product labeling, unfair or deceptive acts and practices, and mail-order marketing. For example, the word *new* can be used to describe a product only for the first six months of its life. To use it afterward is in violation of FTC rules. The FTC offers free booklets on these categories. Every new business should order a set and get up-to-speed on these regulations.

If you take orders through the mail, you need to become familiar with the FTC's Rule Concerning Mail-Order Merchandise (16 CFR 435). The rule is explained in an easy-to-read booklet, "A Business Guide to the Federal Trade Commission's Mail Order Rule." Some of its basic features are summarized here:

➤ You must ship the merchandise within 30 days after you receive a properly completed order and payment, unless your ad clearly states that it will take longer. This rule is strictly enforced, with possible fines of up to $10,000 for each violation.

➤ If there will be a delay, you must notify the customer in writing. You must give the customer the option of a new shipment date (if known) or the opportunity to cancel the order and receive a full refund. You must give the customer a postage-free way to reply. You may assume that a customer who does not reply has agreed to the delay.

➤ If the customer cancels, you must refund the customer's money within seven days of receiving the canceled order. If the customer used a credit card, you must issue the credit within one billing cycle.

Pointers

To obtain pamphlets on FTC rules, go to www.FTC.gov, or write to the Consumer Response Center, Room 130, Federal Trade Commission, 600 Pennsylvania Avenue, NW, Washington, DC 20580.

Crafter Alert

If your ad clearly states that it will take longer than 30 days to ship your merchandise, it's important to put a notice on your order form stating that "orders are shipped within six to eight weeks," for example. You may not need to take that long, but this allows a cushion for unforeseen delays.

> ➤ A customer who consents to an indefinite delay can still cancel the order at any time before its shipment.

> ➤ A customer who cancels or never receives the ordered merchandise does not have to accept a store credit in place of a refund, but that customer is entitled to a cash refund or a credit on the charge card used.

The mail-order rule does not cover mail-order photo finishing; spaced deliveries, such as magazines (except for the first shipment); sales of seeds and growing plants; COD orders; or orders made by telephone and charged to a credit card account.

The Value of Disclaimers

A final precaution: I strongly recommend the liberal use of disclaimers. A few little words, such as "Not recommended for children under five years old," or "This item is not a toy" can mean so much. A disclaimer serves as a warning to the buyer, but much more than that, it may save you from being dragged into court for a product liability claim. The disclaimer should be printed on a label or a hang tag attached to the product.

A good rule of thumb for disclaimers is that if you have even the slightest question of whether you should use one, *use it*. It's a pretty cheap way to have a little extra insurance and peace of mind.

The Least You Need to Know

> ➤ The consumer product safety rules will affect you, especially if you make products for children.

> ➤ You must get written permission to use designer fabrics, logos, and celebrity-related images or words for your product or service.

> ➤ If you use any textiles or fabrics in your products, you must comply with content and care labeling laws.

> ➤ Personal care and aromatherapy products that make any medical claims are regulated by the FDA.

> ➤ Liberally use disclaimers to protect yourself, and attach them to your products.

Chapter 15

Bringing in the Pros

In This Chapter

➤ Finding professional help for your business

➤ Selecting an attorney

➤ Determining the type of accounting services you need

Most business start-ups will need some professional advice to get up and running. While the business owner focuses on the demands of a new business's start-up, accounting and legal issues may be best left to the professionals. As the business grows, you will face new issues that are even more complicated.

There are quite a few self-help books, computer programs, and preprinted forms for the new business owner, but they should not be relied on exclusively. The law can be complicated, and mistakes can be costly. Legal and accounting professionals often point out potential problems that you may not have anticipated and give you guidance in additional ways. Enlisting the help of professionals can improve your competitive edge.

Finding the Professionals You Need

Like selecting a doctor, finding the right attorney or accountant is not as simple as looking in the Yellow Pages. As with any business decision, you must weigh the time and cost of selecting and hiring professionals against the benefits of the advice and other services that they can provide.

It can seem like quite a challenge to find the right group of professionals to meet your specific business needs, but it's really a research process that includes getting references from friends, relatives, local professional associations, the Chamber of Commerce, and other professionals and business owners.

➤ Local community groups and universities may also provide good leads.

➤ Professionals who specialize in helping start-ups often attend local entrepreneur conventions and meetings.

➤ Local colleges and trade schools offering business programs often feature attorneys, accountants, insurance consultants, and business consultants as guest speakers.

The following sections give you some guidelines to help you evaluate your needs and make sound decisions about the professional help that you enlist.

Selecting an Attorney

While any attorney can probably fulfill an entrepreneur's legal requirements, only a small fraction will have the expertise and experience to meet the entrepreneur's specific small business requirements. Would you go to a foot doctor to find out why you have a sore throat? I think not. It is just as important to match the attorney that you decide to hire with your specific type of business.

Finding Attorneys to Consider

In addition to identifying attorneys that you want to consider by getting references from people you know and by attending events where you can see local lawyers in action, you can do some research online at the following Web sites:

➤ **Attorney Find: www.attorney-find.net.** Here you can sort possible choices of lawyers by location and specialty.

➤ **Lawyers.com: www.lawyers.com.** This site offers a wealth of legal information to help individuals better understand the law, make more informed legal choices, and identify high-quality legal representation. From Martindale-Hubbell, this site carries more than 420,000 listings of attorney firms worldwide.

➤ **Business Law Lounge: www.lectlaw.com/bus.html.** This site, the 'Lectric Law Library, is primarily for legal research, but it could help you find out more about attorneys that you're considering.

There is no single way to find a lawyer who is right for your business. One way to start the process is to call several lawyers you've been referred to. Some offer free consultations so you can get an initial feel for the individual and exchange information.

Questions to Ask Attorneys You're Considering

After you set up appointments to meet the attorneys you want to consider hiring, find out everything you need to know to make a fully informed choice. Keep the following list of questions in mind so that you can get the most from your meetings:

1. What is your experience in the area of legal matters specific to my type of business?

2. What percentage of your practice is devoted to my type of business? (For example, as a business owner, you may want an attorney who devotes the majority of his or her time to small business and contract law.)

3. What are your hourly rates?

4. How many attorneys are in your firm? Is it a full-service firm, do any of you specialize in small business legal matters?

5. Does the firm provide tax return preparation, or tax or estate planning?

6. Are you familiar with the following areas of federal and state law: income/estate taxation, corporations, contracts, partnerships, securities, antitrust, product liability, or the Uniform Commercial Code (UCC)?

7. Do you have knowledge about and experience in such nonlegal areas as business finance, financial accounting, management techniques, and ways to work with bankers, brokers, insurers, zoning boards, or industrial development agencies?

Naturally, your questions will be unique, based on your business's particular circumstances and needs, so use this list as a guide for modeling your own set of questions.

After your interviews, review your notes and examine the strengths and weaknesses of each lawyer. No single factor will decide which lawyer to hire; you will need to weigh many factors to determine which is the "best fit" for you and your business needs.

Pointers

Your questions will be unique, based on your business's particular needs, so use this list as a

Factors to Consider

Some of the factors to consider in weighing your choice of an attorney are listed here:

➤ **Availability.** Can the lawyer work with you immediately? Will other lawyers in the firm also work on your legal matters?

➤ **Comfort.** Do you feel comfortable with the lawyer? Do you trust the lawyer not to discuss private matters? Does the lawyer really listen to you?

➤ **Cost.** Do you feel comfortable and informed about the way you'll be charged for the legal services rendered?

➤ **Experience.** Does the lawyer have the necessary experience for your type of business?

➤ **Skills.** Does the lawyer know your specific industry and have connections that will save you time and money?

In the end, you'll have to decide which of these or any other factors are the most important to you.

When to Call in an Attorney

The following list of some of the situations in which complications are more than likely to arise will give you an idea of when you should call in an attorney:

➤ **Business start-up.** An attorney can assist you when you start up a business by clarifying your business objectives and analyzing your business proposal. Your attorney can evaluate the soundness of your business plan, research, and risk analysis. The attorney should also be able to recommend bankers, accountants, insurance professionals, government officials, and financial planners.

Artisan's Corner

If you ever need an attorney and cannot afford one, contact Volunteer Lawyers for the Arts (VLA), 1 E. 53rd St., New York, NY 10022, or call the organization's legal hotline at 212-319-2910. This nonprofit organization provides legal aid for professional artisans.

➤ **Business structure.** When you're considering setting up any form of corporation, partnership, or limited liability company (LLC), an attorney will steer you through all the legal documentation that is required and advise you on the differences between these structures so that you can make an informed decision.

➤ **Contracts.** Consult an attorney *before* you sign a contract, not afterward. Contracts should be drafted in writing to avoid possible misunderstandings. Seek your lawyer's advice before you sign contracts.

➤ **Estate planning.** Attorneys can provide guidance concerning wills; trusts; estates, gifts, and income taxes; S corporations; powers of attorney; family partnerships; healthcare proxies; living wills; and guardianships.

➤ **Formal written opinions.** When a business is sold or borrows money, opinions are often requested relating to specific regulatory problems, the priority of liens, absence of defaults, and other matters. A bank or purchaser of the business may request a formal written opinion from your business's lawyer.

➤ **Litigation.** An attorney can help you avoid lawsuits and legal hassles. If your business is incorporated, you must engage an attorney to represent it whenever it sues or is sued. An attorney is needed in areas of labor and management disputes; debt collection; buying, selling, or merging a business; licensing, copyrights, trademarks, and patents; bankruptcy and reorganization; or criminal matters to name a few.

➤ **Real estate.** An attorney should be consulted before a purchase contract or lease is signed. Consult an attorney regarding local codes; environmental concerns; zoning regulations; assessments against the property; liens that may have been placed on the real estate; the existence, validity, and terms of any leases; tenant and landlord agreements; the purchaser's right to assume existing mortgages; and services that must be provided by the landlord.

How Much Will It Cost?

Hiring an attorney may not be as expensive as you may think. Attorneys charge for their services using one or a combination of these three methods:

➤ **Flat fees.** They are predisclosed amounts usually charged for basic legal matters, incorporation of a small business, real estate closings, basic wills, and bankruptcy.

➤ **Contingent fees.** In the contingent fee arrangement, you pay the attorney a certain percentage of your recovery through a suit if and only if you win, but the attorney cannot guarantee the result. If you sue for $1 million and you recover only $99 after trial or settlement, and there is a one-third contingency fee arrangement, the attorney's fee will be $33.

➤ **Hourly fees.** Generally charged for all other types of cases, including estate planning and defense of lawsuits. Some companies retain an attorney on a monthly basis, whereby the attorney is paid a specified monthly retainer fee regardless of the amount of time spent on the client's matters.

Whatever the fee structure is, the client must pay for all disbursements, such as process service fees, investigations, court costs, travel expenses, long-distance calls, expert testimony, medical reports, appraisals, and all other out-of-pocket expenses.

After you've decided on fee terms, ask for a written fee agreement that sets forth the services to be performed by the attorney, the amount of the legal fee (hourly rate, contingent, or flat), and the anticipated amount of disbursements.

Working with Your Attorney

You need to understand some factors about your working relationship with your attorney. The major ones are covered in the following sections.

Attorney-Client Privilege

It is of primary importance to define the boundaries of your attorney-client privilege, as outlined in the following list:

➤ **A lawyer employed or retained by a corporation or similar entity owes allegiance to the entity.** Allegiance is not owed to a shareholder, director, officer, employee, representative, or other person connected with the entity. Occasionally, a lawyer for an entity is asked to represent a person connected with the entity in an individual capacity (outlined in the following section). In such cases, the lawyer may serve the individual only if the lawyer is convinced that differing interests are not present.

Crafter Alert

Attorney-client privilege does not extend to business advice. In addition, the privilege is lost by the client if any communication with the attorney is intended to further a crime or an illegal act, or if any communication is shared with others or is witnessed by outsiders.

➤ **When hiring an attorney, you should clarify whom the attorney represents.** The attorney-client privilege does not protect communications with a lawyer unless the person making the communication is a client. If the client is a corporation, privilege will protect communications made by any company employee to the attorney, if the communications relate to the employee's duties and are made at the direction of a corporate superior. While the company founders may initially be the only representatives of the company, they are usually not considered the client. Thus, if the board of directors later decides to fire the founder, the attorney cannot represent both the founder and the company. Additionally, any communications between the attorney and the founder would not be privileged.

➤ **The privilege applies only to legal advice, not to business advice.** It does not protect client communications that are made to further a crime or an illegal act. A client also loses the privilege for any communication shared with others or witnessed by outsiders.

Tips on Cutting Attorneys' Fees

You can do a lot to keep your expenses for legal work and advice under control by following these tips:

➤ **Be organized, prepared, and proactive.** Business owners can use an attorney more efficiently and save money, too. For example, if you need a contract drawn up, before you meet with the attorney, draw up a rough draft of all the key points that you want covered. With the draft done, the attorney can go over it quickly with you and just add the necessary legal language to protect your interests.

➤ **Standardize your employment forms, contracts, noncompete or nondisclosure agreements, and any legal forms that your business may frequently use.** This way you pay for only the original legal drafting of the document once, rather than having an original document drawn up each time you have a need for one.

➤ **Take initiative.** You should keep the attorney informed of important business and legal issues that may have seemingly insignificant legal consequences that the attorney may spot. More important, the attorney will have your business at the forefront of his or her thoughts if any relevant legal issues occur.

Crafter Alert

When you are not clear on what a legal term or contract clause means, *ask! You* are responsible for every agreement that you sign, so be sure that it's worded the way you intended it to be.

Selecting the Right Accounting Services

First we will look at some of the differences in accounting services, which will help you select the right one—maybe even at the right price. Remember, accountants are not bookkeepers. You have to supply them with all the figures that they need to prepare financial statements and tax returns. If they do offer bookkeeping services, they charge accordingly.

An accountant can help you understand your total financial picture. A professional can assist you in your business planning by helping you understand such things as the tax implications of the type of business structure you select, and whether you should buy or lease a vehicle, a computer, or other business equipment.

If you require business financing, your accountant can prepare the financial statements and support documentation required by your bank. Accountants can be invaluable in helping you structure your business to take advantage of all the possible tax benefits.

Most small and home-based businesses do not require the full-time services of an accountant, and owners find that their accountants are best used (after assisting with the business start-up) to help them take steps to minimize their tax bills and to prepare their tax returns.

What Accounting Services Are Available?

Several levels and types of accounting services are available, including these:

➤ **Certified public accountants (CPAs).** These accountants are licensed by the state, have a four-year college degree, and, as a result, usually charge more. Most CPAs tend to specialize in corporate work, so be careful—they may not be the best choice for a small or home-based business. A CPA can prepare your financial statements, produce your quarterly reports, do your taxes, and assist in your business financial and tax planning.

➤ **Public accountants.** These pros offer the same services as a CPA. They usually charge less and offer a full range of accounting and tax services.

➤ **IRS enrolled agents (EAs).** EAs are licensed by the Treasury Department. They are qualified to handle complex tax issues, prepare annual tax returns, and represent you before the IRS (the same as a CPA can). They may be the best choice for your annual tax filing. EAs cost less than other accountants but are probably the most educated in the complex tax rules and regulations that a business has to deal with. You can get a list of EAs for your area by calling 1-800-424-4339.

➤ **Tax preparers.** These experts are best used for personal income tax returns only. You need to seek out the most qualified tax specialist possible to make sure that you take full advantage of the tax deductions available to you under the law.

➤ **Payroll services.** These companies handle all your payroll record keeping, prepare all the reports in a timely manner, and send them to you ready to sign and send in.

➤ **Bookkeeping services.** These services are available for small businesses to track where your money is coming from and going to, and to get all the numbers plugged into the right accounts with the proper values. They also offer payroll services and your choice of quarterly or annual financial statements.

➤ **CPA Finder: www.cpafinder.com.** This service focuses on connecting businesses with potential accountants, utilizing a database categorized by state.

Artisan's Corner

Visit the American Accounting Association Web site at www. rutgers.edu/Accounting/raw/aaa/ index.html. You can use this site to locate the regional group serving your area, and then contact the group if you need a referral.

Cutting Accounting Costs

The big question is this (and now you have to be truly honest): Are you the type of person who will take charge of your accounting and keep good, up-to-date records, or is a shoebox stuffed with receipts and invoices more your style? When was the last time you did your personal bank statement reconciliation? Have you ever bothered to prepare a family budget to track where all your money goes? Okay, you get the idea.

If you know deep down that crunching numbers is not your forte, then you should plan to hire someone to take care of that responsibility. This is an area that, if left unattended, will certainly spell disaster for your plan to develop a successful business.

If you opt to keep track of your own financial records, as we told you in Chapter 7, "Using a Computer to Lighten Your Business Load," doing it with a computer and accounting software is the way to go. In that case, you may need only the services of a good tax accountant, so the less you'll have to spend. But whether doing your own accounting or spending the money makes sense for you as an individual is your decision to make.

The Least You Need to Know

➤ Referrals are often the best way to find attorneys, accountants, and other professionals to help you with your business.

➤ Research and interview professionals that you're considering, and select those who are knowledgeable about your specific type of business.

➤ The type of accounting services that you need depends a lot on how much you can or are willing to do yourself.

Part 4

Gearing Up for Profit

Yes, I know you have been waiting to hear about where the profits fit into the total picture. This is it. Profits don't just happen; it takes planning and business know-how. It starts with knowing the tricks of the trade for buying your supplies wholesale, and being prepared for producing your products in volume. Then we delve into how to value your time so that you can make the money you deserve. Plus, this part covers the various ways to price your products or services so that you can cover your costs and make a profit. These chapters provide you with the basics of planning for profits from your business. Wow! That's a lot of ground to cover in one part.

Chapter 16

Tricks of the Wholesale Buying Trade

Wholesale buying is buying in bulk. Usually, items that you purchase wholesale are packaged by the dozen, the case, or perhaps the gross. It is this unit packaging and the no-frills warehouse method of selling that, in part, makes it possible for you to buy merchandise at wholesale rates.

To succeed in the business of producing and selling products, you have to establish connections with reliable wholesale suppliers who will supply the materials that you'll need. Your goal is to buy production materials at the lowest possible price so that you can offer your products to the customer at a competitive price and still make a reasonable profit. In this chapter, we explore the world of wholesale buying.

Wholesale Buying

Buying wholesale is not as difficult as it may seem for a small business owner; remember, wholesalers are in business to sell their goods, and what company doesn't want new customers? The key is that you must *be prepared to do business* before you contact a wholesale company. Because wholesalers generally don't sell to individuals, you'll have to prove that you're in business.

For a new business to qualify for wholesale buying, it first has to have a *business identity*.

Qualifying to Buy Wholesale

Qualifying as a wholesale buyer isn't complicated; it just takes a series of simple steps:

1. Select a business name.

2. Register the name with the appropriate county or state agency.

3. Apply for a sales tax number, or a vendor number or license if sales tax is not applicable to your merchandise. If you're a corporation, your corporate ID number is acceptable. The sales tax or vendor or corporation ID number is the number that you'll put on the *resale certificate form* (explained in Chapter 10, "Uncle Sam and You") that most wholesale companies will require before they'll sell to your business. Some companies won't even send you a catalog without a number signifying that you are an authentic business owner.

4. Open a business bank account in the name of your business.

5. Prepare your printed business stationery: letterhead, envelopes, business cards, and order forms or purchase orders.

Artisan's Corner

To qualify your new business to start buying wholesale, you have to create your business identity. The steps are: get a name, register it, get a sales tax or vendor or corporation ID number, and open a business bank account.

Once you've established your new business, you're ready to contact wholesalers.

Ordering Catalogs

Most businesses find that the wholesale suppliers that they need to supply their materials are not in their local area. This is why using mail order catalogs, ordering at trade shows, and placing orders with sales reps are the most common methods of buying wholesale supplies.

If you want to order wholesale catalogs, here are some tips to make it easier:

➤ When mailing inquiries for wholesale catalogs, always type your request on your company letterhead; *do not hand-write your inquiry.* At the very least, use post-cards that you have stamped or labeled with your name, your business return address and telephone number, and the phrase "Please send your latest catalog. Thank you."

➤ If you contact a supplier by telephone, present the best business image possible. Identify yourself as Mary Jones, of ABC Design Company. Explain that you are interested in purchasing supplies to be used in the manufacture of your products. The more professional you sound when dealing with wholesalers, the more apt you are to win their confidence and cooperation.

Because the cost of printing and mailing catalogs has hit the roof, it's becoming more common for suppliers to charge a fee (usually $3 to $10) to mail a catalog to potential customers. Most companies will deduct the catalog cost from your first order. When you become a regular customer, wholesalers usually send you new catalogs automatically at no charge, along with information on whatever sales promotions they're offering.

Buying Supplies

Buying wholesale means that you must buy each item in the minimum quantity offered by the wholesaler. You may have to buy items packed by the dozen, by the gross, by the case, or in prepacked assortments. The catalog or order form will explain how each item is packaged. Some companies offer several quantity choices per item. Usually, the larger the pack you buy, the lower your unit cost per item will be.

Most wholesale companies require a *minimum order*—that is, a minimum dollar amount for each order placed. This can vary from no required minimum to $5,000 or more. Some companies require a larger amount for the first order than for reorders. In the arts and crafts supply industry, many wholesalers require no minimum orders at all, or minimums starting as low as $25.

Some suppliers will ship orders for less than the minimum required and charge a handling fee to offset the cost of packing and shipping a small order.

> **Trade Terms**
>
> A **minimum order** means the lowest dollar or quantity amount that a company will accept when you place an order. The minimum amount is usually the amount that a company figures is cost-effective to pack and ship. Anything less reduces the company's profit line.

Shipping charges are paid by the company placing the order and are usually freight on board (FOB), meaning that the buyer is responsible for all shipping charges from the company's shipping location to the order's destination. As a perk to gain your business, companies will sometimes waive shipping charges on orders that meet a certain dollar amount, that are placed within a specified time frame, or that are part of a special promotional package.

You may not be able to obtain an open account or credit terms for your orders until you've established a credit presence for your company. In the meanwhile, you may have to order COD or prepay with your company check. In addition, many suppliers now offer credit cards as a payment option, which has made ordering less of a hassle for new businesses. Be patient and persistent in securing good connections with your wholesale suppliers; they'll be the lifeblood of your business.

Wholesale Suppliers

The term "wholesaler" does have a specific meaning, but it is also used generically for several levels of companies from which you can by wholesale supplies:

➤ **Manufacturer.** The prime source for buying wholesale, the manufacturer will usually offer the lowest wholesale price for its own product line. The drawback is that sometimes the minimum order requirements are too high for a small business that is just starting out. It may also take longer to receive your merchandise when you order from the manufacturer.

➤ **Wholesaler.** This type of company buys in very large quantities directly from manufacturers. Wholesalers are usually able to obtain added quantity discounts and price concessions for high-volume purchasing. They then wholesale the merchandise at prices very close to—and sometimes even the same as—those you would get from the manufacturer. Wholesalers usually offer low minimum order requirements, small quantity packaging per item, and quick turnaround time for shipments. This serves as an advantage to small business operators.

➤ **Distributor.** Distributors act a lot like wholesalers. In some cases, they may be the distribution division of a major manufacturer, set up to be the supply channel for its products. Traditionally, a distributor's price is slightly higher than a manufacturer's, around 5 percent to maybe 15 percent higher. In return, a distributor offers a lot of convenience to the small-quantity buyer, such as low to no minimum order or quantity requirements and the ability to ship within 24 to 48 hours. One drawback may be that once the distributors sell out of a particular style or item, it may not be available again or may be replaced with a similar item, possibly from a different manufacturer.

➤ **Sales rep.** Sometimes called a manufacturer's rep, a sales rep (representative) is usually an independent salesperson (sometimes part of a representation company) who represents several manufacturers in a specific territory but gives the impression of working exclusively for each manufacturer. Sales reps are usually paid a straight commission by the manufacturer of 15 to 20 percent on the orders that they write. They typically sell their lines at trade shows and showrooms, and a good rep often makes regular follow-up calls or visits to customers to let them know about new or discontinued items or special promotions.

Each of these wholesale channels serves a useful purpose. Most businesses will find that they'll be using a combination of them, depending on the type and quantity of supplies that they need to buy. The following section offers some guidance on selecting suppliers.

Supplier Preference Checklist

You should consider several factors before you choose one wholesale supplier over another. The following checklist will help you compare potential suppliers' abilities to meet your specific needs:

❑ Order minimums.

❑ Quantity minimums. (Can packs be assorted by colors, sizes, or styles to meet the minimum?)

❑ Shipping *lead time*.

❑ Terms and conditions of return policy.

❑ How credits for damaged or missing goods are applied.

❑ Whether a restocking fee is charged for items returned.

❑ What happens when the quality of an item isn't what you expected.

❑ Distance from the shipping location to your business.

❑ Shipping and handling rates.

❑ How flexible quantity breaks are in the way items are packaged.

❑ How the supplier receives orders. Can you call, fax, e-mail, order online, or mail-order at your convenience?

❑ Whether the supplier has an effective customer service policy to unravel any errors in orders, billing, or shipments.

> **Trade Terms**
>
> **Lead time** is the amount of time that a company needs from the time that it receives your order to the time that it actually can ship it to you.

❏ Whether the supplier maintains a consistent supply of the items offered. You want to be able to rely on reordering items that you plan to use over an extended period of time.

❏ Reputation within the industry. Is this supplier considered reliable?

Use this checklist as a guide when you receive a supply catalog or when you call suppliers for information. (If terms and conditions are not written in a supplier's catalog, find out what they are before you place your first order.) This is part of the research that you need to do when you're planning to move from hobbyist to new business owner.

Crafter Alert

Be sure to check the return policy of the supplier before you order. Some charge a restocking fee, which is a flat fee or a percentage charged for returning products. Others may allow returns only for damaged merchandise.

As you select your wholesale suppliers, remember that although price is very important, it should not be your only consideration. A consistent and reliable source for the main supplies that you'll need in the manufacture of your product line outweighs all other factors. What could be worse than having a major art and craft show coming up and, as you're building up inventory for the show, you suddenly find out that a main component of your hottest selling item is out of stock, or no longer available? You can avoid that kind of panic if you have another supplier lined up.

Make sure that you establish business relationships with several reliable suppliers. Even if you do most of your ordering from only a few of them, have several backup suppliers, especially for the main materials that you use to produce your products.

Finding Wholesale Sources

There are many places to look for wholesale sources, including these:

➤ **Trade shows.** These shows are specifically set up to provide business buyers the opportunity to view and order products directly from wholesalers. For show listings, check Events Lister at www.eventlister.com/; the NCA at www.craftassoc. com/confer.html; Festival Network, at www.festivalnet.com/; or Trade Show Central www.tscentral.com. Also see the section on shopping trade shows, later in this chapter.

➤ **Regional and national wholesale buying centers.** Manufacturers maintain showrooms of product samples in buildings or trade centers, staffed with salespeople ready to display and sell their lines to business buyers.

➤ **Trade publications.** Check out *Urlich's Directory of Serials,* for example, to see if anyone publishes a trade journal in the area of your specific hobby, art, or craft.

➤ **Books and business publications.** Look for publications about industries and hobbies related to your business.

➤ **Magazines and newspapers.** These publications publish profiles as news items—and, of course, advertising is the mainstay of these publications.

➤ **Trade associations.** These organizations have considerable information on the industry they serve and the companies that provide goods and services to the industry. Many also conduct educational seminars and publish source information related to their fields. To help you find the right association, two great resources are *Gale's Directory of Associations* and the *National Trade and Professional Associations* book. See the sampling of major art and craft trade shows later in the chapter.

➤ **The *Thomas Register.*** This is a listing of manufacturers grouped by industry and product. You can find it online at www. thomasregister.com, and in the library.

➤ **Local and national Yellow Pages.** The local Yellow Pages offer listings under specific product lines, such as "floral supplies, wholesale." You also can visit www. athand.com/ for a national directory broken down into regions. In addition, CBS Switchboard at www.switchboard.com/, features a special "find a business" category, and www.bigyellow.com/ claims to have more than 11 million business listings.

Artisan's Corner

Don't forget to search the Internet for additional resources. New Web sites for associations are popping up frequently as more of them go online.

➤ **Internet search engines.** These provide the means to search online by product category (such as "beads, wholesale").

➤ **Networking opportunities.** Meet other business people, join business groups, attend business seminars, and join trade associations.

➤ **Individual detective work.** Look on retail packages of products similar to yours for the manufacturer's name and address, and call or write to that supplier to inquire about buying wholesale. If they don't sell directly, they'll be glad to tell you who the distributor is in your area. Some packages list the distributor. Find the manufacturer or distributor through directory assistance or by using the *Thomas Register* (www.thomasregister.com).

➤ **Free e-mail business discussion groups.** An example is the one that NCA sponsors, A Craft Biz Connection (you can sign up free at www.craftassoc.com/cbcelist.html). Members share business tips and resources, and help each other with business issues common to professional arts and crafts producers working from a home base.

Pointers

Sources for wholesale suppliers are listed in Appendix A, "Resources." Also check there for listings of trade associations and trade publications. Trade publications have a wealth of information and are usually packed with advertising from suppliers related to the industry niche that they serve.

Some comments from members of the A Craft Biz Connection e-mail discussion list (www.craftassoc.com) follow:

From Susan West of SunShine Glass Works–Sun Catchers of All Sorts (www.sunshineglassworks.com): When I first started out, I purchased retail. I very quickly realized that I needed to purchase wholesale. Basically, I have found all my wholesalers on the Web through searches and links and lists. There are still a couple of items that I purchase retail because the wholesalers that I have found sell the product at the same or greater cost than I can get it retail—and that doesn't include shipping! I would imagine that there have to be wholesalers someplace for these items, but as of yet, I just haven't been able to find them.

From Linnea J. Kilgren of California: Some wholesalers have a minimum order requirement; some do not. Some go pretty far with their minimum—let's say, $500 per order—and each calendar year you must meet a larger minimum, such as $5,000. That is at least 10 $500-orders each year. Then you are considered a "stocking dealer." Some want 75 percent or more of your business to use the type of products that they sell. For example, if you apply to a wholesale stained-glass company, your company must be in stained glass, and 75 percent of your product must be in some form of stained glass. But don't become disheartened—many wholesale companies cater to the little guy. You may pay a few cents more per item, but there is no minimum (or a small one of around $50), and you don't have to be a stocking dealer or a big guy.

From Debbie Gragg of Gragg Enterprises (www.homebizprofits.com): I am a wholesaler of imported giftware, including handcrafted items and decorative accents. I require an opening order of only $55 plus 15 percent shipping and handling. With that, I send our beautiful, full-line, 250-plus–page color catalog. After an opening order, I require a minimum of only $25 per order, plus the shipping and handling. My ordering prices have been set with new small businesses without big budgets in mind.

Getting Help from Trade Associations

One of the best places to start your research for wholesale suppliers is with trade associations within your industry. As we've pointed out in this chapter, there are many ways to locate the associations related to your business. To get you started, here's a list of some of the major ones:

Hobby Industry Association (HIA)
PO Box 348
Elmwood Park, NJ 07407
Phone: 201-794-1133
Fax: 201-797-0657
Web site: www.hobby.org

The HIA sponsors large wholesale supply trade shows.

National Association of Manufacturers
1331 Pennsylvania Ave. NW, Suite 1500 North Lobby
Washington, DC 20004-1790
Phone: 202-637-3000
Fax: 202-637-3182
Web site: www.nam.org/

National Association of Wholesale Distributors
1725 K St. NW
Washington, DC 20006
Phone: 202-872-0885

National Craft Association (NCA)
1945 East Ridge Rd., #5178
Rochester, NY 14622
Phone: 1-800-715-9594
Fax: 1-800-318-9410
E-mail: nca@craftassoc.com
Web site: www.craftassoc.com

The NCA publishes wholesale directories that supply wholesale contacts for more than 500,000 art and craft-making supplies. See details at www.craftassoc/dirwhbks.html.

Artisan's Corner

In addition to probably being able to provide wholesale source information, some trade organizations offer training programs and industry certification that will assist you in becoming more professional within your chosen field.

Artisan's Corner

Attending trade shows not only provides you with great product selection, it also improves your competitive edge. This is a learning experience that every artisan should participate in at least once a year. Add it to your list of things to accomplish!

Shopping a Trade Show

After you're up and running, you should put a trade show on your agenda. Obtaining the materials and supplies that you need, at the right price and when you need them, is as important as the products that you make. No supplies, no products, right? You'll also see what new fads and trends there are in the industry—and you'll have fun! So, let's discover how to make the most out of your trip to a trade show.

1. **Preregister whenever possible.** Don't waste time standing in long lines for show badges, seminars, and special events.

2. **Go prepared.** Take either your sales tax or vendor's license or corporation ID number, or copies of your resale certificate, in case you want to do business with a new vendor.

3. **Have a good supply of your business cards.**

4. **Know what your inventory needs are before the show.** Try to plan about six months in advance. This makes your selection easier by establishing an outline of what you need for your product line, holiday items, and promotions. Planning helps you save money by grouping your orders to take advantage of discounts and special offers.

5. **Go to the show with specific goals.** For example, find a more competitive packaging supplier, find a wider range of dried flowers, or find new items to enlarge your merchandise line.

6. **Review the show guide.** Before you begin viewing the show, mark off the vendors that you really don't want to miss so that you don't forget to make time to speak with them.

7. **Carry a small tape recorder or notebook.** Capture the day's details, and make notes on the next day's agenda and on things that you may want to do when you get home.

8. **Check out what's hot.** Ask suppliers what their two or three best-selling items are, and compare notes with others.

9. **Co-op advertising.** Ask if a program is available to you and, if so, what the requirements are.

10. **Ask about show specials.** Many suppliers offer special incentives for placing orders at the show; they're designed to save you serious money.

11. **Know your repayment plan.** Decide before you shop how you will be paying: by check, with credit cards, or on open account.

12. **Check on freight costs.** Ask each supplier what the freight would be to your area on items that you want to buy, and figure it into the cost. Compare before you buy.

13. **Plan shipments.** Sometimes you can take advantage of quantity discount programs by planning split shipments over several months. Check with suppliers; it can save you money.

14. **Delivery times.** Make sure that what you're buying does not have an impossible backorder list, especially if you need it right away. Find out average shipping time for new orders and for reorders. Check backorder policies.

15. **Minimum order requirements.** Find out what first orders and reorder requirements are.

Pointers

As a special offer to this book's readers, the NCA will give you 30 percent off on a membership in the National Craft Association. Just mention the offer when you contact the NCA. Call 1-800-715-9594, e-mail nca@craftassoc.com, or visit the NCA online at www.craftassoc.com. And don't forget to ask for a copy of the *free* "NCA Arts and Crafts Newsletter."

16. **Read the return policy.** Get all the details up front.

17. **Total your orders as you place them.** Make sure that you're not exceeding your budget. It's easy to do if you don't keep track while you're placing the orders.

18. **Review orders before you sign.** In the trade show rush, it's easy to make a mistake. Take a moment to go over your orders to make sure that everything you need is included and that there's nothing you didn't order.

19. **Ask questions!** You are among experts who are willing to answer questions about selling, market trends, business tactics, and more.

Finding the wholesale suppliers that you need takes a combination of a little research and lots of persistence.

So, if at first you don't succeed, just put on your detective hat and dig a little deeper.

The Least You Need to Know

➤ You must first establish your business identity before you can expect to buy from wholesale suppliers.

➤ Always be businesslike and professional when contacting and dealing with wholesale suppliers; they can make a huge difference in the success of your business.

➤ Before you place orders, research the terms and conditions that several suppliers require, and choose the suppliers that best meet your needs.

➤ Try to establish a working relationship with several suppliers, especially for your main product line materials; if your main supplier runs out at a crucial moment, you'll always have a backup.

Chapter 17

Setting Up Shop: The World of Manufacturing

<table>
<tr><td colspan="2" align="center">**In This Chapter**</td></tr>
</table>

In This Chapter

➤ Designing your work area

➤ Planning for efficient manufacturing

➤ Getting organizing tips and shortcuts

➤ Understanding the open-to-buy inventory–buying concept

Even if your business is home-based, when you produce a product, you are a manufacturer, so you need to plan your work space to enhance production. If you plan a service business, you still need to set up an effective and efficient work area, so we need to explore your requirements and how they relate to your overall business operation. In this chapter, we also tell you how to create a long-range open-to-buy plan for maximizing the return on the capital that you invest in inventory.

Your Work Area: Focus on Efficiency

Whether you're just establishing your work area or you've decided that it's time for an upgrade, as you make the move from hobbyist to business owner, focusing on function over style will reap returns by maximizing efficiency and providing flexibility for future growth. Time is money, so it's important to plan your work space to best accommodate your actual work flow.

Even if yours is a one-person operation, you need to start designing your work space by analyzing how you work, what type of equipment you use now or will add down the road, and what goals you have for your business in three to five years. I can't tell you how many times I've heard artisans moan that they wish they had planned their work space rather than just let it happen in a haphazard fashion, or complain that they've outgrown their work area because they didn't plan for growth and expansion. A little planning up front can save you from getting trapped in a work space that doesn't work. Ask yourself, "How will I use the space, and what are my actual requirements?"

Pointers

If you plan a home-based business, rule number one is this: *Create a work area separate from the family living area and free from the normal family traffic.* Use a room with a door that can be closed, or a garage, a basement, or any other space where you can work without unnecessary distractions, interruptions, and noise.

Planning Your Work Space

Ask yourself the following questions to design a work space that's right you:

1. **If you're planning a home-based business, is the product or service one that can be done at home without disrupting the family's lifestyle?** Can you find a quiet area away from the normal family traffic and distractions? Can you designate your work hours and stick to them, or do you need to be in a location away from home to apply yourself wholeheartedly to working? If you plan to rent or buy office space or a storefront location, have you carefully worked out a budget and financing that will guarantee that you'll have enough money to operate for six months to a year? Can you afford the "right" location for the business?

2. **How much will be used for your home office area?** How much space do you need to spread out design plans, page layouts, and research notes; fill orders; do the books, and so on? How much desktop space do you need? What about space for files or storage? What machines or equipment will you need space for? Is the office the key work area? Will you need a conference area to meet with customers? Does your zoning allow for customer traffic? (See Chapter 9, "How It Works: Can I Run My Business from Home?" for information on zoning and other laws and regulations.)

3. **How much is needed for the production area?** Do you need several work surfaces for simultaneous projects? How much? Have you planned the space to include the materials and tools used for each project so that they are within reasonable reach of the work surface area? What projects require you to stand or sit to work efficiently? What is the ideal work-flow arrangement from start to

finish for the items that you make? How can you streamline the work flow for mass production as your volume grows? What business equipment do you need now? What might you need in the future? What electrical, plumbing, telephone, or computer hook-ups do you need to plan with future needs in mind? Do you need separate work spaces for production? For example, perhaps a woodworker would want a separate area for painting and finishing items, away from the dust created by cutting or sanding. A painter may need a special enclosed vented area for spray painting or airbrush work.

4. **Do you need an area for shipping?** Have you planned for where you'll house the shipping cartons, packing materials, sealing equipment, and weight scale? How much of a work surface do you need to pack and seal boxes? Where will they be kept until they're shipped?

5. **How much storage space is needed?** Do you have adequate storage space for production materials and the completed inventory? Is the space convenient to move stock in and out of? Does storage of your materials require light, temperature, or humidity control? (Can you imagine a candle-maker in Arizona storing inventory in a garage without air conditioning when it's 115°?) Is the storage area free of odors from cooking, chemicals, or smoke, which will be absorbed by porous materials that you store? Will you need to include extra storage space to accommodate seasonal inventory build-up, such as when you're producing in advance for the fall holiday selling season?

6. **How much time will you spend in your business?** Have you planned for your creature comforts? Are the work surfaces and seating arrangements set at convenient heights? Is there adequate light and ventilation? Do you need heat or air conditioning? Have you considered your food and drink requirements? What type of flooring will you be walking or standing on all day? Would a fatigue mat or carpet remnant be useful where you stand or walk when working?

Artisan's Corner

Just think how much easier and less costly it will be to organize your work space at start-up rather than when you are in the middle of production rushing to complete orders on time.

7. **Will you be traveling?** What equipment or supplies will you need to take with you? Will you need duplicate equipment at your home base? Do you have transportation suitable for traveling, and is it in good running condition and big enough to meet your needs? What if you plan to do art and craft shows? Will the vehicle hold all your display fixtures and enough inventory to make the trip profitable?

8. **Have you considered safety in your plans?** Have you allowed for enough aisle room between work areas for people and stock to move around without knocking things off work stations? Did you plan where to place fire extinguishers? Is there enough space to use a hand dolly to move shipments or inventory from place to place? Is all your equipment properly vented, if required? Is a proper storage area planned for chemicals, solvents, or combustible materials, if you use them? Do you have a place to keep safety glasses and other protective gear required for your work within the production area? When things are not immediately handy, the temptation is far greater to do one quick thing without going to get protective gear that you know you should be using. And isn't that just when an accident is most likely to happen!

Always try to take a frugal approach to purchasing furniture and fixtures. Unless you have customers coming into your business on a regular basis and you want to look established, you don't need to spend a lot on work surfaces or basic furniture. Focus on functionality rather than appearance. Modular furniture that you can move around to redesign your work space or that you can add to as you grow is a very smart choice.

Carefully plan your work space layout; it's the heart of your business—it's where your work flows from.

Manufacturing Tips

There's more to setting up a home business than furniture, equipment, and storage. Some tips and shortcuts that will save you time and money are listed here:

➤ **Organize your supplies.** Keep all like supplies together. For example, keep all ribbon together, sorted by size and color. This not only speeds your production, but it also helps you control your supply reordering needs. Hanging spools of ribbon from a dowel hung on brackets over your work area is very efficient and saves space.

➤ **Designate specific work areas.** Think of each work station as a mini production line. Set up each work station with places for the tools, materials, and any equipment or fixtures that you need to complete that part of the production phase. Make it a habit to always put the tools back in their designated spots. Looking for a misplaced glue gun or cutting tool costs you time, which is money. Plan enough space in each work area so that all the materials that you require are within easy reach. Think of each phase of the product production from step one to completion, and design the work space to accommodate the natural work flow that you prefer.

➤ **Assemble all the materials that you need.** Before you start production on an item, check to make sure that you have all the necessary supplies assembled in your work area. Every time you have to leave the work area to get more materials, it stops production and disrupts your momentum.

➤ **Never make one item at a time.** The only exception to this rule is if you're creating a prototype for a new design.

➤ **Check your sales records and order log.** Estimate how many of which items you will need for a specific period of time or for a particular sales event. Then decide which items you need to make first so that you'll be sure you have the total quantity produced within the required time frame.

➤ **Work efficiently.** Group all the preassembly steps for producing an item into individual units. Perform all the steps, and then assemble the completed item. For example: If the item you're making requires two pieces each of 12-inch ribbon, one blue and one pink, and you're making a dozen of those items, then cut 12 pieces of each and set them aside. Cut all the ribbon at once, or paint all the same color at once; do all the gluing or sanding at the same time, and so forth. This will save you valuable production time. Repeat the process for each component part required to assemble the item, then you are ready for the assembly process.

➤ **Prepare ahead.** Keep a quantity of prepared component parts on hand for each item that you sell so that you can assemble them quickly when you're pressured to fill orders or to get ready for shows. A good habit to develop for use of your spare time (instead of goofing off) is to prepare ahead for your busy times. What if you were doing a three-day show and sold out of your best-seller on the second day? If you had the components ready, you could whip up some items when you got back and have them ready to take to the show the next day.

➤ **Keep good sales records.** For production planning, you need to keep track of how many of each item you've sold, in what colors, sizes, and so forth. It not only helps you in planning your supply orders, it keeps you on target with any changes in your sales trends. You'll be able to spot increased or decreased sales of items in a specific color or style, for example, so that you can react accordingly. (Chapter 12, "Keeping Financial Records," covers the many uses of financial records in detail.)

Crafter Alert

Unless you're creating a prototype for a new design, never make one item at a time. It's an inefficient use of your facilities and your time.

➤ **Plan your buying.** Purchasing your supplies in a larger quantity usually allows you to get quantity discounts and freight savings. Keep a pad in your work area to write down items that you notice are low, and always recheck your supply inventory and sales records to make sure that you're ordering enough supplies to get you through to your next order period. Plan ahead when ordering; lack of materials for your best-sellers could cost you big money in lost sales. See the following section for a comprehensive look at planning your buying.

Open-to-Buy: A Business Buying Plan

Open-to-buy is the industry term for planning the amount of retail dollars allocated for the purchase of future delivery of merchandise. Many business owners profess to understand the concept but don't actually apply it properly. Most tend to ignore it and assume, incorrectly, that they can operate their buying program based on guessing what their needs will be from season to season.

Although widely referred to as open-to-buy, the more accurate terminology would be *open-to-receive.* While orders may be placed at any time, the delivery times are critical. A working open-to-buy system will give the business a dollar plan for each delivery period as far into the future as necessary. Receiving the right amount of merchandise will ensure that you have the beginning inventories that you need to support actual monthly sales at the highest possible turnover rates.

Trade Terms

Open-to buy is a system of using sales projections to plan inventory purchases and allocate funds for future delivery periods.

Is your operation too small for open-to-buy planning? Is it too large? *Every business, no matter what size, needs open-to-buy planning to maximize the return on the capital invested in inventory.* Smaller retailers particularly cannot afford any mistakes because sales volume and cash flow are critical. Large retailers can get buried by being overinventoried because of the very size of their purchases. There are those who have been in business for many years and will say with an odd sense of pride that they've never done any open-to-buy planning, preferring to buy however much of whatever, whenever. The question to ask them is: How many markdowns did you take in those years? How much merchandise did you donate to charity? How much inventory that can't be sold is currently in stock? And how much money could you have made had you bought "by the numbers"?

Many of the same business owners may turn to their profit and loss statement and say, "But look at the money we made last year." One of the disconcerting things about profit and loss accounting is that in the gross profit calculation, the figures used are for the cost of goods *sold,* not the cost of goods *bought. If they had to account for the amount of excess dollars invested in unsalable inventory, they might revise their assessment of their operating skills.*

People who turn their arts and crafts hobbies into businesses do so out of a desire to work within their chosen product area. Designing, displaying, and selling merchandise is a very creative exercise that can be filled with the pride of a job well done. But what actually constitutes a job well done? *Your business must be viewed as a money machine, an investment.* The investment must be more profitable than if it were put in some other enterprise. The problem is the disparity between creativity and working with numbers. Because the numbers involved in open-to-buy planning can be confusing and difficult to relate to, they are most often ignored. My advice is, ignore the numbers at your peril.

Structuring Your Open-to-Buy Plan

The first step in the process is to organize your products into compatible groupings. Take into consideration product similarities, sales, delivery rates, and other factors that will aid in grouping. Call these merchandise groups departments. One of the most important aspects of merchandise breakdown is that it be done in such a way that it is defined enough to provide information, but not be so narrow that it restricts you in the marketplace.

When you're deciding on your department structure, try to look at everything through the eyes of your customer. For the most part, customers are shopping for a type of item and are coming to you to see what you have available in that department. Consequently, it's crucial to have the amount of merchandise that you need in that department. This works even if you have only one product line; you still need to group or set up the items into departments by type and always have the best available merchandise in each of your departments. If you don't, your competition will gobble up sales that you should have had.

Assign codes (that are easy to deal with) to the departments. They are used to track the merchandise flow in and out. If you're currently using a point-of-sale (POS) system, use the department codes that you've already established. If not, we suggest that you use a simple numeric code (two digits). When you've determined your merchandise breakdown and coding, you're ready to go ahead and develop an annual sales plan on which to build your open-to buy program.

The Bottom Line of Buying

The open-to-buy system projects future buying needs in each merchandise department. It is important to remember that while the items within the departments will change as consumer styles and tastes change, the departments will remain somewhat stable. Creativity can be put into the selection of items within the departments, but *all purchases should be against your previously established open-to-buy (receiving) plan.*

201

Artisan's Corner

A working open-to-buy system will give the business a dollar plan for each delivery period as far into the future as necessary. Receiving the right amount of merchandise will ensure beginning inventories that will support actual monthly sales at the highest possible turnover rates.

Put very dramatically, using efficient open-to-buy planning will change your life. No longer will you have to consider what to do with your excess inventory. No longer will you have to reach into your pocket or go to the bank or take drastic markdowns to raise cash to pay your bills. *Open-to-buy planning will enable you to operate profitably whether the economy in your community is good or bad.* If it can do this for you, isn't it worth your time? Think how much better equipped you are to ward off the competition when you are in control and are steering your business to growth and higher profits.

The biggest challenge in business success today is change. Develop the habit of looking for early signs that something is changing, and adapt your plans and work space accordingly. Consider changes of customer buying patterns in the design or number of products or services that you offer, and create a long-range open-to-buy inventory plan that will keep you solvent and ahead of the competition. Respond to challenges by being flexible in your business operations and keeping an open mind about your products or services and the market.

The Least You Need to Know

➤ Designing your work areas for efficiency will save you time and money.

➤ Plan for future needs by installing sufficient electrical and communications lines and by buying modular, movable furniture and work stations.

➤ Developing a long-range buying plan will keep you stocked with the supplies that you need and will save you from being saddled with unsalable inventory.

➤ Keep your work space and your product lines or services flexible, and you'll have a great advantage over your competitors.

Chapter 18

Time Is Money: Understanding the Value of Your Time

In This Chapter

➤ Establishing a realistic dollar value for your time

➤ Grappling with pricing your products

➤ Knowing what to charge for freelance work

➤ Increasing efficiency and setting priorities to maximize your time

➤ Keeping demanding customers from wrecking your schedule

Henry David Thoreau said, "What is once done well is done forever." This is particularly true when you think of your time as money. If you squander your time in useless or meaningless ways, it is gone, wasted, lost forever. As a business owner, wasting time could have serious consequences. Once you realize the real dollar value of your time, my guess is that you'll think twice about how you spend it. In this chapter, we show you how to determine your actual hourly wage and price your products accordingly, and we explore ways to use your time to maximize your business's potential.

How Much Are You Worth Per Hour?

First, think about how much an hour you need to make. It doesn't matter whether you plan to operate your business full- or part-time, and we're not considering your business expenses or the cost of materials. The following exercise is for arriving at a dollar figure for your time—an hourly labor rate, or what you would pay yourself as a reasonable salary that you could afford to live on. Before you do the exercise, estimate your hourly rate here: $_____.

Now let's determine the actual value of your time. Just follow along and fill in the questions to arrive at your estimated hourly rate:

Part 1: Estimated Salary

What do you want to make as an annual salary?	$_____
Add 30 percent to cover health insurance and retirement benefits	$_____
Total Estimated Salary	$_____

Part 2: Billable Days

Next, using the 365-day year, subtract the number of days that you normally use as days off and days to do indirect labor. Indirect labor is the time that you spend on administrative or marketing tasks (nonproduct production work time). Most artisans estimate that indirect labor accounts for 20 to 40 percent of their time.

Number of sick and personal days per year	_____
Number of official holidays per year (about 10)	_____
Desired number of vacation days per year	_____
Desired number of days off per year (days per week × 52)	_____
Number of days spent on indirect labor	_____
Billable Days (subtract total from 365)	_____

Part 3: Hourly Rate

Divide the total salary that you calculated in part 1 by the billable days from part 2 _____. This is your rate per day.

Divide your rate per day by the number of hours worked per day—say, 8.

Your hourly rate would equal: $_____

How does this number compare with your original estimate? If you had assigned yourself, say, $40,000 yearly and added the 30 percent to cover health and retirement benefits, you need to earn $52,000. If you worked five days a week (260) and gave yourself 10 sick days, 10 holidays, and a two-week vacation (10), and if you then spent one day a week (50) for indirect labor, you would have 180 billable days left in the year.

Divide your salary ($52,000) by the number of billable days (180) to determine the amount that you need to earn per day ($288.88). Divide this number by the number of hours that you plan to work each day (8 hours) for your hourly rate. Using this example, your hourly rate would be $36.11 per hour.

Your Product's *Real* Cost and Pricing

Now that you know what your fair hourly wage is, you can determine the real cost of your product. If it took you 15 minutes to make an item, add $9 ($36 per hour, divided by 4) for labor to the item's cost—say, $6. To be paid fairly, you need to charge $15 per item—its *real* cost.

The dilemma of what to charge for products or services has been experienced by most, if not all, new business owners. The following few comments reflect what many artisans have to say about pricing:

Comments from Cindy Testerink, Testerink Studio, www.testerinkstudio.com:

> "When you price your work, you must take into account that you *are an artist,* and *people are paying not just for material and time, but also for talent.* I've had a hard time with the pricing issue as well, but I have also found that some people think that price is equated to quality, however untrue this may be. My mom, also an artist, couldn't sell her work at the price she was asking, so she lowered her prices and still, no sales. Then she tripled her prices—and sold everything!! Figure that out ...."

> "So, I keep that in mind, and I surf the Web to see what others are charging for similar work. I make little 5-inch polymer fairies and sell them for $55. I've found some selling very similar work for $80, and others for $20. I found one person whose work was much more elaborate, but so was the price—between $600 and $2,800 per item! I hope this will inspire you to some research and rethink your pricing if it seems too low. You can take a look at my little fairies at my Web site if you'd like."

Comments from Alicia Ellis, owner of Been Framed and Design House:

> "When does folk art become crafting? When does a crafter become a designer? When does a designer become an artist? When does folk art become fine art? An artisan is someone who designs or produces something out of his or her own creativity. *You should charge what your talent is worth!*"

Crafter Alert

Most artisans don't make enough income because they make the common mistake of underestimating the value of their time. If you want to make money with your hobby, the first step is to account for all the time that you spend operating your business to see what you're actually being paid. Then, be sure to include a fair rate of pay for your time in your business budget.

Comments from Susan of CraftCatz:

"At one of the Christmas shows last year, I didn't sell a single ornament. They were priced at $3.95 each. For the next show, I upped the price, on someone's recommendation, to $4.95. I sold out! Shoppers have the notion that if it costs more, it must be better."

In the next chapter, you can read all about pricing terms, calculations, and strategies.

What to Charge for Freelance Work

I know some of you artisans are considering making money by writing about what you know. The field of commercial freelance writing and graphics contains a lot of mixed theories as to what ought to be charged because there are no fixed guidelines, restrictions, or standards to setting fees. There are only scattered pieces of information that hint about what should be charged. Because of the freedom in setting your own fees, it's common to hear about one freelance writer getting paid $850 to write a brochure and another freelancer getting paid $400 to write a similar brochure. Some charge by the hour; others charge by the project. Why is one freelancer paid higher than the other?

➤ **Level of experience.** A freelancer who has more experience obviously is in a position to charge more. A beginner might not have the clout or the samples to command higher pay or to attract the type of clients that would pay the big bucks.

➤ **Type of industry.** Corporations pay writers higher than most other industries. The difference in pay between writing a brochure for a corporation and writing one for a small business can be hundreds of dollars.

➤ **What others are charging.** Understand what other businesses are willing to pay you and what others are charging, to help you price your services competitively.

➤ **Type of work involved.** Not every project or assignment is the same. Using the example of a how-to booklet, one freelancer may have been required to do additional research or was required to attend a seminar (which means more billable hours and, therefore, higher pay). Another freelancer may have had the information already at hand to write the booklet in less time.

➤ **Type of economic conditions.** Regional economic conditions can affect what businesses are willing to pay you, as well as how much work is available in your area.

Research Tips

If you plan to self-publish informational books, newsletters, or perhaps hobby guides based on your specific hobby, this type of material is usually priced by the cost of comparable products or services, or what the market will bear (the amount the customer will pay).

Because there are no hard and fast rules, of course, you will have to find out what the going market rates are for the type of freelance work that you want to do. To get started:

Get a current edition of *Writer's Market* (www.writersmarket.com/index_ns.asp), published by F&W Publications. It provides a handful of pages on what commercial freelance writers should be charging for assignments and projects.

In addition, the *Guide to Freelance Rates and Standard Practice,* published by the National Writer's Union (www.nwu.org/), provides some information on commercial freelance writing fees.

A book worth reading is Robert W. Bly's, *Secrets of a Freelance Writer: How to Make $85,000 a Year,* which includes freelance rates. Or, contact the National Writers Association, 1450 S. Havana, Suite 424, Aurora, CO 80012; phone: 303-751-7844; fax: 303-751-8593. This association also publishes a bimonthly magazine called *Authorship.*

Online Resources

Author Link marketplace (www.authorlink.com/) is where editors and agents buy and sell rights to unpublished and published manuscripts and screenplays. Industry news and information also is available.

Inkspot (www.inkspot.com/) is a resource for writers of all ages and levels of experience.

Writers Digest (www.writersdigest.com/) also offers tips and workshops for beginning writers and a guide to the life of writing. This site offers links to some of the best information resources for writers as well.

Maximizing Your Time

Now that you're aware of the real value of your time, let's explore some ways to invest it wisely in running your business. Most new business owners start feeling as if there's always far too much to be accomplished in a given period than is feasible to get done. The key is to maximize the value of your time by setting priorities and focusing on strategies that produce positive results.

Develop a true customer focus. Understand that customers always go where they get good value and go where they are treated well. When the value isn't clear or the level of service slips, they slip away. Take some time to identify your target customer; the more you know about your customers, the easier it is to serve them well and to provide goods or services that they want so that your time is well spent.

➤ **Gather and analyze management information regularly.** You need strategic information on your own business to know what's really going on and to make wise decisions based on accurate, timely information. Use the following four areas: financial, customer, industry information, and market trends.

➤ **Increase the customer's perception of value.** Value is not the same as price. If you position your marketing on value it saves time because you are also building the products image. It also includes considerations of quality (are your products better?) and quantity (do you offer more than others do?). However, most customers are somewhat price-sensitive. Instead of across-the-board markup, consider variable pricing strategies to broaden your market share.

The "value-added" approach to presenting your product or service is very important to increasing your customers' perceived view of your product. It doesn't take much time or work to produce a hang tag with the subtle value-added statement such as "since 1975," which tells the customer that you are established and builds credibility. "100 percent Satisfaction Guaranteed" says you stand behind your work no matter what—a value-added guarantee. "Each Piece Dated and Signed" hints at collectible status, which translates into substantiating the item's value. "Lead Free, Dishwasher Safe, Microwave Proof" adds dollar value to the quality. "Your Design or Ours" offers custom design work, another value-added benefit of doing business with this company.

In addition, of course, is the big hook—"Free Personalization." Is this a value-added benefit or what? As you can see, the product hang tag is a *silent salesperson* for the product. It very carefully builds and adds value to the way customers perceive the product and ultimately to the value that they get for the price.

Pointers

Develop a true customer focus. The more you know about your customers, the easier it is to provide the products and services that they want. Stay on top of the current trends, colors, styles, designs, textures, or whatever drives your product line.

➤ **Position the business uniquely.** You aren't one of the big guys, so don't try to be like them. It is a waste of time. Position yourself in areas where big business can't compete with you, such as friendliness, customer bonding, special orders, original designs, special services, personalization of items, and so forth. Where can you say, "We're better because ..." or "We're unique because ..."? Handcrafted products usually have one major advantage: *They are your own unique design!* That's right, *your product is exclusive*—a product line to which only you have the exclusive distribution rights. You're in a unique position—play it to the hilt!

➤ **Eliminate extra steps.** Time is money, and eliminating time wasters saves you money. Look for areas where you may be duplicating efforts, or where you could streamline the operation; perhaps cut some steps out of your order entry process or your shipping methods. It's just human nature to keep doing things the same way. Every once in a while, you have to stand back and take a hard look.

Pointers

You have to put a hang tag or a label on your product anyway. Isn't it better to use it as a sales tool than as just a decoration with your contact information?

Service Businesses: The Need to Please

If you plan to make money with your hobby by providing a service-based business, I have to warn you that there is a very serious bug going around that many new business owners catch. It's called "the need to please."

You catch the bug from your own misguided sense that when you spend too much time with a needy customer, you're doing a good thing, when the only good thing you may really be doing is feeding your own desire to feel needed and good about yourself. The "need to please" bug slows you way down and causes you to waste valuable time that you should be spending productively. It

Crafter Alert

When you operate a service business, *your time is your income.* If you waste it on nonincome-producing tasks, how will you make any money or achieve your goals? Do what you agreed to do for a customer, and make sure that any additional services are billable.

makes you a slave to people who learn to prey on your good nature and willingness to please your customers, taking advantage of you perhaps without even realizing that they're doing it.

The "need to please" bug has nothing to do with your providing the best service possible, as you contracted to do. But if you have the bug, you do volumes of work for the same initial payment simply because it's demanded of you. You start out doing it to provide good customer service—maybe you even think that it will get you additional referral business. But in the end, overservicing demanding customers is to your detriment: It means the loss of your valuable income-producing time.

It is important to learn the skill of spotting particularly needy customers early on and to deal with the situation up front. The fact is that only a small percentage of people will latch onto you, thinking that by hiring you, they own you body and soul. But beware—they are out there!

The next time you feel the urge to hand over all the fish to feed the multitude, take out a fishing pole and teach your demanding customers how to fish. They may not be happy with you initially, but they may learn something; more important, you'll have more time to nurture your growing business.

The Least You Need to Know

➤ Establish a fair rate for your time, and add your hourly wage to the cost of the items that you sell. Don't sell yourself short; charge what your work is worth.

➤ Freelance rates need to be researched and compared to the going market rates for the particular job that you're doing.

➤ Always try to maximize your time by looking for ways to improve your efficiency.

➤ Learn to recognize and restrain the "need to please" urge; it will rob you of time that you should be spending on your business.

Chapter 19

Playing the Pricing Game

In This Chapter

➤ Discovering the variety of pricing strategies

➤ Learning price-costing terms and how to apply them

➤ Considering market-based pricing

➤ Understanding basic formulas for pricing

➤ Calculating both wholesale and retail prices

➤ Defining deceptive pricing practices

It goes without saying that the goal of any business start-up is profit. If you don't make a profit, you won't be in business for very long. Making a profit is simple really; you just have to make more than you spend. The trick is to know *how* much more. To guarantee profits, accurate pricing is absolutely critical. Your prices must be high enough to cover all costs and enable you to earn a reasonable return, but low enough to remain attractive to potential customers. In this chapter, we describe a variety of pricing methods and guidelines to help you decide which pricing method best suits your particular business.

Pricing Strategies

New entrepreneurs often have difficulty pricing the value of their time and expertise. Some say that they can work cheap because they're fast, so they'll fill in with low-paying jobs between more lucrative opportunities. For this group, the mind-set seems to be that any work is better than no work; this may seem reasonable when you first start out and want to make your mark, but the downside of this short-sighted approach is that customers will think of your business as "cheap"—even after it has become established.

Another group of entrepreneurs takes the approach from the outset that they're worth top dollar. They demand fair pricing for the value they provide, and they won't accept anything less. This group seems to be more successful in the long run. They get off to a slow start, but by setting their standards high to begin with, when their business does become established, it usually has a favorable image and a firm foundation.

Setting prices for products and services is a challenging task for small and home-based business owners. The *best price* is not necessarily the one that will create the most business. The selling price must take cost, market conditions, and perceived value into account. For a business to make money, it must deal with hard economic facts.

Some major considerations in setting prices include these:

➤ Direct costs (materials and supplies)

➤ Indirect costs (overhead)

➤ Adequate salary for the owner

➤ Markup for profit

➤ Prices of comparable products or services, and what the market will bear (the amount the customer is willing to pay)

To begin the process of establishing the best prices for your business offerings, answer the following questions:

➤ How much does it cost to produce your product?

➤ What are all of the costs involved in operating your business?

➤ How much profit do you want to make?

➤ Can you afford to sell this product for that price?

➤ Will the customer buy your product at this price?

➤ Does your price reflect the business image you want to create?

➤ Are there federal, state, and local laws that regulate pricing of your product?

Trade Terms

The **best price** is the market price at which the customer is willing to buy and the seller is willing to sell.

Begin the pricing process by determining the top price (ceiling price) and the bottom price (floor price) that a customer will pay for your product or service. Considering your target customer, your competition, your business image, and information from trade and professional organizations will help you determine your ceiling and floor prices.

The market determines your ceiling price. Your bottom price, or price floor, is determined by all your costs of doing business, the price below which you *cannot sell and make a profit.* If you want to sell to stores, you need to consider whether your floor price would allow the store to double your price and still stay within the average market price for the item.

The price of your product or service needs to include all the costs of operating your business and the amount of profit you desire. Your ability to earn a profit will determine whether you remain in business and bring your dream to reality. You may make a quarter of a million dollars, but if your costs are greater than that, you're losing money.

Crafter Alert

If you exceed the ceiling price by too much, you may lose sales by being over the average market price. On the other hand, if your prices are too low, you may *cheapen the value of the item* from the consumers' point of view because they've probably seen your competitors' similar products at a higher price.

Pricing Policy

There are several approaches to establishing a *pricing policy:* value pricing, competitive pricing, and cost pricing.

➤ **Value pricing.** The uniqueness of your product and your ability to customize and provide special services will allow you to charge more for your goods. If your customers perceive your product to be excellent, and if you are reliable or are highly regarded in your field, this approach can allow for maximum profits. Value pricing is best used when there is little or no competition. If there is competition, you periodically review your market position, and maintain andw lower prices—or perhaps even increase them accordingly.

Trade Terms

Pricing policy (or **pricing strategy**) is the method you use to determine the prices for your products and services. It needs to be continually reviewed and updated to be sure you're always positioned for sufficient profit to build your business.

➤ **Competitive pricing.** If your product is the same or similar to what is being offered by others, you may want to use a competitive pricing approach; that is, price your product in the same price range as the competition. This approach serves to attract and maintain customers. Another way to meet and beat competitive pricing is to offer package pricing to customers. If you produce household accessories, you may offer a lamp and a companion vase at a lower price if purchased together than if purchased separately, or special discounts for buying several mix-and-match pieces. A service business could offer something free that would normally be billable, such as a bonus when certain services are purchased, or that business could package some services together, offering a saving over buying them separately.

➤ **Cost pricing.** Cost pricing is one of the most commonly used approaches. It figures the cost of goods sold times three, or the cost of goods sold plus a predetermined markup of 25 to 50 percent. Be careful if you choose to use this approach: It often overlooks the effects of competition, changes in costs of overhead and materials, and current trends in the market, so it may not provide you with a maximum profit.

Unit Cost Per Item

To arrive at the unit cost per item, you have to establish the total cost for the *labor and materials used to make one item.* Do not include your labor in your calculations for designing the prototype (first one); because designing the prototype will take much longer to produce than the final product; use the average time it takes to make the products after you've made four to six of them. If your work is always one-of-a-kind, however, such as the work of a painter, sculptor, woodcarver, or other artist, then of course you should use the actual time that it takes to make the original piece.

There are two methods for figuring unit cost per item:

➤ **Time log.** You need a method of keeping track of production time. It can be as simple as a notepad where you jot down each start and stop time, and then add up the totals to arrive at the actual amount of time that it took to make each item. Some artisans like to use an electric clock, the type with hands. When they start an item, they set it at 12:00 and then unplug it when they stop. By doing this each time

Pointers

An easy way to have your material costs ready for unit pricing is to figure them out as each new shipment arrives. Break down the bulk purchase into measurements used for that type of material. For instance, if you buy a spool of ribbon that is 25 yards, add the freight and then divide the total by 25 to arrive at the cost per yard.

they start and stop, if the clock says 6:00 when they finish the item, for example, they know that it took six hours. Even with this method, you should keep a written log of the total time used to produce each item.

➤ **Materials log.** There are two ways to track materials used for each item: Write down exactly what you used in each item, or do an estimate based on the cost of the materials divided by the number of items that you can make. The advantage to this method is that it includes waste. Either method will give you accurate unit costs. Experiment to see what works best for you.

Costing Terms

Become familiar with terms used in costing a product. Knowing what costs are included in the terms can help you better understand pricing formulas.

Direct Costs

Production costs figured in direct costs include ...

➤ **In a wholesale operation.** This cost includes the materials and supplies for production, labor for production, and any incoming shipping fees. (If you are the production unit of your business, the labor is your time in the actual production.) Labor costs should include salary and related expenses.

➤ **In a retail operation.** The cost of goods includes the wholesale cost of the product, plus the shipping and handling costs.

Indirect Costs = Overhead

Include the costs (overhead) of running the business, *excluding* the cost of goods sold. If you produce several different products, you will want to distribute indirect costs to all of them. The easiest way for you to do this is to divide your total indirect costs by the total number of units produced. This will give you your indirect cost per item.

Indirect costs include both fixed and variable costs:

➤ **Fixed costs.** Those costs that remain the same during the month or year, regardless of the number of units produced or sold. These costs include items such as the following:

Allowance for the space used in your home, or rent, or other cost of your work space

Labor cost for administrative duties

Equipment payments, auto payments, interest, and bank fees

215

Accounting, insurance, and legal costs

Utility payments, telephone bill, water bill, and laundry expenses

Business licenses, membership dues, and subscriptions for trade publications and magazines

Artisan's Corner

As a home-based or small business owner, you will probably fill many roles: designer, producer, administrator, and so on. Each role requires different talents and tasks, so each could be figured at a different wage rate. For example, when you are in the designer role, you may charge $50 an hour for your expertise, but in your roles as production worker or office staffer, you may want to calculate your salary at a lower rate.

➤ **Variable costs.** The costs that vary during the month or year depending on goods produced or goods sold. These costs include items such as these:

Office and shipping supplies

Business travel (to customer locations, art and craft or trade shows, buying trips, and so forth)

Advertising or promotion, and photography

Booth rentals at shows or craft malls, or consignment fees

Merchant account fees, bad debts, or other losses

Shipping and handling

Determining Costs

To determine a price, you need to figure the cost of your materials, the amount of time needed to make the item, the amount of money needed to pay for the time (direct costs), and the operation expenses necessary to run your business (indirect costs or overhead). Be realistic! If the business uses materials, there has to be some waste. Failure to allow for waste will reduce your profit.

Your direct and indirect costs can be recorded on a break-even analysis worksheet. Your total direct and indirect costs are used to figure your *break-even point*.

The break-even point can give you a realistic picture of the financial aspect of your business offering, and it must be considered before you set your price. When they start out, so many artisans feel uncomfortable charging as much as everyone else. Don't let your lack of self-confidence fool you into settling for a lower income. Take the time to figure out exactly what it costs you *to produce a piece and sell it.* Avoid the mistake of making a product just because you like it, or like to make it, if the numbers don't work. Make that favorite item in your spare time instead, for fun.

Trade Terms

The **break-even point** is the point at which you will neither lose money nor make money.

Market-Based Pricing

This type of pricing is based on a price comparison of similar products or services using the current selling prices for a specific market area. This method assumes that a competitive market exists! Prices are set by market activity, not by a particular vendor or group. Terms and discounts in the market, the degree of competition, and many other factors should be taken into consideration. Be alert to where in the life cycle a product may be in your price comparison. This method requires knowledge of the current market conditions and the ability to accurately compare same or similar items. For a detailed look at the phases in the life cycle of a product, see Chapter 30, "Staying Ahead of Your Competition."

Start by carrying out a competitive analysis. Find out how your product compares with your competitors' on the basis not only of price, but also of costs. If you were going to source this information by approaching competitors directly, a word of caution—don't. It could be considered an attempt at *price fixing*.

Crafter Alert

The Sherman Act in the United States (and similar legislation in many other jurisdictions) prohibits businesses of any size from entering "contracts, combinations, or conspiracies" in restraint of trade. Making deals with competitors about what price you'll charge—in other words, **price fixing**—is illegal. This is one area where you just don't want to give even the whiff of an impression of doing anything along those lines.

Instead, to keep tabs on what your competition is up to, read their ads, talk to their suppliers, engage mystery shoppers in conversation about your competitors, or play consumer and ask them to send their brochures and price lists (to your cousin, of course). Also check retail prices for similar items in stores and galleries (you can usually assume that the wholesale price is half of the asking price).

When you've completed your research on the competition, analyze your competitive advantages and disadvantages. If you learn that you have an advantage over your competition, then this advantage is something that your customers will likely pay more for. Adjust your prices accordingly.

Product Pricing Formulas

There is a variety of formulas for pricing. You may want to examine several of them before you select one. You may also find that you will need to use more than one pricing formula.

As you use these formulas, keep in mind that *the easiest formula to use may not always be the best.* Pricing formulas serve as guides for you to make a fair profit. Then, whatever final price you arrive at will need to be compared with the going market price. If you cannot realize a profit once you've factored in labor and materials and overhead (direct and indirect costs) and added a percentage for profit, consider dropping that particular item, or find a way to cut the expenses or reduce the production time for it.

You can use several basic methods or formulas to determine the wholesale price of your product. Work through the formulas with your own facts and figures. Remember that no single formula will work for all products or ensure maximum profit. Putting your data into these formulas should enable you to compare the different ways to price your product.

If you don't know what your overhead is because you're just starting out, you can figure that, as a general rule, it should be 20 to 25 percent of your labor and materials. If you know the figure you need for labor costs, use it; if not, complete the worksheet in Chapter 18, "Time Is Money: Understanding the Value of Your Time," to compute a fair and reasonable labor rate.

The following example illustrates the use of each of the formulas:

An artisan manufactures lamps and wants to work 40 hours per week operating the business. Twenty lamps can be produced in 40 hours. The indirect costs have been figured at $40 per week, and the materials to manufacture the lamps cost $40 per week. The business owner wants to make $12 per hour, or at least $480 per week in wages (labor). A $40 profit per week is needed for inflation, business expansion, and investment.

Formula 1

Materials + labor = $_____ ÷ number of units = $_____: wholesale selling price per unit

Example: ($40 + $480 = $520) ÷ 20 units = $26 per item. This pricing method is frequently used, but there is no allowance for overhead costs, inflation, or profits.

Formula 2

Materials × 3 = $_____ ÷ number of units = $_____: wholesale selling price per unit

Example: $40 × 3 = $120 ÷ 20 = $6 per item. This formula is easy to calculate, but profit margin is slim or nil unless production time is very efficient and materials are relatively inexpensive and readily available.

Formula 3

Materials + indirect costs + production time × hourly wage = $_____ ÷ number of units = $_____: wholesale selling price per unit

Example: $40 + $40 + (40 hours × $12 = $480) = $560 ÷ 20 = $28 per item. This approach does not include a profit factor.

Formula 4

Materials + indirect costs + desired weekly wage + profit = $_____ ÷ number of units = $_____: wholesale selling price per unit

Example: $40 + $40 + $480 + $40 ÷ 20 = $30 per item. This is the most individualized method because you are deciding on the wage you want and the amount of time you spend earning that wage.

Formula 5

Materials + labor + (50 percent of materials and labor) = $_____ ÷ number of units = $_____: wholesale selling price per unit

Example: $40 + $480 + (.50 × 480 = $240) = $760 ÷ 20 = $38 per item. This direct cost approach depends on establishing a contribution percentage that will cover (contribute to) all your overhead expenses plus your profit. This example is figured on direct costs (materials and labor) but can also be figured per labor hours, per pound of raw materials, or per machine hours.

Pointers

When you use any of these formulas, you will arrive at the wholesale price per item. See the "Retail Pricing" section that follows to calculate the price for selling at the retail level.

Formula 6 (My Favorite)

Labor + materials + overhead = $ _____ (subtotal here) + profit (take 20 percent of the subtotal to arrive at the profit figure) = $_____ : wholesale price

Example: $480 + $40 + $40 = $560 ($560 × 20% = $112) + $112 = $672 ÷ 20 = $33.60 per item. This formula is very accurate because it contains all the actual costs and provides a 20 percent profit allowance as a constant factor.

Formula 7 (Percentage Markup Basis)

This is calculated by dividing the original cost into the amount of markup and then multiplying the result times 100. The amount of money that a business adds into a product's price, over and above the cost of the product, is expressed as a percent. A piece of candy costing $.05 to produce that has a markup of $.10 (meaning that the price to the consumer is $.15) has a percentage markup of 200 percent.

Retail Pricing

If you decide to sell your product at retail, you must first establish the wholesale price and then establish a retail price. You can use two basic methods to price for retail: the keystone method and the dollar markup method.

➤ **Keystone method.** Assumes that you will double the wholesale price of the product to obtain a retail price. Formula: Wholesale price × 2 = retail price.

➤ **Dollar markup method.** Begins when you determine the markup in dollars needed to cover your operating expenses and provide your business with a profit. Formula: Wholesale price + dollar markup = retail price.

The following example illustrates how to determine a retail price using these methods:

A manufacturing business decides to retail its teddy bears through craft shows. Using one of the previously illustrated pricing formulas, the owner has figured the wholesale price (cost) of one of the bears to be $21. The owner will need to recover costs associated with attending the craft show (booth rent, travel, retail license, lodging, and so on). The owner needs to achieve at least a $19 markup on each bear sold. Use these figures to compare the two methods.

Keystone Method	
Wholesale price × 2 = retail price	$21 × 2 = $42

Dollar Markup Method	
Wholesale price + dollar markup = retail price	$21 + $19 = $40

It's important to keep your own retail prices the same whether you sell at craft shows, craft malls, or galleries; via sales reps; on the Internet; or at your own studio. Wholesale buyers need to feel assured that you will not undercut their efforts to sell your work. Undercutting is a quick way to build a negative business image and destroy the business relationships that you're working hard to build.

Crafter Alert

The easiest price formula to use may not always be the best. Price formulas serve as guides to what an item should be priced at for you to make a reasonable profit. To realize a profit, you need to include labor, materials, and overhead (direct and indirect costs), and add a percentage for profit. Then compare the final price with the going market price.

Test each of these formulas using a piece of your work. Ask yourself whether you think you can sell the item at that price. If you can't, where can you cut some of the costs? Do you think that you can sell it for more based on the average market-based price? The most important consideration is to make sure that you're charging enough for each item you make so that you can earn a livable wage and stay in business. The fastest way to go out of business is to sell a lot of work but lose money on every sale.

Deceptive Pricing

The Federal Trade Commission (FTC) has jurisdiction over deceptive pricing practices. At the state level, it's usually the attorney general's office or, in bigger cities, the district attorney's consumer fraud unit that enforces laws dealing with deceptive trade practices. The two biggest problems that enforcers encounter concern merchants' incorrect price comparisons with prices of other merchants or with their own regular prices, and merchants who offer something advertised as free but that has a hidden cost.

Price Comparisons

Offering a reduction from your usual selling price is a common and powerful sales technique. To satisfy legal requirements, however, it's essential that the former price be the actual, bona fide price at which you offered the article. Otherwise, the pricing is misleading.

Example: Woodworks, Inc., produces design software and announces a new product for $129. The company sells the product to wholesalers as if it were a $79 product and similarly discounts it to direct customers. The $129 price has never really existed except as a device to mislead customers into thinking that they were receiving a discount.

Price comparisons often use words such as "regularly," "usually," or "reduced." For example, it's common to see a price tag that says, "Regularly $200. Now $150." On the other hand, sometimes a sign says "40 percent off our regular price." These comparisons are fine, legally, if you in fact offered the sale merchandise at the old price for a reasonable length of time. They're not okay if you've bought or produced a special batch of merchandise just for the sale and created a fictional "regular" price or one that you adhered to for only a day or two.

If your ad compares your price with what other merchants are charging for the same product, be sure of two things: that the other merchants are selling the identical product, and that there were a sufficient number of sales at the higher price in your area to make your offer a legitimate bargain. In other words, make sure that the higher comparison price isn't an isolated or unrepresentative price.

Free Offers

If you say that goods or services are "free" or "without charge," be sure that there are no unstated terms or conditions qualifying the offer. If there are any limits, state them clearly and conspicuously. Let's assume that you offer a free paintbrush to anyone who buys your kit, "How to Paint Natural Roses," for $8.95, and you describe the kind of brush. Because you're disclosing the terms and conditions of your offer, you're in good shape so far. But there are pitfalls to avoid. If the $8.95 is more than you usually charge for this kind of kit, the brush clearly isn't free. You can offer free products or services, *as long as there are no strings attached.*

As you can see, setting the *right price* for your products and services is absolutely crucial to the profitability of your business. With careful calculations and a methodical approach, you should be able to arrive at fair prices without too much difficulty, but don't stop there: Your prices operate within a constantly changing environment, and you need to be ever vigilant to ensure that your prices remain at their best competitive position.

One final piece of advice: If you're in doubt, price high rather than low. It is much easier to reduce prices than it is to increase them.

The Least You Need to Know

➤ Your pricing strategy should include consideration of the perceived value and the going market rate as well as the product cost.

➤ Market-based pricing is determined by how much the customer is willing to pay for a particular product or service.

➤ Usually more than one pricing strategy is used because no single strategy is appropriate for all products or services.

➤ The retail price is usually figured by doubling the wholesale price.

➤ When in doubt, price higher; it's easier to reduce prices than to raise them.

Part 5

Where Do I Start Selling My Product Line?

Now that you know how to make a profit, you need to know where and how to sell your product or service to make that profit. You need a plan of action. In this part, we introduce you to the many ways available to sell and market your work, such as arts and crafts shows, consignment shops, art galleries, craft malls, private venues, boutiques, and wholesale avenues. We even give you an overview of what it takes to open a retail store and how to market a service business. Products are not the only way to make money from your hobby experiences, as you'll discover in this section of the book. It's a real eye-opener, and it's fun to read what entrepreneurs say about their experiences along the path to business success. Their advice will help you down the same path.

Chapter 20

Selling at Art and Craft Shows and Fairs

In This Chapter

➤ Selecting the "right" shows for your products

➤ Being prepared to sell at art and craft shows

➤ Learning how to handle the application process

➤ Gearing up to sell at shows

➤ Finding art and craft show listings

Everyone knows that arts and crafts are big business all over the country. *SAC News Monthly,* an art and craft show list publication, covered more than 6,700 professionally produced shows in 1999. That number doesn't include the thousands of local churches, civic groups, schools, and clubs and organizations that have shows every year! In this chapter, we tell you everything you need to know to select the right shows for you, how to apply, and how to sell at these events. We also show you how to decide which kinds of shows you should sell at, and tell you how to locate them. Art and craft shows are a natural marketplace for most of the products produced by today's artisans, so it pays to learn as much about them as you can.

Choosing the Right Art and Craft Show

Art and craft shows can be among the best marketing tools available to artisans. They provide you with direct selling access to the purchasing customer. Show costs vary widely depending upon region, attendance records, and advertising support provided. There are differences among the types of shows you see advertised all over the country, but they can be divided into three general groups:

➤ Bazaars/flea markets

➤ Festivals and fairs

➤ Arts and crafts shows

Bazaars/Flea Markets

This type of show is usually sponsored by churches, schools, clubs, or other organizations as a fund-raiser. Included in this group are open-air markets; antique and craft shows; and theme events such as car shows, bake sales, sporting events, air shows, and so on. Although the cost of entering these shows is usually very low, the return in sales is, too—generally this is not worth two or three days of your time.

The National Craft Association survey of professional artisans found that this type of show tends to attract more fun-seeking browsers than buyers, and if "flea market" is included in its description, it draws bargain hunters looking for "super-low-low prices."

The merchandise that does sell is usually low-end, from $1 to $15, so unless this is the type of merchandise you specialize in, or unless it's a special holiday show with a good reputation, you can usually find more profitable shows to spend your time and money on. Shows that try to mix crafts and antiques don't work out very well, either. The antique buyer and the buyer of handmade arts or crafts are two distinctly different groups. If the show is mostly crafts with a few antiques mixed in, it may be worth your while, but if it's the other way around, skip it and go to a real art and craft show.

Crafter Alert

When "flea market" is attached to an event's name, it usually attracts bargain hunters looking for the lowest-priced buy-sell or imported stuff, not the real art or craft buyer.

Here's what Evelyn Villegas, of Crystal Star Works Magic Gems, has to say about bazaar/flea market shows:

"I think these venues are often perfect for the 'hobby crafter.' Lots of the sales come from other club members, and local promotion is sometimes kind of 'inside.' I'd be delighted to leave the entire market to the folks who do it just to 'get enough money to do it some more.' What I wish, though, is that the hobby crafters not come into the larger, better markets with their 'just to re-coup costs' pricing strategy. That's what often confuses buyers and makes it difficult for the artist who spends a fortune on supplies and works on the projects 12 to 14 hours a day. Making jewelry is not my hobby; it's my career. What would be great is if we could all find our target 'buying crowd' without having to hurt one another. Just occasionally I might want to buy a pine cone spray-painted gold and hung on a rattail cord. I'd be glad to know where to look for that. I'd also appreciate knowing where to find unusual gems in one-of-a-kind settings."

Festivals and Fairs

This type of show is usually sponsored by a civic group, a merchant or neighborhood association, or a municipality. The shows are usually put on by a professional promoter and are well organized, well advertised, and well attended. They're often located right on the sidewalks of main streets, or on the grounds of places such as museums and town halls, or in public parks. The deciding factor here is to understand the content of the event. If it's advertised as an arts and crafts show, be sure that handmade products dominate in the show's promotion and that the arts and crafts booths are integrated with the entertainment and food stands, where the main traffic is, not isolated in a remote area.

Many of these shows have enjoyed a solid reputation for many years, and our survey finds that arts and crafts do well at these events as long as the show promotion features and advertises them. On average, the best selling price is up to around $50, though higher prices do sell, depending on the item. Of course, selling prices do vary from region to region and from rural to urban areas.

Art and Craft Shows

These are all the organized, professionally produced shows for the specific purpose of promoting the sale of handcrafted art or craft items. The show can be inside or outside, at a convention center or shopping mall, in a commercial building, and so forth.

Art and craft shows are usually broken into categories by type: fine art, fine craft, and traditional art and craft. Some shows allow a mix of fine and traditional, while others have specific definitions of what they allow, which you can usually determine by reading their information and application package. If you're interested in selling to the wholesale market, you'll need to apply to wholesale trade shows, not retail consumer shows.

Artisan's Corner

Shows are usually categorized by type: fine art, fine craft, and traditional art and craft. Some shows mix fine and traditional, and others have specific limitations. Get applications and show information to determine which shows would be best for you.

Whatever show you're considering, be sure that it's one that attracts the kind of customer most likely to buy your type of work. If you do a country theme, then a show that caters to an upscale, modern, trendy crowd probably won't work for you, and vice versa. If you're not sure about the show, talk with the promoter and other vendors to find out more about it. Best of all, visit the show and check it out for yourself.

Some of the things you'll want to find out about a show that you're considering are these:

➤ Number of years running

➤ Average attendance and previous year's attendance

➤ Number of vendors allowed within each category (jewelry, wood, fiber, paintings, and so on)

➤ Customer parking and admission fees

➤ Handcrafted items only, or imported or commercially produced items allowed

➤ Size of booth space provided

➤ Extra costs such as electricity, door prizes, special uniform booth requirements, and transportation of displays

➤ Setup and breakdown arrangements and/or costs

The organized art or craft show is usually the best place to start when you decide to sell your hand-crafted work as a business venture.

Selling at Art and Craft Shows

Selling at art and craft shows has some benefits, especially for home-based business owners. It gives you a place to sell directly to the customer; an opportunity to test new products, colors, and ideas; and a variety of selling locations, locally and out-of-town.

The following are just some of the tips that can help you evaluate which shows to consider:

1. Select a show that is compatible with the type of merchandise you plan to sell. Find out what type of customer a show usually attracts: average age group; income; urban, suburban, or rural; singles or families. Is there a particular theme, such as country or modern art? Ask the promoter, check with vendors that do the show, or visit the show whenever possible.

2. Select a show that is sponsored by a reputable group or a professional promoter. At least that way, you'll usually find a well-organized, well-advertised show that has a consistent attendance record year after year.

3. Be prepared to apply to sell at the show. Dealing with show applications is fully covered in the next section.

4. Prepare for the show you are accepted into. Check the attendance average for prior years so that you can plan to have enough items to sell to justify doing the show. Plan ahead: Can you do the show alone, or do you need someone with you to set up and break down, or to cover for you during breaks or help with rush hour crowds? Does the show provide selling tables and chairs, or do you have to provide all your own display setups and materials? Some shows offer both. Do you know what you need to display your merchandise? Is your display portable, and will the vehicle you have be able to transport it and the inventory you'll be taking to the show?

5. Have you established all of your selling policies and procedures? What if a buyer approaches you wanting to buy wholesale or to place your work on consignment in a shop or gallery? Will you offer special order? What is your return policy? Do you want to take orders for custom-designed work?

Pointers

The best way to check out a show that you're thinking of applying for is to see it for yourself. When it's feasible, do it.

6. What form of payment will you accept: cash, check, credit cards? You can increase your selling options by offering to accept checks and credit cards. Some companies offer check guarantee service and credit card processing to home businesses.

7. How will you keep track of sales and expenses for each show? Most artisans use a duplicate sales receipt pad or a form they create that provides information that they need to keep track of sales and inventory.

8. What about a money box or a portable cash register? Most artisans use a cash box available at any office products store. Start with at least one roll each of quarters, dimes, nickels, and pennies, plus at least 25 singles and five $5 bills for $50. For a larger show, start with 25 singles, 7 $5 bills, and 4 $10 bills for $100 in cash.

9. Are your printed handouts ready? Always have a business card, brochure, price list, or show schedule ready to use as a bag stuffer or a handout to potential customers. This often leads to future sales and is especially important if you're usually away from your home base marketing at craft shows and can be reached only by phone.

Dealing with Show Applications

Crafters generally agree that a very time-consuming part of the business is just completing the show promoter's application requirements, especially when you start

Trade Terms

Before your application is accepted, **juried craft shows** have the promoter or a jury committee view your work (usually through slides or photos) to determine whether it's acceptable based on their guidelines. Some promoters charge a "jury fee" in addition to the show fee.

Artisan's Corner

Most show promoters require their show applications far in advance of the actual show date. Popular shows often have waiting lists, and artisans do sign up for the following year at the current show to be guaranteed their booth space. That's why you have to contact the show promoters as early as possible to receive their show applications and requirements.

doing a lot of craft shows. A very important thing to understand is that most promoters require their show applications far in advance of the actual show, so you have to really plan ahead for the shows that you want to participate in. Contact the show promoters as early as possible to receive their show applications and requirements. Pay special attention to the type of show it is, and apply only to shows that cater to the type of work you do.

Some show promoters want to see slides of your work. Others require photos. One promoter will want two photos of three or four pieces of your work. And so on—the combinations are endless and frustrating. Also, slides and photos usually need to be labeled or numbered in a variety of ways. Some promoters of *juried craft show*s require a nonrefundable jury fee before they'll review your work. Jury fees typically range from $5 to $50.

Then there's the application itself. An application may ask for anything, from a list of shows where you've displayed to what kind of vehicle you own, to your license plate number, but keep this in mind: Many promoters have a rule that if you omit one piece of information, your application goes into the trash! Or, if you send the wrong size photos or fail to label them as required, the same fate could await your application packet. Also make sure that you send the required money, or you may never hear from them at all!

Understandably, all promoters want to receive applications far in advance of the show; some even require them a year or more before the show! Some pass out the next year's applications at their current show, offering vendors ample opportunity to reserve space. Some promoters offer a discount for applying by a specified date. Discounts can add up to considerable savings if you plan to do a lot of shows. Most promoters require that your show fee be included with your application.

There are numerous things to be aware of and to consider when you're thinking about exhibiting your goods at an art and craft show. The next sections discuss them in more detail.

Deadlines

If you attend more than 10 or 12 shows a year, sort all your applications by deadline date. Pick a date to review applications once a month so that you won't miss any deadlines, and stick to it!

Photos and Slides

Make sure that you have plenty of high-quality slides and photographs on hand to send with your applications so that you won't have any delays in getting them completed. Remember that your photos are very important because your work will be judged on them—as they say, first impressions count!

I always took my own photos. I set up indoors so that I could control the lighting, and I used a neutral, plain background (soft blue or beige wrinkle-free bed sheets or a piece of fabric work great). About twice a year, I set up a photo session and took lots of rolls of high-quality 35mm film, photographing a large variety of stock. That way, I knew I'd get plenty of good shots. I had the negatives developed as photos, so I could pick out the best, and then have slides made from the negatives of the photos I'd selected. If you don't have the time or don't like your own photography attempts, you can hire a professional photographer to do the work for you. Whether you take your own pictures is unimportant. What is important is having good-quality pictures on hand before your application deadlines.

Cristiana Kinzle, of A Joy to Sew, shares her rejection blues:

"I was rejected from a show two years ago. My little heart was broken. After all these years of never having to send in a completed application and of promoters calling me, all of a sudden I was rejected! It really broke my heart to think a show didn't want me. Then, I realized, it's not 'me,' it's my representation of my crafts. They'd asked for some quality photos to jury my crafts, and I'd sent some that I'd printed from my not-so-good printer. Worse, they were photos that I'd taken, and I'm not a photographer or even close to it. The following year, I sent in a very nice representation of my work (even if I do say so myself), and I got into the show. It was an outside space, but I was in. After seeing my work, the sponsors added me to their inside show. It is a great thrill for me. I learned my lesson: Be sure that your application pictures give juries the best view of your products."

Crafter Alert

The photos or slides that you send in with your application should be of the highest quality possible. This is not a place to skimp. Your work will be judged based on those pictures—it could be the deciding factor in whether your application is accepted.

Find out what each promoter's labeling requirements are by checking the show application packet. Be sure that yours are properly labeled for each show. If a promoter requires a self-addressed, stamped envelope (SASE) to return your photos or slides, comply, and be sure to put enough postage on the envelope. You can save some bucks by getting your pictures back so that you can use them again.

The Application

Your application should be typed or neatly printed so that all of your information can be clearly read. It never hurts to read the entire application before you start to enter the information so that you can avoid messy corrections. Be sure to completely fill in all the information requested. Remember that some show guidelines are so strict that a single piece of missing information will send your application directly to the circular file. A time-saving trick is to make a copy of the completed application before you send it, and file it in the promoter's file so that you can just copy it to the next year's application, making any changes needed to update it.

Show Fees

One way to help take some of the sting out of paying advance show fees is to be sure to plan for them up-front in your cost projections and budget. Think of your show fees as rent for your selling space, and the promoter as your landlord. If you don't pay the rent, where will you sell?

Show Calendar

When you start applying for shows, be sure to set up a show calendar. You could use a monthly planner book or just use a wall calendar that has boxes large enough to write in. There are two key dates to enter: the show application approval-rejection notification date, and the actual dates of the show. You'll also want to enter the date that the promoter says it will be sending out notification of approvals or rejections. It's important because you may have to follow up on your an application if you haven't received your notification within one week of the date you were told to expect it.

Keep a copy of your show schedule in your work area to help you plan your supply and material purchases and your product production schedule. You'll want to have enough inventory on hand to meet your scheduled show requirements.

Getting Started Selling at Shows

Small, local art and craft shows, fairs, and festivals offer an inexpensive and easy-to-manage environment for selling crafts. They also provide a low-stress way to learn the ropes before investing lots of dollars in major events. It's like learning to walk before you run. The show fees are usually moderate, so it's a desirable way for beginners and seasoned veterans alike to sell crafts. After all, lower expenses equals higher profits.

When you're starting out, take the time to know your customers. Small craft shows have smaller crowds, so you can discover which of your designs or products are the most popular. That way, you'll be sure to have enough of them on hand, especially for major events. *Selling out* is a phrase often heard used to describe great shows, but the reality is that when you sell out of a particular product line it means you weren't prepared, and potential sales have been lost. Consider the first 5 to 10 shows you do as your training or your trial phase. It takes *doing* the shows to refine not only your method of selling, but also your products. Listen to what customers say, and learn. Observe how other vendors work, and learn.

Crafter Alert

Selling out is a phrase often used to describe great shows, but selling out of a particular product line means that you weren't prepared and that you consequently lost sales.

How Do I Find Art and Craft Shows?

There are many ways to research the different categories of shows:

➤ **Search locally.** Your local Chamber of Commerce, civic groups, and charitable or trade organizations are great places to start. Contact them to find out if they publish lists or are sponsoring any events where crafts are sold. Check your local newspapers and upcoming event listing guides.

➤ **Search the Web.** Online resources are another way to get information about craft shows. The Internet makes it easy to find craft-related events if you're willing to do the research!

➤ **Trade show publications.** This industry, like most others, has specific trade publications that serve a niche market. Listings of art and craft shows have developed into a category of their own. Hundreds of quality publications, both regional and national, do an excellent job of specializing in this field. Some of the more popular publications are ...

> *The ABC Directory.* Editor Phil Reed says, "At *ABC*, we are dedicated to serving the needs of exhibiting artists, craftspeople, and food vendors—from beginner to professional, with our nationwide coverage of events." You can usually pick up a copy at your favorite craft store. Contact PO Box 400, Walland, TN 37886-0400; phone: 1-800-678-3566 or 865-983-1374; Web site: www.theabcdirectory.com/.

> *Arts and Crafts Show Guide Magazine.* Free online source for event listings, founded in 1986. Web site: www.acnshowguide.com/acn/.

Choices. The art-and-craft-show Yellow Pages for craftspeople and artists. It lists art and craft shows in Connecticut, Massachusetts, New Jersey, New York, Pennsylvania, and Vermont. Contact PO Box 484, Rinebeck, NY 12572; phone: 1-888-918-1313; Web site: www.smartfrogs.com.

Craft Master News. Covers the western United States, including California, Arizona, Nevada, Oregon, and Washington. Contact: PO Box 39429, Downey, CA 90239; phone: 562-869-5882; Web site: www.craftmasternews.com/page2.html.

Festival Network Online. A subscription-based online database for art and craft events and more. Web site: www.festivalnet.com/.

Mid-Atlantic Craft Show List. Your craft show listing guide for Pennsylvania, New Jersey, New York, Maryland, Delaware, and Virginia. Contact PO Box 161, Catasauqua, PA 18032-0161; Web site: www.craftassoc.com/redwards.html.

Midwest Art Fairs. Regional art & craft shows in North and South Dakota, Minnesota, Wisconsin, and Iowa. Contact PO Box 72, Pepin, WI 54759; phone: 715-442-2022.

National Craft Association. The association publishes nationwide art, craft, and wholesale trade show listings, free online at www.craftassoc.com/confer.html.

SAC News Monthly. Lists more than 6,700 shows nationwide with complete details. Contact PO Box 159, Bogalusa, LA 70429-0159; phone: 1-800-925-3722 or 504-732-5616; Web site: www.SACNewsmonthly.com/.

Sunshine Artist Magazine. Dedicated to the professional exhibitor of handmade items with national coverage of events. Contact 2600 Temple Dr., Winter Park, FL 32789; phone: 407-539-1399; Web site: www.sunshineartist.com/.

TSNN.com. An online trade show locator, segmented by industry. Web site: www.tsnn.com/tsnn2000/careercenter/tsjobs.html.

Where It's at Magazine. Coverage for Alabama, Arizona, Arkansas, Colorado, Georgia, Kansas, Louisiana, Mississippi, Missouri, New Mexico, Oklahoma, Tennessee, and Texas. Contact 7204 Bucknell Dr., Austin, TX 78723; phone: 1-800-972-8589; Web site: www.whereitsatmagazine.com/.

Start collecting information on the art and craft shows that you're interested in participating in as soon as possible. Good shows fill early, and you don't want to be left out. The only way to make money with your hobby is to get your plans in gear and act. As Harry Truman said, "The buck stops here!"

The Least You Need to Know

➤ Art and craft shows provide you direct, immediate access to the buying public.

➤ It is important to select shows that are suited to the type of products that you plan to sell.

➤ Usually small, locally promoted shows are the most cost-effective and the best place for beginners to get started.

➤ Trade show publications have the most comprehensive listings and information about art and craft shows that you may want to participate in.

Chapter 21

Batteries Not Included: Preparing to Sell at Professionally Promoted Shows

In This Chapter

➤ Setting up an attention-grabbing display

➤ Discovering where to find display fixtures and equipment

➤ Learning what you need to take to a show

➤ Protecting yourself, your cash, and your products at shows

➤ Getting along with other show vendors

Art and craft shows are where most artisans get their first experience selling their handmade products. They soon discover that, just as in any other sales venture, there's a lot to learn about marketing through shows before you can become truly successful at it. In this chapter, we show you how to prepare for selling at shows, teach you the tricks of the trade for making money at it, and caution you about pitfalls to avoid. Selling at professionally promoted shows is a very exciting, lucrative way to start making money with your hobby.

Display with Pizzazz

Most customers browse a craft show or shop by strolling up and down the aisles. They give your merchandise a casual glance (about 20 to 30 seconds) as they pass by—or is that what really happens? What *can* happen is that *customers stop at the displays that catch their attention* and spend some time and, let's hope, some money there.

Many factors are involved in creating a display that will beckon the buyer. We'll look into these in the next sections.

Visual Appeal

First, the customer must be able to see what you're selling. Don't let your display area look like a cluttered rummage sale. If it looks jumbled, it's confusing, and customers won't take time to figure out what you have. They'll pass you by without a second look. Your display should have height, depth, and layering. Center your best-selling items in the shoppers' main line of vision, the area between eye and knee level. Keep items off the floor by using crates, ladders, boxes, or any prop that you can think of that ties into your display theme. Don't forget to allow for a traffic flow pattern so that people can easily browse your merchandise displays.

Lighting

Lights will optimize your display and attract attention to indoor displays, especially where shows use fluorescent lighting; adding spotlights helps.

The difference that lighting makes in sales is tremendous. *Lights bring out the true colors of your work.* They make your display stand out and look inviting. Check your local hardware or discount stores for clip-on lights or small unit track lighting that holds flood light bulbs.

Crafter Alert

To get customers to stop at your display, it needs pizzazz, creative marketing, and an attention-grabbing idea. If you can't get browsers to stop long enough to discover what you have to sell, you just won't sell.

Sound

Sound attracts attention. Consider playing soft music, or a tape (perhaps in your own voice) describing the history of your art or craft or the techniques used to create it. If you use soft music in the background, tie it to the type of work that you sell to enhance your total display theme. Be creative with music: Selling children's items? Try children's songs. Country items? Try country music. If you're selling home decorating items, make a tape of suggestions for ways to use them (with soft music). Dare to be different!

Color Basics

Your display colors should complement your products, not overpower or detract from them. Colors evoke emotions. The cool colors, such as blues and greens, are relaxing; hot colors, such as red, orange, and yellow, are energizers and tend to attract attention.

Earth tones and pastels work well for seasonal themes, as do red and green for a holiday season theme. Using white or black backdrops will sharpen the definition of your products, providing dramatic visual impact. In a confined area such as a display booth, white has the advantage of visually enlarging your space because it reflects light.

Layout Concepts

The height, depth, and layering of your display will create visual impact and give individual attention to the different items that you'll display. Height can be achieved by using your display backdrops as a merchandising display area. If you have hanging things, hang them. If you have sitting items, have a shelf arrangement on the walls. The backdrop or walls that you create to separate your area from another vendor's are important display areas for your products. Pegboard also makes an effective backdrop.

Artisan's Corner

In displaying your products, use color to your sales advantage. Group your items by color for visual impact. This helps customers see that you have many items grouped in the same color range, which promotes multiple or add-on sales. Display your color variety beginning on the left with cool colors, moving to warm colors, and ending on the right with bright, or hot, colors.

Two shutters or screens hinged together can make a corner. Two six-foot ladders with boards between them create instant shelves. Plastic snap-together shelves are light to carry and take very little room to transport. Wooden or plastic crates can be stacked or placed pyramid style.

Layering can be accomplished by creating risers or a step effect on your flat surface areas, such as tabletops. Layering increases your display surface area, creates depth, and provides more visibility for individual products. L-shaped hooks added to shelf edges, or ladder-and-crate sides, increase your merchandising space for hanging items. You can add wooden slats across the top of your booth area to hang items from the ceiling. Baskets, boxes, mini ladders, and benches are other display props to consider. The possibilities are as endless as your own creativity.

Check out your local hardware or discount stores, garage sales, and used store fixture and equipment dealers for additional ideas.

Signs

Signs are very important sales and display aids. First, make sure that your signs are *professional-looking and readable* at a glance. There should be price tags on every item, but if you do sell items that you can't tag, use a sign. Customers resent having to ask, which irritates most of them. That's not a good way to build customer relations. If your product needs some explanation, make sure that your sign clearly states it in the briefest possible way. Use signs to suggest sales ideas (such as, item A goes with item B). If you're offering special orders, say so with a sign. Run out of a color or size? Post a sign offering to take orders for it.

Artisan's Corner

Display items in a setting or grouping as they might be used. Tell a picture story so that customers can visualize just how great the grouping would look in their home. You can use creative ideas to set up your display inexpensively, or you can purchase items from display manufacturers. Use the back and side walls to screen out other views and to keep your booth *visually self-contained* so that customers can stay focused on your product display.

Motion

Motion attracts attention. Either you or your display should have some motion going on at all times. Whenever possible, be working on your art or craft so that customers can see what you do.

If you can't produce your products in your display area, create motion in your display. It's as easy as having a small turntable to rotate one small tabletop display. If one of your items has movement, set it up at the center of your display area to show it in action.

Crafter Alert

Never sit in your booth just reading or looking bored. Don't leave your booth unattended for extended periods of time. Be ready to greet customers with a smile, a nod, or a cheerful hello that makes them feel comfortable and invited.

Aroma

Let us not forget that smell is another big attention-grabber. *Aromatic displays add to sales appeal.* They say in the trade, "If it smells, it sells." If your items have no fragrance, you can add some. You could use room fragrance stick-ups or potpourri concealed in your display props. Food aromas such as vanilla, apples, and cinnamon are pleasing to most people. Outdoor aromas of fresh county bouquets or pine trees are also popular.

Table Covers

Table covers are required by some promoters and must cover the top and three sides of your table. You can purchase table covers that meet this specification. An alternative is to purchase a piece of fire-retardant polyester material, 60 inches wide. This fabric washes easily and does not wrinkle the way cotton does. A plus to a table cover that goes to the floor is that you can store stock or boxes under it out of sight and keep your display area looking neat. Select a color for your table cover that complements your merchandise by contrasting with your products so that *they* are the focal point.

Your products must be shown off to their best advantage. The use of a brightly colored or printed table cover may work if the product is plain in itself, such as wooden shelves, for example. If the background color or design is too busy or bright, however, it may actually detract from the product, making it look less attractive.

Pointers

To add interest to a plain table cover, you can selectively position a few lace or crocheted doilies or some woven place mats on it to add contrast or enhance the look of certain items—enhance, not overpower.

Promotion

Promotion demands that you allow space in your display area for your brochures, fliers, business cards, and guest sign-up log. This is an important marketing tool for future mailings. Be sure to ask them to sign up before they leave your booth. Always have a bag stuffer that includes your future show schedule, company name, address, phone number, and mini product description. Place some where visitors can pick them up, but most of all, make sure that one goes in every customer's bag.

Plan Your Booth

You can plan your booth to be your silent sales rep. If it's not doing the job, you could be losing sales. Ask yourself what the main items that you want to sell are. Do they project a theme? What color will complement them? Do they vary in size and shape, and how does that affect your display requirements?

Make a list of the items that you plan to sell and how they need to be placed: sitting, hanging, or standing. Now go shopping: Visit gift shops, boutiques, and department stores. Study how items similar to yours are displayed. Stores have professionally trained display technicians to make sure that every inch of space is working as a silent salesperson. *Learn from the professionals.* Visit craft shows to see how vendors display merchandise.

When you have some ideas, make a simple layout of your display space using a scale of $1/4$ inch equals 1 foot. Make a diagram of a typical 10-inch × 10-inch booth with three walls and floor space. You have total flexibility to design the interior layout of your booth. Plan to use as much of the back and side wall space as possible. You're paying for this space; don't waste it. Remember to design a traffic flow for customers. A booth filled from top to bottom and cleverly arranged will attract the customers.

Basics to Bear in Mind

Some other bits of advice to help you set up your display are listed here:

➤ Keep your display pieces flexible so that you can arrange them in various ways based on the shape and size of the display area you're given. Display setups vary from show to show.

➤ Keep your display pieces light and easy to transport. Consider multifunctional pieces that could serve as containers to pack products in and that can be converted to a display unit.

➤ If you use a table as part of your display, you can buy light, folding ones. It's cheaper than renting tables at every show, and you have control over its size. *A chair should be used sparingly.* It's better if you're standing or working around your booth than if you're sitting. A high director's chair is recommended; it gives you a clear view of your booth, and people can see you.

Where to Get Display Stuff

The following list of suppliers stock display fixtures, equipment, and retailing (store) supplies that you may need to merchandise your product line.

➤ **AMAC Plastic Products.** Clear plastic box displays. Contact PO Box 750249, Petaluma, CA 94975-0249; phone: 1-800-852-7158 or 707-763-3700; Web site: www.amacbox.com/.

➤ **Armstrong Products, Inc.** Carpeted displays. Contact PO Box 979, Gunthrie, OK 73044; phone: 405-282-7584 or 1-800-278-4279; Web site: www.armstrong-products.com.

➤ **Clear Image, Inc.** Crystal-clear acid-free packaging bags for image impact. Contact 1919 Windplay Dr., Suite 7, El Dorado Hills, CA 95762; phone: 916-933-4700 or 1-800-233-2630; Web site: www.clearbags.com.

➤ **Dealers Supply, Inc.** Complete show supplies. Send for a free catalog. Contact PO Box 717, Matawan, NJ 07747; phone: 1-800-524-0576.

➤ **Display Warehouse.** Sixty-eight-page catalog of store supplies. Contact 8820 Kenamar Dr., San Diego, CA 92121; phone: 1-800-842-5501; Web site: www. displaywarehouse.com/.

➤ **Fetpak, Inc.** Display, packaging, and retailing supplies. Call for a free 48-page catalog. Contact 70 Austin Blvd., Commack, NY 11725; phone: 1-800-883-3872.

➤ **Garment Racks Etc.** Sean James Enterprises, Inc. Contact 425 Tribble Gap Rd., Cumming, GA 30040; phone: 1-888-866-9826; Web site: www. garmentracksetc.com/index.html.

➤ **MD Enterprises.** Display panels. Contact 9738 Abernathy, Dallas, TX 75220; phone: 214-350-5765; Web site: www.propanels.com.

➤ **Nu-Ease.** Portable displays and accessories. Contact 264 West 40th St., New York, NY 10018-1574; phone: 212-840-0025 or 1-800-840-0095 (outside New York State); Web site: www.travelautobag.com/tab_home001.htm.

➤ **Roberts Colonial House, Inc.** Table-top and small displays. Contact PO Box 308, South Holland, IL 60473; phone: 708-331-6233.

➤ **The Wood Factory.** Wood display fixtures. Contact 21 Musick, Irvine, CA 92718; phone: 1-800-842-9663.

➤ **Woodland Marketing.** Portable wooden displays. Contact 555 Jensen Dr., Medford, WI 54451; phone: 715-748-4004 or 1-800-762-1796; Web site: www.woodlandmarketing.com/.

Getting Organized: Craft Show Checklist

You can cut down on your show preparation considerably if you do just a few simple things:

➤ Assemble all the supplies that you'll always need to take with you for each show; store them in a designated spot so that they are ready to load into your vehicle as you pack to leave.

➤ As items run low, jot them down on your supply list so that you can replace them before the next show.

I always liked to break my list into three groups and pack each separately: business supplies, display supplies, and personal items. The following checklist will help you get organized and ready for your craft show season:

Business Supplies

❏ Business cards and holder

❏ Gift boxes, tissue or newspaper for fragile items, bags in several sizes for customer purchases

❏ Receipt book, sales log, guest book (to develop a mailing list), notepad or extra paper

❏ Extra hang tags or price tags besides those already on the merchandise; extra care instructions (if required)

❏ Cash box with change and assorted small bills

❏ Printed show schedule to use as a bag stuffer and handout, brochures or catalogs, wholesale order forms and price list, special order forms

Pointers

Always make it convenient for customers to contact you. For shows, I always made up a $5^1/_4 \times 8^1/_2$-inch form to use as a handout and a bag stuffer. At the top is a copy of my business card, followed by a little PR about my products, and then a list of the craft shows that I was participating in. It's cheaper to make these than to give out business cards. And just think how much more information you can get into the consumers' hands! Never let a bag leave your booth without stuffing it with promotional literature.

❏ Calculator and extra batteries, stapler, pens, tape, sales tax chart (if it's easier than figuring it out with each sale)

❏ Copy of your sales tax certificate of authority (you're required to display it in your booth)

❏ Credit card equipment and supplies; cellular phone (optional)

❏ Company name sign, any product information signs necessary, return policy sign, payment policy sign, check handling policy sign

❏ Inventory with all merchandise clearly priced (best done before the show), show confirmation documentation

Display Requirements

❏ Display fixtures or folding tables, fabric for table or display prop coverings (clean and pressed), chair(s)

❏ Lights and extra bulbs, extension cords, power strip

❏ Push pins and extra tacks or nails, display wire or fishing line, small display items such as easels, plate stands, and racks

❏ Mirror for customer use, if applicable

❏ Indoor/outdoor carpeting cut to the size of the booth (optional, but helps keep dust and dirt away from your inventory)

❏ Glass cleaner and other cleaners, paper towels

❏ Rubber bands, a package of clip-type clothespins to anchor plastic tarps, table covers, and other items in wind and rain

❏ Masking and duct tape, box cutter or knife, scissors, wire cutter, hammer or mallet, bungee cords, and rope

❏ Extra ground stakes, plastic tarps in case of rain, canopy, and related supplies (see the following section on canopies for details)

❏ Large trash bags for emergency packdown and to cover boxes of inventory in case of sudden rain

> **Crafter Alert**
>
> Don't forget to make sure that you have complete contact information on your business cards and all the printed material that you plan to hand out. Include the business name, your name, your address, your phone and fax numbers, and your e-mail and Web sites. If you don't want to use your home-based business address, rent a PO Box and use it instead.

❏ A bundle of wood shingles to use as shims (they break into pieces easily), or pieces of paneling or thin plywood (You'll probably never set up outdoors on level ground.)

❏ Dolly or cart to transport heavy stock to your booth; craft supplies to demonstrate your crafts when feasible

Personal Items

❏ Thermos or cooler with drinks and food, napkins, box of tissues, toilet tissue, wet wipes or wet wash cloths in a plastic zip-bag, hand soap

❏ Change of clothes and shoes, extra socks, waterproof boots, umbrella, raincoat, jacket or sweater, gloves, blanket, big brim hat, sunglasses, sunscreen, towel, aspirin (plus any medications that you may require), and a first-aid kit

Be prepared—your creature comforts are important, too!

Surviving the Show

Plenty can go wrong at an art and craft show. This section tells you what to prepare for and how to do it.

Canopies for Outdoor Show Survival

The most expensive piece of equipment that you need to have for doing outdoor shows is the canopy (tent). If you're planning on doing shows alone, look for a canopy that one person can set up. The size 10 × 10 feet is considered standard for art and craft shows. White is the best color; any other color will cast a tint of color on your products, and their true colors won't show up properly. You may want to visit a few craft shows and speak with artisans to see how they like the style or brand that they own.

There are a lot of canopy suppliers—here are three companies that make styles popular with artisans:

> **Pointers**
>
> When you're shopping for a canopy, don't just consider price—also consider quality. You want a durable waterproof and fire-retardant canopy that will last you many years.

➤ **Elaine Martin Co.**, PO Box 274, Deerfield, IL; phone: 1-800-642-1043; Web site: www.emartin.com/canopies/index.html.

➤ **EZ-UP Canopies**, 1601 Iowa Ave., Riverside, CA 92507; phone: 909-781-0843 or 1-800-457-4233; Web site: www.ez-up.com/.

➤ **K D Canopy**, 3755 W. 69th Place, Westminster, CO 80030; Phone: 303-650-1310 or 1-800-432-4435; Web site: www.kdkanopy.com/.

Show Travel Safety

It doesn't take much effort, just a higher level of awareness, to ensure your safety on the road and at shows. The following pointers should become part of your show routine:

1. The day before a show, and again before you leave, do a quick walk-around of your vehicle to check your tires and make sure that there's no puddle of liquid underneath. You can save a lot of grief by repairing or replacing tires, or taking care of other problems before you're stranded.

2. At the show, park near a light. If it's not dark when you arrive, it may be at the end of the day.

3. Try not to be the last person leaving at the end of the show.

4. Wear a fanny pack in front of you as a belly-bag, low and loose. There shouldn't be very much in your cash box at any time ($50 worth of singles, and $5 bills and change). As the day progresses, remove your checks, charges, and large bills from your cash box and put them in your belly-bag.

5. Don't latch your cash box. One of the tricks thieves use, especially at outdoor shows, is to reach over, grab the cash box, and run. If the box isn't latched, it

will open, and the contents will be dumped onto the floor. The rest of your cash should be tucked away on your person.

Crafter Alert

"Even a fanny pack can disappear when an experienced pickpocket slices through the belt with a utility knife. Several models of "undercover security wallets" are available from many sources, including Travel Smith (1–800–950–1500, www.travelsmith.com). Don't leave your booth neighbor to watch your cash, either. Remove cash and checks from your cash box if you leave your space. Your neighbors will probably be willing to watch your booth while you're absent, but if they get busy, they may forget."

—Betty Chypre

6. At restaurants and gas stations, don't discuss the show and how busy you were. You may as well be carrying a sign that reads, "Mug me."

7. Get rid of the show badge. Put it in your pocket when you leave the show. It's a little piece of paper that advertises that you're carrying money. Put it out of sight!

8. If you stay at a motel, leave the TV or radio on while you're away. Leave a "Don't Disturb" sign on the door so that it looks as if someone is in the room at all times, especially if you store your extra inventory there.

9. Set up your booth with secure corners so that no one can come into your private space. Make sure that valuables are tucked out of reach and out of sight.

10. Even though it's a secure place, when you leave your booth overnight, remove your most valuable pieces and cover the rest of your merchandise with sheets or large covers. In the morning, arrive early when the doors open.

Safety in Your Vehicle

Several simple precautions can help to make your road trip secure. Here are a few items to have in your vehicle:

➤ A flashlight with new batteries.

➤ A fresh can of Fix-a-Flat (it goes hard after a year or two).

➤ Quarters for phone calls and tolls.

➤ Maps.

➤ A 3 × 5 card with written directions to and from the location.

➤ Pen and paper.

➤ Cell phone, if possible.

➤ A blanket, for winter traveling, in case you're stranded on a back road.

➤ At least a half-tank of fuel in winter; the larger the air space in your tank, the more likely that your gas line will freeze. Put a can of dry gas in your tank with each fill-up when the weather is below freezing.

These safety suggestions were contributed by Betty Chypre, editor of *Choices: The Art & Craft Show Yellow Pages for Craftsmen & Artists,* which publishes art and craft shows in Connecticut, Massachusetts, New Jersey, New York, Pennsylvania, and Vermont. For more information call 1-888-918-1313, or visit the *Choices* Web site at www. smartfrogs.com.

The key to your success in doing any type of show is to *be prepared.* Even if the show is just across town, you still need to have all your supplies, equipment, fixtures, and inventory with you for the day.

The Exhibitors' Golden Rule

When you attend art and craft or trade shows, keep in mind some basic things that will make you a better neighbor. Remember that the other vendors at the event are there because they paid for their space and want to make money, just as you do. When you participate in any event, you should try to *acknowledge and respect the needs and rights of your fellow exhibitors:*

➤ **Stay within your allotted space.** If your display needs a little extra space, buy it from the promoters before the event. Quite often this means that you'll need to purchase a double booth or at least an additional half space. Check with the show promoter to see what options you have regarding measurements. If you don't want to incur that added expense, you should redesign your display so that it will fit into the space that you purchased. Use display fixtures that can easily be adapted to various booth layouts. Whatever you do, don't extend your display into your neighbor's space! The quickest way to make an enemy at a show is to steal extra space from a fellow exhibitor or to set up in such a way that you partially block a neighbor's booth entrance. Think about it: When you put your display into another vendor's booth space, you're taking space that someone else paid for, which is stealing—it's also inconsiderate and downright rude.

➤ **Be prepared.** Take everything you need to set up your booth. Don't expect to borrow tools or equipment from your neighbors—they brought them because they plan to use them. Make a checklist for yourself of all the things that you need for your booth setup, and refer to it when you pack up for each show.

➤ **Design a flexible display.** One of the best ways to avoid problems is to plan your original booth setup with flexible display components. That way it's quick and easy to adjust your display to suit various size or layout arrangements that you'll encounter as you work different shows. If you're side by side in a row with other exhibitors, your booth will be accessible only from the front. Because there are always more of these spots available at shows, this is the typical setup to plan for. You'll find that most shows (especially outdoor ones) offer a 10 × 10-foot space. Some indoor shows, however, provide only 10 × 8-foot, or 8 × 8-foot spaces. Check the show application for the space size when you apply for a show so that you'll be prepared.

➤ **Set up at the right time.** Give yourself enough time to set up before the show begins. Setting up a booth at a show takes a reasonable amount of time to get everything just the way you want it.

Whether it takes you a few minutes or several hours, be sure to allot yourself enough time to finish before the gates open. Boxes blocking aisles not only keep customers from visiting booths, but they also can be a violation of the fire code regulations. Even if you're not still in the aisles, continuing to set up your display when the show is open distracts customers. It can hurt your sales and even your neighbors' sales. Also remember that most show promoters set aside specific setup times, and you're required to complete your setup within them.

➤ **Respect your fellow exhibitors.** Be friendly and courteous to fellow exhibitors, but don't be a pest. It's fine to visit with other exhibitors at a show; in fact, meeting and networking with fellow artisans is sometimes as important as developing new customers. However, don't stand around talking if a customer walks in. Bear in mind that what may work best for you may infringe on other exhibitors. Remember: Every exhibitor is there to make money. They can't do that if someone is always visiting or blocking customers from viewing their display.

Pointers

Always make sure that you're prepared to set up within your allotted booth space without infringing upon or blocking any space that belongs to your neighbor.

To sum up, when selling at professionally sponsored shows, be aware that you're there first and foremost for a business purpose, as are all the other vendors. Too many un-neighborly oversights can make enemies of your fellow vendors; worse yet, they could even get you banned or bounced from a show. By being professional and treating others with the same respect that you would expect, you'll make new friends and perhaps develop some important contacts that will benefit you in the future.

The Least You Need to Know

➤ To sell, you need to design an attention-grabbing product display that will *stop customers at your booth.*

➤ Use display fixtures that can easily be adapted to various booth layouts and that are easy to transport.

➤ Always make sure that you're prepared to set up within your allotted booth space, without infringing on or blocking any space belonging to your neighbor.

➤ Don't make yourself a target for muggers or thieves. Be alert to those around you, and be cautious in handling your cash.

➤ Selling at art and craft shows is one of the best ways to start making money with your hobby.

Chapter 22

Other Sales Outlets

In This Chapter

➤ Using craft malls to increase your income

➤ Evaluating and choosing the craft malls to sell your products in

➤ Understanding what selling on consignment is all about

The secret to making money with your hobby is to plan a marketing strategy that includes as many different ways as possible of presenting your product or service to customers. The other obvious advantage is that when you're selling in a variety of markets, if one market is slow, you should still have sales from your other venues to provide an income stream. As they say, "Don't put all your eggs in one basket."

To build a business with growth potential, you need to activate a selling strategy centered on getting your products into every possible sales venue that exposes your line to your target customer. In this chapter, we explore some of the popular ways artisans are selling their work. You can design and produce the most fantastic widget that the world has ever known, but if you don't have your sales channels in place to put it into the hands of the potential buyer, guess what? The world will never know!

Selling in Craft Malls

A *craft mall* is a retail store that rents space to artisans so that they can display and sell their own original handcrafted items. The term "mall" in this case means that the retail store is like a shopping mall because it is made up of many different vendor booths selling their work under one roof, similar to the way that a craft show is set up.

Craft malls either assign a specific "booth" space or operate more like a boutique by grouping your crafts with other vendors' compatible items and mixing your items throughout the store. This marketing method tends to give the craft mall a cozy, gift boutique atmosphere.

Artisans have mixed opinions on both methods.

➤ **Booths.** Some want a "designated booth" where they can control the display of their work. These artisans feel strongly that they know how to merchandise their line and that, as long as the store brings in traffic, they'll sell. Others argue that if the individual crafters don't do a good job of displaying and maintaining their booths, then the shop loses customer appeal and everyone's sales will reflect it.

However, most shops have strict policies in place about the quality of the displays and are vigorous about policing the booths. They know that the survival of the shop depends on the image that it projects to the customers.

➤ **The boutique look.** Artisans who prefer the boutique look argue that sales increase when a customer walks into a store with a floral arrangement in mind and can find all the floral designs tastefully displayed together rather than scattered in individual booths around the store. Others argue that this merchandising method takes the individuality away from vendors and just tosses them into the competitive ring with everyone else. I think that if the shop is artfully designed and well maintained by the management, this is a powerful way to sell.

> **Trade Terms**
>
> A **craft mall** is a retail store in which artisans rent display space for their handcrafted products.

> **Artisan's Corner**
>
> A craft co-op is similar to a craft mall, but you're usually required to work in the store for a specified amount of time each month. Because the shop is staffed mainly by the vendors, the rent is usually lower than at a shop that provides all the staff.

So what are we saying? Both methods work. What it really comes down to is which you prefer and how well the store management maintains the store's image.

Craft malls charge rent for the space that you decide on and usually do not charge a commission on your sales. There are year-round craft malls and seasonal craft malls that operate for a few months or weeks at the prime holiday season. They differ from consignment shops (covered later in this chapter), which usually do not charge monthly rent but charge a commission on each item sold instead.

Craft Mall Benefits

Most craft malls are open six to seven days a week. They provide the staff and collect and pay sales tax. They'll usually take special orders for you, provide a layaway program and accept major credit cards as a convenience to the customers. You get all the benefits of a retail store without the hassle of owning or operating one. Most craft malls offer *stocking and display setup programs.*

The craft mall should provide you with a contract that spells out all the terms and conditions of your agreement so that there is no misunderstanding of the arrangements. The management provides you, the vendor, with a statement of your sales at each pay period and generally pays you every two weeks or on a monthly basis. The mall should do regular advertising and promotions, and some craft malls add a percent-per-month fee for an advertising fund because advertising costs are so high. Artisans don't seem to mind—as long as the money is used for advertising. After all, what store doesn't want to attract more customers?

Trade Terms

Stocking and display setup programs are arrangements provided by shops outside your area that will store and set up your entire display for you. They are generally offered free to encourage out-of-town artisans to exhibit. One advantage that artisans find in selling through remote locations is that their products may be new or different from those offered by local artisans, which often gives the new items a selling advantage.

Choosing a Craft Mall

There are no hard and fast rules for choosing a craft mall. Your research and your value judgments are important here. If the mall is local, pay a few visits at different times of the day or evening, on weekdays and weekends. Observe the store traffic, see how the staff interacts with the customers, see if the exhibit booths are well maintained, and check the traffic flow for the area. Is parking convenient? Collect a few business cards from vendors, and call them. Get input on how they think the shop works for them, and ask if their statements and payments are timely. Check to see if the owners, managers, or staff members are experienced in craft sales. Make sure that the shop doesn't allow commercially made or imported products. All the merchandise offered should be handcrafted if the shop is marketed as an art and craft shop.

Ask about the advertising and promotions program. Be cautious, however, when evaluating what other vendors tell you about their sales. Remember that a craft mall is just like a craft show: Some vendors' sales will be terrific, some will be okay, and others will bomb—because a major part of sales is the quality and salability of the product.

If the mall is out of state, check it out with the local Chamber of Commerce or Better Business Bureau, and get vendor references. Create and use an evaluation sheet to compare the advantages and disadvantages of each mall. If the craft mall is part of a chain, be aware that good sales in one location don't guarantee equally good sales in another. All the stores may operate under the same policy, but consider other variables such as the on-location manager and the store's physical location. Just because a shop is near or on a busy major traffic artery or in a large shopping center doesn't guarantee traffic. Most retail experts agree that malls need foot traffic to survive.

Crafter Alert

Most malls offer a security system but are not responsible for theft or damage. This should be covered by your craft business insurance policy.

The Contracts

Most malls require a three- to six-month minimum contract for the space that you decide to rent, and most offer a variety of space-size options, which will be determined by the number of items you want to display, as well as how much you want to spend. A few malls may offer a month-to-month rental. Be sure that you know what you're getting before you sign. The written contract should detail the what, where, when, and how. The owner or manager should be happy to explain all charges and services to you, or mail you complete information on them, and should be willing and able to answer any questions you may have. Beware of promises: Find out what your legal obligations are before you sign any contract or deliver your products. Remember, if you don't have it in writing, you're not protected.

How to Be Successful in a Craft Mall

Be realistic in what you want to put into the craft mall. If the mall's crafts have mainly a country theme, and your items don't, then skip it and select a mall with your type of merchandise. If you have items that sell well at craft shows, they should sell just as well at the craft mall; the same goes for slow-moving items.

Take time to plan the design and layout of your space. Your space must be attractive, inviting, and attention-getting to make a shopper stop at your booth. Make it convenient for shoppers; have everything clearly priced. Coordinate colors and items that will enhance your craft sales with add-on sales. Think of your rent-a-space exhibit as a gift boutique displaying your handcrafted products. Make sure that your signs, hang tags, business cards, or brochures are professional and on hand.

Monitoring Your Booth Space

After you've set up your display at a craft mall, establish a regular routine to monitor your booth area. Visit your booth weekly or on any regular basis to check sales, restock, clean, and rearrange products. The more attention you can give to your booth, the more you'll sell. You have to replenish stock. If it isn't there, you can't sell it, and you could be paying rent for an empty space. The lower your inventory gets, the fewer choices the shopper has, so you'll never know how much more you could have sold if you'd had sufficient inventory.

Your best-selling items will not stay best-sellers forever. You need to create new items to add to your line or replace items that have lost appeal. You'll begin to build a customer base at a craft mall, shoppers who will continually come in to see what's new. If you're on the ball and you regularly show new merchandise, you're apt to sell a lot more.

Many craft mall owners have said that their main problem is getting vendors to keep their booths stocked, and continually restocked with seasonal items. To keep your sales up, you must add new items that are on-target for selling throughout various seasonal changes and popular holidays. When a season is over, pull the seasonal items out and replace them.

Keep Good Records

Set up a record system for items that you take to the mall, your sales, and items that you remove. This inventory information will give you proof of sales and any loss due to shoplifting. If you keep good records, most times you'll find that your losses are less than you thought. With rare exceptions, most retail stores would love to have the low percentage of theft that a craft mall has.

Your records are also important because they'll tell you your selling trends, including choices of color, style, price ranges, and what or how much sells and when. Buying patterns usually differ depending on what region of the country the craft mall is in, so it's a good idea to keep separate records for each mall location that you sell in. The fact is that sales will fluctuate. Most craft malls will provide you with detailed computer records of your sales at each pay period, so it will be easy to compare their records with yours.

Crafter Alert

You must monitor sales on a regular basis to be sure that you have sufficient inventory. Not everything you put in your booth will sell, so remove slow-moving items and try them again later or in a different market. Be sure to replace stock regularly with items based on seasonal changes and holidays.

There seems to be a consensus among mall owners that the typical crafter will have four to five inventory turns per year. That means that if you stock $1,000 in inventory (retail value $2,000) at a craft mall, with five inventory rollovers, you would gross $10,000 for the year, about average with the inventory turns at a typical retail gift shop.

Plan Properly

You're paying rent every day in a craft mall. Don't rob your merchandise from the mall to take it to craft shows on the weekends. It puts wear and tear on your products and is time-consuming, and you could spend that time making more products. Weekends usually provide the highest traffic at a craft mall. That's when you want your booth to look its best.

For your business to be more profitable, you may need to focus on fewer rather than more locations. Choose your most profitable place(s), and give them the attention they need. It will be cash in your pocket. Success rarely just happens—it takes proper planning. It's okay to be aggressive in building your business, but don't overextend yourself; it's better to take it one step at a time.

It's up to you to make your booth work for you. Provide the display and the merchandise that will make customers want to buy from you. The efforts that you put into keeping your mall space neat, attractive, and well stocked will make a difference in your bottom-line profits.

Crafter Alert

If you're continually taking items out of your mall locations to do craft shows you're doing a disservice to yourself, your customers, and the craft mall. You're spreading yourself too thin. Your overall gross sales will go down, but the rent and fees you're paying will still be there!

Be Optimistic

When you decide to make a commitment to be in a craft mall, go in with the attitude that you're going to make it a success. Give it your full attention. The idea that you're just trying it out can give you an easy excuse to pull out when the first little problem arises. Then you'll never know if craft mall selling could have worked for you. It takes time to get established at any location. It is a building process, gaining new customers one at a time, and building a repeat customer base that adds volume to your sales figures. Craft malls deserve a closer look because of the profit potential they offer. While the concept is only about 10 years old, artisans have built the craft mall business into a multibillion-dollar industry.

Craft Mall Research

You can contact these craft malls and request information and details on their costs, services, and various locations.

➤ **American Craft Malls, Inc.** Five locations: four in Texas, one in Oklahoma. Contact Box 799, Azle, TX 76098-0799; phone: 817-221-1099 or 1-800-335-2544, e-mail: azle@ctelcom.net; Web site: www.procrafter.com.

➤ **Coomers.** Thirty locations in nine states. Contact 6012 Reef Point Lane, Suite F, Fort Worth, TX 76135-2056; phone: 817-237-4588 or 1-888-362-7238; e-mail: coomers@coomers.com; Web site: www.coomers.com.

➤ **Crafters Showcase.** One shop, founded in 1992 by owners Gary and Shelley Wain. Southland Shopping Center, 653 Clairton Blvd. (Route 51), Pittsburgh, PA 15236; phone: 412-653-4222 or 1-800-414-3521; e-mail: crafts@cscrafts.com; Web site: www.cscrafts.com.

➤ **Craftworks.** Founded in 1994, there are now 20 locations in Connecticut, Delaware, Florida, Massachusetts, Maryland, New Hampshire, New York, Pennsylvania, Tennessee, South Carolina, and Virginia. Phone: 1-888-296-7577; e-mail: info@craftworksonline.com; Web site: www.craftworksonline.com.

➤ **First Capital Craft Mall.** One shop. Contact 400 Chamber Dr., Chillicothe, OH 45601; phone: 740-773-0099. Web site: www. imagineifyouwill.com.

➤ **The Handcrafters Barn.** One shop, owned by Chuck and Carol Guilbeault. Contact Route 16, Main St., North Conway Village, NH 03860; phone: 603-356-8996; e-mail: info@handcraftersbarn.com; Web site: www.handcraftersbarn.com.

➤ **Homespun Crafters Mall** Nine locations in Idaho, Oregon, Tennessee, and Washington. Contact 856 NW Bond, Bend, OR 97701; phone: 541-463-8853 or 1-888-463-7786; e-mail: homespun@homespuncrafters.com; Web site: www.homespuncrafters.com.

Artisan's Corner

The National Craft Association (NCA) publishes a "Craft Mall Directory" with nationwide listings of craft malls. Visit www. craftassoc/mktsourc.html, or call 1-800-715-9594 for information and a free brochure.

➤ **Peddler's Village Craft Malls.** Nine locations in Florida, Illinois, Ohio, Oklahoma, Indiana, and Texas. Contact 1881 W. Henderson Road, Columbus, OH 43220; phone: 614-791-9166; e-mail: kevin@antiquelandusa.com; Web site: www.peddlersmall.com.

➤ **The Quilted Bear.** Seven locations in California, Idaho, Oklahoma, and Utah. Contact 145 W. 7200 S. Midvale, UT 84047; phone: 801-566-9382 or 1-800-792-4530; Web site: www.quiltedbear.com.

Selling on Consignment

When you place items in a shop on consignment, you're sharing the risk of whether your merchandise will sell with the retail shop or gallery owner. Shops that sell on consignment usually do not charge monthly rent, instead taking a commission on each item sold. Commissions are usually about a 60/40 split. The shop owner earns the 40 percent in lieu of rent by providing you with all the amenities of the retail store. Be sure to get a written contract that spells out all the terms and conditions of your arrangements.

Consignment is a good way to test the market salability of new designs or high-end one-of-a-kind items that a shop owner is not quite sure fits the shop's particular type of customer. Consignment selling gives you about the same profit as if you were selling wholesale. Use the same rules outlined in selecting a craft mall for deciding whether a retail shop, or gallery, is a good fit for your products.

However, you have some things to consider when selling on consignment:

1. Who sets the selling price, you or the shop? Can the shop sell it for whatever price it can get?

2. Exactly how much commission will you get from sales?

3. Do you get paid when the item sells, or within a week, two weeks, or a month?

4. What's the duration of the consignment term? One month, three months, or until your work is dusty and shop-worn?

5. Who pays shipping, handling, packing, insurance, or other costs if the item has to be delivered to the customer?

6. Will the shop or gallery be responsible for loss or damage? Will you receive the same amount as if your work had been sold?

7. Will the shop or gallery lend your work out, take it off the premises, or sell it on approval without your permission?

8. Will the shop or gallery take special orders? Under what conditions?

9. Does the shop agree to display the items in the sales area during the contract term, not stuff it in a stock room?

10. Do you have a prepared, detailed inventory list for the owner to sign as acknowledgment of receiving the merchandise?

Before you sign a written consignment agreement, review the items in the preceding list, and be sure that they're covered. It's always a good idea to have the owner sign photos of the work that you place on consignment, acknowledging the date and the condition that the items were in when they were delivered.

Selling in craft malls and selling on consignment in shops or galleries are both popular marketing ventures for artisans. Do your research first, and then choose the best options for getting your handcrafted products into your customers' hands.

Pointers

If an owner suddenly shuts down a shop, or the shop's assets are seized for nonpayment of taxes, for example, the photos and contract would be valuable documentation to help you get your items released by the courts.

The Least You Need to Know

➤ Craft malls are a good way to increase your income by selling directly to consumers.

➤ Research each craft mall carefully before you sign up to make sure that it's right for your product line.

➤ Selling on consignment is another good way to sell your products directly to consumers through retail shops and galleries.

➤ Always get a detailed, signed contract when you place your products in a craft mall, shop, or gallery.

Chapter 23

Selling Through Private Venues

In This Chapter

➤ Increasing your income through seasonal and home shows

➤ Using an open house or studio tour to sell

➤ Giving make-it/take-it parties for fun and profit

Selling through studios, workshops, open houses, home shows, and parties is just another way to get your products into the consumers' hands. Artisans are working together to make these sales events pay off for them, big-time. In this chapter, we fill you in on the details so that you can decide whether any of these marketing methods should be added to your bag of tricks.

Home Shows and Seasonal Boutiques

Artisans across the country report that home shows are a very successful way to market their arts and crafts. A group of artisans joins together and sets up a craft show, either at someone's home or at a temporary rental location, such as a party room or a space at a church or fire hall. The group's members contribute their time, share the expenses, and sell their merchandise at the show. They send invitations to their customers and advertise the event locally. They usually serve light refreshments and make the event fun with door prizes and grab bag gifts for customers who bring along a friend or two. These events are particularly popular during the selling seasons; in spring, around Easter; at Mother's Day; and in the fall, which covers Halloween, Thanksgiving, and the holiday season.

Artisan's Corner

An enterprising group of 37 artisans set up their canopies in a large backyard every summer and invite their customers to a free hot dog roast and craft show. The customers loved the special treatment, and the continuing success of this annual event proves it.

Pointers

When a group of artisans teams up to do a series of home shows or home parties, there's a wider selection of merchandise to offer and more people to cover the scheduled events.

Shows can vary in length, with some lasting just a weekend and others running one to three weeks. During the holiday season, some groups of artisans set up series of shows in different localities spanning the same three-week period. The artisans then work together to run the two- or three-week event. Other groups of artisans set up several shows on the same date in a single locality, offering shoppers a marathon of shows to visit on the scheduled dates. The invitations to the shows include all the show dates and maps with directions to each location.

An extension of this concept is the in-home host-sponsored parties that go on throughout the year. Artisans book a party at a private home, and the person hosting it invites his or her own guest list of family, friends, and co-workers. The host or hostess receives credits based on the total sales made at the party that can be applied toward any items offered for sale. Some artisans sell only what is on display, while others may only take orders—and, of course, some combine both.

To increase sales, it's helpful to give the person hosting the party a catalog or perhaps an album of photos with descriptions and prices before the event. You'll be amazed at the number of extra sales that the host will get by showing it to family, friends, and co-workers who can't attend. Artisans who sell this way also report that they can always plan on additional sales from the ripple effect of the party plan (people admiring an item bought at a party and wanting to buy a similar one, and so on). That's why it's so very important to have all your contact information on your hang tags and on every piece of literature that you give out. Think of them as extra sales staff working for you.

Artisans' Open House or Studio Tour

If you have a working studio or shop location large enough to allow customers to visit, you should plan to have an open house at least four times a year. Customers love to see how an artisan works. This trend is becoming very popular in many parts of the country and has even extended to group studio tours, coordinated by several artisans who live near each other and who open their studios on the same date and share the promotion costs.

Whether or not you also advertise to the general public in addition to sending invitations to your customers really depends on how large an area you have to accommodate visitors.

Be sure that your work area is ready for customers—it should be clean and safe. Put away any sharp or dangerous objects or tools, make sure that there are no cords to trip over, and see that all your displays are secure and can't be tipped over easily. Sales from these events are reported as being very strong, and a good way to move some odds and ends of inventory that wouldn't work as show merchandise.

Artisan's Corner

A clever way to show customers what processes you go through to produce your products is to create a story board. Just take photos of an item at each stage of production, mount them on a poster board with a description for each photo, labeled "Stage 1," "Stage 2," and so on. A story board is a good PR piece, not only at your studio show, but also to display at craft shows so that your customers can understand how much work goes into the products that you are selling. It will enhance their perceived value.

Customers seem to really like the idea of being able to visit a variety of private showings, and they especially enjoy hearing artisans explain and show their work. You'll be surprised to see how customers turn out for these events and even bring along some friends (be sure to note on the invitations that guests are welcome). What you do is probably not novel to you anymore, but for people who are not artisans, it can be pretty exciting to get an opportunity to peek at what goes on behind the scenes.

Planning a Group Event

Some tips for planning a group event include ...

1. Select artisans for the group who do quality work in a nice range of crafts that complement each other but that are different enough to enrich the overall merchandise mix.

2. Consider the space available to display the crafts and the type of crafts that will be shown. Jewelry, for instance, may not require too much space, but a wood crafter with wall shelves, curios, or small furniture to show would need a lot of space.

3. You should have a written agreement that all the artisans sign agreeing to the terms and conditions of how the show will be handled, who is responsible for what, and how the shows costs and income will be handled.

4. Most groups share equally in all the show costs and receive the money derived from the sale of their own merchandise. Artisans mark their price tags with their initials or a code number so that the person who cashes out customers can record the sale on the individual artisan's sales sheet. It's a good idea to use per-forated two-part sales tags or a duplicate sales receipt book. Either provides a backup record in case the cashier gets busy and forgets to record a sale on a sales sheet. Artisans are usually responsible for reporting and paying the sales tax collected for their sales.

5. When your group is formed, you should have an organizational meeting to iron out all the details, set the show date(s), assign responsibilities, and set the work schedule. This should be at least six to eight weeks before the actual show. At this time, you should also decide on the theme and name for the show, and on decorations, refreshments, invitations, the mailing list, how the space will be used to display the products, and who will be responsible for bringing items such as tables, chairs, display pieces, and so on. Whether it's a single event or you're planning a series, you need to work out every detail in advance so that each event runs smoothly. This happens when everyone works as a team.

Pointers

Save the event checklists and or-ganizational meeting notes from the first event that your group plans. That way, more than half the work is done for planning your next event. You may have to make some changes, but you already have established the basic operating formula.

6. If you decide on grab bag or door prize gifts, being the crafty people that you are, you should be able to come up with inexpensive but clever handmade items to give out. You could use index cards to have guests sign in (to keep the mailing list updated for the next event) and then use the same cards for the drawings. Also decide what phone number(s) and information will be on the invitations. For instance, if you offer door prizes or gifts for bringing a guest, say so, along with any other information that will entice customers to want to come.

7. So that no one person bears all the up-front costs of the printing for flyers, invitations, postage, signs, and possible advertising, each participant should kick in some money to estab-lish a start-up expense fund. Someone should be assigned the responsibility of keeping a record of the up-front costs.

8. If a private home is used for the event, be sure that it has been cleared with everyone living there. If there are pets, find a place for them away from the rooms used for the displays or any area where customers will go.

9. Set your policies in advance on how to handle refunds and exchanges, cash, insurance, order-taking versus direct selling of the stock on hand, and the deposit policy for special orders. If it's a holiday show, customers may want the convenience of being able to take their purchases with them rather than having to wait for delivery.

10. Refreshments at a home show can make it seem comfortable and inviting; the option is yours. A good rule of thumb to follow is to have simple foods that can be prepared in advance, that do not require silverware, and that can be left out at room temperature for an extended period: things such as mini muffins, sliced date or banana bread, cookies, cheese and crackers, grapes and so on. Try to set up the food and beverages away from the sales area, and provide some seating, if possible. Tie the refreshments into the show theme and time of year. If you're having an evening high-end art show, perhaps wine with cheese and crackers and some finger sandwiches would be fitting. If you do serve something with alcohol in it, such as punch, make sure that it's clearly labeled, and also offer alcohol-free beverages.

11. If the area is residential, be careful about where you post signs directing people to the show ("Santa's Workshop" or "Spring Open House," for example). You could probably put them at the street corners and on the front lawn without any repercussions. Also post signs in the house to direct customers to refreshments, displays, and bathrooms so that they feel comfortable knowing where they should and should not go.

12. Use common sense about security. Block off rooms that you do not want strangers in, remove extra cash from the cash box as it accumulates, and put small expensive items in an area where you can watch them.

13. Always plan to have enough helpers to assist customers, monitor the sales areas, straighten up displays that get disturbed, and replenish stock as it sells.

14. Have plenty of customer merchandise bags and packing material for fragile items, plus your PR bag stuffers, on hand at the checkout area.

15. Don't forget to post policy signs about your return or exchange policy, returned check fees, or special order requirements near the checkout area. Private sales are subject to the same rules and regulations as those at a store or a commercially held craft show.

16. Be ready to open the doors at least a half hour before the show opens; there's bound to be an early bird or two. Make sure that the outside walkways are clear of

obstacles, snow, and ice. Double-check to make sure that displays are anchored securely and that there are no scatter rugs or extension cords anywhere that someone could trip over.

17. Plan on enough help for setup and breakdown of the show so that the host's home can be returned to normal after the show.

Artisan's Corner

Make-it/take-it craft parties for children's birthdays are a great promotional angle and can be inexpensive when paper or clay crafts can be used. The parties are profitable, and you gain exposure to a whole new group of potential customers with every party.

Artisan's Corner

Craft parties do not even have to involve making craft kits. They can be as simple as the "paint your pots" idea that's so popular. Just supply a range of unfinished bisque or wood items and an assortment of patterns, stencils, and paints that the party participants may select from to make whatever they like.

Make–It/Take–It Craft Parties or Classes

Make-it craft parties and classes for all ages are sweeping the country, and they can help you earn extra income, build sales, and develop repeat customers. You don't need a storefront location; you can offer craft parties or classes in your home, or go to a party location. These get-togethers are happening for birthday parties, club meetings, hobby groups, social entertainment, church groups, and the one-night-a-week-out crowd.

Joining this growing trend is easy. Develop several craft ideas covering a variety of age groups, interests, and price ranges. The wider the variety, the better. Offer a full-range program to build in repeat business and appeal to different age groups, including some that parents and children can participate in.

Write the instructions for each craft, and include a detailed materials list. Then test the instructions and list by following them to make the craft item. When you're sure that the instructions and materials are complete in an easy-to-follow, step-by-step format, you're ready. A good marketing ploy is to make up a sales brochure that features all the kits and kit prices, and photos of the finished items.

There are many ways to market craft parties. Contact local retail craft shops, and offer to hold classes for their customers. Contact church groups, clubs, senior citizen groups, scout groups, and other organizations. They're always looking for new ideas to use for meetings. Advertise in-home craft parties for children or adults, or start craft clubs that meet on a regular weekly or monthly basis. Local weekly newspapers are a good place to advertise, along with community bulletin boards and community activities' bulletins often offered by the local Chamber of Commerce or civic groups.

When the party business eats into your own time schedule, think about training others to offer your party plan. Fall and winter are great times to start. People are looking for activities to fill their leisure time, and there are endless possibilities as to the types of craft projects that you can offer. With a little creative thought, you can develop a program to take advantage of this exciting growing trend. Show and sell the fun that drives make-it/take-it craft party sales.

Follow-Up Pays

One of the most neglected areas of the sales process is follow-up. A customer is the most valuable asset that a business has. Yet so few business owners make a serious effort to cultivate an ongoing relationship with their customers. Some ways you can improve your follow-up are …

➤ When you're talking with a customer and there's some little thing that you know you could do for that person, or if you need to find out about something, keep a special notebook to write it down in, or write it on the back of your copy of the sales receipt. Right after the show, make it your number-one priority to take care of these little details. It may seem small and insignificant to you, but people will be impressed and pleased with your prompt response. It goes a long way in building your image and reputation with your customers.

➤ When you're working events, as you see methods or setups that should be changed to make things run more smoothly, make a written note of them. After the event, take the appropriate corrective action before the next one is scheduled. Experience is always the best teacher. As you do more events, you'll see things that can be done faster or more efficiently, or perhaps even eliminated altogether. Reacting quickly can save you time and money. And you know what that means—more profit!

➤ After every event, do an inventory, and not just of your stock; include all the other supplies and sales materials that you use. When you know what needs to be replaced, work it into your schedule to do it so that everything you need is ready for the next event. Trust me: Procrastination doesn't pay, especially if you have to place orders with suppliers to get the job done.

➤ Once you have even a small a network of customers, you should establish a regular newsletter. It doesn't have to be more than a one-page, three-fold self-mailer. Include some crafty tips and news about what you have to offer, such as special promotions or new items. Newsletters are also good vehicles for customer appreciation coupons.

Think of the home shows, studio tours, and craft parties as more than merchandising ends in themselves. Think of them as great ways for artisans to form customer relationships that they can build on far into the future.

The Least You Need to Know

➤ Private and seasonal shows are a viable way to increase your income.

➤ Artisans are increasingly using open houses or studio tours to market their work.

➤ Make-it/take-it parties are fun and can increase your exposure to new customers as well as add to your profits.

➤ Artisans working together as a team can enhance their customer base as well as their bottom line.

Chapter 24

Am I Ready for Selling Wholesale?

> ### In This Chapter
>
> ➤ Learning why timing is critical in selling wholesale
>
> ➤ Getting a handle on how selling wholesale works
>
> ➤ Finding the right sales reps for your business
>
> ➤ Selling directly to shops or galleries

As a consumer, I bet you've gone shopping during the back-to-school sale season and have been bombarded with the Halloween, Thanksgiving, and even Christmas and Hanukkah merchandise displays. And you think to yourself, "Good grief—that's months away!" But did you stop to realize how far in advance the manufacturers were working just so that these products could be on the retail shelves months in advance? This is what wholesaling is about, working in advance of the selling seasons. The major advantages of selling wholesale are repeat business and larger quantity orders. In this chapter, we give you an inside look at what it takes to meet the demands of making money at selling wholesale.

Timing Is Everything

Timing is critical to survival in the wholesale market. Your products must be ready in time for the wholesale trade season. Your spring and summer line must be ready for the January and February trade shows. Your fall through holiday line must be ready for the trade shows in July and August. Whether you elect to sell at the trade shows, use sales reps, or contact retail buyers directly, you must adhere to this schedule. Store buyers are programmed to plan their bulk purchasing during the established trade show time periods.

Artisan's Corner

Spring and summer wholesale lines are sold at the January and February trade shows. The fall through holiday season lines are sold at the wholesale trade shows in July and August.

Your reps may sell all year long, traveling their territory, visiting their store accounts, or working through temporary or permanent showrooms, but they usually contact the core of their customer base at trade shows or during the trade show season.

Wholesaling requires careful advance planning on your part. Keep a watchful eye on the styles, colors, and trends associated with your product lines. To sell successfully, your products must reflect each season's popular colors and designs. Store buyers generally want to purchase groupings of related products or products with companion items. I'm not saying that they won't buy a single, unique standalone item—just that, if that's all you have to offer, you'll limit your earning capacity. Stores look for product lines that will offer them add-on and multiple sales opportunities. They want repeat sales just as much as you do.

If you're wholesaling, you also have to work with your suppliers to ensure a consistent flow of raw materials and supplies so that you'll be able to fulfill the bulk orders that you receive.

Trade Show Marketing

Are you thinking about selling your products at a wholesale trade show? The major advantages of selling wholesale are the repeat business and the larger quantity orders. Trade shows are where a majority of buyers make their bulk purchases.

If you sell wholesale, you can be a vendor yourself, or you can opt to hire a sales rep to represent your line. (There's more on sales reps later in the chapter.) But the shortest route to success in wholesaling is via contacts that you can make at trade shows. There are large and small trade shows. When you're new to the business and you're doing the selling yourself, it's usually best to start out with the smaller regional shows.

Handmade, originally designed art or craft products are a perfect fit for the gift and home decor markets. Stores want new and different merchandise to offer their customers. This is especially true of the smaller or independent retailers. Their market is created by their ability to offer specialty products to their customers.

Although many exhibitors do well at trade shows, it's often costly, and unless your products have been market-tested and have a proven selling track record, you can sometimes be taking a chance. A trade show is *not* the place to test-market your line. It can cost anywhere from $500 to $800 for a small regional show to several thousand dollars for a major show. Then you've got to add the travel, lodging, food, and perhaps the cost of shipping your display and products. For artisans accustomed to "cash in hand" from retail markets, writing orders to fill in the future can seem like a letdown, but it's important to keep in mind that many exhibitors will take in many thousands of dollars in orders booked at trade shows.

Trade show numbers will dwarf what even the best retail show can offer you. You must realize, though, that it's a gamble, the same one that you take when you attend a retail show, but on a larger scale. If you invest, let's say, $3,500 in one trade show and don't reach above your breakeven point, you might cut into your cash reserves to the point of slowing down your other marketing avenues. Even if you do very well at a trade show, the production expenses are immediate, but the money received from the orders could be stretched out over a long period of time.

Large corporate buyers don't pay for their shipments up front. Most will only work from a 30-90/net payment plan, which means that they pay, at the earliest, 30 days after receiving your invoice, but that they have up to 90 days to do so.

Many of the large chain stores have their own fixed terms, so you must either accept them or forget them altogether. Can you accept their terms and wait for the payment? If you can't take the risk of overextending yourself financially, you may be better off turning down the business.

Crafter Alert

A retail art and craft show is a good test market for new items. A trade show is not the place to test the market with your line. Only items with a proven sales track record should be considered for inclusion with the product line that you assemble for a trade show.

Make sure that you state your payment policies clearly. And keep in mind how far you can afford to bend your own rules to make a sale.

When you're starting out, if you don't have the cash flow to go to wholesale trade shows or the money to risk on them, you may want to try other alternatives, such as selling via sales reps, selling directly to shops and galleries, or perhaps selling on consignment.

Wholesale Biz Tips

There's a lot to know about the wholesale business, and there's not enough space in this book to go into all the details. This section gives you tips on how wholesaling works in the areas of pricing, selling terms, orders, shipping, and scheduling.

Pointers

The difference between your suggested retail price and what the buyer actually pays is the wholesale markdown. So, for example, if your retail price is $20 and your wholesale markdown is 50 percent, the buyer's cost is $10. The average buyer expects a 50 percent markdown from retail, sometimes referred to as "keystone" pricing.

Whether you display wholesale or retail prices at a trade show is up to you. You may want to check with the show promoters beforehand to find out the norm for their particular event. Either way, prices need to be easy to find. If your displayed prices are retail, make sure that the wholesale price structure is in clear view. If you're displaying wholesale prices, be sure to make it clear to your customers so that they don't have to ask. The quickest way to lose a sale is to have to tell a potential buyer that the price he or she thought was retail is actually the wholesale price (therefore double what the person thought it would be).

If you plan to show both prices, I recommend displaying the wholesale price prominently and showing the retail price as the "suggested retail price" on your display tags. Always state "Wholesale Order Form" on your order forms, along with your terms and conditions, to prevent any misunderstanding. In Chapter 19, "Playing the Pricing Game," we covered including a 20 percent profit factor in your wholesale price. Make sure to do it before you start quoting any wholesale prices to buyers.

Selling Terms

Small businesses usually require payment by credit card, cash on delivery (COD), or prepayment by check for first-time orders. After several reorders from an established customer, some sellers allow a 30-day "credit line."

Credit card payment has become the most feasible way for small wholesale companies to take payment because it maintains cash flow without the risk of losses.

When you offer *open account terms* (a credit line that allows the buyer to pay in 30 days from your invoice date), it means that you've shipped the order and created an open account receivable (money payable to you). The result is that you're acting like a bank, extending credit to the companies that are buying from you, but having no guarantee of repayment. This could severely cut into your cash flow, so until you have sufficient cash available to take the risk, it's better to avoid offering open account terms.

Prepayment by credit card or check can be handled in several ways: The total amount could be due with the order; you could require a 50 percent deposit at the show, with the balance due before your shipment date; or you could split the payment into thirds, with the last payment due before your shipment date. If you ship COD and want to reduce your risk, you can require that payment be in cash or by certified check only.

Keep in mind that some buyers, especially those from larger organizations, will balk at prepayment terms. They usually require an invoice before they can get their accounts payable department to send payment. Plus, they're set up to make payment on their billing schedule, which could mean 30 days, 60 days, 90 days, or even longer before you get paid. Although most retailers are reputable and do pay on time, many small businesses can't wait too long to be paid because of their own overhead costs.

If you're not comfortable using someone else's payment terms, you may be able to work something out with individual companies. Negotiation is always an option. The worst thing that they can do is say no, but at least you tried.

Another payment option for larger organizations is a *pro-forma invoice* (the customer is invoiced when the order is ready to ship). In these cases, you could offer a 5 to 10 percent prepayment discount incentive if your cash flow situation makes it worth your while. Whatever you decide your terms are, decide on them beforehand and stick to them as closely as possible. Remember that an order is just a piece of paper until you're paid.

> **Trade Terms**
>
> A **pro-forma invoice** is an advance invoice. The company pays upon receipt of the invoice, and you ship after payment is received. Because the customer pays in advance, companies usually offer a prepayment discount. **Open account terms** extend credit to the buyer by agreeing to ship the order before payment is received.

Minimum Order Amounts

A minimum order amount is a certain dollar amount or number of products that must be purchased before a wholesale order will be taken. It can be $150, a dozen pieces of just one product—it's up to you to decide what it's worth for you to sell your products at wholesale. It's standard in the industry to set some sort of minimum order requirements to ensure that the buyers are buying for their businesses and not just shopping for themselves. People who are simply buying products for themselves will not reorder like a buyer who's stocking a store.

At trade shows, display your minimum opening order so that buyers know it without having to ask. If you don't require a minimum opening order, be sure to let customers know that, too. The more information you can give without explanation, the better. A few signs spread around your booth should easily do the trick.

Shipping Charges

State your shipping terms up front. Wholesale customers don't like surprises when it comes to the bottom line. Shipping costs are a big concern, especially on large items, such as furniture, that may cost quite a bit to deliver. Buyers must take shipping charges into consideration when pricing their products, so be sure to let them know what they'll be paying. If you give a total price on an order, include shipping, COD, insurance, and any other charges that may apply. Also include shipping costs in any price sheets or order forms that you hand out. This information will help the buyers decide whether they can purchase your product. Without it, they may just order from your competitor.

The standard wholesale shipping terms are "FOB (freight on board) your city/state." This means that the shipping charges the buyer pays will be to transport the shipment from your business location to the buyer's place of business. On your order form for shipping charges you can simply state "FOB your city/your state."

Scheduling Order Shipments

Give yourself enough time to fill orders. Let your customers know when an order will ship, and then ship it on time. Be careful not to overbook. If you can produce only 500 wood shelves in a month, don't schedule shipments for 1,500. Set up a scheduling book to help you know your available lead times for shipments in advance.

Using a Rep

The average sales rep commission for the gift and home decor markets is 15 to 20 percent. Select your sales rep or rep company carefully: Don't hesitate to ask for a resumé or references, and make sure that your product line fits with the merchandise the rep sells. Remember, you're contracting for the rep to work for you. Start with one good rep, and begin building a foundation before you start hiring reps for other territories.

Artisan's Corner

Professional reps do more than sales, and a good rep will give you feedback on how your work will sell in major markets, what new or add-on items you might produce, and what buyers have on their minds. This kind of input can help you make more informed decisions about your product line.

You need to hire a working rep who's a professional, who is talking with customers every day, in person, on the phone, or at a showroom. A good rep will give you feedback on how your work will sell in major markets, which can be a valuable asset if you don't live near any of them. Listen to your rep, who can be helpful in steering you to new or add-on items that you can produce and can tell you what buyers are thinking. That kind of information can have an impact on how you refine or add to your line.

Many reps who work with small volume producers report that each vendor they represent will do an average of $10,000 in wholesale sales at trade shows. If you don't have stock on hand, ready to ship, or if your items take considerable time to produce, then it's wise to seek these lower-volume sales reps. Don't start with a high-volume rep until you're ready.

A high-volume rep usually means about $50,000 to $150,000+ in annual wholesale sales. Ask the rep firm how many accounts it handles. Unless you're ready for high volume, don't start with a firm that handles 10,000 accounts; go for one that handles several hundred or a thousand.

To help maintain their cash flow, shops are buying closer to their margin and are holding less back-up stock, so they like to buy from producers who can replace stock quickly on fast-moving items. The shops make more money, and so do you. You must be able to meet the shipping times that you agree to. Shops can't sell your merchandise until it's on their shelves, and they won't reorder until they see how it moves off their shelves. You can sell twice as much if you can ship within two weeks rather than four to six weeks. The key is to select a rep who's in line with your production ability.

Contract negotiations with your sales rep are a primary issue. Be aware that reps usually want an exclusive territory. It's not wise to sign a territory agreement for commission on all sales in an area(s) before the rep can prove that he or she can sell your merchandise. Include a provision that you can retain any accounts that you've already established. Be sure to include reasonable performance time lines within the agreement, so that if the rep signs on but doesn't produce sales, you can replace him or her with someone who can.

Some reps sometimes sell a single item, not the entire line. When that item's sales fall off, the rep moves on to another item or line. This leaves the producer without effective representation.

Clearly define commission rates and payment terms, and pay the rep on time. Establish good communications and be reliable. Keep your rep informed whenever something happens that affects your mutual customer. If you run into production delays or shortages, be sure to inform the rep as well as the customer. The rep is your partner in maintaining good customer relations and should be treated with respect and professionalism.

Pointers

It's your job to provide the product samples, sales materials, order forms, and whatever else the rep needs to properly represent your products to the customers. It's also your responsibility to adhere to all government regulations concerning product safety and labeling.

Selling Direct

If you decide to sell direct to shops or galleries, choose those you want to approach carefully. Particularly if you're going to do the marketing in person, don't spend your valuable time on wasted sales calls. Make sure that the items you want to sell fit into the general merchandise format of the store. For example, if your items are country, there's no sense in approaching a modern, upscale trendy boutique.

Prequalify before you visit. Call to find out who the buyers are and when they are in the store. This will save you time and money. You have several options in approaching a store for the first time. You can call and make an appointment, mail a letter introducing yourself and then follow up with a phone call, or just drop in.

Crafter Alert

A store buyer is interested only in items that fit the store's image, theme, and price range. Stores have a specific customer base and want items suited to their customers' buying habits.

Be prepared and organized on each sales call. Have your product catalog, pictures or sales sheets (and a set to leave with the buyer), order forms, price lists, selling terms, and business cards. On direct sales calls, product samples are a plus—if at all possible, take a sample of each item. Have your sales pitch rehearsed, and move right along. When you're finished, ask for an order. Don't be intimidated; that's why you're there.

If you don't get an order on the first call, follow up with a phone call or a second visit. To avoid impulse purchasing, some buyers don't buy on the first presentation. Send a business thank-you card or postcard to thank the buyer for taking the time to review your line, whether you receive an order or not.

The Mail Approach

Contacting buyers by mail is fast, efficient, and cost-effective, and it gives you a wider range of exposure in less time than direct sales calls. To do it effectively, you should design a mailing package. To get steady results, try to mail from 25 to 100 pieces each week, but not more than you can handle following up.

The key component in the package is the sales letter, which should introduce you and your products in the most favorable PR manner and close by asking for the sale. Along with the letter, include a business card, sales literature, a price list, and an order form. The sales brochure must contain photos of your products of the best possible quality. Direct mail to a target market produces about a 1 to 5 percent response rate. To enhance the numbers, you must do follow-up. The most effective way to follow up is a quick call to the buyer about 10 days after the mailing.

As you can see, there are some important differences between selling to the wholesale market and selling retail. When you're new to the world of business, it's often best to use the as your training ground. When you're comfortable with it, you can move into the wholesale market. Many business owners are perfectly content with the income that they can achieve selling retail, and they never approach the wholesale market. Each business and each business owner has a different set of variables to consider when weighing the option of selling wholesale. Consider your choices, and make the decision that's best for you and for your business.

The Least You Need to Know

➤ To sell wholesale, your products must be ready far in advance of the selling season and in time for the trade show schedule associated with your target market.

➤ Trade shows are where most buyers do the bulk of the wholesale purchasing for their shops and galleries.

➤ Hire a sales rep that's compatible with your business size and the products you produce.

➤ Successfully selling to shops or galleries requires being prepared with a meaningful presentation and doing follow-up.

Chapter 25

More Ways to Make Money with Your Hobby

In This Chapter

➤ Making money publishing your own designs

➤ Profiting from licensing your designs to pattern companies

➤ Selling designs to book publishers and manufacturers

➤ Learning how to avoid the most common information–selling mistakes

---

Throughout this book, we've given you countless ideas on how to make an income with products. *Products are not the only way to make money with your hobby.* You can sell your original designs to magazines or book publishers, license the line to pattern companies, make pattern or design kits, design for manufacturers, write how-to books, or even self-publish your own informational materials. In this chapter, artisans who became successful at doing these things tell you in their own words how they did it.

Enterprising artisans just like you are building their incomes by selling their work in multiple markets. It's pretty exciting when you consider that there are so many opportunities to make money.

Publishing Your Designs

The best way to learn is from your own experience and the experience of others. In this section, artisans share what they've learned about extending sales of their products into new areas.

Nancy Olson, contract in-house designer for Delta Technical Coatings, in Whittier, California, started out as a freelance decorative tole (sheet metal or tinplate) painter and became a designer for a major manufacturer.

"I work my own hours as needed. I also freelance my designs to craft magazines.

"In 1993, I had been tole painting for seven years. In those seven years, I had managed a retail tole painting shop for two years and founded a chapter of the National Society of Tole & Decorative Painters. Like many of you, I have purchased more than my share of books about my chosen habit. Believe it or not, my love of craft magazines of all kinds is what led me to designing.

"The magazine *Decorative Woodcrafts* was new to the publishing world in 1993, and to show support for the decorative arts, it established a yearly Christmas Ornament Contest. The winning ornaments would be displayed at the Society of Decorative Painting Convention being held in St. Louis, Missouri, that year. Money would be raised by selling raffle tickets on individual decorated trees and would go to the Society's Decorative Arts Collection. I entered a silly-looking reindeer. My thought was that I would be contributing the ornament, and the Society would benefit from my participation.

"All thoughts aside, I went about my daily schedule of being a mom—carpooling, homemaking, and so on—when one morning in late February, I received a call from the editor of *Decorative Woodcrafts,* Bev Rivers. I knew that name. She told me that I had not won the contest, but that because of the overwhelming response, the publishers had decided to put out a holiday book of 50 designs. *Wow!* ... I'm going to be published .... Then she says, 'We will pay you the usual two-fifty for the use of your design and directions.' (Directions? Oh ... I never kept a copy of the reindeer, or the colors I used. Panic set in.) So I thought, two-fifty, that's nice. Just being published was enough. I discovered later that the 'two-fifty' was not $2.50, but $250. Wow! I was hooked! Now that's the way to go! Do you know how many things you have to paint to make that kind of money? Of course you do; that's what we're all trying to do, right?

Artisan's Corner

Publishing a design in a magazine can bring you additional income. If you include the use of a company's product in the design instructions, quite often the company will pay you an endorsement program fee. Sometimes you can double your income for the article.

"But wait, there's more. Not only did I receive $250 from the magazine, but by mentioning the Delta Paint Company, I got a check for $150, and then a $100 check from the company whose brushes I used. Now are you following this? That's $500, and it was so much easier than hauling things to a craft show!

"Since that time, I've entered all kinds of contests. I was in the *Decorative Woodcrafts* Holiday Book again in 1994, and then I went on to be one of five winners in the *Michael's Arts & Crafts Magazine* Holiday Ornament Contest in 1996. I had two winning entries in the list of five. I must have had a hundred crafters contact me for wood and directions, which I made money on, and then I received $100 from *Michael's,* $300 from Delta, and $200 from the brush company. Are you catching my drift?

"Here's how you begin to send your designs in to any magazine: Take lots of pictures of your work. Write a cover letter, just a few words, that gives your name, address, and phone number, saying something like, 'Thought you might like to see what I am designing now … does it fit in with any of your future publications?' Put the note together with a picture of the project and a self-addressed, stamped envelope, and send it to the editor of the magazine. Within a month to six weeks, you'll have your answer. Never send the same project to more than one magazine at a time.

"So, if I were to give you advice on becoming a designer, I would say, never give up, because rejection is the name of the game. What one magazine sends back to you, another one will take. The ornaments that won the *Michael's Arts & Crafts* contest were rejects from *Decorative Woodcrafts.*"

Licensing a New Line

Sharion Cox, of Crafters Gateway, licensed a line to Cross The Lilliebridge Publishers, after being discovered at a trade show. We asked Sharion to tell us about it.

"The little BEE-ANGEL 'GG' that I started with was introduced at the January 1998 International Needle Art Retailers Guild show in Nashville, Tennessee. Thanks to Cross The Lilliebridge Publishers, the cross-stitched BEE-ANGELS are now in many stores across the country.

"We are currently working on kits for the cross-stitch lover for more little BEE-ANGELS. I am producing new paint packets for these adorable BEEs with Donna White, who's doing the painting instructions, and we're working with the Homespun Woodshed to cut the wood. We are also negotiating licensing the line with companies that produce dolls, paint, and stamps. You can view the GG cross-stitch kits from the Cross the Lilliebridge site, www.crossthelilliebridge. com."

Freelance Designing for the Consumer Craft Market

Nancy Worrell, Nancy Worrell Designs, is an artist, author, and designer of personal, home decorating, and gift projects. Visit her at hometown.aol.com/designsby/.

"I've been designing for publication for about 10 years. My work has appeared in Mary Engelbreit's *Home Companion, Handcrafts Illustrated, McCalls, Needlework, Arts & Crafts, CraftWorks,* and *Popular Crafts* (a U.K. publication), and in Oxmoor books. I have two books currently on the market: *Paper Plus* and *Beautiful Wedding Crafts.* I currently have projects on the Kunin Felt Web site, www.kuninfelt.com.

"The following suggestions are in three parts: magazines, books, and manufacturers.

"**Magazines.** Research craft magazines to determine which ones suit the technique, style, and level of expertise that readers need to complete your project. Some magazines publish only quick and easy projects.

"When you've determined which magazines you're interested in contacting, look in the front for the name of the craft editor or senior editor. Write to the editor at the editorial address, and request guidelines for submitting projects, along with an editorial calendar. Most magazines work 6 to 20 months ahead, so you always find yourself thinking Christmas in May, June, and July.

"Each magazine has its own guidelines for submitting projects. When you first start out, most want to see photos of your projects, and some request samples of your written instructions. It's a good idea to send swatches of fabrics or small samples of painting or stitching, too. Editors can't afford to contract with someone and then find that the work isn't up to the magazine's standards. Submit your projects to only one magazine at a time.

Crafter Alert

"Most magazines buy all rights. This means that you no longer own the design. You can usually continue to create the project and market it at craft fairs, but that's all. Some magazines buy first rights, which means that they're the first to publish it. Then, after a specified time, the project can be published again."

—Nancy Worrell

"Fees paid vary widely, from $25 to $600 for a project. It depends on the magazine, the technique and complexity of the project, the reputation of the designer, and so on. Most projects are purchased for $50 to $150 for the completed project and instructions.

"**Books.** Again, research is very important. There's no point in contacting a publisher that specializes in tole painting books if you quilt. Also, note whether the books contain the work of more than one designer; being one of the designers is a great way to get published. The book publication process is very much like that for magazines. Booklets (6 to 20 pages) are usually handled in much the same way as magazine articles. The following is information on getting your hardcover book published.

"Here it's a little more difficult to find out who to contact. Most book publishers have acquisitions editors. Call the publisher and tell the receptionist that you're interested in receiving guidelines for submitting a book proposal, and ask for the name of the acquisitions editor for books in your craft area. If you attend major trade shows, such as those of the Association of Crafts and Creative Industries (ACCI) or Hobby Industries of America (HIA), you can visit the booth of the publisher and often get this information from someone there.

"Write a letter of inquiry to the acquisitions editor. This is preferably a one-page letter briefly describing your book proposal and giving some background information about yourself. I usually include a resumé. The resumé can include publications, exhibits, teaching and demonstrating experience, education (if appropriate), and organizations and guilds that you may belong to. If the publisher is interested, it will send you format requirements and ask that you complete your proposal.

"Book proposals usually require an introduction, which may be anything from an ad-type blurb to the introduction of the book. You'll also need to develop a chapter outline, a list of projects, the projected number of photographs and illustrations required, and a description of your target market. Some publishers ask for several writing styles: narrative, instructional, descriptive. They also want to know who you are, who you know, what you say, and why you think it's important.

"If a publisher is interested, contract negotiations begin. Have a publications lawyer review the contract; the $200 per hour is expensive, but it's money well spent, particularly when you first start out. A lawyer will help you understand what you're selling, what you're getting, and what your publication rights are, now and in the future.

"Some publishers will want to photograph the steps in the step-by-step instructions for your project, which may require completing many of the stages of a single project. This is extra work, so keep that in mind during negotiations. They may also want extra materials and equipment to photograph. For one of my books, I was responsible for the photography and illustrations, and I was given a budget for them. Publishers all work differently, and individual publishers may have different arrangements for different books.

Pointers

"Most publishers offer an advance on royalties. Royalty payments don't kick in until the advance has been covered, so unless the book is a very good seller, you may never see any royalties."

—Nancy Worrell

"An important question to ask during contract negotiations is what the budget and marketing plans are for the book. It's good to know up front how much selling you need to do to make the book a success. Of course, if you teach or have a following at galleries or craft fairs, you already have a local market. Most publishers have a trade account that allows you to purchase your books at wholesale and sell retail to students and in other nonprofit areas.

"**Manufacturers.** Many manufacturers have their own in-house design teams and occasionally use freelance designers to promote specific products. Some manufacturers form design teams using freelance designers. Manufacturers also pay endorsement fees if their product is included in a published article for a magazine or book.

"Manufacturers need projects for store/product project sheets, for Web projects (see my felt jewelry roll and box at www.kuninfelt.com), and for use in ads and trade show booths. The easiest way to begin working with manufacturers is through designer endorsement programs, which many manufacturers now have. If you use a specific product for all your projects and a magazine publishes one of your projects using a specific description of the product (with paint, for example, its name, color, type, and so on), you're probably eligible for an endorsement fee. Call the company and ask if it has a designer endorsement program, or ask to speak with someone in marketing. If it does, you'll be sent guidelines for submitting your work for the endorsement fee. Usually, the only requirement is a tear sheet (within six months of publication) and your name, address, and Social Security number.

"After you build a portfolio of designs using the company's product, you're ready to initiate a discussion about designing for that company. Or, if you've been doing great work and are amenable to using that company's products exclusively for the projects, then approach someone there with your portfolio.

"Payment for this type of work varies greatly from manufacturer to manufacturer. Other opportunities with manufacturers consist of doing in-store and trade show demos. For any of these avenues of work, it's helpful to attend trade shows and to belong to trade organizations."

The All Rights/Electronic Rights Issue

Barbara Brabec is a nationally known authority on home-based business and the author of several books on the topic. Her two best-known titles are *Homemade Money* (Betterway Books) and *Creative Cash* (Prima). Brabec has her own Web site at www.barbarabrabec.com/. She offers the following advice:

"Writers and designers have always been reluctant to sell all rights to a magazine for an article or a how-to project because no one likes to completely relinquish all the rights to their creative work. But as many have learned, sometimes you don't have a choice in the matter. It can be either sell all rights or sell nothing.

"But the Internet has greatly complicated things. Now, when a magazine buys all rights to your work, it not only has the right to publish it in the magazine, but it also may republish it in a book or on the Web. Sadly, some do this even when they don't have the right to do so. As I've stated in an article on my personal domain:

"'Professional writers in the nonfiction field first encountered the electronic rights issue several years ago when consumer magazines began to put the whole content of back issues on the Internet in spite of the fact that most of the articles in those issues had been originally sold to them on a first rights (one-time use only) basis. Many writers were shocked to discover their copyrighted articles floating on the Internet when they had sold only first rights to the magazines in question. I don't know how most professional writers are handling this problem today.'

"Designers and writers of how-to projects for craft consumer magazines are really having a tough time of it today because print magazines want the right to publish both in print and on their Web sites, but they don't want to pay anything extra for this. Because many professional designers and writers have their own Web sites today, this is presenting quite a problem for them. If they insist on retaining electronic rights, they'll probably lose sales.

"This is a complex topic that can only be touched on in a book like this. If you're interested in knowing more about it and the peculiar 'electronic pitfall' that I fell into when I began to provide content for an e-commerce site, visit my personal domain at www. barbarabrabec.com to find a feature article on this topic, along with feedback from others who are also being affected by this problem."

Crafter Alert

"I'm sure the amazing growth of the Internet and the flagrant disregard of copyright laws by both publishers and individuals has greatly complicated writers' lives and made it more difficult to earn a living from their work."

—Barbara Brabec, from an article on her personal domain

Making Money Selling How-To Information

Selling your how-to information couldn't be any easier than it is today. Computers and the Internet have made it easy to self-publish and sell your own material, right from your own Web site. Artisans find that selling information can be quite profitable. But there are hazards involved in planning, creating, producing, and marketing information, which can result in wasted time and money.

A Dozen Mistakes That You Don't Want to Make

In the hope that we can save you from some of the frustration and disappointment that other artisans have experienced, here we describe the dozen most common mistakes artisans make and tell you how to avoid them.

➤ **Mistake #1: Expecting to make real money with one product.** Many novice information entrepreneurs expect to make sufficient profit with one product, but unfortunately, in the real world, relatively few products will make a significant profit by themselves. Unless you stumble across one of them, you'll need to offer a line of related products or services to make any real money. Building a line of related products may seem harder than it is: Just review what you know and want to write about, break it into segments, and package each segment as an individual item.

Artisan's Corner

Getting an International Standard Serial Number (ISSN) lends credibility to your publication. Customers who see that it's archived by the Library of Congress will be somewhat assured that you're not some fly-by-night. The ISSN is used by libraries as a standard form of reference.

➤ **Mistake #2: Failing to sell related products/ services.** Some information entrepreneurs who are smart enough to recognize the value of offering several products make the mistake of selling a mixture of unrelated offers, appealing to different types of prospects in various scattered markets. This spreads their limited resources too thin, and they fail to reap the full benefits of offering more than one product or service to the same customer. Your goal should be to turn more prospects into buyers, increase the average size of each order, and convert more customers into repeat buyers.

➤ **Mistake #3: Failing to give marketing top priority.** Frequently, entrepreneurs put marketing on the back burner, but its importance can't be over-stressed. Marketing, or the lack of it, can make or break a business. Or, as the saying goes: "Marketing is everything." Therefore, give it a high priority.

➤ **Mistake #4: Using ineffective marketing.** A large percentage of marketing communications fails to stress the benefits of the products or services, and stresses the features instead. Customers want to hear "What's in it for *me*?" Make sure to tell them.

➤ **Mistake #5: Failing to use persistence in marketing efforts.** Many artisans fail to realize that marketing is most effective when the marketing message is repeatedly brought to the attention of the target audience. For whatever reason, a sizable number of prospects won't respond to marketing communications the first time. Presenting the message repeatedly will eventually convince more potential consumers to act on offers. The key is using marketing methods that you can afford to use repeatedly without breaking the bank.

Pointers

In the United States, information about getting an ISSN is available at the Library of Congress site at lcweb.loc.gov/issn/. The application form for electronic serials is located at lcweb.loc.gov/issn/ISSN.html.

➤ **Mistake #6: Trying to sell when no market exists.** Inexperienced info-marketers are often too optimistic about making money from information products. In their haste, they rashly jump headlong into investing too much time, effort, and expense to produce and market their products without first considering whether any sizable or expanding markets exist. They often find that they've wasted their time and money, which may have been avoided had they first researched viable markets.

➤ **Mistake #7: Failing to revise or update products.** Updating can inject new life into a product, and its newness can be used as a hook to gain valuable free publicity. Unfortunately, many products are pulled from the market after just a few years because they become dated. As long as worthwhile markets exist, it's possible—and smarter—to keep profiting from information products for years by keeping them current.

➤ **Mistake #8: Failing to reuse written material.** Developing a line of related products is more or less essential to real info-marketing success. The best products to add to your line are those that you create or otherwise control. This doesn't mean that you always have to create new material from scratch. Usually some information from one product that you've created can be reworked to create a distinctly new product.

➤ **Mistake #9: Pricing information products too low.** The value of an information product is often underestimated by its creator. Underpriced products don't profit you very much, and their value may be undercut in the customers' eyes. Price your products high enough so that you can afford to market them through

289

whatever channels seem necessary. This way, your potential for profit is considerably increased.

Pointers

In Canada, information about getting an ISSN can be obtained at the National Library of Canada Web site at nlc-bnc.ca/issn/e-issn.htm. To obtain an ISSN outside of North America, the best place to start is www.issn.org/.

➤ **Mistake #10: Not offering solid value.** A notable percentage of information-product creators fail to develop products that offer true, solid value for the money. Instead of creating products with detailed, step-by-step guidelines that help their audiences achieve what they want, too many products deliver vague, nonspecific information that leaves their audiences disappointed. It may result in returns for refunds and could discourage future sales to the same customers.

For your own good—and the customers'—your objective should be to do more than just profit from writing, publishing, and selling information—although that's a good incentive! It should be to also deliver solid, useful information that gives real value to your audience, even if it's a simple product such as a report or a booklet.

➤ **Mistake #11: Failing to test-market.** Even if you're fairly certain that a sizable market exists for a product before you create it, it's recommended that you develop your initial version in as simple a form as possible. This is particularly important during the start-up phase of your business, when you have less experience and capital. As you test-market a product and gather feedback on it from others, you'll find mistakes and identify areas for improvement. Improvements and corrections can be made easily and inexpensively while the product is in a simple form. It's not wise to tie up substantial amounts of money in a product until it's a proven seller. You could have big money invested in an untested, unproven product that may never sell.

➤ **Mistake #12: Overlooking low-cost marketing methods.** Particularly if you're new to information marketing, you need to be extra cautious with the way you use your limited capital. You can quickly lose a lot of money. A print ad in a large-circulation magazine can run several thousand dollars for just one issue, but it may not pay for itself in sales. On the other hand, free publicity and other forms of low-cost promotion cost next to nothing, yet can be valuable marketing tools.

While there are no foolproof formulas for success in the information market, now that you're equipped with some knowledge of common mistakes made in planning, creating, producing, and marketing information products, you have a much better chance of striking real gold, not fool's gold.

The Least You Need to Know

➤ Magazines will pay you for writing about your art or craft designs.

➤ You can profit from licensing your designs to pattern companies, and from selling pattern or do-it-yourself kits.

➤ Book publishers and manufacturers pay artisans for the use of their designs and how-to information.

➤ Anything that you really know about can be turned into a written information product or service.

Chapter 26

Should I Open a Retail Store?

In This Chapter

➤ Determining a retail store's profits

➤ Considering a store's location

➤ Selecting your product mix

➤ Ensuring success in retailing

Today, opening a retail store usually means operating seven days a week. Most stores are open six days from about 10 A.M. to 9 P.M., and on Sundays from noon to 5 or 6 P.M. But that's just half the story. There's the buying, receiving, merchandise pricing, stocking, completing paperwork, staffing, maintaining displays, and cleaning that goes on behind the scenes. Am I trying to discourage you? No, I'm just trying to alert you to the fact that running a store is a full-time *plus* commitment, not one to be taken lightly. In this chapter, we acquaint you with the basic factors that you need to consider to make an informed decision about whether a hobby-related retail store is right for you.

The Store

The most successful merchants are those who enjoy the challenges that come with the retail trade: learning about their customers, finding out how to meet customers' needs, creating something and seeing it succeed, and building a presence in the community. Profit motivation and an interest in arts and crafts are important, but they're only a part of the larger picture. The retail supply business has grown to more than $14 billion yearly! The yearly sales figures for a few of the big players in this retailing arena, including the stores that sell fabrics and accessories for home sewing, are ...

1. **Fabri-Centers of America:** $890 million
2. **Garden Ridge:** $197 million
3. **House of Fabrics:** $277 million
4. **Michael's stores:** $1,341 million
5. **Old America stores:** $131 million
6. **Tandycrafts:** $249 million
7. **Trend-Lines:** $206 million

Look impressive? Don't get excited yet; these are major chain store operations. Let's look at what makes a retail store work.

The Margin

In retailing, you know that if you've paid $1 for an item that you've sold for $2, you have a 50 percent margin. Half of the sale pays for the product, the other half must pay for all the other costs of operating your business—*plus profit*. Since store prices range from full price to many variations of discount prices, the margin of markup is usually figured at what percentage of markup a store requires to satisfy its pricing strategy.

The margin is calculated by dividing the original cost into the amount of markup and then multiplying the result by 100. The amount of money that a business adds into a product's price, over and above the cost of the product, is expressed as a percentage. A candle costing $.05 to produce that has a markup of $.10 (meaning that the price to the consumer is $.15) has a 200 percent markup.

Artisan's Corner

Some retailers operate successfully with margins as high as 55 percent or as low as 25 percent. Full-service, higher-cost retailers tend to operate at the high end of the margin scale; self-service, discount retailers operate at the low end.

Inventory Turns

The second basic is the turn of your inventory. For example, all of a product for sale at your store was purchased at a wholesale cost of $50,000. Your store has an overall margin of 50 percent, meaning that when all of the inventory has sold, $100,000 has run through the cash register. This is one inventory turn. Therefore, at five inventory turns, $500,000 is rung up.

Why are turns so important? Because a higher turn keeps your cash flow moving. But don't forget that with five turns, the first $250,000 is cost—the cost of inventory. Then you have to deduct all the overhead, wages, and taxes from the $250,000 left before you'll see a profit. Most experts agree that a healthy annual turn figure begins at four, though some retailers aren't happy unless they hit eight or more. What an average, well-managed retail store can expect in sales is usually four to six times its inventory turn.

Opening a retail store requires a sizable investment in start-up costs and inventory, plus a big advertising budget, particularly in the beginning to build customer traffic. I think that you can see by these numbers that the smaller your store is and the less inventory it has in stock, the less potential income you'll have. Most major retailers acknowledge that about 70 percent of their annual business is made during the fall through holiday buying season. Poor holiday season sales can wipe out a small retailer without sufficient back-up cash reserves.

Pointers

To open a store, you have to have financial resources. A lot of artisans choose to operate a home-based business first and then, by building the profits steadily with the help of lower overhead, they can eventually make the move to a retail store.

You can boost your inventory turn by dealing with suppliers that can replace stock quickly. This means that you can avoid having a large supply of product that just sits there in your warehouse. That's considered dead money; it's not working for you. This is why it can often be worth paying a slightly higher price to a vendor that keeps your stock flowing and turning, instead of getting a big discount on a large supply of a product that will sit in your warehouse for months or maybe years. Smart buyers at retail stores try to keep only enough stock to get them through about a month. By using speedy suppliers, they can do it, and keep those important inventory turns high.

Technology Is the Answer

A point-of-sale (POS) system integrates your cash register with your inventory database. Every time stock arrives from your suppliers, it's entered in the database. Then every customer purchase is tracked, and the items sold are deleted automatically from the database. True, a learning curve comes with a POS, but the advantages of having one can far outweigh the challenge.

The major advantages, in brief, are …

➤ **Inventory management.** A POS system gives you instantaneous information about your turns, which products are selling well, and which ones need help to get them moving.

➤ **Customer database.** You can create a valuable self-maintaining customer database that tells you which customers are buying what products and when. You have the ability at your fingertips to develop promotions that can be targeted to exactly the right customers at exactly the right time.

➤ **Savings of time and money.** When a POS system is up and running, most of your routine inventory tasks become automated, freeing you up to concentrate on other important functions that will bring customers to your store.

Location, Location, Location

What real estate agents say is true: There really *isn't* anything more important than location. It's particularly true when you're looking for a location for your retail business. A poor location can kill your business, even if you do everything else absolutely right; a great location *and* doing everything right gives you a big head start toward achieving success. There are two main factors to consider when you're choosing a location:

➤ **Demographics.** Who are your target customers? Which neighborhoods are filled with these potential customers? Which commercial areas cater to upscale shoppers, and which are for the budget-minded? If your target is the upscale customer, your store needs to be situated with other upscale retailers, and the same applies to attracting the cost-conscious.

➤ **Traffic flow.** Traffic flow is the heart of any business, so the answer is simple: An art and craft products store must be in a location with heavy foot traffic. Drive-by traffic is not as important and can sometimes even be a detriment; people don't like to have to get in and out of heavy traffic. If the location has a good, steady, walk-by traffic flow, four of every five people who walk past your store are potential customers or are shopping for potential customers.

The Sales Team

After location, people are what make a store work. The success secret of retailing hobby and art and craft supplies is showing, or teaching, the customer how to use them. Retailers must take responsibility to ensure that the customer will enjoy and will successfully use the products that they buy. If they don't, you won't be able to build a solid repeat business.

Because of the long hours that retail stores are required to stay open, you'll have to plan on enough employees to cover all the hours effectively, and have enough people capable of offering classes to teach customers how to use the products that you sell. This is an important factor in building a loyal repeat customer base.

Artisan's Corner

Gone are the days of putting products on the shelf and letting the customer figure out how to use them creatively. This means that you and the staff that you select must be knowledgeable, trained in the products and their uses, able to communicate effectively, committed to customer service, and, most of all, able to put themselves in the customers' place and bring enthusiasm and empathy to their dealings with customers.

Managing your staff can be one of the most challenging areas of your business. Make certain that your staff members know what they're aiming for. Set the pace for their success and for great customer service:

➤ Require that every customer is welcomed with an open-ended greeting, which is nothing more than a simple, "Good morning," or "Good afternoon," giving the customer a chance to respond openly and in kind. "May I help you?" is *not* an open-ended greeting because the customer almost always replies, "No thanks, I'm just browsing."

➤ When customers seek help, make it part of the sales staff's job to ask enough questions to find out exactly what they want to know, or to do, and help them do it. If a salesperson can't locate a specific item that a customer asks for, make it his or her job to do the research necessary to find a substitute product or an alternative solution.

➤ Mandate that the staff members treat every customer with the same respect that they themselves would expect as customers.

Time spent training staff is always time well spent. Your customers need a great deal of support as they develop their creative skills, so a high level of staff expertise and flexibility is critical to the success of your store.

Why Retail Arts and Crafts Products?

According to a survey commissioned by the Hobby Industry Association, 80 percent of all families in the United States have at least one family member who enjoys making arts and crafts. The people who enjoy arts and crafts make for a tremendous potential market for any retailer. It's a market that offers great diversity—from independent specialty stores that focus on one niche area, such as ceramics, beading, needle crafts, or woodworking, to large, multicategory retailers.

Can Retail Be Profitable?

Retail can be profitable if you can juggle an extraordinary set of skills: a love of dealing with the public, the courage of a lion, the insight of a teacher, and the vision of a psychic, not to mention a lot of financial smarts and hard work. In addition to your love and knowledge of hobbies, you'll find that you'll need to develop a sophisticated range of business skills and retailing know-how. Some tips for making your retail store profitable are …

➤ **Define your customer.** First, you must know everything possible about the people you're trying to attract. Start by doing the market research that we covered in Chapter 4, "Make Contact: Doing Your Market Research."

➤ **Supply the right product mix.** After you understand the demographics and interests of your target customers, then decide on the image of the store. Will it be focused on entertainment and creativity, or efficiency and bargain pricing? It's equally important to know the trends in your area and the interests that your customers have outside of their hobbies. These factors will influence your target customers' lifestyles and interests.

➤ **Determine value.** New retailers often mistake low pricing for "value." Experienced retailers understand that "value" for the customer is a complex mix of factors, and pricing is only part of it. Value is what will keep customers coming back, repeatedly—for instance:

➤ **Convenience.** Are you conveniently located? Do you make it easy to buy? Do you make it easy to return merchandise?

➤ **The right product mix.** Do you have the products that match your customers' interests?

➤ **Selection.** Are you well stocked? Do you have all the related products on the shelf that a customer may need for a project?

➤ **Display.** Do you show off your products with exciting, tempting display techniques that say "Buy me"?

➤ **Timing.** Do you offer new ideas as they happen and keep your product mix current with the ever-changing trends?

➤ **Service.** Will you do whatever is necessary to make certain that the customer will be successful with the products you sell? Will you offer classes? Are you prepared to answer any question?

If you focus on the items on this list, customers will pay a higher price for the privilege of doing business with you. If you don't offer much in the way of presentation, selection, or service, you'll need to offer convenience and efficiency, and be prepared to sell at a lower price.

Researching the Product Mix

No matter what else you do right, what keeps customers returning to an art and craft store is an irresistible dynamic product mix, plus the activities associated with the products. Your goal has to be finding out what your potential customers can't resist.

To gather information and ideas that will help you create the best possible product mix, follow these tips:

Pointers

Before you open your store, find out what crafting groups are active in the area. Learn what activities are popular and which customer interests or needs are not being met.

1. Visit the local schools and colleges, and speak with art teachers about their activities. Check with local arts and crafts guilds, and contact trade associations for research information.

2. Visit all the stores within your market area that are related to hobbies and arts or crafts. Evaluate what their merchandising plans are. Look for areas that they're not serving or that they serve in only a limited fashion. Compare what you observe to the research material that you gathered on your target customer to try to determine the kinds of products that may be needed and wanted in your market area.

3. Learn what products are everyday staples that your customers will expect to see on the shelf all the time.

4. The Hobby Industry Association's study showed that 77 percent of artisans give their finished items as gifts, so find out what popular gift trends are in your area.

5. How will seasonal products figure into your product mix? Studies show that 59 percent of artisans decorate their homes for the holidays with things that they make.

6. Pay attention to other related markets. Know what's happening in the home decor, computer, and do-it-yourself markets. Look for opportunities for crossover applications. The more you know about other markets, the better equipped you'll be to identify potential crossover opportunities.

Store Layout and Design

Being a creative person, you probably don't have to be told just how much a visually exciting, colorful retail environment can do to capture your customers' attention, or how that translates into sales.

Retail store layout and design is a huge subject, which we can only touch on here. There are some other sections about it in this book; for example, Chapter 21, "Batteries Not Included: Preparing to Sell at Professionally Promoted Shows," which is about arts and crafts shows, contains a lot of useful advice about how to display handcrafted products to their best advantage. In Chapter 30, "Staying Ahead of Your Competition," we take a look at future influences on design and the use of color.

How Color Affects Your Displays

Depending on your target customer for a particular activity, using one color scheme versus another can be the difference between a display that sells and one that's ignored. If you're targeting children, for instance, you'll want to use the primary reds, blues, and yellows. If you're targeting an upscale customer, you may want to use colors that send an elegant signal, perhaps regal purples, rich earth tones, or dignified blues. Color isn't the only criterion for great displays. Don't forget about adding texture, composition, and the proper lighting and signs.

➤ Warm colors, such as red, yellow, orange, and pink, impress the eye and enhance the appearance of most merchandise. To the eye, they move items forward in a display.

➤ Cool colors, such as blue and green, appear calm and soothing. To the eye, they enlarge the display area.

➤ America's favorite colors are blue, red, green, white, pink, purple, and orange.

➤ Certain colors affect our emotions. When considering colors for your display themes, signs, and backgrounds, keep the following in mind.

  ➤ **Red.** Powerful, exciting, the attention-grabber. It appeals to the emotions. It's more difficult, however, for the brain to process, and it has a negative connotation when associated with money.

  ➤ **Yellow.** A dynamic color. It's associated with happiness and sunshine. Too much of it can be testy, though, so yellow should be used in moderation.

  ➤ **Blue.** Soothing, tranquil, and calming. It's associated with water and is considered conservative. Blue is one of the least exciting colors, but it's one of the most popular ones in the United States market.

  ➤ **Green.** Puts people at ease and has a positive connotation associated with money, the ecology, and nature. It was *the* color for the 1990s. It makes people feel secure and more creative.

➤ **Orange.** Communicates informality and unisex style. It quickly catches the eye, so it works to call attention to something that you want people to notice.

Arranging Merchandise

Displaying your merchandise in a store is not as difficult as it may seem because there is a standard formula to follow. And what makes it easier is that it works for all types of products. The basic strategies for arranging merchandise are …

➤ **In a vertical presentation.** Light down to dark, small down to large, warm down to cool.

➤ **In a horizontal presentation.** From left to right, light to dark, warm to cool, small to large.

If you follow this basic formula you'll be able to plan your merchandise layout in a logical and eye-pleasing manner.

Artisan's Corner

Few people can walk past a mirror without "sneaking a peek," so include mirrors in your displays—behind a product or under a product—and you're guaranteed to stop traffic.

Store Traffic Flow

The placement of your shelving and display units will play a powerful role in determining what may or may not happen in your store. Rather than just using straight aisles, consider diagonal placements of display units and circular directions for traffic flow. This traffic flow circulates customers in subtle patterns that may lead them to discover areas of the store that they may not have seen if the store had traditional straight aisles, predictably stocked.

With these ideas in mind, go shopping in a variety of stores, large and small. Pay attention to how they make use of color, texture, traffic patterns, displays, signs, and other things to project their image and boost sales. Store design is a profession in its own right. It may be worth the investment to hire a store design consultant to help you create an effective ambience that will translate into sales and repeat customers.

Advertising and Promotion

Advertising is essential to your survival. How else will the public know that you exist? Most retailers budget between 3 and 5 percent for advertising and marketing. A Yellow Pages ad is important. Beyond that, different retail markets usually require different methods of reaching potential customers.

Many successful retailers swear by direct mail and newsletters; others find that newspaper and radio advertising pays, while still others rely on cable television to reach their target audience.

Offer Classes and Training

The majority of consumers who take classes make most of their purchases at the store where the class was offered. There's no question that seminars, workshops, and ongoing classes are proven business builders. They bring regular customers and new ones into the store and introduce people to new projects and products. A well-run activities and education program will help build your bottom line.

Targeted Promotions

Attention-getting events are very effective. You could have a T-shirt or sweatshirt painting event, a family scrapbook night, a floral arranging event for every season, or an ornament-making contest, or you could even let your customers participate in creating the event. Have a suggestion box, and reward customers whose ideas are used with free supplies. Manufacturers will often help by providing a representative to meet with customers and put on demonstrations.

Staying on Top

Becoming successful is just the beginning. Staying successful is the ongoing challenge. The arts and crafts industry is an ever-changing market. It's more important than ever that retailers stay current on trends and new products while watching for opportunities that may be just around the next corner. There's no secret to staying current other than to constantly be doing your market research. Spend time tracking your customers' interests, and survey them regularly to stay on top of any changes that may be in the wind.

Artisan's Corner

Many very successful merchants will tell you that the most valuable information they get each year comes from sitting down and swapping ideas with non-competitive peers at the trade shows.

Attend Trade Shows

Where else but at a trade show can you find such a concentration of products and retail know-how? Most trade shows offer retailing seminars and training programs to boost your store's success—and don't forget the big benefits of networking and meeting new contacts to help you build your business. Sharing information and ideas can make or break your business.

Manufacturers and distributors clearly understand that if you're successful, they will be, too. Many vendors offer assistance and support for their customers.

Retail Resources

You're not in this by yourself. A wealth of resources can help you build a successful retail store operation. Here are just a few:

The Hobby Industry Association, www.hobby.org, focuses its attention on the creative products retail store. Visit the www.i-craft.com for project sheets, ready to download. During the annual National Craft Month in March, your customers can win gift certificates that they can redeem in your store.

Gifts and Decorative Accessories magazine (www.giftsanddec.com) is the trade publication for retail stores of ready-to-sell gift and accessory products, loaded with store retailing tips, trends, and tons of supplier information. 345 Hudson Street, New York, NY 10014. For subscription information, call 1-800-309-3332.

Wholesale suppliers: Call NCA at 1-800-715-9594, or visit www.craftassoc.com/dirwhbks.html. Also look up wholesale suppliers in the section on your craft in Appendix A, "Resources."

The Small Business Administration (SBA) (www.sba.gov) is a top-notch place for new store retailers to get start-up assistance and financing information. Or, call your local SBA office.

The Gift Association of America (GAA) serves as a trade association for gift and decorative accessories retailers. Contact 612 West Broad St., Bethlehem, PA 18018-5221; phone: 610-861-9445; fax: 610-861-0948.

Crafts and Needlework Age (*CAN*) is the trade publication for retail stores, featuring craft and needlework supplies. Call 1-800-258-0929 for subscription information. CAN Creative Data Service, 650 S. Clark St., Chicago, IL 60605-1702.

For additional information on store retailing see the following books:

> Antoniak, Michael. *The 21st Century Entrepreneur: How to Open Your Own Store: Everything You Need to Know to Succeed in the Retail Marketplace.* New York: Morrow, William & Co., 1994.

> *Stores and Retail Spaces 2.* The Institute of Store Planners and Visual Merchandising and Store. New York: Watson-Guptill Publishing, 2000.

> Varley, Rosemary. *Retail Product Management: Buying and Merchandising.* New York: Routledge, 2000.

As you can see, if you're thinking about opening a retail store, there's a lot to consider, and a lot of research to do before—and when—you take the plunge.

The Least You Need to Know

➤ Margin and inventory turns are ways to determine the financial success of a retail store.

➤ Retail stores should be located close to the target customers' neighborhoods.

➤ Your product mix needs to satisfy the interests of your customers.

➤ The staff and educational programs that you offer build good community relations and are key to the success of a retail hobby and arts and crafts store.

Part 6

Marketing Strategies That Will Help You Build Your Business

This part covers the stuff you need to know to keep your business up and running as you continue to grow. Building a business is like laying a foundation, one block at a time. Each one you put in place adds structure to what you already have in place. Marketing is like that; the more you expand your efforts, the more opportunities you have to build your profits. The chapters in this part prepare you for running an ongoing, growth-structured business using marketing tactics that you can take to the bank. We also included a special chapter on how to put the Internet to work for you and how to avoid letting the competition eat up sales that you should have had. Marketing your product or service is as critical to your business success as having the right product or service at the right time. That's why we devoted the entire closing part of this book to helping you get a grip on the keys to success in marketing your business now and in the future.

Chapter 27

The Big Marketing Secret

In This Chapter

➤ Grabbing attention for your marketing message

➤ Using your printed materials as silent sales partners

➤ Finding ways to market your products or services

➤ Learning how confidence counts in your marketing efforts

The big marketing secret is that there is no single successful marketing technique, no magic wand or magic bullet that will catapult you to financial success. Successful marketing is a *combination of marketing techniques* carefully planned to work together to achieve the desired results. It goes without saying that you can have the best product or service in the world, but if you don't project that message to your potential customers, how will they know that you exist or be encouraged to buy from you?

For small businesses, and particularly home-based ones without storefront visibility, this is a major, ongoing, uphill battle. Major media advertising costs are almost prohibitive for a small start-up business, so what do you do? Get creative and put together a marketing strategy that your budget can handle and that is focused on your niche market. This chapter gets you started by telling you about some of the marketing techniques that are working for arts and crafts entrepreneurs—and that can work for you, too.

Getting Attention

Do you remember when the game show *Let's Make a Deal* first premiered? In those early shows, no one wore goofy costumes (as later became the standard), and contestants were picked from the audience at random. One day, an audience member tried to increase her odds of being picked by wearing a goofy costume—and it worked! There's an important lesson in effective advertising here: Before you can sell to someone, you must *first* get that person's attention. Common sense, right? It's surprising how often we fail to spend enough time getting the prospect's attention before we jump into the sales pitch.

With the amount of direct advertising mail, ads, commercials, and e-mail messages increasingly crowding our lives, most of us tend to ignore anything that doesn't stand out from the pack. You don't need to dress up in a goofy costume like the game show contestant, but you *do* need to work at making your ads a little different. It's the key to getting attention, the first step in selling.

Crafter Alert

Don't look for a magic bullet to achieve your marketing target. Create a plan using a *combination of marketing techniques* that will work together to capture your market's attention.

Know for a fact that you can increase your marketing profits 5, 10, or even 15 times just by concentrating on creating heart-stopping, desire-creating titles and headlines. What is the number-one most critical element in your marketing piece? It's your *headline*. Think about it: When people read the subject line in your e-mail messages, they're reading a *headline!*

The power of headlines will make or break you on the Internet, just as it will in print advertising and sales materials. Create a powerful, captivating headline, or you'll lose out to other people's attention-grabbers.

Your Silent Sales Partners

Your sales materials, catalogs, brochures, signs, bag stuffers, hang tags/labels, stationery, and product packaging are your sales partners. They should be designed as an integral part of your advertising and marketing strategy.

I'm going to say this first because it's the most important thing to consider in designing all your printed materials: *Put complete contact information on everything!* Okay, I hear the home-based business owners pushing the panic button. You don't want people showing up at your door unannounced. Release the button. The answer is simple: get a PO Box. If you want customers to believe that yours is a credible business, you must give them complete contact information. You can't create a professional business image without it. In fact, the more convenient you make it for them to reach you, the better. That means by phone, fax, e-mail, regular mail, and your Web site. Put all this information on every piece that you create and on your Web site.

The second reason why complete contact information is so important is: *more sales!* When someone buys your product and shows it to a friend who then wants one or wants to know what else you carry, or when the customer gets home from your shop or show and decides to buy that matching piece after all, if your contact information is attached to your products, you may just have made another sale—or two.

Complete contact information is essential, but it's not your only silent sales partner:

➤ Try to select a business name that reflects what your business does. You'll save a lot of time and money in marketing if you start with a name that tells customers what you're selling. For example, if you were a candle maker and named your business Crafty Candles and Accessories, just think how much more quickly a potential customer could identify with your product line than if you'd named it Crafty Designs.

➤ Use a hang tag or label on your products. It gives them a packaged finishing touch that singles you out as a professional merchant. The hang tag identifies you (the manufacturer) and your product. It should reflect the image that you want to project for your products and business. To do this, you should consider color, size, logo or graphic, information needed, method of attaching it, and type of product(s).

If you have a product line that varies widely in material composition or size, consider using the same design in several sizes, colors, or font styles. Put creativity in your hang tags just as you do in your products. Make them stand out and serve a useful purpose. The goal is to have your hang tags reflective of your actual products for more emphasis.

➤ Print catalogs, sales sheets, and Web pages need to have the best possible close-up photos of your products. Rather than put prices in a catalog, use a separate price list. This will save you printing expense. Prices do change; when they do, you need to replace only the price list. Make sure that the product descriptions and the order form are complete and leave no unanswered questions. Nine times out of ten, once a potential customer gets stopped at any stage of the ordering process, the buying impulse dissolves and the sale is lost.

➤ Bag stuffers and show schedules or craft mall locations are very important PR tools. Always have an adequate supply on hand wherever your merchandise is on display. If you do shows and sell at shops, list them both on

Crafter Alert

All your contact information must be included on *all* your printed materials. If you operate a home-based business and don't want to use that address, get a PO Box.

the same flyer, and include all your contact information. There are great bag stuffers that can also be used in your customer mailings. Make up coupons to use as incentives to draw customers back for repeat sales.

➤ Use e-mail or direct mailings to keep your name and products on your customers' minds. Send at least four a year. Whatever you do, try to get one out to kick off the spring and the fall through the holidays seasons. Send news about new products and your selling locations, and perhaps include an incentive coupon.

➤ Product packaging can be a vital part of your sales message. It has two objectives: It should be designed to enhance sales appeal by making products attractive and customer-friendly, and it's another place to advertise your company contact information.

➤ Proudly display "Handmade (or handcrafted) in the USA" somewhere on your labels, hang tags, or the packaging. It will build the perceived value of your products and make them stand out from the commercially made and imported products that flood the marketplace.

➤ Get a separate phone line for the business, and put an answering machine or voicemail system on the line for times you're not available to answer in person. Use the recording to play a brief PR message to greet your callers. For example: "Thanks for calling Mollie's Dollies, producers of fine handcrafted porcelain collector series dolls." I called an NCA member, got voice mail, and was really impressed by the message. It went something like: "Thanks for calling ABC Woodworks. Leave your name and number at the sound of the beep, or stop by and see us today from 10 A.M. to 6 P.M. at the Apple Festival on Main Street." Now is that a proactive marketing message, or what?

➤ If you sell by mail or via the Internet, use a guarantee: "If for any reason our product doesn't meet your expectations, we'll exchange it or give you a 100 percent refund." You'll be amazed at how much more business you'll get with that simple guarantee. Removing the risk breaks down your customer's resistance and instills confidence that your claims must be true because you stand behind your products. It enhances your credibility because you certainly wouldn't guarantee a full refund if your product wasn't as advertised.

Removing the risk by providing a money-back guarantee works well when a product is involved, but how do you provide a guarantee when the transaction involves a service? Your customer can't return a computer programming job; the work was already performed. In lieu of offering a money-back guarantee, a service business can provide a guarantee to solve the customer's problem. For example, you can guarantee to come back without charge as often as necessary to get the program working properly.

Maybe you're reluctant to provide a money-back guarantee because you're afraid that some people may take unfair advantage of it. Businesses have learned by experience that you don't have to worry about refunds if you offer a quality product or service at a fair price. The buyers who take advantage of such guarantees represent only a tiny percentage of the overall increase in business generated by the security and credibility that a guarantee provides.

➤ Ask for the sale. When you sell by mail or via a Web page, you have to motivate customers to take action. Your words have to move them from passively reading about your offer to taking the next step, so tell them what to do next: "Don't Delay, Order Today!" or "Order Now and Take Advantage of Our Special Limited Offer." These are simple words, but they're powerful sales messages because they transport the potential customer into thinking about the next step—ordering.

How to Reach Your Target Market

To increase sales and your selling marketplace, you have to be aggressive and seek out new areas that you haven't explored. For example, sales reps do find artisans, but you have to be out there in the marketplace for them to find you. It won't happen if you stay at home. Sales reps find most of their new accounts in shops and galleries, at consumer and trade shows, in trade publications, in consumer magazines, and on the Internet. If you want new business, you have to make sure that your product is shown in all possible markets. The key is exposure. Only you can make it happen by getting into action. Most artisans recommend arts and crafts shows as the first place to put your sales emphasis when you plan to start selling handmade products.

Chapter 20, "Selling at Art and Craft Shows and Fairs," is full of information about how to choose the right shows for your product line and how to show your products in the best possible light.

➤ Corporate buyers are another marketplace that you should consider. There are several ways to access this market. Include corporate gift information in your catalog or sales flyer, add "executive gifts" on your business cards, let galleries and shops know of your corporate gift items, collect names and addresses from industrial and business guides, work through sales reps, and look for local businesses that give gifts to employees and customers. The corporate buyer is eager to find new and unique gift items. This is an area often overlooked by businesses, and it is a particularly viable one for handcrafted products.

Artisan's Corner

"With thousands of arts and crafts shows being held each year, how do you choose which ones to exhibit at? Start by thinking about what you plan to sell. Who will be interested in buying your work? Are your products impulse items, or will your customers need time to think about their purchase? Are your products large and difficult to carry? The answers to these questions will tell you a lot about what type of show will provide a successful marketplace for your work."

—Mary Reed, Editor of *The ABC Art & Craft Event Directory* (www.TheABCDirectory.com)

➤ Consider teaching a class at a local school or adult education program. The idea here is to broaden your exposure in your local area and gain recognition as an expert in your field. The more you're noticed in your community, the more people will be aware of you and of your products.

Pointers

Learn to use articles and press releases to obtain free media exposure for your products or business. Media coverage is a potent force in marketing because people are more inclined to believe what they read or hear in an editorial context than in an advertisement.

➤ Write an article relevant to your particular expertise, and submit it to local newspapers or entertainment magazines. In a small business, you have to be proactive in your PR—that is, take the initiative in creating and managing newsworthy situations, stories, and events to encourage news media to develop stories of their own about you and your business.

You can create a news story by presenting a new product or service that you've developed, by marking the anniversary of your business, or by something as simple as issuing a position statement about a community, national, or industry issue. Generate interesting information about your products or work. Provide useful advice, tips, techniques, strategies, or instructions. Position yourself as a local expert, and encourage media people to contact you to tap your expertise.

➤ Mark Fitzgerald, President of Sales Training Institute, Inc. (www.saleskills.com), trains professional salespeople and speaks nationally about sales and business development topics. He shares the following tips for achieving success in sales:

> Prospects become customers for *their* reasons, not *your* reasons.
>
> Your prospects love their own ideas and find them persuasive.
>
> Your prospects will resist your ideas and find objections to them.
>
> Prospects seldom initially share the real reasons that they would want to buy from you.
>
> The real reason that people buy may have nothing to do with the product or service offered.
>
> The real reason that people buy always has more to do with their feelings than with facts.
>
> The best salespeople develop the skills to get the prospects to do their own presentation of why they would buy before they spend a significant effort trying to sell them.

Believe in Yourself

Do you feel uneasy presenting your products or services to potential customers? Do you feel crushed when someone rejects your services or decides not to buy your products? Many experts agree that having such doubts is one of the greatest obstacles to success.

In marketing, it's important to believe in yourself and in the products or services that you provide. The best way to strengthen this belief is to make sure that you're as knowledgeable an expert as possible in your chosen field. If you harbor lingering doubts about your abilities, they may translate into insecurity when you speak with potential customers. In business dealings, the unspoken word can be very powerful. Customers sense when a person doesn't feel secure about his or her abilities, and it can ruin many a sales presentation. If you still have lingering doubts, turn your attention to improving your knowledge and overall expertise. It may require researching for more information, taking specific classes, or consulting or networking with other experts in your field.

Enjoy the process of becoming successful. Don't take yourself too seriously when things aren't going exactly as you planned. Maintain balance by cultivating the understanding that achieving success is an ongoing experience of personal and business growth, not an easily reached overnight accomplishment.

Crafter Alert

If you're taking rejection personally, you need to understand that you're not alone in this. To overcome negative responses, professionals fall back on their training and on the knowledge that they're practicing their professions as well as they possibly can. When you do the same, no matter what business you've chosen, you can begin to take rejection less personally and look at it as something that is inevitable in the ordinary course of conducting business. Shrug it off and move on.

Remember, you know your product best, so you are its best spokesperson. Take every opportunity to promote your work. You can't afford to be shy in business. Be aggressive! Get started immediately by drafting that press release that you need to announce the opening of your new business.

The Least You Need to Know

➤ Every sales message needs to start with an attention-grabbing headline to capture the attention of your targeted market.

➤ Design your printed materials to work for you as silent partners that project your marketing message.

➤ Successful marketing is using a combination of marketing techniques coordinated to achieve your objectives.

➤ In marketing, it's vitally important to believe in yourself and in the products or services that you sell.

Chapter 28

Effective Local Marketing on a Shoestring

In This Chapter

➤ Putting on your marketing hat

➤ Creating a local market for your product or service

➤ Learning the latest marketing techniques

➤ Developing a successful marketing campaign

Whether you're just starting a new business or you're already operating one, if you're an artisan, chances are good that you're limited to using "shoestring" tactics. Don't despair: Simple, down-to-earth marketing techniques have worked wonders for many small businesses. What's more, the latest trend in business development is based on building relationships within the community—with customers, other business owners, community organizations, and the media. Communicating with people and giving them real information about your products or services, real benefits, and outstanding customer service are low-cost techniques that work.

It's not how much you spend on marketing, but your ability to get your message to your target audience that can put your business on top and keep it there. In this chapter, we acquaint you with some shoestring marketing ideas that you can bank on.

Don't Overlook Opportunities

Any routine day presents you with countless opportunities to market your business. You may be missing them because you're not seeing everyone that you communicate with—whether by telephone, in person, by mail, or via the Internet—as a potential customer or someone who knows a potential customer. You'll want to learn to effectively market to these people. Never waste an opportunity for more exposure for your business. Every time you take some hours off from your business, put on your marketing hat; don't leave it behind! Wherever you happen to be, seize the moment. The following ideas can get you started:

➤ **Off-hours marketing.** Gain new exposure and potentially increase business by making your off-hours pay, too. Make sure that you're always armed with business cards or brochures. Remember, if you don't promote your business, who will? You never know when you'll be introduced to someone new, so keep a stash of cards with you at all times. If a new introduction includes mention of your business, great! If not, work it in. You should not let the person you met depart before you place one of your business cards in his or her hand.

➤ **Spread the word.** When you're at a cookout or out on the golf course with friends or business acquaintances, what do you talk about? Yes, sharing a leisure activity can provide a great opportunity to discuss your business. Perhaps not all of your friends and acquaintances know what your business is all about. Some of them may not buy from you, but they may have friends and acquaintances who could use your product or services. Make sure that you keep them filled in on what you're doing so that they can help spread the word. Haven't you asked friends if they know where you can get this or that product or service, and been glad to get good referrals? The Yellow Pages is okay, but a recommendation from someone you trust is the best.

➤ **Make it happen.** You're continually in circumstances that can be used to increase your business exposure—at the bank, the post office, a store, the dentist, the doctor, church, and meetings. Be creative; work your business into the conversation. Ask a question that prompts a response that you can use to work in your hot new product or benefit. The first few times, it may feel a little awkward, but after a few tries, it will feel as natural as saying, "Hi, how are you today?" Do some planning for the encounters that you expect to have—then speaking to people is really easy. After all, you're the expert on your business.

➤ **Take direct action.** The following are perfect examples of creating a market where none existed:

A crafter decided to enclose a business card in the envelope along with her check when she paid her bills, rationalizing that in most large companies, the likelihood of the same person opening her payment every month was pretty slim. She was rewarded with three inquiries the first month, which resulted in sales from two of them. Found business, right? Creating a market where one did not exist, that's the point.

Another clever artisan who sells florals purchased a bunch of inexpensive plastic business card holders. She filled each to capacity with a card that had one photo of her best-selling item and her contact information on the front, and a brief list of other products on the back. Then she visited local businesses (except floral shops), and asked if she could leave one card holder near the cash register. She placed these in 12 business locations in just one morning.

She was so encouraged by how easy it was to get cooperation from other business owners that she went right out and bought more card holders so that she could build on her marketing idea. Now, once a week she makes the rounds to keep them full. Why? Because it works! The increased exposure is bringing her a steady flow of new business she would not have had.

There are lessons to be learned here: Be creative, and never be shy about marketing your business everywhere you go! If you don't do it, who will?

Artisan's Corner

When you close up shop for the day, keep your marketing hat on! Wherever you go, make sure that you're always armed with business cards or brochures. Your business card is one of the most powerful marketing tools that you'll ever use. Be sure to leave one with everyone you meet.

The Business–Builder Marketing Approach

The trend in business development is toward relationship-based marketing, through networking and referrals, developing a niche or two, offering value-added sales, and generally being customer-driven.

Don't use a scattershot marketing approach; communicate with individuals. Act, react, and interact with them for your mutual benefit. No matter how many day-to-day problems you may have to solve, always give time and thought to building your business. Marketing is the foundation of its growth and financial success.

Pointers

A product or service is no greater than the market's desire and ability to purchase it! Learn everything about what your customers may want or need, and send the messages that they want to hear. Sell the benefits; answer the "What's in it for me?" question first.

Product Originality

NCA member Jack Wolcott of Handcrafted by Jack and Barb Wolcott, in Fleetwood, Pennsylvania, stresses that originality pays.

"I have been in the crafting business for a short five years. Because my experience is somewhat limited, I feel like a novice among professionals on this subject. At the same time, I feel that I'm able to see the business with new eyes.

"My sales over the past years have at least quadrupled each year. I attribute this to gaining access to bigger and better shows, producing a better product than I did each previous year, presenting my products better, and giving the buying public what it is willing to pay for.

"When I first started, I had one of those booths that had the same thing everyone else did. If I did $200, I was fortunate. I'd been in the sales profession for most of my life, so I recognized that I had a serious problem: There was no way I was going to get the sales I wanted while selling a product similar to what several other vendors sold.

Crafter Alert

Jack Wolcott's advice is right on target. Don't waste your time making and trying to sell what everyone else has; create your own original designs. As Wolcott says, eliminate your competition by producing something that your competitors don't have. The essence of any artisan's business is "specialty." It's why consumers spend money for your products. If your product or service is original, you'll have the business-builder marketing edge that's working for Wolcott's business.

"I began walking the shows and actually looking to see what everyone else had to sell. I went home, and I found, designed, reconfigured, and reworked products that no one else had. And, if it was similar to someone else's product, I made it in a way that it would present itself better and more uniquely. Basically, I was eliminating my competition by producing something that my competition did not have. Is that not what people want? Something different, something new, something they can have the first of in their neighborhood or group of peers? And the buying public doesn't mind paying more for something different or newer or better.

"I guess what I'm trying to say is that I'm learning to be unique, but I'm staying with what I feel people are looking for. I try to improve the quality of my designs, craftsmanship, and presentation—and I'm willing to change my product to suit the buying public as long as I work in the medium that I wish to use."

Increased Perceived Value

Selling your product at a higher price is what most people associate with increasing its perceived value, and it's true that many people assume that the higher-priced product is better. However, there are additional ways to increase the perceived value of your services or products:

➤ Service businesses can offer a free trial or sample of a service, such as a copy of your newsletter. This increases the perceived value because people think that you're confident in your product, so it must be good.

➤ Including testimonials about your products in your ad copy or sales materials increases their perceived value because you have actual proof of other people's positive experiences with your product. Testimonials can be as simple as a one-line sentence or a short paragraph. New business owners want to be on the alert for positive comments from their customers and should collect them to use in their copy. If you do this, be sure to get customers' permission first.

➤ Load your ad copy and sales materials with benefits. This increases the perceived value of your business or service because people see that your business is solving their problems.

➤ Give people a strong guarantee. It increases your perceived value because it shows that you stand behind your products.

➤ Get your product endorsed by a local or national celebrity. This increases the perceived value of your product because people think that famous people wouldn't want their names associated with a poor product. Getting such an endorsement is more feasible than you think, but you won't know unless you try contacting some of them.

Artisan's Corner

Selling your product at a higher price tends to increase its perceived value. People usually associate the higher-priced product with better quality. Pricing too low may cost you sales.

Reach Out

There are many other ways that you can use low-cost business-building techniques in your community to increase exposure and sales for your business:

Pointers

A big part of marketing success is creating a market, expanding into other sales venues. That means finding more opportunities to present your offerings to a new, untapped target audience. In other words, create a market for your products or services where none existed.

➤ **Sticky marketing.** This is a low-cost way to promote your business over and over for pennies. These promotional products have been around for decades, but they're so obvious that we often fail to think of them. *They are labels.* They come in all shapes, sizes, paper stocks, adhesive types, and inks. You can print them on your computer. You can buy a wide range of sizes and colors of stick-on labels in sheet form. *They are miniature billboards.* Put anything on them that you want—name, phone number, slogan, and product or service offer. Stick them on catalogs, sales flyers, craft show schedules, envelopes, product packages, cassettes, video tapes and business card backs, magnets, and mini calendars, just to name a few. Pass them out or mail them. Just use your marketing imagination. Days, weeks, months, and yes, even years from now, potential customers will see your sticker and call.

➤ **Business publications.** Scan local trade publications for announcements of promotions and special achievements in the business community. Send congratulatory notes and your catalog or brochure to members of the Realtor's Million-Dollar Club or to real estate salespeople who just got their brokers licenses, newly appointed vice presidents and managers, and so forth. Enclose your brochure or catalog with photos or line drawings of products that could make you the special local resource for business gifts!

➤ **Newspaper announcements.** Engagement and birth announcements represent another viable market for artisans. If you have your direct mail package ready ahead of time, it's easy to address a few every day as you follow up leads.

➤ **Hospital gift shops.** These shops are usually run by volunteers but have someone on staff who's in charge of buying. This is another market that's often overlooked. If you have a product that children, new mothers, or recuperating patients would enjoy, follow up on this marketing opportunity.

➤ **Museum shops.** These gift shops support the museum and its projects, and they can help support your marketing efforts if you have a product related in some way to art or history. You can create items based on a detail from a specific time period, carvings, replicas, models, cards and stationery, miniatures, jewelry, games or puzzles, or clothing or accessories with historical embellishments, to name a few. Unless a product is very familiar to customers, it will need a label or a hang tag explaining its association with the museum's collection or special exhibition.

➤ **Networking with other businesses.** Getting together for efforts such as the following can save each business considerable time and money:

> ➤ **Cooperative mailings.** If you know several people with the same customer profile or gift category (items for home decor, brides, or parents or grandparents of newborns, for example), you can share mailing envelopes for your sales material with certain businesses or a target group of businesspeople.

> ➤ **Home shows, studio tours, and party plans.** This is a simple but effective marketing strategy. For the how-to details, review Chapter 23, "Selling Through Private Venues."

➤ **Photo postcards.** These are inexpensive to produce and even cheaper to mail than a letter or brochure. They make great handouts and are a terrific way to introduce yourself by mail.

➤ **Yellow Pages ad.** You're never too small or too new to benefit from the exposure gained by an ad in the Yellow Pages of your phone directory. Check the subject guide in your local directory, and list all the possible headings that your product or service matches. Then narrow your list and select the one or two that you think will be the ones people will use to find your product or service. To be included in most Yellow Pages, you need to contact the publisher about six months before the next directory is scheduled for publication.

➤ **Sales reps.** Is a rep for you? Carolyn Spray, of CSpray & Associates, a sales rep company, has this advice:

"A good rep will take your product into his or her clearly defined territory and show your product to appropriate retail locations. Some—but not all—reps will include your products in their booths at trade shows. Most require the payment of a participation fee to help offset the cost of doing the show. The shows expose your product to a large number of people and can have lasting benefits in addition to the orders written. Your rep can be your best ally in providing customer service. They can correct small problems

Artisan's Corner

Modern Postcard (www.modernpostcard.com; phone 1-800-959-8365) offers 500 full-color promo cards for $95.

quickly before they become major ones; they also can turn a problem into a positive customer relationship. Long-term good customer relationships benefit everyone. Reps can also give you ideas. They're in touch with customers' taste in their area."

Pointers

If you're seeking a sales rep for handcrafted items, you may contact Carolyn Spray, at CSpray & Associates (1-800-378-3437; e-mail: CSpray2@msn.com). Be sure to have a wholesale price list, catalog, brochure, or good photos of your products ready to send her.

Ad Copy and Sales Brochures

Your ad copy and sales brochures should reflect and enhance your personal presence and the standing of your business in the community. Consider using some of the following tips:

➤ Use a handwritten quote or note in your ad copy with the printed text. You can use this for printed or electronic sales materials. Write it on a piece of paper, scan it, and add it to the copy that you're designing.

➤ Show before and after photos of how your product or service improved a condition or problem.

➤ Include an article or review that was written about you or your business, product, or service. This will show people that your business is respected, and it will increase your credibility.

➤ If you offer a free bonus incentive, also list its dollar value. It will increase the perceived value of the offer.

➤ Include your own picture in your copy. It makes your business seem like more than an invisible entity if customers see a real person representing it. Under the photo, include the business's contact information and a brief statement or quote.

The Four Marketing Keywords

Developing and actually getting through the course of a marketing campaign while trying to maintain your sanity involves a great deal of thought and appropriate action. Four keywords best describe the elements required of an entrepreneur in implementing a successful marketing program: plan, content, patience, and perseverance.

The Plan

Your marketing campaign must begin with a well thought-out plan, or strategy. Begin by determining exactly what you want to market and who you want to market it to.

Your carefully structured plan will include a budget, or how much you can afford to spend on your marketing campaign. When you determine approximate cost, you can pick and choose how you'll target your audience. Whether it's through a direct-mail campaign involving a sales letter and a brochure, or a well-structured press release sent to targeted media, you'll want to make sure that your documents are soundly and professionally written and printed. A plan ensures that you stay on course in your marketing efforts.

The Content

Your marketing tools must be packed with powerful content and graphics that will grab the attention of your audience and command action. Content is definitely *boss* when it comes to producing the perfect marketing materials. Fill your Web site, brochures, sales letters, press releases, and other marketing tools with positive statements and action words. Include testimonials and success stories as they are available. The bottom line is that you want your audience to know that you're the best and to choose you over your competitors!

The Patience

If you possess an ounce of patience, you have more to work with than most, and you'll need every bit of it—and more—during your marketing campaign. You're not usually going to see immediate results. You're not going to rake in your first million instantly. Every customer you deal with is not going to be easy to please. When you find your patience wearing thin, stop: Get yourself together and slow down! Think! Is it really worth a panic attack? Of course not. Just continue to take it one step at a time, and you'll accomplish your goals.

The Perseverance

Perseverance, along with persistence, tenacity, determination, and steadfastness, is what it takes to follow through on your marketing plan. As you implement your plan, you're going to likely run into roadblocks along the way; people may tell you that your plan will never work; you may have doubts or wonder if you're doing the right thing. Don't allow fears to determine the outcome of your challenges. Everything worthwhile is worth working for. You must make the commitment in your heart and in your mind that—no matter what—you'll persevere!

Artisan's Corner

Creating a market for a product is a vital part of marketing. Businesspeople do it successfully all the time. That means you're a salesperson, even if it's not the way you think of yourself. Sales equals marketing. When you understand this concept, you're on the way to building your business.

By combining your ongoing business-building techniques with your well-planned and powerful content-marketing campaign, as long as you have patience and perseverance, you'll have a formula that will take your business anywhere you want it to go.

The Least You Need to Know

➤ Market your business on a shoestring by creating opportunities to talk about it wherever you go, and then follow through by passing out your business cards.

➤ A big part of marketing is creating sales opportunities and then consistently following up on them.

➤ Marketing works when you have powerful content in your sales materials, and have the patience and perseverance to implement your plan.

Chapter 29

Put the Internet to Work for You

In This Chapter

➤ Putting together a good Web site

➤ Marketing from your own domain

➤ Using e-mail effectively

If you live in the real world, you know that you can't turn on the television or radio, or flip through any print media without being hit with the .dot-com explosion.

According to Nua Internet Surveys, (www.nua.ie/surveys/how_many_online/) as of September 2000, the world's number of online Internet users was estimated to be 377.65 million, with Europe accounting for 105.89 million, and the United States and Canada 161.31 million users. The numbers are increasing every day. At this stage in the game, it's not a question of *whether* you should have a Web site, but how soon you can get one working for you. When you consider what a Web site can do for your exposure, the cost of designing and maintaining one is minimal and, as major marketing investments go, affordable for a small business. In this chapter, we give you the basics on the elements of a good Web site and what you need to know to take full advantage of this incredibly powerful marketing tool.

Web Site Start-Up

The Internet is the great equalizer. The *Web* (*World Wide Web*) levels the playing field and offers your small business an equal opportunity to compete with the major players.

If you have a truly professional-looking Web site, visitors have no way of knowing whether you're a one-person business or whether you have a staff of a hundred and a 10,000-square-foot warehouse. How you handle this great opportunity is what will make or break your *Internet* marketing plan.

Trade Terms

The **Internet** is the electronic superhighway composed of millions of interconnected computers and servers that exchange massive amounts of text and images on a worldwide basis. The **Web,** short for **World Wide Web** (**WWW**), is loosely defined as the portion of the Internet with pages that are interconnected by hyperlinks that allow us to access other Web pages with just a click of the mouse.

Your site needs to look like it's a commercial Web site rather than an amateur home page. The design needs to be consistent from page to page and should be easy to navigate. Contact details, including physical address, phone numbers, and e-mail address, need to be clearly displayed. You can buy Web site creation software and do it yourself, or hire a Web page designer, or Webmaster (person who designs and maintains Web sites). In Chapter 7, "Using a Computer to Lighten Your Business Load," you can find sources for software and search engines. But whether you design and maintain your Web site yourself or you hire someone, you need to know the basics of what makes a good one.

➤ **Figure out your plan.** First you need to determine the purpose of your Web site. Is it for selling, information, customer support, or mainly a catalog to support other marketing efforts? Then decide on the layout and design. Content is everything on a Web site. You must take time to prepare good content before you start. Most online shoppers are attracted by a casual-style presentation of information. Imagine how you would pitch your product if the customer were seated right in front of you. Everything needs to be coordinated to present the image that you want in a professional manner. This is your storefront.

➤ **Examine your product.** The first area to review is the product or service that you're offering. Does a market exist for it? To answer this question, you need to find out whether similar products are being sold successfully on the Internet. If they aren't, you may need to rethink your Internet strategy. If others are selling a similar product successfully, then this would tend to confirm that there is a market for your product. Next, look at the strategy and pricing being adopted by your competitors. How do you compare? Why should your visitors buy from you rather than from one of your competitors? In other words, do your market research. Also take a critical look at your product quality. Does it live up to the claims that you're making? If not, improve your product so that it does, or modify your Web page content to be more realistic about it.

➤ **Avoid graphics.** To ensure that your page downloads quickly and that your Web host provides a dependable, fast connection to the Internet, graphics must be minimized. Net surfers won't wait for a slow-loading Web page; they'll just move on to a competitor's page. Skip all the flashing, gimmicky stuff—most viewers find it distracting. Keep your site simple and easy to navigate. The rule is two clicks maximum to reach the desired destination on a site.

➤ **Craft catchy titles.** Ensure that your Web page has a strong headline that grabs your visitors and makes them want to read more. Your headline should in effect say, "You have this dilemma; here is the solution." For instance, if you sell gifts, "Gifts for All Occasions" is strong. It says what you offer. Follow that by suggestions such as birthdays, anniversaries, graduations, showers, and so on to demonstrate that you can solve their gift needs.

➤ **Make it easy to order.** A great number of people abandon a Web site in the middle of the order process. Common reasons for this are that the order process is too time-consuming or complicated, or, worse yet, that there wasn't enough product detail for the potential buyer to make a purchasing decision. Anything that stops the buying impulse can kill the order right then and there.

Pointers

A merchant credit card program is critical to generating sales from a Web site. It is the preferred payment method used by online shoppers. Chapter 13, "Money Matters," covers information on obtaining a merchant credit card account.

Artisan's Corner

Take every opportunity to gather comments from your customers about how your product has helped them. Get their permission to publish the comments as testimonials. An easy way of getting comments is a customer feedback survey, which can also be used to identify ways to improve your product or to develop additional products that your customers may need.

➤ **Welcome credit cards.** The number-one preferred method of payment by on-line shoppers is the credit card. Susan Grant, of Internet Fraud Watch, says that it really *is* okay: "Paying with a credit card is the safest way to shop online. Federal law protects credit card users if they don't get what they were promised or if unauthorized charges are made on their accounts." Now, pass on that reassurance to your visitors. State your credit card security policy, and emphasize how safe the new encryption technology is.

➤ **Provide solutions.** Your visitors are looking for a solution to a dilemma about a service, product, or gift. Do you know what dilemmas your visitors need to solve? You'll need to put yourself in their shoes to better understand what they're seeking so that you can provide it. When you've done that, design your Web page content to show that your product will provide the solution that they need.

➤ **Provide testimonials and guarantees.** Testimonials and guarantees can have a huge impact on your level of sales. On the Web, a main priority is to build credibility. For example: "Loved your online basket-weaving course!" M. Berry, Tulsa, Oklahoma. Then put those quotes in high-traffic locations. The common components of a Web site are a privacy statement, a newsletter, testimonials from satisfied customers, a strong guarantee, and full disclosure of your contact information. Introduce yourself or another key person in the company by using a real name and a photograph. This brands the site as belonging to a real, live person and creates a subtle bond. An "About Us" page is the perfect place to build on that feeling. Here's where you explain what compelled you to start your business, what your goals are, what your business ethic is, and why customers should deal with you instead of your competition.

By building trust, you can slowly but surely turn your window-shoppers into e-shopaholics, which will give *you* more time and money to build your business!

Web Site Marketing

The giants of consumer e-commerce have it all figured out. Their sites are sticky with customer interaction and follow-up tricks. They send a thank-you e-mail after every purchase and they deliver sales coupons weekly. Regular customers get newsletters and breaking product information. But only 16 percent of these retailers bother to send a simple re-marketing e-mail within 30 days. In addition, only half of them ask the simple question, "Would you like to be notified about related products?"

A recent report on e-commerce *stickiness* (marketing techniques used to keep customers returning) by Rubric, a provider of e-marketing applications in San Mateo, California, indicated that personalization (the heart of Internet marketing) would increase the likelihood that customers would purchase.

Rubric concludes, "The leading e-commerce sites are missing a large opportunity to increase their 'stickiness' by not effectively re-marketing to their own customers." The Rubric report restates the obvious in its conclusions on what's effective in e-commerce:

➤ Use interactive marketing to cross-sell, up-sell, and re-sell products. Want fries with your order?

➤ Apply database marketing principals of targeting and segmentation. For example, if Mom orders stuff to decorate the nursery, guess what—maybe she also needs infant clothes.

➤ Use personalization to broaden and deepen relationships: "Thanks for buying again! Do you want to use the same credit card that you used last time? By the way, you get a 5 percent discount for coming back." Face it, customers like to be recognized.

➤ Use continuous relationship marketing to build customer loyalty. The Internet offers astonishing powers of connectivity and communication. The e-commerce winners will ultimately be the retailers who put these powers in play. The more time people spend at your Web site, the more time you'll have to persuade them to buy your product or service.

Pointers

Web pages should be visually appealing. Encourage customer participation by offering interactive ways for them to use your site, and ask for the sale. Motivate the browser into action!

Keeping Visitors at Your Site

These are some powerful ways to keep visitors at your Web site longer:

➤ Provide your Web site visitors with content that they can't read anywhere else. People will stay longer to read original content.

➤ Remind your Web site visitors that they can print out your content. They may browse around your online store while it's printing. Provide targeted information that your visitors can use. Jewelry sites could give jewelry fashion and care information. Apparel sites could offer color coordination ideas and tips for clothes care. Wood products sites could explain different wood finishes and how to preserve them.

➤ Offer your Web site visitors a freebie if they take the time to fill out your online survey. They'll be at the site longer and might buy something afterward.

➤ Offer visitors free software that they can download right from your Web site. There's tons of it available on the Internet that you can use. While they're waiting, they might read your ad.

Pointers

Use headlines and subheadlines all over your Web site that will grab visitors' attention and get them to explore your Web site longer.

➤ Tell your visitors what's offered at your Web site at the very beginning. If people are confused about what's being offered, they may leave too early.

➤ Carefully proofread Web pages. People will get turned off and leave if they see a lot of spelling and grammar mistakes.

➤ Make your site text easy to read. Most people won't strain their eyes trying to read text that's too small, too light, or too bright.

➤ Use autoresponders to follow up your basic inquiries. An autoresponder automatically sends the message that you prepared after a customer filled out the inquiry form.

Why People Don't Buy

Some of the reasons why people don't buy are …

➤ They don't feel safe when they order. Remind people that they are ordering through a secure server. Tell them that you won't sell their e-mail address and that all their personal information will be kept confidential.

➤ You don't make your ad copy attractive. Your ad lists features instead of benefits. The headline does not attract your target audience. You don't list any testimonials or "guarantees included" on your Web pages.

➤ You don't remind people to come back and visit. People usually don't purchase the first time. The more times they visit your site, the greater the chance that they'll buy.

➤ You don't let people know anything about your business. They'll feel more comfortable if they know who they're buying from. In the "About Us" section, include your business history, profile of employees, contact information, and so on.

➤ You don't give people as many ordering options as possible. Accept credit cards, checks, money orders, and other forms of electronic payment. Take orders by phone, e-mail, Web site, fax, mail, and so forth.

➤ You don't make your Web site look professional. You want to have your own domain name, and the graphics should be related to the theme of your Web site.

Diane Morgan, of Morgan Mailboxes and More (www.dianemorgan.com), shares her views as an artisan and Web site owner.

"I think that your Web site has now become your first impression to your invisible customers. I almost picture my home page as the front of the house or my storefront, and that's the page that you want to have neat and tidy—that's what people see when they "ride" by your house. Don't clutter up your first page with free banners, advertising, frogs jumping across the page, or stars bursting, and so on, because that's like letting the weeds and grass grow too high in your yard. Make it appealing to first-time customers so that they'll open your door to come in and visit.

"I have learned by trial and error and many mistakes. I had checks only for purchases; people had to print out the order form, fill it out, write out a check, put it in an envelope, find a stamp, and mail it, or call me with orders. And I can guarantee you that if I wasn't home, I lost a sale. I then went to the merchant account, and shopping cart, and sales have increased dramatically. I know that when you're first starting out, the money isn't always there for expenses such as this, but make these things part of your business plan and goals, and save up.

"These are all things that make you look like a legitimate business and make your customers feel confident that you're going to create something really nice for them and deliver it, not take their hard-earned money and run! First impressions matter a lot, even more so on the Internet."

Artisan's Corner

"My first Web address was about three feet long because we had a free server, and I was at a site off of my husband's site, www. morganic.com/geocities/ TLCCreations/index.html. I look at that now and think, how in heaven's name would my hard-found customers remember all that? So we invested and bought separate *domain names* that reflect very simply what our sites want to be."

—Diane Morgan

Domain Name Game

Then there's the issue of domain names. A domain name is the text link name used to identify your Web site (also called a URL). It is like a phone number; no one else has exactly the same one. Although you may have been successful at getting the corporate name or assumed business name that you wanted, you may go to register your name on the Internet only to discover that someone got there before you and now owns what you thought was yours. We can't stress this strongly enough: *Thousands of*

Pointers

You can check for domain name availability and even register for a name at the National Craft Association Web site: www.craftassoc.com/ domainamecheck.html. If you need assistance with Web site design or hosting, go to www.craftassoc.com/wpdesign. html, or call 1-800-715-9594 for a free brochure and information.

names are disappearing every day. If there's an available version of the name that you want, grab it! You can always build the Web site pages later.

A question that we frequently hear is, "Do I really need to have my own domain name?" The answer in one word is: *yes!* If you put up your site with some of the free Web hosting services, the only company that benefits is the Web hosting company.

When you have your own domain name, the address of your Web site will be www.yourcompany.com or something similar. On the other hand, if you put up your site on one of the free servers that will put their big flashy advertising banners at the top of your home page, the address of your Web site will be something like www.somebigfreeWebsite.com/members/ yourcompany/. Which of these two sounds more professional? Your customers will feel more comfortable buying whatever it is that you're selling if you have your own domain name. It makes them feel that they're dealing with a large, established company, not some fly-by-night operation.

E-Mail Rules

If you do nothing else, learn how to use e-mail correctly. No matter what size your business is, e-mail has become a major communications and marketing vehicle for businesses. It's imperative in this business environment that you learn it and use it. Not only does it speed communications, but you'll also save time and money. E-mail is sent and received free worldwide.

➤ **DON'T WRITE IN ALL CAPS.** On the net, this type of writing is considered to be shouting or yelling at your recipient. If you send an e-mail to someone in all caps, the recipient will have one of two opinions of you: You're extremely rude or maybe angry about something he or she did, or you're a beginner who doesn't know any better yet. I doubt that you want to give people either of these impressions. If you want to add emphasis to what you're saying, try one of the following instead of caps: Use a * symbol; use quotes around your text; add dashes, as in "----"; or use "...."

➤ **Hit the Reply button.** When someone sends several questions about a product or service, use the Reply button to respond, copying the queries from the sender's e-mail and adding your responses beneath them. (Just make sure not to cut out anything that your recipient will need to remember.) This is the simplest way to avoid sending "mystery" e-mails that just result in further unnecessary e-mails to deal with the matter.

➤ **Use a hard return.** After 60 or 65 characters, hit the Enter key. Some e-mail software will destroy the formatting of your message if you don't use a hard return—you never know what your recipient may end up seeing. It's also much easier to read an e-mail with short lines than an e-mail with lines that stretch all the way across the computer screen. You want to send a professional-looking e-mail.

➤ **Personalize your e-mail.** Everyone is busy, and *spam* is rampant (spam is defined as bulk unsolicited mail, usually containing an ad for something of no interest to you at all). Many people bypass messages that are not personalized, or read them long after they've taken care of their personalized mail. Always try to start your e-mail with "Hi," "Hello," or "Dear," and insert the name.

Crafter Alert

We probably run into this e-mail problem more than any other. Someone will ask the NCA a question. The NCA responds. Then the person sends a new e-mail back saying something like, "Could you give me a little more detail? Signed, Name Withheld to Protect the Guilty." The NCA responds to hundreds of e-mails daily. Now we have no idea what to "give details" on. Use the Reply button!

➤ **Keep your *signature file* short.** A signature file is a little five- or six-line note that your e-mail software can add to the bottom of every outgoing message. The signature file should not exceed six lines and should include your name, contact information, and a benefit phrase (written like a headline) of why someone should contact you for more information on what you can do.

➤ **Never send spam.** No matter how tempting all the hype is about buying e-mail lists to use for marketing, don't fall for it! Spam is considered an invasion of privacy by most active Net users. You can't start off on the right foot with your e-mail marketing campaign by annoying your audience. First impressions do count on the Net, just as in any other venue. Set up your Web page and post a free sign-up form to collect your e-mail list. This is called *permission-based e-mail*—and it works.

E-mail and the Internet are valuable marketing and research tools. The Internet is a powerful form of communication and sales that can put even the smallest business and the major players on a level playing field. More important, the *annual* cost of owning a Web site is probably less than you would pay for *one* good retail art and craft show. Having a Web site with your own domain name is an opportunity that you can't afford to miss!

Trade Terms

Spam is the term used to describe unsolicited e-mail, or "junk mail" as we call it when we receive it in our regular mail box. Spam is the opposite of **permission-based e-mail,** which is e-mail you signed up for or agreed to receive. A **signature file** is a closing to your e-mail that identifies you and provides your contact information, just as a letterhead does on your business stationery.

The Least You Need to Know

➤ A good Web site has quality content, is easy to navigate, builds customer confidence, and projects the image that you're building for your business.

➤ A Web site is another major spoke to add to the marketing wheel that will move your business toward continued growth and profits.

➤ As a businessperson, you need to use e-mail correctly, and use it as another business-building tool.

Chapter 30

Staying Ahead of Your Competition

> ## In This Chapter
>
> ➤ Avoiding the pitfalls of the comfort zone
>
> ➤ Developing and maintaining your creativity
>
> ➤ Planning for profits
>
> ➤ Keeping ahead of the competition by responding to change

Preparing this book for you has been exciting, sometimes exhausting, and very rewarding. In this last chapter, we concentrate on ways to ensure that you're in touch with your market, as well as ways to avoid letting the competition eat up sales that you should have had. We look at a variety of techniques that can help you stay ahead of the competition while you build your business.

Is Your Comfort Zone a Rut?

Your personal comfort zone is where you're comfortable in what you're doing, in your business, your job, your life, and your experiences. It is having no feelings of risk or anxiety.

Feeling comfortable is a nice idea, but it could turn into being in a rut. You may be thinking, what's so bad about that? Well, maybe nothing—unless you're in business: If you're in business, it can be dangerous. While you lounge in your comfort zone, the competition will more than likely be leaving you in the dust.

Beware of the comfort zone! In our fast-paced, competitive world, complacency can severely limit your personal and professional growth and can be fatal to your business. You need to keep your edge, which is the unique character of your products or services. To do that, you have to keep your ideas fresh and be open to diversification and change. You also have to be profit-oriented and keep your eye on social trends and your market's taste in arts and crafts. Doesn't sound very comfortable, does it?

So how do you step out of the comfort zone? Try some simple things: Drive home a different way, shop at a different store, sleep on the other side of the bed, try a new craft medium that you haven't worked in, use different colors to work with, or design a new item. Make a conscious effort to experiment.

Artisan's Corner

Experiment with a new marketing method. Allow your anxiety level to increase, and allow the adrenaline in your body to make you sharp, creative, and quick. As we try new things, we gain confidence in our ability to survive and to implement new ideas.

Here's the challenge to you: Make a list of 15 to 20 things that, if you could do them successfully, would help you feel more stimulated, energized, and productive—things such as give a speech, write and publish a design, start an exercise program, meditate daily, teach a new class, feed a homeless person, volunteer, try a new product, learn to work in a new medium, sign up for a craft class, start a new project that you've been meaning to get around to, and so on.

Choose one or two things from your list that you're willing to do within the next 30 days. Schedule them, and then go for it. Afterward, choose one or two more, and do it again. Make personal and professional growth a lifelong habit. Don't park in your comfort zone. It's bad for business; your competition *will* creep up on you.

Keep Creative Thinking Alive

A talk radio host told a story that he swore he had read in the local newspaper. Whether or not it actually happened, the anecdote provides a great example of *thinking outside of the box*. It seems that a man was driving home one afternoon when he got a flat tire. He happened to pull over in front of the city's largest mental institution. The man noticed one of the patients watching him from behind the fence as he grabbed the jack out of his trunk.

The driver loosened each of the four lug nuts on the wheel and placed them inside the hubcap that he had put on the ground. He put the spare tire on, but as he turned to grab the lug nuts, he kicked the hubcap and caused them all to roll into a sewer opening a few feet away. Dismayed, he screamed, "Oh no! Now what am I gonna do? I'm ruined. There's no way I can go anywhere now!"

A voice came from behind the mental institution's fence: "You still have four lug nuts on each of the other three wheels. Why not take one nut off of each one and put those three on the tire that you're changing. That should at least get you to a gas station or somewhere where you can get more lug nuts." The driver was relieved—and impressed. "Wow," he said, "that's amazing. How did you think of that?" The patient replied, "I may be crazy, but I'm not stupid."

Think about this story the next time you're faced with a challenge that seems insurmountable, or the next time you experience some type of creative block. *Don't focus on the problem area only.* Ask yourself, "What opportunities to remedy this situation are right here in front of me?" Look for a way over, under, around, or through the obstacle. Thinking outside of the box can keep you head and shoulders above the competition and in touch with your market.

Brainstorming

Brainstorming can help you come up with scads of new ideas; it can help you decide which are the best ones. Here are a few tips to help you get into the brainstorming mode:

Pointers

When you feel overwhelmed by challenges, or when your creativity seems to be at a standstill, think outside of the box. Get your mind off your anxieties, and look for ways to move forward.

➤ Always have a small notebook and a pen or pencil with you and on your nightstand. If you're struck by an idea, you can quickly jot it down. Go window-shopping in gift shops and department stores—just take in the sights, or browse home decor and gift catalogs. New, unrelated ideas are often sparked in creative minds by being exposed to a multitude of products, colors, shapes, and styles. Write down anything that pops into your mind. When you reread your notes, you may discover that about 90 percent of your ideas are off-the-wall. Don't worry, that's normal. What's important is the other 10 percent, the ideas that are workable.

➤ If you're stuck for an idea, open a dictionary, randomly select a word, and then try to formulate ideas that incorporate the word. You'd be surprised how well this works. The concept is based on a simple but little-known truth: Freedom inhibits creativity. There's nothing like restriction to get you thinking.

➤ When you have a problem, define it. It could be, "We need a new product for the holiday season." When you write it out concisely, you'll probably find ideas positively spewing out of your head.

➤ If you can't think, go for a walk. A change of atmosphere is good for you, and gentle exercise helps shake up the brain cells.

➤ Exercise your brain. Like bodies, brains need exercise to keep fit. If you don't exercise your brain, it will get flabby and useless. Exercise your brain by reading a lot, talking to creative people, and disagreeing with people—arguing can be a terrific way to give your brain cells a workout. But note this: Arguing about fashion trends or politics is good for you; bickering over who should take out the trash is not. If you work alone, hop on the computer and network with some other artisans to get those creative ideas flowing.

Brainstorming can generate lots of ideas. It's most effective with a group of people and should be performed in a relaxed environment.

But whether you brainstorm alone or in a group session, save all your notes; make it a practice to review them from time to time, and keep building on the list. You'll be amazed to find that looking at notes about your ideas weeks later can spark a whole new set of ideas. Continually generating new design ideas and marketing directions is the way to stay ahead of your competition.

Your Competitive Edge

The home-based arts and crafts business is no different from a storefront on Main Street in that sellers can sell only price, service, or product. Michael Treacy and Frederik D. Wiersema in *The Discipline of Market Leaders,* describe it well as *best price, best service,* or *best product.*

You can't be all things to all people—if you want to survive, you have to pick one and be the market leader in that area: lowest price, best service, or differentiated product.

Have you tried competing with the local Wal-Mart lately? So what's new? As one nursery business owner with a Wal-Mart nearby said:

"We have a simple business differentiation: If the big guys carry it, we don't. We grow the specialized plants that they can't find in the wholesale trades, and we make a reasonable living doing it. We know that we can't sell peat moss, bedding plants, or a common whatever, at their price, and we don't even try.

"Mom-and-pop operations have no business directly competing with the big guys, whether it's on Main Street or on a Web page. If they can't compete on price (and they can't), then they have to compete either on service or on product. If service differentiation is eliminated by the nature of your services (and usually this is not the case with artisans), then the only way that a small operation can compete and make money is by offering the *best products* or *best services*—the ones that the big dogs don't have, don't want, or can't find fast enough. If you sell something they don't, it isn't competition. Build in better service or better product to survive.

"Being a small producer of specialized products means that I'll survive quite nicely, thank you—well out of the range of the big dogs—either on the Net or on Main Street. They can't do what I can do, and I don't want to do what they do."

This is the built-in *competitive edge* that artisans have, the ability to use their original product designs to create their market niche.

The Customer Service Edge

In looking at the competitive challenges of being in the arts and crafts business, we eliminated the possibility of competing with chain store prices. Our nursery owner said that there was only one way that artisans could complete: with the best service or product. Customer relations was probably not a "service" that this person had in mind, but it is an area in which the small arts or crafts business owner can build a loyal return customer base.

The truth is that no business is exempt from the occasional customer complaint, and as sales volume increases, the odds are good that so will the number of complaints. This is an inevitable part of doing business. Even if you're doing absolutely everything right, someone will complain. Accept the fact that it's impossible to please everyone, no matter what you do. What's important is how you handle troublesome customer matters.

Trade Terms

When it comes to competing with chain stores, artisans have a built-in **competitive edge:** They have unique and original product designs that chain stores do not, which gives them a market niche.

Remember that the customer is always right. Never be confrontational, and remain calm (you can let it all out later). One grumbling customer can do more harm to your business image than 10 totally satisfied ones will do good. Why? People love to gossip about the bad stuff; it's just human nature. Treat your customers with courtesy, solve their problems quickly, and turn every negative situation into a positive one. Give them the attention and responsiveness that a chain store can't provide, and you'll have an edge on the competition. Plan to outperform your competitors in every area of customer service.

Crafter Alert

Don't hang on to products or services that are slow sellers. Take them out of your line, or re-design them.

Plan for Profits

The secret to success in your business is to *think profit* in everything you do. Profits don't just keep happening. Continually evaluate every aspect of your business operation, and *plan for profits!*

➤ **Provide a variety of price ranges.** Use inexpensive items as attention-grabbers to stop traffic. This is particularly important when you sell at art and craft shows or craft malls. You want to have something to stop traffic at your booth. When you have the customer stopped, your chances are greatly improved that people will browse your full line and buy something.

➤ **Be cost-effective.** Don't spend five hours producing an item that you can retail for only $30. Set a dollar amount for your labor, and factor it into every item that you make. Design products that keep the time investment low and the profit margin high. Learn to group tasks to save time, not only in product production, but also in all your daily routine business tasks. Pay all the bills at once, enter all the orders together, and set aside a specific time to pack and ship orders or order more supplies.

➤ **Be professional.** Don't be emotionally tied to your product or service. If a product or service is a slow seller or is not cost-effective, take it out of your line.

➤ **Follow market trends.** Stay updated on color trends, styles, themes, and lifestyle changes. Use these ideas to adapt your products to the hot-selling trends. Use your creative imagination to create new items or redesign some existing products or services. Remember, a small business has an advantage over big business; it can usually react to market changes much faster and reap the rewards. There's more on fads and trends in the next section.

➤ **Think about collectibles.** Create one unique design or pattern once or twice a year that is a signed, dated, limited edition. This builds repeat business and helps you sell companion products. A lady who made teddy bears did this. She sent an announcement about the limited edition to all her customers along with her show schedule. After a few years, she developed such a following that many of her customers called and placed orders sight unseen, just to make sure that they'd be able to get the next edition.

➤ **Have a hot seller.** Be prepared to ride the wave of a hot seller. Promote and feature your best-selling products. Look at what you can make in the way of compatible products to sell that will ride on the coattails of your sales leader.

➤ **Know your numbers.** Keep good records that can provide you with information to determine exactly where your actual profits come from. Review them to determine how to address unprofitable areas and then focus on the profit-making areas of your business. Sell in as many different markets as possible. This way, if one market is soft, you have alternative sales working to keep your income rolling in. Plan to make the time to evaluate all aspects of your business on a regular basis to guarantee a profitable, steady growth pattern.

Pointers

Always be on the alert for new items to add to your line. Nothing remains a "hot seller" forever. Have new items worked into your line on a regular basis, or modify an existing product to the current selling trends.

What Are Fads and Trends?

The latest styles, the hot new looks, new technology, or a new way of doing something … yes, they are as important to your product production as they are to the services that you may plan to offer.

What's the Difference Between a Fad and a Trend?

A *fad* is fleeting—here today, gone tomorrow. It might be a new color, such as hot pink, or a garden bug, or a woodland critter. I doubt that many people would want to decorate their entire house in hot pink or even live with it for the long term, but fads are fun touches for updating the home or for gift-giving. They're an important part of your business.

Trade Terms

A **fad** comes and goes; a **trend** has staying power. Some, but not all, trends, and even classics, started out as fads.

A *trend* has staying power. Some trends start out as fads and then move on to become trends, or even classics. Fads and trends can very quickly create consumer demand, and your sales numbers will reflect this if you keep your line up to date.

Artisans need to be aware at all times of what is happening in the home decor and gift industries. If you're unable to attend trade shows, a quick and easy way to keep up with the latest news is to go to your local craft supply store and take a look at the newest pattern books. Really examine what's on the shelves and in the sales circulars. It's a way to take advantage of the trend research that's already been done by professional buyers. Study trade publications, find out what's new, and then continue monitoring products to see what has staying power and what's on the way out. It's important to keep checking because trends, and even the classics, may eventually evolve and change over time. Just look at how country decor has cleaned up its act: It's lighter, has less clutter, and has more of a contemporary edge. Use industry trends and forecasts to help you with design ideas.

The Color Story and Social Trends

Color, and the direction it's taking, has always been a major factor in product design. CMG (Color Marketing Group) is a nonprofit organization made up of 1,600 color designers, founded in 1962 and based in Alexandria, Virginia. CMG members forecast *color directions* one to three years in advance for all major industries, manufactured products, and services for both consumer and commercial goods. CMG's forecasts serve as a guide for designers developing new colors for new and existing products.

CMG points to blue as an example of how color is influenced by social trends. Blue is both soothing and spiritual. It is also the favorite color of most Americans. In addition, blue is closely linked to symbols of our heritage and history, not to mention our favorite item of clothing. Blues have hit the marketplace in products ranging from dresses to dishes, but the clue to its lingering importance lies elsewhere. A variety of blues is now emerging in product categories where color longevity is valued. "Mass media and the Internet are changing the speed with which colors and trends move within our society, and around the world," says Sue Hannah, co-chairman of the Consumer Color Directions Committee. "A design launched in Tokyo today can be purchased in Des Moines tomorrow. It no longer takes years for a color trend to move from one continent to another."

With these important influences in mind, CMG members identified four color clusters that will be important to consumers during this next decade:

➤ **Techno-colors.** From gray to taupe to black and pure white, these colors are both from and for technology. Neutral colors are required for products that must work in widely differentiated environments.

➤ **Chromatic adrenaline colors.** These energetic hues will brighten color combinations and add punch to product lines.

➤ **Serenity colors.** These are colors influenced by consumers' desire for more balance and harmony in their lives. They are pale, soft, and reassuring; some come from nature, inspired mostly by water.

➤ **Mediterranean culture colors.** These are a group of rich, earthy, spice colors most often seen in textiles dyed with centuries-old natural methods.

Designing Trends Forecast

Forecasters of trends that will be influencing design in the new millennium point to the following:

➤ **Individualism.** People increasingly want to customize or personalize an object or their environment.

➤ **Simplicity.** People seek a more humanized way of living as a result of the recent incorporation of many new technologies into daily life. Softened, calm, and livable are strong themes surrounding the concept of simplicity, and they lead to forecasts for softer and lighter colors, as well as more neutralized color.

➤ **Spirituality.** Lead the spirit, lead the eye. Approach life with optimism and hopefulness. We are more comfortable expressing ourselves through intuition and our spiritual sides.

➤ **Water.** Cleansing and pure, water is a physical symbol of our themes of simplicity and spirituality. Water is the final evolution of nature's influence on the world's color palettes.

➤ **Ethnic and cultural blending.** Interest in colors of various skin tones is evidence of increased acceptance of cultural blending resulting from increased globalization. Christine Dickey, CMG Consumer Color Directions Committee co-chairman, says, "There is an expectation of interest in all things Australian, due to the 2000 Olympics. This will inspire a continued interest from all industries in browned oranges."

➤ **Texture and finish.** Visual and actual texture, patterns, and finishes increase the perception of quality and value. For example, smooth and soft textures can complement or act as a counterbalance to coarse textures.

Fads, trends, colors, and textures are a vital part of what keeps designing new products fun and interesting—*and what keeps your customers coming back for more!*

Product Life Cycle

All products and services go through a *life cycle.* They are the evolutionary four phases: infancy, growth, maturity, and decline. This starts from infancy (when it is developed) and moves to decline (when it is taken off the market). The perceived value and sales volume change throughout the life cycle. It's essential that you keep track of where your products or services are in their life cycle. It directly affects the amount of sales and income that you will receive during each phase, and it tells you when you need to update or cancel an item or create a new one.

➤ **Phase 1.** In infancy, the product or service is first introduced to the market and needs time to build customer awareness and confidence.

➤ **Phase 2.** Growth is the period in which sales are gradually building and competition usually starts to show up

➤ **Phase 3.** Maturity is the peak, the leveling-off period at which consumer demand has reached a saturation point in the market and competition is usually intense.

➤ **Phase 4.** Decline happens when customer demand is gradually reduced because improved variations, new technology, or other factors make the product less desirable or obsolete.

The life cycle plays an important role. A few years ago, for example, "garden decorative" products were new to the gift industry and home decor market. The market seemed to be able to absorb every decorative bird house, yard sign, and stepping stone produced. Today, however, buyers are selecting only the truly unique, distinctive items from this category because the market is maturing. In contrast, sales for home accessory categories are growing by leaps and bounds.

The 1999 market was estimated at almost $20 billion in wholesale dollars. This underscores how the gift and home decor market is apt to be driven by consumer attitudes and lifestyles that translate into consumer demand.

The Challenge of Change

Most new business owners often expect to devote a lot of time and effort to getting their businesses established. Then they plan to relax as the business "runs itself" and continues to grow. Maybe this was achievable in the past. It isn't today. Aggressive, innovative competitors and rapidly changing technology make it impossible to establish a system that will automatically meet all future challenges.

Expect Change

Develop a "change is normal" attitude. Realize that you're never going to reach the point at which you know your business so well that you can stop learning or being innovative. Just when you think you've mastered operating it, something will change and disrupt your growth.

Make it a habit to look for changes that may be part of a developing trend. Then try to determine how this trend may impact the growth of your business. You can develop the best solution to a problem when you catch it early and take your time to carefully work out your response. There's nothing more difficult than trying to make good long-term business decisions while you're trying to rescue rapidly falling sales.

Take Defensive Action in Advance: Diversify

Diversification is your best defense against the impact of change. This applies in two major areas:

➤ The products or services that you offer

➤ Your marketing activities

The primary reason that you want to offer a variety of related products or services to your customers is to maximize your income. But there's a second reason: Changing market conditions or an aggressive competitor can cause sales for a product or service to decline, often suddenly. The impact won't be devastating if a variety of other products or services continue to produce sales for you.

The same rule applies to marketing. You'll reach more prospects and generate more sales by using a variety of marketing methods than you will by using just one or two. This policy also protects you from suddenly losing a substantial volume of business because one of your marketing methods stopped producing results.

Look for Opportunity Hidden in Change

The challenge of change often forces you to discover a hidden opportunity that you can exploit to gain more business. I recently spoke with Ron Gallo, the owner of a small computer store near a fast-growing city in the Northeast. Two years ago, a large retail computer chain started building a new superstore nearby. Ron realized that he wasn't going to be able to compete with that store's prices and stay in business, so he set up a used computer equipment section in his store and started advertising that he would upgrade, refurbish, and buy or sell used equipment. Today most of Ron's income is generated by sales of used equipment. His total income has almost doubled, and he's even planning to expand his used equipment business to the Internet. It's an opportunity that Ron wouldn't have recognized without the challenge of competition.

The biggest challenge to business success today is change. Staying ahead of your competition is easy if you're aware of what you need to do and you then take the appropriate action. As you've discovered in reading this book, there are many artisans just like yourself who followed their dream of making money with their hobby. They've set up businesses and are dedicated to achieving their goals. My goal in writing this book was to pass on to you what my colleagues and I have learned

Artisan's Corner

Keep looking for and testing new marketing tools and some old ones that you haven't tried yet. Make it a habit to look for changes that may signal a developing trend, and then try to determine how the trend may impact the growth of your business.

from our experiences of working inside this industry for many years. Only you can decide what the right path is for you. Whatever your decision is, we wish you continued success in all your endeavors.

The Least You Need to Know

➤ Always staying in your comfort zone can be very limiting. In our fast-paced competitive world, complacency can limit your personal growth and be fatal to your business.

➤ Think outside of the box to develop and maintain your creativity. Originality gives you a competitive edge.

➤ To stay ahead of the competition, expect change, and respond to it quickly and creatively.

➤ Being successful in business means skillfully weaving all the components of your business together in harmony, guided by your vision.

Resources

This appendix begins with listings of general resources related to arts, crafts, and hobbies. It includes organizations and associations; publishers of books, videos, and designs; trade publications and catalog sources; and wholesale suppliers of materials. Following the general section, there's a section on the arts and crafts business—trade associations, business books, office supplies and computer equipment, legal issues, and more. In the alphabetical listings for specific industry segments, you'll find detailed information on every major area of your art or craft.

General Listings: Arts, Crafts, and Hobbies

In addition to the listings in this section, see the listings by specific art or craft category, and don't forget to refer to the chapters in this book, which contain a wealth of additional contacts and sources.

Arts and Crafts Show Listings

Chapter 20, "Selling at Art and Craft Shows and Fairs," contains a list of ways to find out about art and craft shows to participate in nationwide.

Associations

American Craft Council (ACC)
21 S. Eltings Corner Road
Highland, NY 12528
Phone: 1-800-836-3470

A national educational organization dedicated to the advancement of the American craft movement.

American Indian Arts and Crafts Association (IACA)
122 La Veta N.E., Suite B
Albuquerque, NM 87108
Phone: 505-265-9149
E-mail: iaca@ix.netcom.com

Supports the effective protection and ethical promotion of authentic Native American art and material culture.

Canadian Craft and Hobby Association (CCHA)
Phone: 403-291-0559
Web site: www.cdncraft.org/

Center for Safety in the Arts (CSA)
2124 Broadway, Box 310
New York, NY 10023
Web site: artswire.org:70/1/csa

Provides information on hazards and precautions in the arts.

Craft Emergency Relief Fund (CERF)
Box 838
Montpelier, VT 05601
Phone: 802-229-2306
Web site: www.craftemergency.org/

CERF provides immediate support to craftspeople suffering career-threatening emergencies such as fire, theft, natural disaster, and illness.

The Crafts Center
1001 Connecticut Ave., NW, Suite 525
Washington, DC 20036
Phone: 202-728-9603
E-mail: craftsdc@erols.com

A nonprofit organization serving the interests and needs of low-income artisans, the Crafts Center provides technical assistance and information to help artisans achieve greater quality, production, and sales.

Miniature Industry Association
Phone: 740-452-4541
Fax: 740-452-2552

National Craft Association (NCA)
1945 E. Ridge Road #5178
Rochester, NY 14622
Phone: 1-800-715-9594
Fax: 1-800-318-9410
Web site: www.craftassoc.com
E-mail: nca@craftassoc.com

The NCA is the information and resource center for the arts and crafts industry. It is a trade organization for beginners as well as seasoned professionals who are seeking business and marketing education and resources to build their art or craft business. The NCA helps entrepreneurs advance their business expertise and encourages them to network and build strong relationships with other artisans, the industry, and the community. NCA membership includes receiving the monthly *NCA Arts and Crafts Newsletter* and taking part in online discussions. *Mention that you discovered the NCA by reading this book, and you'll receive a 30 percent membership discount on an NCA membership.*

National Guild of Decoupageurs
Phone: 407-951-3929
Fax: 407-725-9792

Society of Craft Designers (SCD)
Box 3388
Zanesville, OH 43702
Phone: 740-452-4541

The SCD is an international, nonprofit organization serving designers in the consumer craft industry.

Surface Design Association
Box 360
Steastotol, CA 95473
Phone: 707-829-3110

The SDA promotes professional opportunities and education in the field of surface design, educating the public, and improving communication and dissemination of information among artists, designers, educators, and industry.

Publishers of Art and Craft Books

Contact the following publishers to obtain listings of their latest art and craft books and videos.

Allworth Press
Phone: 212-777-8395
Web site: www.allworth.com/

Publishes many books that provide practical information for artists, crafters, photographers, designers, and authors. More than 30 titles are listed that pertain to arts and crafts.

Alpha Books
Macmillan USA, Inc.
201 W. 103rd St.
Indianapolis, IN 46290
Web site: www.idiotsguides.com

Publishers of *The Complete Idiot's Guides* and other books related to arts, crafts, and operating a business.

The Astragal Press
5 Cold Hill Road, Ste. 12, PO Box 239
Mendham, NJ 07945-0239
Phone: 201-543-3045
E-mail: astragalpress@ibm.net

Publishers of books on metalsmithing, such as blacksmithing, silversmithing, tinsmithing, and goldsmithing, both modern and traditional.

Chester Book Company
Phone: 860-526-9887
Web site: www.chesterbookco.com

Full line of how-to craft books.

Design Originals
Phone: 1-800-877-7820
Web site: www.d-originals.com/

How-to craft books and videos.

Dover Publications
Phone: 516-294-7000
Web site:
www.doverpublications.com/dpubw/
index.html

Copyright-free designs and motifs.

Larks Books
Phone: 1-800-284-3388
Web site: www.larkbooks.com/

Hundreds of how-to art and craft books on all subjects.

Picture Perfect Productions
Phone: 310-838-5624
Web site: www.craftassoc.com/
makebows.html

Bow-making and gift-wrapping how-to videos.

Prima Publishing
Phone: 916-632-4400
Web site: www.primalifestyles.com

How-to business and hobby books.

Storey Books
Phone: 802-823-5810
Web site: www.storey.com

How-to art and craft books on all subjects.

Suppliers

Accu-Cut Systems
Phone: 1-800-288-1670
Web site: www.accucut.com/

Action Bag and Display
Phone: 1-800-824-2247
Web site: www.actionbag.com

Agora Online Supply
Web site: www.agora-
gallery.com/links/supplies.html

Bags and Bows
Phone: 1-800-225-8155

BJ Craft Supplies
Phone: 956-262-3719
Web site: www.bjcraftsupplies.com/

Box Co./Gift Box It
Phone: 1-800-654-2932
Fax: 954-424-1801

Colonial Crafts
Phone: 1-800-966-5524
Web site: www.colonialcrafts.com/

Craft Catalog
Phone: 1-800-777-1442
Call for a 200-page supply catalog.

Craft King
Phone: 813-648-2969
Web site: www.xmission.com/
~arts/ck/items.html

Craft Sources Online
Web site:
www.craftsitedirectory.com/supplies/

Crafter's Choice Magnets
Phone: 1-800-421-6692
Fax: 310-390-4357

Crafts Galore
Phone: 360-330-0200
Web site: www.craftsgalore.com

Creative Express
Phone: 1-800-563-8679
Web site: www.creativexpress.com/

Creative Paperclay
Phone: 1-800-899-5952
Web site: www.paperclay.com/

Creative Wholesale
Phone: 1-800-347-0031
Web site: www.creative-
wholesale.com/

Darice, Inc.
Phone: 404-238-1526
Web site: www.darice.com/

Decorator and Craft Corp.
Phone: 1-800-835-3013

Papier-mâché and rusty tin shapes and
surfaces.

Delta Technical Coatings, Inc.
Phone: 1-800-423-4135

Creamcoat acrylics and other
paintable surfaces.

Duncan Enterprises
Phone: 209-291-4444

Acrylic and dimensional paints.

Eagle Brush
Phone: 1-800-832-4532
Fax: 770-419-4855

EverGreen Bag Co.
Phone: 1-800-775-3595

Poly bags and shipping supplies.

Factory Direct Craft Supply
Phone: 1-800-252-5223
Web site: mir.spaceports.com/~fdcs/

Fiskars
Phone: 608-233-1649
Web site: www.fiskers.com

Cutting tools.

Frame Fit Co.
Phone: 1-800-523-3693
Web site: www.framefit.com

Picture frames.

Frame Mica Corp.
Phone: 516-567-8889
Web site: www.framemica.com

Picture frames.

Hampton Roads Wholesalers
Phone: 757-596-0684
Web site: www.hrws.com/

J and R Industries
Phone: 1-800-999-9513
Fax: 913-362-7421

King Craft Company
Phone: 315-866-5500
Web site: www.craftassoc.com/
kingcrft.html

Full line of craft supplies.

Kunin Felt
Phone: 603-929-6100
Web site: www.kuninfelt.com/
index.htm

KymLar Craft Supply
Phone: 303-660-6609
Web site: www.kymlarcraftsupply.
com/wholesale.htm

Lowell-Cornell, Inc.
Fax: 201-836-8110
Web site: www.loew-cornell.com/

Maple Ridge Paints
Phone: 1-888-214-0062
Web site: www.mapleridgepaint.com/

Maple Ridge Supply
Phone: 517-356-4807
Web site: www.craftassoc.com/
mapler.html

National Artcraft Co.
Phone: 1-888-937-2723
Web site: www.nationalartcraft.com

Online Supply Catalogs
Web site: www.buyersindex.com/

Pearl Paint
Phone: 1-800-221-6845, extension
2297
Web site: www.pearlpaint.com/

Plaster House
Phone: 1-888-822-2006
Web site: www.plasterhouse.com/

Slate Supplies
Phone: 315-597-2739
Web site: www.christmascottage.
homestead.com/

Strathmore Paper
Phone: 413-568-9111

Greeting card stock.

Sunshine Discount Crafts
Phone: 1-800-729-2878
Web site: www.sunshinecrafts.com/

**The Tree Mover Tree and Gourd
Farm**
5014 E. Ave. N.
Palmdale, CA 93552
Phone: 661-947-7121
E-mail: treengourd@aol.com

Forty varieties of gourds.

The Tool Peddler
Phone: 1-800-344-8469
Web site: www.toolpeddler.com/

Wangs International
Phone: 1-800-729-2647
Web site: www.wangs.com

Welburn Gourd Farm
Phone: 760-728-4271
Web site: www.welburngourdfarm.com

Woodworks
Phone: 1-800-722-0311
More than 1,200 wood items.

Wyla
Phone: 1-800-995-2352
Web site:
www.wylalaces.com/shop_wyla/
supplies/

Zim's, Inc.
Phone: 1-800-453-6420
Fax: 801-268-9859

Craft supplies.

Trade Magazines and Catalogs

You can use *Urlich's Directory of Serials* (in your library) to see if anyone publishes a trade journal about your specific hobby.

Country Business
Phone: 904-446-4873
Web site: www.sampler.com/cbiz/
subscribe.html

Country Register
Phone: 602-942-8950
Web site: www.countryregister.com/

Craft and Needlework Age
Phone: 1-800-258-0929
Web site: www.krause.com/crafts/cn/

Crafts Report
Phone: 1-800-777-7098
Web site: www.craftsreport.com/

Subscription: $29 for 12 issues.

Gifts and Decorative Accessories
Phone: 1-800-309-3332
Fax: 212-683-7929

Gifts and Stationery Business
Phone: 1-800-950-1314
Web site: www.giftline.com

Krause Publications
Phone: 715-445-2214
Web site: www.krause.com/crafts/

The Arts and Crafts Business

This section lists basic resources you can draw on to help you set up and run your arts and crafts business. Included are trade associations, books on business subjects, and sources of office supplies and equipment.

Associations and Organizations

The Friedman Group, Retail Training And Development
720 Corporate Circle, Suite C
Golden, CO 80401
Phone: 1-888-611-4315

Offers a free one-year subscription to *On the Floor,* retail newsletter for store owners and managers. Good source for seminars, and retail management, supervision, and staffing information and more.

National Association of Manufacturers
1331 Pennsylvania Ave. NW, Suite 1500 North Lobby
Washington, DC 20004-1790
Phone: 202-637-3000
Fax: 202-637-3182
Web site: www.nam.org/

National Association of Wholesale Distributors
1725 K St. NW
Washington, DC 20006
Phone: 202-872-0885

National Craft Association (NCA)
1945 East Ridge Road #5178
Rochester, NY 14622
Phone: 1-800-715-9594
Fax: 1-800-318-9410
Web site: www.craftassoc.com
E-mail: nca@craftassoc.com

The NCA publishes wholesale directories that supply wholesale contacts for more than 500,000 art and craft-making supplies. NCA also publishes marketing directories with national contact information for shops and galleries, sales reps, mail-order catalogs, and craft malls. For more details, go to www.craftassoc/dirwhbks.html.

Small Business Administration
Web site: www.sba.gov/

Provides a wealth of valuable information for new business owners.

Business Books

Brabec, Barbara. *The Crafts Business Answer Book and Resource Guide*. New York: M. Evans and Company, Inc., 1998.

———. *Creative Cash*. Rocklin, CA: Prima Publishing, 1998.

———. *Homemade Money*. Cincinnati, OH: Betterway Books, 1997.

———. *Make It Profitable*. New York: M. Evans and Company, Inc., 2000.

Also check out www.barbarabrabec.com/ or order at www.amazon.com.

Caputo, Kathryn. *How to Produce a Successful Crafts Show*. Mechanicsburg, PA: Stackpole Books, 1997.

———. *How to Show and Sell Crafts*. Cincinnati, OH: Betterway Books, 1997.

———. *How to Start Making Money with Your Crafts (Revised edition)*. Cincinnati, OH: Betterway Books, 1999.

Dillehay, James. *The Basic Guide to Selling Your Arts and Crafts*. 1994, Warm Snow Publishers, PO Box 75, Torreon, NM 87061; 505-384-1102.

———. *The Basic Guide to Pricing Your Craftwork*. Torreon, NM: Warm Snow Publishers, 1997.

Encyclopedia of Associations. Available at your library.

Ford, Jill Poulsen. *Gift Trade Marketing: The Handbook for Developing, Exhibiting, and Selling Giftware at Wholesale Trade Shows*. Capistrano, CA: J. Ford Company, 1997. Available by calling 949-240-3333.

Gerhards, Paul. *How to Sell What You Make*. Mechanicsburg, PA: Stackpole Books, 1996.

Hutchinson, Betty, and Warner A. Hutchinson. *Business Letters Made Simple*. Garden City, NY: Doubleday Made Simple Books, 1985.

Hynes, William G. *Start and Run a Profitable Craft Business, Sixth Edition*. Bellingham, WA: Self-Council Press, 1996, reprinted 1999.

Kamoroff, Bernard. *422 Tax Deductions for Businesses and Self-Employed Individuals.* Laytonville, CA: Bell Springs Publishing, 1999.

———. *Small-Time Operator: How to Start Your Own Business, Keep Your Books, Pay Your Taxes, and Stay Out of Trouble.* Laytonville, CA: Bell Springs Publishing, 1995.

National Trade and Professional Associations of the U.S. Available at your library. Check to see if there is an association for your specific business venture.

Oberrecht, Kenn. *How to Start a Home-Based Craft Business, Second Edition.* Gilford, CT: Globe Pequot Press, 1994.

Ramsey, Dan. *The Crafter's Guide to Pricing Your Work.* Cincinnati, OH: Betterway Books, 1997.

Rosen, Wendy. *Crafting as a Business.* New York: Sterling Publishing, 1998.

Sager, Susan Joy. *Selling Your Crafts.* New York: Allworth Press, 1998.

The Standard Periodical Directory. A guide to U.S. and Canadian periodicals.

The Thomas Register, at www.thomasregister.com and at libraries; a source book for locating manufacturers.

West, Janice. *Marketing Your Arts and Crafts.* Fort Worth, TX: The Summit Group, 1994.

Business, Office, and Packaging Supplies

Refer to listings in this appendix under "Product Display and Packaging" and to Chapter 27, "The Big Marketing Secret," for gift wrap, gift boxes, and other retail packaging suppliers.

Mac Paper Supply, Inc.
Phone: 1-800-486-5783
Web site: www.macpaper.com/

Paper Mart
Phone: 1-800-745-8800
Web site: www.papermart.com/

Rapp's Packaging
Phone: 1-800-722-9727
Web site: www.rappspackaging.com

S. Walter Packaging Co.
Phone: 1-800-523-8888
Web site: www.SWalter.com/

Business, Office, and Secretarial Outsourcing Services

The following companies offer mailing lists, databases, letters, flyers, brochures, business cards, resumés, and word processing, transcription, and consulting services.

Accurate Office Services
Nancy Hayes
Phone: 1-877-895-1060
E-mail: AccOfcServ@aol.com

Certek Software Designs, Inc.
Phone: 1-908-561-7700
Web site: www.certek-software.com

POS (point of sale) software for craft malls, retail stores, and wholesalers. Customer and inventory tracking, mailing lists, and labels; supports electronic cash drawers and bar code readers; exports data to Quicken, Quickbooks, and Peachtree.

Home Office Connection
Angela Leisner
Phone: 716-723-5889
Fax: 716-723-5888
E-mail: hocwp@aol.com
Web site: www.craftassoc.com/hoc.html

Computer Hardware and Software

Resources are listed in Chapter 7, "Using a Computer to Lighten Your Business Load."

Copyrights, Trademarks, and Patents

Refer to Chapter 8, "Placing Value on Your Intellectual Property," for more information and sources.

Books

Elias, Stephen, and Goldoftas, Lisa. *Patent, Copyright & Trademark: A Desk Reference to Intellectual Property Law.* Berkeley, CA: Nolo Press, 1999.

Miller, Davis. *Intellectual Property, Patents, Trademarks and Copyright in a Nutshell.* Blemont, CA: West/Wadsworth, 2000.

McQuown, Judith H. *INC Yourself: How to Profit by Setting Up Your Own Corporation.* New York, NY: Bantam Doubleday Dell, 2000.

Trademark Register of the U.S. (available in the library); lists trademarks currently listed with the U.S. Patent and Trademark Office.

Warda, Mark. *How to Register Your Own Trademark with Forms, Third Edition.* Clearwater, FL: Sphinx Publishers, 2000.

Copyright Forms

lcweb.loc.gov/copyright/forms/

Trademarks and Patents

For more information or to do a patent or trademark search: www.uspto.gov/Web/menu/tmebc/index.html and www.uspto.gov/ebc/index.html or www.uspto.gov/.

Legal

Refer to the chapters in Part 3, "Legal and Financial Stuff You Need to Know," for additional information and resources.

Philadelphia Volunteer Lawyers
Web site: www.libertynet.org/pvla/resources.htm.

Visit the Web site for a map listing Volunteer Lawyers for the Arts locations throughout the country.

Volunteer Lawyers for the Arts
1 E. 53rd St., Sixth Floor
New York, NY 10022
Phone: 212-319-ARTS (212-319-2787)
VLA Art Law Line: 212-319-2910
E-mail: vlany@vway.net

A legal hotline for any artist or arts organization that needs quick answers to arts-related legal questions.

Books

Crawford, Tad. *Business and Legal Forms for Crafts.* New York: Allworth Press, 1998.

———. *Legal Guide for the Visual Artist.* New York: Allworth Press, 1999.

DuBoff, Leonard D. *Business Forms and Contracts (in Plain English) for Crafts People.* New York: Allworth Press, 1993.

Paulson, Ed, and Marcia Layton. *The Complete Idiot's Guide to Starting Your Own Business.* New York: Alpha Books, 1998.

Mail Order

National Mail Order Association
Phone: 612-788-1673
Web site: www.nmoa.org

Web Site Development and Hosting

National Craft Association
Phone: 1-800-715-9594
Web site: www.craftassoc.com/wpdesign.html

Product Display and Packaging

The companies in the following sections supply display materials, fixtures, equipment, product packaging supplies, and labels for displaying and selling your products.

Display Fixtures and Materials

The following companies supply display fixtures and materials for selling at shows. For additional resources refer to Chapter 21, "Batteries Not Included: Preparing to Sell at Professionally Promoted Shows," and to the following section, "Store Fixtures and Props."

Brightman Design
Phone: 1-800-995-1723
Web site: www.displaybright.com/

Dealers Supply
Phone: 1-800-524-0576
Web site: www.dlrsupply.com

Arts and crafts show and retailing supplies.

Flourish Co.
Phone: 1-800-296-0049
Web site: www.flourish.com

Canopies and flame-retardant sidewall drapes, tablecovers, pedestal covers, art panel covers, and fabric by the yard.

MD Enterprises–Pro Panels
Phone: 214-350-5765
Web site: propanels.com/

Carpet-covered display panels, desk, and pedestals.

National Artcraft Co.
Phone: 1-888-937-2723
Web site: www.nationalartcraft.com

Fountain-making parts.

Seigel Display Products
Phone: 1-800-626-0322

Literature holders, booth display systems, and tabletop and floor display racks.

Southern Perfection Fabrication, Inc.
232 Hwy 49 S., PO Box 628
Byron, GA 31008
Phone: 1-800-631-4442
Fax: 912-956-4001

Bakery racks, garment racks, retail and textile racks, and more.

Store Fixtures and Props

The following sell retail store fixtures, merchandise displays, and props in addition to supplies such as clothes hangers, signs, price tags, price guns, and the like.

Advance Fixture Mart, Inc.
Phone: 1-800-621-2500
Web site: www.advancefixture.com/

AGAM Group Ltd.
Phone: 1-800-645-0854
Web site: www.agam.com/store/

Donnelly Display
Phone: 212-997-9261
Web site: www.donnellydisplay.com/

KC Fixture and Display
Phone: 1-800-862-0899
Web site: www.kcfixture.com/default.htm

Murdock Mendelsohn Co., Inc.
Phone: 615-226-6424
Web site:
www.murdockmendelsohn.com

Newood Display Fixture Mfg. Co.
Phone: 1-800-233-9663
Web site: www.newood.com/

Store Fixtures
Phone: 1-877-9DISPLAYS
(1-877-934775297)
Web site: www.storefixtures-
online.com/

Used Store Equipment
Phone: 1-800-494-1648
Web site:
www.usedstoreequipment.com/

Display Product Packaging

DCI Marketing
Phone: 1-800-778-4805
Web site: www.dcimarketing.com/
custom_merchandising.htm

Product display systems.

Nashville Display
Phone: 615-743-2900
Web site: www.nashvilledisplay.com/

Package Concepts Assoc. LLC
Phone: 561-364-0014
Web site: www.packagingconcepts.
com/

Product Containers and Packaging Suppliers

Anchor Box
Phone: 1-800-522-8820
Web site: www.anchorbox.com/
packtoc.htm

MAC Paper Supply, Inc.
Phone: 1-800-486-5783
Web site: www.macpaper.com/

xPackage.Com.
Phone: 1-800-832-7372
Web site: www.xpackage.com

Product Labels and Hang Tags

Charm Woven Labels
Phone: 1-800-843-1111
Web site: www.charmwoven.com/

Name Maker, Inc.
Phone: 1-800-241-2890
Web site: www.namemaker.com

Sterling Name Tape Co.
Phone: 1-800-654-5210
Web site: www.sterlingtape.com

Ribbon Suppliers

Atkins and Pearce, Inc.
One Braid Way
Covington, KY 41017-9435
Phone: 1-888-272-7243

Braided decorative tinsel cords, wire
cords, elastic cords, tapes and ribbons.
Metallic, nylon, acrylic, polypropylene, polyester.

Berwick Industries, Inc.
Bomboy Lane and 9th Street,
PO Box 428
Berwick, PA 18603
Phone: 570-752-5934

Full line of ribbon supplies.

Equality Specialties
41-T Madison Ave.
New York, NY 10010-2202
Phone: 1-800-959-0116
Fax: 212-686-2164

Poly-Satin, embossed Poly-Satin, iri-
descent, printed, metallic, high-gloss
polypropylene, and fancy woven ribbons.

Lawrence Schiff Silk Mills, Inc.
590 California Road
Quakertown, PA 18951
Phone: 215-538-2880
Fax: 212-538-2798

Ribbons, bows, rosettes, narrow fabric labels, tapes, trims, bindings, webbing and cords for packaging, cosmetics, gift wrap, apparel and fashion accessories, shoes, floral, craft, home furnishings, and toys.

Lion Ribbon Co., Inc.
Route 24, Box 601
Chester, NJ 07930-0601
Phone: 908-879-4700
Fax: 908-879-4588

Full line of ribbon supplies.

Offray, C.M., and Son, Inc.
Route 24, PO Box 601-T
Chester, NJ 07930
Phone: 1-800-563-3729
Fax: 212-279-9794

Ribbons and narrow fabrics. Product line includes satins, grosgrains, wired ribbons, printed ribbons, and specialty all-occasion ribbons.

Listings by Art, Craft, and Hobby Category

The following sources are broken down by the type of products you are making. You may want to check several categories because product lines often overlap.

Aromatherapy, Toiletries, Soaps, and Personal Care Products

Associations and Organizations

The Cosmetic, Toiletry, and Fragrance Association
1101 17th Street, NW, Suite 300
Washington DC 20036-4702
Phone: 202-331-1770
Web site: www.ctfa.org/

The Handcrafted Soap Makers Guild, Inc.
1920 Apple Road Street
Paris, OH 43072

The National Association for Holistic Aromatherapy
Phone: 1-888-275-6242
Web site: www.naha.org/

Soap and Detergent Association
475 Park Ave. South
New York, NY 10016
Phone: 212-725-1262
Web site: www.sdahq.org/

Publications

Check out the following Web sites for publications available online:

Allured Publishing Corporation
Phone: 630-653-2155
www.store.yahoo.com/allured/

The cosmetic, skin care, perfume, and flavor industries' one-stop bookshop.

Herbage Online Herb Database
www.herbweb.com/herbage/

iSmell Digital Scent Technology
www.digiscents.com/

Medicinal Plants and Herbs Information
world.std.com/%7Ekrahe/

Online Guide to Medicinal and Aromatic Plants
biodiversity.uno.edu/delta/www/data.htm

Two recommended books are ...

Maine, Sandy. *Creating an Herbal Bodycare Business.* Pownel, VT: Storey Books, 1999.

Nerius, Maria Given. *Soapmaking for Fun and Profit.* Rocklin, CA: Prima Publishing, 1999.

Suppliers

The following companies supply soap bases, oils, fragrances, herbs, potpourri, naturals, molds, colorants, containers, equipment, books, accessories, and the like.

Absolutes and Oils
Phone: 316-758-1012
Web site: hometown.aol.com/absolutesandoils/

Amaranthine Aromatics
Phone: 1-800-842-8609
Web site: www.aaroma.com/

Aphrodisia Products
Phone: 1-800-221-6898
Web site: www.aphrodisiaproducts.com/

Astral Sea, LTD
Phone: 573-729-7280
Web site: www.jmw.net/products/wholesale.html

Incense, bath salts, oils, and more.

Creation Herbal's Wholesale
Phone: 828-262-0006
Web site: www.creationsoap.com/wholesale/

Creative Designs Enterprise
Phone: 909-369-8232
Web site: www.sweetscent.com/

E. D. Luce Packaging
Phone: 562-997-9777
Web site: www.essentialsupplies.com/index.htm

Bottles, jars, vials, and more.

Environmental Technology, Inc.
Phone: 707-443-9323
Web site: www.eti-usa.com/

From Nature with Love
Phone: 718-822-6873
Web site: www.from-nature-with-love.com/soap/

Herb Net
Phone: 717-393-3295
Web site: www.herbnet.com/

Intercontinental Fragrances
Phone: 713-896-9991
Web site: rampages.onramp.net/~scents/ifimain.htm

Lebermuth Co. Inc.
Phone: 1-800-648-1123
Web site: www.lebermuth.com/

Pourette Manufacturing
Phone: 1-800-1-888-9425
Web site: www.pourette.com/

Rain Shadow Labs
Phone: 1-800-543-9133
Web site: www.rainshadowlabs.com/

The Scent Source
Phone: 1-888-388-2418
Web site: www.scentsource.com/

Scentastics
Phone: 603-536-1824
Web site: www.scentastics.net/

Sunburst Bottle
Phone: 916-348-5576
Web site: www.sunburstbottle.com/

SunFeather Natural Soap Company
Phone: 315-265-3648
Web site: www.sunsoap.com/

Wholesale Supplies Plus
Phone: 1-800-359-0944
Web site: www.wholesalesuppliesplus.com/

Art

Associations and Organizations

Americans for the Arts
Phone: 202-371-2830
Web site: www.artsusa.org/

Art Dealers Association of America (ADAA)
Phone: 212-940-8590
Web site: www.artdealers.org/

ArtLine
www.artline.com/

An online resource for artists.

Publications

AmericanStyle
Phone: 1-800-272-3893
Web site: www.americanstyle.com/

A quarterly guide on the arts scene (subscription: $18.78).

Art in America
Phone: 1-800-361-4132
Web site: www.enews.com

A magazine for artists and dealers who want the latest news, show reviews, event schedules, updates on genres, literature, and materials (subscription: $29.95).

Mayer, Ralph. *The HarperCollins Dictionary of Art Terms and Techniques*. London, UK: HarperPerennial, 1991.

Patin, Thomas. *Artwords: A Glossary of Contemporary Art Theory*. Westport, CT: Greenwood Press, 1997.

Suppliers

2000 Art Supplies
Fax: 954-255-7849
Web site: www.2000-art.com/

Art Supplies Wholesale
Phone: 1-800-462-2420
Web site: www.allartsupplies.com/

Artist Club
Phone: 1-800-845-6407
Web site:
www.artistsclub.com/ac/Lobby.asp

Designer Moulding
Web site:
www.designermoulding.com/shop/default.asp

Dick Blick Art Materials
Phone: 1-800-447-8192
Web site: www.dickblick.com/homepage/a/

Discount Art Supplies
Phone: 1-800-547-3264
Web site: www.discountart.com/

Dixie Art Supplies
Phone: 1-800-783-2612
Web site: www.dixieart.com/

Graphic Art Supplies
Phone: 714-739-0981
Web site: www.dduck.com/

Rex Art
Phone: 1-800-739-2782
Web site: www.rexart.com/

Sax Arts and Crafts
Phone: 1-800-558-6696
Web site: www.saxarts.com/

World Wide Art Resources, Inc.
Phone: 614-221-7661
Web site: wwar.com/categories/Commercial/Art_Supplies/

Basket Making

Trade Magazines

Basket Shop News
Phone: 603-286-8927
Web site: www.basketshop.com/

Contains articles about basket makers and basket making, reports on new products, patterns, and basket tips, and class listings (subscription: $15.95 for four issues).

Basketry Information
Web site: www.ulster.net/~abeebe/basket.html

A must-see for basket makers. Contains books, CDs, videos, and information on guilds, magazines, suppliers, classes, workshops, and more.

Just Patterns
Web site: www.justpatterns.com/

The idea magazine for basketmakers (subscription: $17 for four issues).

Basket-Making Supplies

Everything you need to create your own beautiful baskets and chair bottoms. Excellent quality reed, chair canes, kits, dyes, books, tools, handles, mini stencils, accessories, and more!

Basket Basics
Phone: 812-825-4447
Web site: www.basketbasics.com/

Baskets of Joy
Phone: 207-725-5899
Web site: www.basketsofjoy.com

The Country Seat, Inc.
Phone: 610-756-6124
Web site: www.countryseat.com/

GH Productions
Phone: 1-800-447-7008
Web site: www.nctc.com/~ghprod

Summer Meadow Basketry
Phone: 231-798-3034
Web site: www.summermeadow.com/

V.I. Reed and Cane
Phone: 1-800-852-0025
Web site: www.basketweaving.com/

Baskets, Ready Made

The Basket Peddler
Phone: 1-888-740-0733
Web site: www.thebasketpeddler.com/

King Craft Company
Phone: 315-866-5500
Web site: www.craftassoc.com/kingcrft.html

Baskets and general craft supplies.

Mid Island Floral Supply
Phone: 631-586-6111
Web site: basketswholesale.com/~categories.shtml

Royal Imports
Phone: 718-256-1640
Web site: www.royalimports.com/Docs/utility.html

United Basket
Phone: 718-894-5454
Web site: www.craftassoc.com/ubasket.html

Beads

Associations and Organizations

Bead Society of LA
Phone: 310-450-8939
Web site: home.att.net/~beadsla/

The oldest ongoing bead society (25 years) in the United States, a nonprofit organization dedicated to the study of beads and to the dissemination of knowledge about beads.

National Bead Society
Phone: 1-888-273-6298
Web site: nationalbeadsociety.com

Suppliers

Accents Beads
Phone: 301-881-2003
Web site: accentsbeadshop-md.com/

The Bead Link
Phone: 248-474-8141
Web site: www.thebeadlink.com

Eastwest Dyecom, Inc.
Phone: 1-800-407-6371
Web site: www.eastwestdye.com

For color-anodized aluminum in wire, beads, jumprings, sheets, shapes, and more. Services include custom anodizing.

JS Beads
Phone: 407-836-2070
Web site: jsbeads.safeshopper.com/

Myron Toback, Inc.
Phone: 1-800-223-7550
Web site: www.myrontoback.com

Rings and Things
Phone: 509-624-8565
Web site: www.rings-things.com

Candle Making

Associations and Organizations

International Guild of Candle Artisans
Phone: 503-589-0650

National Candle Association
Phone: 202-393-2210

Suppliers

The following suppliers sell waxes, oils, fragrances, colorants, molds, wicks, containers, books, equipment and accessories, and the like.

Barker Candle Supplies
Phone: 1-800-543-0601
Web site: www.barkerco.com/

Belmay, Inc.
Phone: 914-376-1515
Web site: www.belmay.com/

Cajun Candle Factory
Phone: 1-800-667-6424
Web site: www.cajuncandles.com/

Candlewic Co.
Phone: 610-847-2076
Web site: www.candlewic.com/

Lebermuth Company
Phone: 219-259-7000
Web site: www.lebermuth.com/

North Valley Candle Mold
Phone: 530-247-0447
Web site: www.moldman.com/

Paramold Mfg. LLC
Phone: 1-877-527-4461
Web site: www.thomasregister.com/olc/paramold/

Pourette Manufacturing
Phone: 1-800-888-9425
Web site: www.pourette.com/

The Scent Source
Phone: 1-888-388-2418
Web site: www.scentsource.com/

Scentastics
Phone: 603-536-1824
Web site: www.scentastics.net/

Walnut Hill Enterprises, Inc.
Phone: 215-785-6511
Web site: walnuthillco.com/

Wholesale Supplies Plus
Phone: 1-800-359-0944
Web site: www.wholesalesuppliesplus.com/

Wick Store
Phone: 1-800-343-8114
Web site: www.wickstore.com/

Ceramics and Pottery

Associations and Publications

American Ceramic Society (AcerS)
Phone: 614-890-4700
Web site: www.acers.org/

Dedicated to the advancement of ceramics.

Clay Times Magazine
Phone: 540-882-3576
Web site: www.claytimes.com

Clay Times is designed to inform ceramic enthusiasts at all levels of the latest developments in the clay world. Features useful information on pottery forming, decorating, firing, glaze recipes, and more (subscription: $23 for 12 issues).

National Council on Education for the Ceramic Arts (NCECA)
PO Box 1677
Bandon, OR 97411
Phone: 503-347-4394

The NCECA is a professional organization of individuals whose interests, talents, or careers are primarily focused on ceramic arts.

Suppliers

Contact the following for ceramic and pottery supplies, including kilns, wheels, glazes, clays, raw materials, bisqueware, books, tools, and tips.

Aftosa
Phone: 1-800-231-0937
Web site: www.aftosa.com/

Bisqueware, pottery, ceramic, and display supplies.

American Art Clay Company, Inc.
Phone: 317-244-6871
Web site: www.amaco.com

Ceramic USA
Phone: 1-888-221-CUSA
Web site: www.ceramicusa.com

Cridge, Inc.
Phone: 1-888-801-4438

Glazed and bisque porcelain.

Highwater Clays, Inc.
Phone: 828-252-6033
Web site: www.highwaterclays.com

House on the Hill
Phone: 618-344-4543
Web site: www.craftassoc.com/rwhite.html

National Artcraft Co.
Phone: 1-888-937-2723
Web site: www.nationalartcraft.com

Ranchhand Originals
Phone: 1-800-380-3095
Web site: www.rocnp.com/

SuperCal Ink Jet Decals
Phone: 847-520-4699
Web site: www.supercaldecals.com/

Clothing Blanks, Apparel, and Accessories for Embellishing

A2Z Wholesalers
Phone: 1-888-828-2525
Web site: www.a2zwholesalers.com/

Ladies fashions for every season or reason.

Absolute Caps, Hats, and Clothing!
Phone: 1-800-488-4546
Web site: www.virginiamag.com/
clothingsource/index.html

Barr Wholesale
Phone: 1-800-831-TEES
Web site: www.barrwholesale.com/

Resort apparel and quality blank sportswear.

Carolina Manufacturing
Phone: 1-800-845-2744
Web site: www.carolinamfg.com/

Bandannas, handkerchiefs, aprons, tote bags, scarves, and more.

Dalee Book Co.
Phone: 914-965-160

Paintable canvas surfaces.

Hanes Printables
Phone: 1-800-685-7557
Web site: www.hanesprintables.com/

Full line of printables for the professional embellisher.

Heartway International
Phone: 808-626-8043
Web site: www.craftassoc.com/
heartway.html

Ladies' silk apparel.

Imprints Wholesale, Inc.
Phone: 1-800-634-2945
Web site: www.imprintswholesale.com/

Complete line of apparel and accessories.

Mission Imprintables
Phone: 1-800-480-0800
Web site: www.missionimprintables.com/

T-shirts, fleecewear, sportswear, denim, towels, hats, and more.

T-Shirt City Inc.
Phone: 1-800-543-7320
Web site: www.t-shirtcity.com/

Sportswear apparel and imprintables, including hats, aprons, bags, umbrellas, and many other items.

Western Pacific International
Phone: 213-747-7088
Web site: www.wpioffprice.com/

Wholesale off-price ladies' apparel.

Decorative Painting

Associations and Organizations

International Faux Finishers Association
Phone: 407-688-9121
PO Box 837
DeBary, FL 32713

Silk Painters International, Inc. (SPIN)
Phone: 301-474-7347
Web site: www.nurlnet.com/

A nonprofit organization dedicated to increasing public awareness of contemporary silk painting.

Society of Decorative Painters
Phone: 316-269-0300
Web site: www.decorativepainters.com

Stencil Artisans League, Inc. (SALI)
Phone: 215-564-3484
Web site: www.sali.org/

A nonprofit organization dedicated to the promotion and preservation of the art of stenciling and related decorative painting.

Books

Decorative Artists Book Club
PO Box 424
Devault, PA 19432
Phone: 610-640-2787

Books of interest to decorative painters.

Moyer Design and Silk Painting
Phone: 1-800-990-6377
Web site: www.moyerdesign.com.

The books, *Silk Painting* and *Silk Painting for Fashion and Fine Art;* supplies; and classes.

Screens of Silk
Phone: 1-877-718-9986
Web site:
www.craftassoc.com/ssilk.html

Screen painting kits and books.

Tolemarketplace
Phone: 760-747-2167
Web site: www.tolemarketplace.com

Tole painting information and links of interest.

Viking Folk Art Publications
Phone: 507-835-8009
Web site: www.viking-publications.com

Painting instructional books.

Window Painting for Profit
(A how-to book)
Web site: www.craftassoc.com/bachman.html
E-mail: glassact@gateway.net

Suppliers

Tole and decorative painting supplies and equipment.

American Traditional Stencils
Phone: 1-800-448-6656
Web site: www.amtrad-stencil.com

Art Craft Etc.
Phone: 1-800-537-2738
Web site: www.artcraftetc.com/

Barb Watson, MDA
Phone: 909-653-3780
Web site: www.barbwatson.com/

Binney and Smith
1100 Church Lane
Easton, PA 18042

Liquitex paints and other products.

Cellar Craft Woodworks
Phone: 603-673-3615
Web site: www.cellarcraft.com/

Daler-Rowney
Phone: 609-655-5825
Web site: www.daler-rowney.com

DecoArt Paints
Phone: 606-365-3193
Web site: www.decoart.com

Decor Delights
Phone: 801-262-9451
Web site: www.decordelights.com/

Donna Dewberry
Phone: 1-800-536-2627
Web site: www.onestroke.com/

Faux Effects, Inc.
Phone: 1-800-270-8871
Web site: www.aquafinishing.
com/aqua.html

Heritage Brush
Phone: 314-845-2216
Web site: www.craftassoc.com/
heritage.html

Heritage Saw Co.
Phone: 1-800-682-6686

Paintable saws and blades.

Painting Place
Phone: 913-888-5414
Web site: www.thepaintinplace.com/

Plaid Enterprises, Inc.
Phone: 1-800-842-4197
Web site: www.plaidonline.com/

Stenciling
Phone: 1-800-449-1655
Web site: www.stenciling.com/

Tole Mart
Phone: 1-800-923-9663
Web site: www.tolemart.com/

Doll and Critter-Making Supplies

Association

National Institute of American Doll Artists (NIADA)
Box 656693
Fresh Meadows, NY 11365
Phone: 970-824-8407

Suppliers

Apple Valley Doll Works
Phone: 1-800-635-7933
Web site: www.applevalleydolls.com

BJ Craft Supplies
Phone: 956-262-3719
Web site: www.bjcraftsupplies.
com/dolls_menu.htm

Doll parts and accessories.

Cloth Doll Supplies
Phone: 1-800-250-5075
Web site: www.sistersanddaughters.
com/

Creative Wholesale
Phone: 1-800-347-0031
Web site: www.craftswholesale.com/
sub-doll.htm

Doll Parts and Accessories
Phone: 1-800-252-5223
Web site: mir.spaceports.com/
~fdcs/dolacs.html

Maplewood Crafts
Phone: 717-384-5555
Fax: 717-384-2500

National Artcraft Co.
Phone: 1-888-937-2723
Web site: www.nationalartcraft.com

Syndee's Crafts
Phone: 702-564-8118
Web site: www.craftassoc.com/
syndees.html

Teddy Bear Making Supplies
Phone: 905-770-3173
Web site: www.bearingredients.com

Electric and Musical Parts for Lamps, Clocks, and Similar Items

Lamp Specialties, Inc.
Phone: 1-888-225-5526
Web site: www.lamp-specialties.com/

National Artcraft Co.
Phone: 1-888-937-2723
Web site: www.nationalartcraft.com

Floral Crafts

Publications

Florist Magazine
Phone: 1-800-383-4383
Fax: 810-948-6420

Flowers
Phone: 1-800-321-2665
Fax: 310-966-3610

Suppliers

Anderson Floral Supply
Phone: 716-665-5197
Web site: afloral.com/ushop/

Best Buy Floral Supply
Phone: 1-800-553-8497
Web site: www.bestbuyfloral.com/

Birch Bark
Phone: 715-374-2135
Web site: www.craftassoc.com/
birchbark.html

Chelsea Farms Dried Flowers
Phone: 757-787-4410
Web site: www.chelseafarms.com/

Dried Flowers Direct
Phone: 315-536-2736
Web site: www.keukaflowerfarm.com

Floral-Connections Online Directory by State
Web site: www.all-connections.com/
floral/by_state.html

Floral Supply Syndicate
Phone: 1-800-347-9994
Web site: www.fss.com

FS Imports
Phone: 618-797-1818
Web site: www.fs-imports.com/

Holiday Foliage, Inc.
Phone: 619-661-9094
Web site: www.holidayfoliage.com/

J and T Imports
Phone: 858-481-9781
Web site: www.driedflowers.com/

K2 Freeze Dried
Phone: 1-800-525-7597
Web site: www.ktwo.com/
supplies.shtml

Mosses Galore
Phone: 715-374-2135
Web site: www.craftassoc.com/
mogal.html

Nature's Best Dried Flowers
Phone: 440-572-1138
Web site: www.nbdriedflowers.com

Also sell wreath forms.

North American Floral Supply
Phone: 1-888-249-9996
Web site: www.nafps.com/

Gift Basket Making

Trade Shows

Confections West or **Confections South**
Phone: 610-687-3426

Dallas National Gourmet Food Shows
Phone: 214-655-6100

International Fancy Food and Confections Show
by National Association for
Specialty Food Trade
Phone: 212-482-6440

Jubilee
by Festivities Publications
Phone: 1-800-729-6338

Nowco
Phone: 1-800-233-8302

Philadephia National Candy, Gift, and Gourmet Shows
Phone: 610-265-4688

Publications

Frazier, Shirley George. *How to Start a Home-Based Gift Basket Business*. Old Saybrook, CT: Globe Peqot Press, 1998.

Gift Basket Review
Phone: 1-800-950-1314
Web site: www.giftline.com

Gourmet Retailer
Phone: 305-446-2868

Suppliers of Packaging

For baskets and containers see the preceding sections, "Baskets, Ready Made" and "Floral Crafts."

Action Bag and Display
Phone: 1-800-824-2247
Web site: www.actionbag.com/ giftbpro.html

Bags and Bows
Phone: 1-800-225-8155

BoxCo/Gift Box It
Phone: 1-800-654-2932

Clayville Imports, Inc.
Phone: 315-839-555
Web site: www.craftassoc.com/ clayvill.html

Rapp's Packaging
Phone: 1-800-722-9727
Web site: www.rappspackaging.com

S. Walter Packaging Co.
Phone: 1-800-523-8888
Web site: www.SWalter.com/

Suppliers of Products

These suppliers are reps that carry a variety of products from many manufacturers that are suitable for gift basket contents.

Chase Collection
Phone: 301-468-2388
Fax: 301-468-1218

Commito Company
Phone: 1-800-530-8245
Fax: 303-293-3865

Hod Turner and Co.
Phone: 1-800-899-4826
Fax: 404-581-1921

J. Rouse Sales
Phone: 1-800-600-2521
Fax: 714-995-3657

Simon and Cohen
Phone: 213-763-5714
Fax: 213-763-5715

Glass Arts and Crafts

Trade Organizations and Publications

The Enamelist Society
Phone: 606-291-3800
Web site: www.craftWeb.com/ org/enamel/enamel.htm

For those interested or active in making art by fusing glass to metal.

Glass Art Society
Phone: 206-382-1305
Web site: www.glassart.org/

International Guild of Glass Artists, Inc.
Fax: 856-428-1199
Web site: www.igga.org/menua.htm

Also has an online supply directory.

Stained Glass Association of America
Phone: 1-800-888-7422
Web site: www.stainedglass.org/
main_pages/sgaamain.html

Books

The following books are available at www.amazon.com:

Bray, Charles. *Dictionary of Glass Materials and Techniques*. Shippensburg, PA: University of Pennsylvania Press, 1996.

Dayton, John F. *The Discovery of Glass, Experiments in the Smelting of Rich, Dry Silver Ores, and the Reproduction of Bronze Age-Type Cobalt Blue Glass as a Slag*. Shippensburg, PA: University of Pennsylvania Museum, 1993.

Houston, James. *Fire into Ice: Adventures in Glass Making*. Toronto, ON, Canada: Tundra Books, 1998.

Jenkins, Cindy, and Dierks, Leslie. *Making Glass Beads*. Asheville, North Carolina: Lark Books, 1997.

Lui Fyson, Nance. *Decorative Glass of the 19th and Early 20th Centuries: A Source Book*. Portland, OR: David & Charles Uk, 1997.

Lundstrom, Boyce, and Daniel Schwoerer. *Kiln Firing Glass: Glass Fusing Book One*. Camp Colton, OR: Vitreous Group Publications, 1989, revised 1994.

———. *Advanced Fusing Techniques: Glass Fusing, Book 2*. Camp Colton, OR: Vitreous Group Publications, 1989.

———. *Glass Casting and Moldmaking: Glass Fusing, Book 3*. Camp Colton, OR: Vitreous Group Publications, 1989.

Suppliers

Armour Products
Phone: 201-847-0404
Web site: www.armourproducts.com/

Glass etching and sandblasting supplies.

Arrow Springs
Phone: 530-677-1400
Web site: www.arrowsprings.com/

Everything for making glass, plus tools, glass, ovens, supplies, books, and videos.

Delphi Stained Glass
Phone: 1-800-248-2048
Web site: www.delphiglass.com

Stained glass-making supplies and tools.

Ed Hoy's International
Phone: 1-800-323-5668
Web site: www.edhoy.com

Distributor of glass, tools, and supplies for the stained glass and art glass industry. Also, patterns, books, videos, tools, lampbases, forms, jewels, and fusing and lampworking materials.

Glass Crafters
Phone: 941-379-8333
Web site: www.glasscrafters.com/index_dw1.html

Glass-making supplies, tools, glass lamps, books, and videos.

Glass Web-Mart
Phone: 847-589-1642
Web site: www.glassmart.com/

All glass-crafting and glass-etching supplies and tools.

Khue Co.
Phone: 707-442-4203
Web site: www.khue.com/

Glass supplies, cutters, and tools.

Sunshine Glassworks Ltd.
Phone: 716-668-2918
Web site: www.sunshineglass.com

Supplier of tools and materials for work in stained glass.

Uroboros Glass Studios
Phone: 503-284-4900
Web site: www.uroboros.com/

Decorative sheet glass.

Warner-Crivellaro Stained Glass
Phone: 1-800-523-4242
Web site: www.warner-criv.com

Jewelry-Making Resources

Trade Organizations

Gemological Institute of America
Phone: 760-603-4000
Web site: www.gia.org

For gemology education and more.

International Colored Gemstones Association (ICA)
3 East 48th St., 5th Floor
New York, NY 10017
Phone: 212-688-8452
Web site: www.gemstone.org/index.html

Also see the "Metal Arts" section in this appendix.

Revere Academy of Jewelry Arts
Phone: 415-391-4179
Web site: www.revereacademy.com

Classes and diploma programs on jewelry making, as well as jewelry books and videos.

Trade Publications

JCK Magazine
Phone: 1-800-662-7776
Web site: www.jckgroup.com

Trends, shows, industry news, and suppliers (subscription: $39.95 for 12 issues).

Lapidary Journal
Phone: 1-800-676-4336
Web site: www.lapidaryjournal.com

Trends, jewelry supplies, trade shows, and industry news (subscription: $29.95 for 12 issues).

Jewelry-Making Supplies

Best Crystals
Phone: 1-800-859-4001
Web site: www.bestcrystals.com

Fire Mountain Gems
Phone: 1-800-423-2319
Web site: www.firemtn.com

Gem Market
PO Box 631
Paoli, PA 19301
Web site: www.gemmarkets.com

Kassoy
Phone: 516-933-6878
Web site: www.kassoy.com

Jewelers' tools and supplies.

Kitco
Phone: 877-775-4826
Web site: www.kitco.com

Gold and precious metals.

Kingsley North
Phone: 1-800-338-9280
Web site: www.kingsleynorth.com

Lapidary and jewelry supplies.

Land of Odds
Phone: 615-292-0610
Web site: www.landofodds.com

Jewelry supplies, beads, and books.

Pisces Trading
Phone: 916-344-2323
Web site: www.dabeadbabe.com

Rings and Things
Phone: 509-624-8565
Web site: www.rings-things.com/

All jewelry-making supplies, tools, and books.

WigJig
Phone: 1-800-579-9473
Web site: www.wigjig.com/

Wire design and jewelry tools, beads, kits, chains, wire, and more!

Wire Sculpture
Phone: 504-649-6505
Web site: www.wire-sculpture.com/

Jewelry-making tools, gems, classes, books, beads, findings, videos, and more.

Leather Craft Suppliers

CLPW Leather
Phone: 901-728-5551
Web site: www.shopforleather.com/wholesale.html

Just Leather
Phone: 207-641-8313
Web site: www.justleather.com/

Leatherman
Phone: 858-481-6984
Web site: www.shoplite.com/leatherman.htm

Springfield Leather
Phone: 1-800-668-8518
Web site: www.springfieldleather.com/

Tandy Leather
Phone: 1-800-890-1611
Web site: www.tandyleather.com/

Metal Arts

Artist-Blacksmith's Association of North America (ABANA)
Phone: 706-310-1030
Web site: www.abana.org/

Focuses on art metalwork, contemporary and traditional.

ArtMetal Project
Web site: www.artmetal.com/

The ArtMetal Project is an educational resource to help educate the general public and promote the various art metal disciplines. The ArtMetal Village is a cybervillage for the metal trades with "centers" dedicated to specialized fields within the metal crafts: wrought iron, designer furniture, metal sculpture, custom jewelry, metal suppliers, architectural metals, and design.

FOUNDRY Management and Technology
Phone: 216-696-7000
Web site: www.foundrymag.com/

The leading metalcasting industry trade publication, is published monthly by Penton Media, Inc.

Society of American Silversmiths (SAS)
Phone: 401-567-71-800
Web site: www.silversmithing.com

For anything related to the silversmith's art and devoted to the preservation and promotion of contemporary silversmithing—specifically in the areas of hollowware, flatware, and sculpture.

Society of North American Goldsmiths (SNAG)
Phone: 630-579-3272
Web site: www.snagmetalsmith.org

For jewelers and metal artisans; it sponsors *Metalsmith* magazine.

Suppliers

Ametco
4326 Hamann Pkwy.
Willoughby, OH 44094
Phone: 216-951-4300 or 1-800-321-7042

Supplier of fine copper mesh, perforated metals and plastics, metal grating, fencing, and wire cloth.

Arizona Specialty Metals
4020 E. Washington
Phoenix, AZ 85032
Phone: 602-276-8407

New and surplus ferrous and nonferrous metals, including tool steels of many kinds.

Armco, Inc.
Phone: 201-316-5200

Suppliers of carbon steel, draw plate, electrical and stainless steel, and steel products.

Atlas Metal Sales
1401 Umatilla St.
Denver, CO 80204
Phone: 303-623-0143 or 1-800-662-0143

Specialty metals, including aluminum, brass, bronze, copper, lead, nickel, pewter, tin, and zinc.

Belmont Metals
337 Belmont Ave.
Brooklyn, NY 11207
Phone: 718-342-4900 or 1-800-654-2152

Various nonferrous metals, including aluminum, antimony, arsenic, babbitt, bismuth, beryllium, boron, bronze, cadmium, calcium, chromium, cobalt, gallium, indium, lead, lithium, magnesium, manganese, mercury, molybdenum, nickel, pewter, selenium, silicon, solder, telurium, tin, tungsten, zinc, and zirconium. Various grades, compositions, alloys, and shapes are available, both standard and custom.

Bovano of Cheshire
830 S. Main St., PO Box 250
Cheshire, CT 06410

Suppliers of European imported leaded enameling stock.

Green Industries, Inc.
Green Boulevard
Mexico, MO 65265
Phone: 1-800-887-5555

Suppliers of high-temperature refractory materials of all types.

Mold Making, Resin Castings, Liquid Latex Rubber, Casting Waxes, Finishes, Sealers, Rug Backing, Clear Coatings, and Adhesives

Blended Waxes, Inc.
Phone: 1-800-294-4692
Web site: www.blendedwaxes.com/index.html

Casting and packaging waxes, specialty greases, and wax emulsions.

Calwax Corp.
Phone: 626-969-4334
Web site: www.calwax.com/casting.html

Environmental Technology, Inc.
Phone: 707-443-9323
Web site: www.eti-usa.com/

Polymer Clay

Association
National Polymer Clay Guild
Phone: 202-895-5212
Web site: www.npcg.org/

Suppliers
Clay Factory of Escondido
Phone: 760-741-3242
Web site: www.clayfactoryinc.com/

Rings and Things
Phone: 509-624-8565
Web site: www.rings-things.com/

Rubber Stamps, Paper Arts, and Scrapbooks/Memorybooks

Art of Origami
Web site: ccwf.cc.utexas.edu/~vbeatty/origami/folding/

Learn the art of paper folding at this site.

Associations

Hand Papermaking, Inc.
Box 77027
Washington, DC 20013-7027
Phone: 301-220-2393 or 1-800-821-6604

A nonprofit organization dedicated to advancing traditional and contemporary ideas in the art of hand papermaking through publications and educational formats.

International Scrapbook Trade Assn.
Phone: 972-318-0492

Original Paper Doll Artists Guild (OPDAG)
Phone: 207-265-2500
Web site: www.opdag.com/

For beginners and professionals.

Publications

Creating Keepsake Scrapbook Magazine
Phone: 1-800-815-3538
Web site: www.creatingkeepsakes.com

Design Originals
Phone: 1-800-877-7820
Web site: www.d-originals.com/

Rubber stamp and scrapbook how-to books and videos.

Suppliers

Art Paper
Phone: 828-251-0028
Web site: www.artpaper.com/

Crescent Supplies
Phone: 413-637-0156
Web site: www.crescent-cardboard.com/TopDown.htm

Framing and papers.

Hyway Sales
Phone: 860-236-0737
Web site: www.hywaysales.com/

Rubber Tree Stamps
Phone: 413-585-0875
Web site: www.rubbertreestamps.com/home.htm

Supplies and specialty papers.

Sax Arts and Crafts
Phone: 1-800-558-6696
Web site: www.saxusa.com

Specialty papers.

Stampendous
Phone: 1-800-869-0474
Web site: www.stampendous.com

Sewing, Fiber Art, and Needlework Arts

Associations

American Needlepoint Guild
Phone: 602-816-4139
Web site: www.needlepoint.org

American Quilters Society
Box 3290
Paducah, KY 42002
Phone: 502-898-7903
Web site: www.AQSquilt.com

Craft Yarn Council of America
Phone: 704-824-0630
Web site: www.craftyarncouncil.com

Knit, crochet, and more.

Crochet Guild of America
Phone: 1-877-852-9190
Web site: www.crochet.org

Embroiderers' Guild of America
Phone: 502-589-6956
Fax: 502-584-7900

Handweavers Guild of America, Inc.
Phone: 770-495-7702
Web site: www.weavespindye.org/

Dedicated to encouraging excellence, inspiring creativity, and preserving fiber traditions through education.

Home Sewing Association
Phone: 212-714-1633
Fax: 212-714-1655

Knitting Compendium Online
Web site: www.woolworks.org/

Knitting Guild of America
Phone: 865-524-2401
Web site: www.tkga.com/

The National Needlework Association (TNNA)
Phone: 614-455-6773
Web site: www.tnna.org/

A trade organization comprised of professional designers, manufacturers, publishers, retailers, mail-order companies, manufacturers' representatives, and wholesalers of upscale needle art products and services.

Publications and Online Resources

Fiberarts Magazine
Phone: 1-800-284-3388
Web site: www.fiberartsmagazine.com

Subscription: $22 for 12 issues.

Knitting-Crochet Online
Web site: www.knitting-crochet.com/

Knitting News
PO Box 1612
Carolina Beach, NC 28428
Web site: www.craftassoc.com/knitnews.html

They also offer a full range of knitting books, patterns, yarns and kits.

MacNulty, Shirley. *Knitting for Fun and Profit*. Rocklan, CA, Prima Publishing, 1999. (Available at www.craftassoc.com/knitbook.html.)

The Needleworker
Phone: 415-458-8672
Web site: www.needleworker.com

Bimonthly magazine for lovers of beautiful handwork. It brings designs and projects for cross-stitch and other needle arts, step-by-step instructions for specialty stitches, and new techniques to add texture and dimension to your work (subscription: $19.95 for 12 issues).

Patternworks
Phone: 1-800-438-5464
Web site: www.patternworks.com

Knitting software.

Quilt Patterns Online
Web site: www.nmia.com/~mgdesign/webhome.htm

World Wide Quilting Page
Web site: ttsw.com/MainQuiltingPage.
html

Online information and resources for quilters.

Suppliers

Cross Stitch Store
Phone: 1-800-591-1863
Web site: www.gostitch.com/

Cutting Edge Concepts
Phone: 661-822-6585
Web site:
www.cuttingedgeconcepts.net/

Quilt and sewing supplies.

Dharma Trading
Web site: www.dharmatrading.com/

Full line of textile craft supplies, fabrics, dyes, clothing, accessories, and the like.

Duncan by Design
Web site: www.duncancrafts.com

Fiber paints.

Embroidery Supplies
Phone: 606-887-3168
Web site: www.threadartist.com/
embroidery_supplies.htm

Fabric Club
Phone: 1-800-322-2582
Web site: www.fabricclub.com/
store/Default.asp

Fabric Gallery
Web site: www.fabricgallery.com/

Online fabric store.

Fabric Stash
Phone: 1-888-594-8187
Web site: fabric-stash.com/

Fabric World
Phone: 1-800-845-8723
Web site: www.Hancocks-Paducah.com

Fiber Shop
Phone: 760-436-6119
Web site: www.fiberartshop.com/

Knitting and more.

Foothill Fabric and Sew On
Phone: 1-888-878-5803
Web site: www.foothill-fabric.com/

Lace Supply
Phone: 650-949-1096
Web site: www.lacemaking.com/

Nancy's Notions
Phone: 1-800-245-5116
Web site: www.nancysnotions.com

Sewing notions and equipment.

NW Tag Co.
Phone: 503-234-1054
Web site: www.nwtag.com/

Tags and labels.

On-Line Fabric Directory
Web site: www.fabdir.com/

Fabric sources.

Personal Threads Boutique
Phone: 1-800-306-7733
Web site: www.personalthreads.com

Accessories for knitting, weaving, spinning, and needlepoint.

Quilt House
Phone: 1-800-660-0145
Web site: www.ezquilt.com

Sew True
Phone: 1-800-739-8783
Web site: www.sewtrue.com/

Sewing supplies and equipment for tailors, dressmakers, home sewers, and crafters, as well as dry cleaners, bridal shops, and alteration specialists.

381

Sewing-Needlework Supplies Online
www.buyersindex.com/brca/42.htm

Fabrics, textiles, and equipment.

Smocking Store
Phone: 707-995-9337
Web site: www.smockingstore.com/

Stencil Co.
Phone: 716-656-9430
Web site: www.quiltingstencils.com

Sweet Gum Fiber Farm
Phone: 843-726-9271
Web site: www.craftassoc.com/
sweetgum.html

Spinning, weaving, knitting supplies, and yarns.

Thread Artist
Phone: 606-887-3168
Web site: www.threadartist.com/

Trims and Notions
Web site: www.netics.com/findex/
manufacturing/trims_and_notions/

Velona Needlecraft
Phone: 1-800-972-1570
Web site: www.velona.com

Yarn and books.

The Woolery
Phone: 1-800-441-9665
Web site: www.woolery.com/

Woolstock
Phone: 1-800-242-5648
Web site: www.woolstock.com

Yarns, books, videos, patterns, blockers, and the like.

Yarn Barn
Phone: 1-800-468-0035
Web site: www.yarnbarn.com

Soap-Making

See the "Aromatherapy, Toiletries, Soaps, and Personal Care Products" section earlier in this appendix.

Surface Materials, Equipment, Finishes, and Clear Coatings

Acrilex, Inc.
Phone: 1-800-227-4539
Web site: www.acrilex.com/

Acrylic sheets.

Aqua Finishing Solutions
Phone: 1-800-270-8871
Web site: aquafinishing.com/

Artistic Endeavors
PO Box 20448
Oakland, CA 94611
Phone: 510-594-0789

Suppliers of patina chemicals, many superior waxes, and clearcoats.

Environmental Technology, Inc.
Phone: 707-443-9323
Web site: www.eti-usa.com/

Imagine Tile
Phone: 973-771-0977
Web site: www.imaginetile.com/
index.html

Imprints Plus
Phone: 1-800-563-2464
Web site: www.imprintplus.com/

Nevamar Decorative Surfaces
Phone: 1-800-638-4380
Web site: www.nevamar.com/
home.html

Plasti-Kote Co.
Phone: 1-800-251-4511
Web site: www.plasti-kote.com/

Woodworking

Associations

American Association of Woodturners (AAW)
Phone: 612-484-9094
Web site: www.woodturner.org/

A nonprofit organization dedicated to the advancement of woodturning. Its mission is to provide education, information, and organization to those interested in turning wood.

Furniture Society
Phone: 804-973-1488
Web site: www.furnituresociety.org/

Organization whose mission is to advance the art of furniture making by inspiring creativity, promoting excellence, and fostering understanding of this art and its place in society.

National Woodcarvers Association
7424 Miami Ave.
Cincinnati, OH 45243
Phone: 513-561-0627

Woodworking Association of North America
PO Box 478, Depot Road
Tamworth, NH 03886
Phone: 603-323-7500

Dedicated to the advancement of woodworking as an industry, a hobby, and an art.

Publications

Karen, Reed. *The Complete Idiot's Guide to Woodworking*. Indianapolis: Alpha Books, 2000.

This may be the best basic guide to woodworking out there.

Woodworker's Journal
Phone: 1-800-765-4119
Web site: www.woodworkersjournal.com

A great source for woodworking tips, techniques, tool reviews, and literally thousands of great plans (introductory price of $19.95).

Suppliers

Aged Woods, Inc.
Phone: 1-800-233-9307
Web site: www.agedwoods.com/html/home.html

Art Craft Etc.
Phone: 1-800-537-2738
Web site: www.artcraftetc.com/

Cupboard Distributing
Phone: 1-800-338-6388
Web site: www.cdwood.com

The Cutting Edge
Phone: 541-832-2736
Web site: www.thecuttingedge-wood.com/

Rockler Woodworking and Hardware
Phone: 612-478-8201
Web site: www.rockler.com/

Teaberry Farm
Phone: 509-468-5985
Web site: www.teaberryfarms.com

Patterns.

Unfinished Furniture Mart
Phone: 310-539-3631
Fax: 310-539-4895

Viking Woodcrafts, Inc.
Phone: 1-800-361-0115
Web site: www.vikingwoodcrafts.com

Wood, papier-mâché, and tin pieces.

Walnut Hollow
Phone: 1-800-950-5101

Unfinished wood products.

Wood-N-Crafts
Phone: 1-800-444-8075
Web site: www.wood-n-crafts.com

WoodCraft
Phone: 1-800-225-1153
Web site: www.woodcraft.com/
woodcraft/assets/html/homepage.asp

Woodworking hand tools, power tools, hardware, lumber, sharpening supplies, wood finishing, and more.

Woodcrafts and Supplies
Phone: 618-592-4907
Web site: www.woodcraftssupplies.com

Woodworker's Choice
Phone: 1-800-892-4866
Web site:
www.thewoodworkerschoice.com/

Glossary of Art and Craft Industry Terms

accounting period   A period of time used to correlate revenues and expenses; usually defined as a day, week, month, quarter, or year.

accounts payable   Money that a business owes to others. Also called short-term liabilities.

accounts receivable   Money that others owe to a business.

accrual basis of accounting   A method of accounting that relates revenues and expenses based on when the commitments are made, as opposed to when the cash is spent or received.

a.k.a.   Abbreviation for "also known as."

articles of incorporation   Documents filed with the Secretary of State's office to formally establish incorporation in that state.

artisan   Skilled craftsperson.

artist   Person skilled in any of the fine arts.

assets   Items of value that the company owns, such as cash in its checking account, accounts receivables, fixtures, equipment, and property.

balance sheet   A type of financial statement that shows all the company's assets, liabilities, and equity owned by investors. For the statement to balance, the value of the assets must equal the value of the liabilities plus the equity.

bank statement   A monthly statement provided by the bank that details the various deposits, withdrawals, and fees or charges associated with your account.

bookkeeping   A system for accurately tracking where your money is coming from and where it is going.

break-even point   The quantity point at which the gross margin equals the fixed expenses for the period in question. Above the break-even point, the company makes money; below the break-even point, the company loses money.

browser   A software program that runs on a computer and allows Internet HTML pages to be viewed properly.

business plan   A document that outlines the business's overall business objectives, its viability, and the steps necessary to achieve those objectives.

C corporation   The business structure used primarily by major corporations so that they can sell shares of stock to the public.

calendar fiscal year   A financial year that starts on January 1 and ends on December 31.

cash basis accounting   A method of accounting in which expenses and revenues are tracked based on the date that payments enter a business account as cash.

cash flow analysis   A financial statement that shows how much money the company had at the beginning of the month, how much money came in through sales and payments, how much went out in the form of payments, and what was left at the end of the month.

chart of accounts   A list of all the categories that a business uses to organize its financial expenditures and sales.

copyright   The exclusive right to publication or sale of a literary or artistic work.

corporation   A legal entity that is created as an umbrella under which business operation can occur.

cost of sales   The costs directly linked to the production or sale of a product or service, also called the cost of goods sold. These generally include the cost of raw materials, the cost of labor that produced the item sold, and other expenses that were required to sell the product or service.

craft   A special skill or art.

crafter   An artisan who produces a craft product. Alternate term for craftsman or craftsperson.

craftsman   A skilled worker, an artisan.

credit card transaction processing company   An organization that processes the typical credit card transaction and handles the transfer of funds from a credit card account into a company's bank account.

current assets   Company assets that are liquid or that can be converted to cash in less than one year.

demographics   A set of objective characteristics that describes a group of people. Includes characteristics such as age, home ownership, number of children, marital status, residence location, job function, income, and other criteria.

depreciation   An accounting procedure that deducts a certain amount of an asset's worth for each year that it operates.

doing business as (d/b/a)   The form issued to a sole proprietor when a name other than the proprietor's is used for a business. Also called a fictitious name statement.

domain name   A name registered on the Internet as the name of a Web site. An Internet home address unique to an individual or business.

earned income   Income attributed to business operations during a specific period of time.

e-commerce or **electronic commerce**   Buying and selling over the Internet.

e-mail or **electronic ail**   A method of sending mail from one location to another using an electronic delivery medium such as the Internet.

employer identification number (EIN)   A number issued by the IRS to any company with employees.

endcaps   Display units placed at the end of a shelving row.

entrepreneur   Someone who is willing to take personal and financial risks to start a new business.

exchange rate   The rate at which one country's currency is converted into another's.

fictitious name statement   *See* doing business as (d/b/a).

fine arts and crafts   Usually used to describe objects that are completely handmade, such as the work of a potter, glass-blower, artist, or sculptor. The objects require a high-end market, and as a result, they generally sell in the more limited or specialty markets.

fiscal year   The period of time over which a company tracks its annual business accounting operations.

fixed expenses   Business expenses such as rent, equipment leases, and utilities that do not vary each month based on the amount of sales.

FOB   Freight on board. A standard wholesale shipping term meaning charges paid for shipping from the manufacturer's business location to the buyer's place of business.

franchiser   A company that has created a successful business operation and concept and then offers to sell the rights on a limited geographic or market basis. The buyer of the franchise rights is called the franchisee.

freelancer   An individual who works for several different companies at once, helping out on specific projects.

freight forwarder   A company that specializes in shipping, duties, customs, and other administrative complexities related to international commerce.

FTP (File Transfer Protocol)   FTP looks and acts a lot like a giant file manager for Windows. It is commonly used to transmit software, share files, or send pages to a Web site.

gross profit   The amount of money left after all costs of sales are covered. Operational expenses are paid out of gross profit.

HTML   Hypertext Markup Language, used to define text, graphics, layout, fonts, and hypertext links when writing for the World Wide Web.

hyperlinks   Items on the World Wide Web pages that take the visitor to another Web location when they are clicked. Hyperlinks can take the form of text called hypertext, or graphics called hypermedia. When the mouse pointer turns into a hand with one finger pointing, it is in the correct position to click the hyperlink.

income   The amount of money left over after expenses are deducted from the amount of sales revenue.

income statement   A type of financial statement that reflects all the income and expenses for a particular period of time, generally a year.

independent contractor   Roughly interchangeable with "freelancer."

initial public offering (IPO)   A stock trading event in which the stock for a corporation is offered to the general public for the first time.

Internet   The electronic superhighway composed of millions of interconnected computers and servers to exchange massive amounts of text and images on a worldwide basis.

Internet service provider (ISP)   A company that provides access to the Internet for users with a computer, a modem, and the appropriate software.

inventory   Stock on hand, either raw materials or finished goods.

lead time   The amount of shipping time between the time an order is received and the time the order is actually shipped.

liabilities   Amounts owed. Typical liabilities include loans, credit cards, taxes owed, and so on. Short-term liabilities, which are paid back within 12 months, are also called accounts payable. Long-term liabilities include mortgages and equipment loans.

life cycle   The four general phases that a product or service goes through between being introduced to the market and being discontinued or taken off the market.

limited liability company (LLC)   A type of business structure available in almost every state that has many of the advantages of a partnership or Subchapter S corporation, but fewer of their disadvantages.

limited partnership   A special form of partnership in which a partner invests money and does not participate in the daily operation of the business. This partner is also liable only for the amount of money that he or she has invested.

liquid assets   Anything the company owns that can be sold quickly and turned into cash.

market niche   A segment of the market that has an existing need for a specific product or service.

market value   The value of a product or service as determined by what the market will pay for it.

marketing   The presentation (selling) of good or services to a particular target customer or market.

markup   The amount of money added to the cost of producing a product or service to pay for overhead expenses and profit.

mass merchandisers   Companies that sell mass-produced products in high volume; they are also sometimes called discounters.

merchant account   A status available only to businesses for the purpose of being able to accept credit cards as payment for products or services.

mission statement   A statement that clearly defines the overall purpose of a company.

net income   Money left over after all company expenses have been paid out of revenues. Net income can be either positive or negative.

officers   Senior members of a management team or board of directors elected to serve as secretary, treasurer, president, and vice president of the corporation or board.

open-to-buy   The amount of retail dollars allocated for the purchase of future delivery merchandise.

operational expenses   Expenses associated with running a business.

outsourcing   The term for hiring outside help such as individual freelancers or companies to provide services rather than hiring employees.

owner's equity   What is left over after the liabilities are subtracted from the assets.

partnership   One or more people forming a business alliance in which debts and assets are legally linked from the start. Any partner can make a commitment for the business, thereby committing all the other partners.

patent   A document issued by the United States Patent Office granting certain rights to the inventor.

perceived value   The overall value that the customer places on a particular product or service. In addition to an item's price, it is influenced by such factors as delivery lead time, quality of salesmanship, service, style, and other less tangible items.

percentage markup   The amount of money that a business adds to the cost of a product, expressed as a percent.

pro-forma invoice   An advance invoice. The company pays upon receipt of the invoice, and shipment is made after payment is received.

publicity   Working with the media to have a company covered by media such as magazines, newspapers, television, and radio.

registered agent   The official contact point for all legal matters. The registered agent is located at the registered office, which is the official address for corporate business.

registered trademark   Grants exclusive rights of ownership and is issued by the federal government's Office of Trademarks and Patents.

remote stocking   Stock sent to another location to be displayed for sale at the destination site.

retained earnings   Earnings from a company that are reinvested in operating it. An item usually found on a company's balance sheet.

S corporation   A Subchapter S type of corporation that has a limited number of shareholders and in which the profits are passed directly through to the owner.

sales   All the steps taken to get a customer to buy the product or service.

scattershot or shotgun marketing   Marketing that sends the information everywhere in the hope that someone somewhere will buy; the opposite of a targeted or focused marketing plan.

search engines   Sites that help World Wide Web users find information on the Web.

secured line of credit   A line of credit that is a type of loan, with an asset such as real state, fixtures, or equipment as collateral.

server   An Internet service provider's (ISP) fast, high-powered computer that is used as the repository and distributor of data and that controls access to e-mail and various applications. Using a modem to connect to the Internet logs the customer on to one of the ISP's servers.

shareholders   Individuals or organizations that own shares of stock in a company.

short-term goals   Goals that can be met within a short period of time, often the steps that lead to the completion of a long-term goal.

short-term loan   A loan that is to be paid off within one year.

SIC   Standard identification code to identify manufacturers.

software   Computer programs used to accomplish tasks.

sole proprietorship   The owner, personally responsible for all the business's obligations and actions.

storyboards   Sample boards that show customers a finished activity along with the products that were used to create the particular item.

strategy   The art of planning and directing; the skill of devising or managing plans toward a specific goal.

target marketing   An approach that focuses marketing efforts on the groups of potential customers most likely to buy a specific product or service.

tasks   Things or jobs that need to be accomplished as part of completing a project.

tax accounting   A type of accounting concerned solely with how much money will be available to pay in taxes. The goal is usually to minimize the tax bill.

trade name   The business name of a company.

trademark   A word or symbol used to distinguish a product. A registered trademark grants exclusive rights to the use of the trademark, whereas an unregistered trademark does not.

traditional arts and crafts   Usually refers to handmade items, but may include some manufactured products to create the finished item—for example, using purchased silk or dried flowers to make floral arrangements, making ceramics from commercial molds, or doing decorative painting on items that were bought for that purpose.

unearned income   Payments made by a customer for work that has not yet been performed but that is included as income on financial statements.

unsecured line of credit   A line of credit such as a credit card that a company can turn to for cash; it is not backed by any collateral.

variable expenses   Costs that vary according to the amount of a product or service produced. Just as things usually cost less when purchased in bulk, producing a product in large quantities costs less. The price per product generally varies according to how much is produced.

Web hosting   A service performed by an ISP or other organization in which outside companies put their Web sites on computers owned by the ISP, or put servers directly into their facility.

World Wide Web (WWW)   Loosely defined as the portion of the Internet whose pages are interconnected by hyperlinks. The World Wide Web is viewed through a program called a Web browser and is the most popular part of the Internet.

Index

A

accountants
  costs, 179
  selecting, 177-178
  types of services, 178
    bookkeeping services, 178
    Certified Public
      Accountants (CPAs), 178
    IRS enrolled agents (EAs),
      178
    payroll services, 178
    public accountants, 178
    tax preparers, 178
accounting, 136
  accrual method, 136
  cash method, 136
  payroll, 139
  setting up a system, 136
    accounts payable, 137
    accounts receivable, 137
    charts of accounts, 137
    depreciation, 138
    fixed assets, 137
    general ledgers, 137
    liabilities, 138
    liquid assets, 137
  software packages, 76-77
    DAC Easy, 77
    M.Y.O.B. Premier 1.0, 77
    Microsoft Money 2000
      Business & Personal, 77
    Peachtree 7.0, 77
    QuickBooks Pro, 77
accounts payable, 137
accounts receivable, 137
accrual method (accounting), 136
ad copy, 322
Adobe Software Products, 78
advertising, 301-302
agents, registered, 57
agreements, partnership, 51
all rights, 286-287
apparel labeling
  Care Labeling Law, 162
  Content Labeling Law, 162
  disclaimers, 170
  Federal Fair Packaging and
    Labeling Act, 161-162

requirement inquiries (FTC
  Web pages), 164
  Wool Products Labeling Act,
    162-163
applications (art and craft shows),
  231-232
  application forms, 234
  deadlines, 233
  photos and slides, 233-234
  show calendars, 234
  show fees, 234
aromatherapy
  organizations, 361
  products, 167
    Good Manufacturing
      Practice Guidelines, 167
    production and labeling
      regulations, 168
  publications, 362
  suppliers, 363
aromatics (art and craft show displays), 242
art
  organizations, 364
  publications, 364
  suppliers, 364
art and craft shows
  application process, 231-232
    application forms, 234
    deadlines, 233
    fees, 234
    photos and slides, 233-234
    show calendars, 234
  craft show checklist, 245
    business supplies, 245-246
    display requirements,
      246-247
    personal items, 247
  displays, 239-240
    aromatics, 242
    booth planning, 243-244
    color basics, 240-241
    general tips, 244
    layout concepts, 241-242
    lighting, 240
    locating supplies, 244-245
    motion, 242
    promotion, 243
    signs, 241-242

    sound, 240
    table covers, 243
    visual appeal, 240
  Exhibitors' Golden Rule,
    250-252
  locating, 235-236
  selecting, 227-231
    bazaars/flea markets, 228
    festivals and fairs, 229
  starting out, 234-235
  survival tips, 247
    outdoor shows, 248
    travel safety, 248-249
    vehicle safety, 249-250
artisans, 4-5
  trends
    current popular culture, 5-6
    identifying and filling
      needs, 6-7
  White House Crafts
    Collection, 5
arts and crafts
  book publishers, 349-350
  organizations, 348-349
  suppliers, 350-352
assets
  fixed, 137
  liquid, 137
associations (trade), 41
attorneys
  costs, 175
    contingent fees, 175
    flat fees, 175
    hourly fees, 175
    tips on cutting attorneys'
      fees, 177
  selecting, 172
    factors to consider, 173-174
    questions to ask prospec-
      tive attorneys, 173
    research suggestions, 172
  situations suggested for legal
    consultation, 174-175
  working relationship factors,
    176
    attorney-client privilege,
      176

B

balance sheets, 140
banks
    business account guidelines
        and special circumstances,
        143-144
        bounced checks from cus-
            tomers, 144-145
    selecting, 141
        checking accounts, 142-143
basket making
    governmental food regula-
        tions, 165
    suppliers, 365
    trade publications, 365
bazaars, 228
BCA (Business Corporation Act),
    57-58
BCL (Business Corporation Law),
    57-58
beads
    organizations, 365-366
    suppliers, 366
Bedding and Upholstered
    Furniture Laws, 163
best prices, 212
bookkeeping services, 178
booths
    art and craft show displays,
        243-244
    craft malls, 257
BOP (business owner's policy)
    insurance programs, 131
bounced checks, 144-145
boutiques, seasonal, 263-264
brainstorming, 337-338
break-even points, 217
brochures, 322
brokers, merchant, 154
budgets, 149
    operating, 150
        creating, 70
        reducing business costs,
            151
    start-up, 70, 149-150
building codes, home-based busi-
    nesses, 105
Bureau of Consumer Protection
    (Textile Fiber Productions
    Identification Act: Content
    Labeling Law), 162
Business Corporation Act (BCA),
    57-58
Business Corporation Law (BCL),
    57-58
business owner's policy (BOP)
    insurance programs, 131

business plans, 70
    advertising and public rela-
        tions considerations, 71
    element descriptions, 63-69
        business description, 64-65
        competition, 65
        cover sheets, 63
        current financial situation
            and financial manage-
            ment plans, 66-67
        executive summaries, 63,
            69
        marketing plans, 67-68
        operating plans, 67-68
        personnel issues, 66
        products or services, 64-65
        statements of purpose or
            mission statements, 63
        supporting documentation
            inclusions, 68-69
        table of contents, 63, 69
        target markets, 65
    outline example, 62
    pricing and sales considera-
        tions, 70
    start-up capital determination,
        70
Business-Builder Marketing
    Approach, 317
    ad copy and sales brochures,
        322
    increased perceived value, 319
    outreach, 320-322
    product originality, 318-319
businesses
    accepting credit card pay-
        ments, 145
    accounting, 136
        accrual method, 136
        cash method, 136
        payroll, 139
        setting up a system,
            136-138
    banking concerns, 141
        account guidelines and spe-
            cial circumstances,
            143-144
        bounced checks from cus-
            tomers, 144-145
        checking accounts, 142-143
    books, 354-355
    budgets, 149
        operating, 150-151
        start-up, 149-150
    business plans, 62-70
    employer identification num-
        bers (EINs), criteria and steps
        for obtaining, 56

home-based
    building codes, 105
    government regulations,
        107-108
    licensing and permit
        requirements, 105-107
    popularity, 110
    safety issues, 108-110
    taxes, 119-120
    zoning laws, 102-105
income and expenses (profit
    and loss), 139-140
    cost-of-sales expenses, 139
    gross profit, 139
    income, 139
    miscellaneous income and
        expenses, 140
    net profit after taxes, 140
    net profit before taxes, 140
    operating expenses, 140
    owner's equity, 140
insurance, 126
    BOP (Business Owner's
        Policy) insurance pro-
        grams, 131
    business income, 127-128
    Cause-of-Loss Form,
        126-127
    health, 132-133
    liability, 128-131
inventory, 138
    categories, 138
    inventory control systems,
        138-139
key financial statements, 140
    balance sheets, 140
    cash flow analysis state-
        ments, 140-141
    income (P&L) statements,
        140
legal structures, 50
    corporations, 52-58
    partnerships, 51-53, 56-58
    sole proprietorships, 50-51
mistakes to avoid, 288-291
organizations, 352-353
retail, 293-294
    advertising and promotion,
        301-302
    arts and crafts products,
        297-298
    employees, 296-297
    inventory turns, 294-295
    location selection, 296
    margins, 294
    profitability factors,
        298-299
    researching products, 299

resources, 303
store layout and design, 300-301
technology advantages, 295-296
service
need to please (quotes), 209-210
small business responsibilities, 24-26
start-up costs
financing, 151-152
researching, 148-149
taxes
deductions, 116-124
time maximization, 207-209
workers' compensation, 128
buying wholesale, 184
locating sources, 188-191
ordering catalogs, 184-185
qualifications, 184
shopping trade shows, 192-193
suppliers, 186-188
supplies, 185-186

C

calendars (art and craft shows), 234
candle making
organizations, 366
suppliers, 366-367
canopies, 248
capital
expenses, 118
start-up, 70
cards (credit), 145, 155
accepting from customers, 145
e-commerce, 155
point-of-sale terminals, 155
real-time processing, 155
technical compatibility, 155
Care Labeling Law, 162
cash, digital, 153
cash flow analysis statements, 140-141
cash method (accounting), 136
castings, organizations, 378
catalogs (wholesale buying), 184-185
catering, governmental regulations, 168-169
cause-of-loss insurance, 126-127
Celebrity Rights Act, 166
ceramics
organizations, 367
suppliers, 367-368

certificates, resale, 114-115
Certificates of Occupancy, 104
Certified Public Accountants (CPAs), 178
change challenges, 344
diversification, 345
expecting change, 344
hidden opportunities, 345-346
chargebacks, merchant accounts, 156
charts of accounts, 137
checking accounts, 142-143
checklists, preference, 187-188
checks, electronic, 153
classes, make-it/take-it crafts, 268-269
clay (polymer), organizations, 378
closed-ended questions, 46
clothing banks, 368
codes, building (home-based businesses), 105
colors
art and craft show displays, 240-241
fads and trends, 342-343
retail store displays, 300-301
comfort zones, 335-336
commerce service providers (CSP), 153
commercial sales, 95
commercial use issues, 165
Celebrity Rights Act, 166
designer fabrics and logos, 166
communications (computer utilizations), 78-80
e-mail, 80
hyperlinks, 79
World Wide Web (WWW), 79
comparisons, price, 221-222
compensation, workers', 128
competition (business plan descriptions), 65, 338-339
competitive pricing, 214
comprehensive general liability insurance, 129-130
compromise, 15
computers, 82-83
business research, 80
directories, 80
search engines, 80-81
buying, 74
communications utilizations, 78-80
e-mail, 80
hyperlinks, 79
World Wide Web (WWW), 79

market research, 81-82
software, 75
accounting packages, 76-77
image-editing and design, 77-78
Lotus SmartSuite Millennium Edition, 75-76
Office 2000 Standard: Microsoft Office, 76
WordPerfect Office 2000—Small Business Edition, 76
"concealed fillings" (State Bedding and Upholstered Furniture Laws), 163
consignment selling, 260-261
Consumer Product Safety Act, 160
lead testing for food or drink containers, 161
paints and surface coatings, 161
safety guidelines for making toys, 160
Consumer Product Safety Commission (CPSC), 160-163
Content Labeling Law, 162-164
contingent fees (attorney charges), 175
contracts, craft malls, 256
copyrights, 88-89
books, 357
copyright law, 88
forms
Web site, 357
notice of copyright, 90
owners' rights, 89
proof of ownership, 89
registering, 89-90
corporations, 52
benefits over general partnerships, 53
corporate kits, 56
deciding where to incorporate, 54
employer identification numbers (EINs)
criteria and steps for obtaining, 56
formation steps, 53-54
name selection, 55
trademark implications, 55-56
S corporations, 53
state regulations and fees, 57-58
tax structures, 54-55
trade name registration, 87
versus limited liability companies (LLCs), 52-53

cosmetics, 167
aromatherapy products and
herbal remedies
production and labeling
regulations, 168
Good Manufacturing Practice
Guidelines, 167
soap labeling, 167-168
cost of goods sold
deductions for business
expenses versus deductions
for cost of goods sold, 118
IRS Publication 538,
"Inventories," 118
necessary expenses, 117
ordinary expenses, 117
cost pricing, 214
cost-of-sales expenses, 139
costs, 215
accountants, 179
attorney consultation, 175
contingent fees, 175
flat fees, 175
hourly fees, 175
tips on cutting attorneys'
fees, 177
determining, 216-217
direct, 215
indirect, 215
fixed costs, 215-216
variable costs, 216
merchant accounts, 156-157
chargebacks, 156
discount rates, 156
gateway access fees, 156
high-risk processors, 156
MAP fees, 156
monthly fees and mini-
mums, 156
setup and equipment fees,
156
transaction fees, 156
real, 205-206
reducing business costs, 151
start-up
financing, 151-152
researching, 148-149
unit cost per item, 214-215
materials logs, 215
time logs, 214-215
cotton products, labeling requirement inquiries (FTC Web pages),
164
cover sheets (business plans), 63
covers, table (art and craft show
displays), 243
CPAs (Certified Public
Accountants), 178
CPSC (Consumer Product Safety
Commission), 160-163

Craft Biz Connection e-mail business discussion group, 190
craft malls, 253-254
benefits, 255
booth space monitoring, 257
contact information, 259-260
American Craft Malls, Inc.,
259
Coomers, 259
Crafters Showcase, 259
Craftworks, 259
First Capital Craft Mall, 259
Handcrafters Barn, 259
Peddler's Village Craft
Malls, 259
Quilted Bear, 260
contracts, 256
National Craft Association
(NCA) Craft Mall Directory,
259
record systems, 257-258
selecting, 255-256
stocking and display setup
programs, 255
tips for success, 256, 258
crafts, fine arts versus traditional
crafts, 21
craftspeople, 11
creative thinking, 336-337
brainstorming, 337-338
competitive edge, 338-339
customer service edge,
339-340
credit cards
accepting from customers, 145
e-commerce, 155
point-of-sale terminals, 155
real-time processing, 155
technical compatibility,
155
CSP (commerce service providers),
153
customer service, 339-340
customers
accepting credit card payments, 145
bounced checks, 144-145
cycles (life), products, 343-344

D

DAC Easy accounting software,
77
deceptive pricing, 221
free offers, 222
price comparisons, 221-222
decision making, 14-15

decorative painting
books, 369
organizations, 368-369
suppliers, 369-370
deductions
business, 116, 120
avoiding restrictions, 117
business trip meals, 123
capital expenses, 118
cost of goods sold, 118
criteria for deductibility,
117
entertainment, 121-122
equipment, 121
hobby versus business dis-
tinctions, 116
home phones, 122-123
IRS Publication 334, "Tax
Guide for Small
Businesses," 116
keeping records, 124
membership dues, 122
personal expenses, 119
vehicle usage, 120
home-based businesses, 119
home-office storage deductions, 119-120
IRS Publication 587,
"Business Use of Your
Home," 119
defining your dream, 14
life choices, 14-15
quiz, 15-16
depreciation, 138
designs
freelance designing
books, 284-286
consumer craft market,
283-286
magazines, 284
manufacturers, 286
publishing, 281-283
retail stores, 300
color effects, 300-301
merchandise arrangement,
301
traffic flow, 301
digital cash, 153
direct costs, 215
direct selling, wholesale products,
277-278
directories, 80
disclaimers, 170
discount rates, merchant
accounts, 156
disintermediation, 153
displays, art and craft shows,
239-240
aromatics, 242
booth planning, 243-244
color basics, 240-241

general tips, 244
layout concepts, 241-242
lighting, 240
locating supplies, 244-245
motion, 242
promotion, 243
requirements, 246-247
signs, 241-242
sound, 240
suppliers, contact information, 359
table covers, 243
visual appeal, 240
doll-making
National Institute of American Doll Artists (NIADA), 370
suppliers, 370
dollar markup method (retail pricing), 220-221
domain names, 331-332
dreams, defining, 14
life choices, 14-15
quiz, 15-16
drink containers, lead testing, 161

E

e-cash, 153
e-Charge Corporation, 155
e-commerce, 152-153
accepting credit cards, 155
point-of-sale terminals, 155
real-time processing, 155
technical compatibility, 155
commerce service providers (CSP), 153
digital cash, 153
disintermediation, 153
electronic checks, 153
electronic wallets, 153
extranets, 153
hard goods versus soft goods, 154
high-risk processors, 154
immerce, 154
merchant accounts, 154-155
costs, 156-157
merchant brokers, 154
microtransactions, 155
phone-cash, 155
telephone billing systems, 155
e-mail rules, 80, 332-333
signature files, 333
spam versus permission-based e-mail, 333-334
EAs (Enrolled Agents), 178
efficiency, work area, 195-200

EINs (employer identification numbers), 56
electronic
checks, 153
rights, 286-287
wallets, 153
embellishments, apparel and accessories, 368
employees, 296-297
employer identification numbers (EINs), 56
engines (search), 80
enrolled agents (EAs), 178
entertainment expenses, tax deductions, 121-122
entrepreneurs
Richards, Torrie example, 16-19
strategy suggestions, 18-19
traits associated with success, 11-12
craftspeople, 11
creative phase, 12
organizational phase, 12
planners, 11
productive phase, 12
self-assessment, 28
visionaries, 11
equipment expenses, tax deductions, 121
executive summaries (business plans), 63, 69
Exhibitors' Golden Rule, 250-252
expenses
business, 120
business trip meals, 123
entertainment, 121-122
equipment, 121
home phones, 122-123
keeping records, 124
membership dues, 122
vehicle usage, 120
capital, 118
cost-of-sales, 139
necessary, 117
operating, 140
budgets, 150-151
ordinary, 117
personal, 119
start-up budgets, 149-150
extranets, 153

F

fabrics
commercial use issues
designer fabrics and logos, 166

labeling
Care Labeling Law, 162
Content Labeling Law, 162
Federal Fair Packaging and Labeling Act, 161-162
Flammable Fabrics Act, 163
requirement inquiries (FTC Web pages), 164
fads
colors, 342-343
forecasters, 343
social trends, 342-343
versus trends, 341-342
fairs, 229
FDA (Food and Drug Administration), food product safety
gift baskets, 165
resale and catering, 168-169
feather and down products, labeling requirement inquiries (FTC Web pages), 164
Federal Fair Packaging and Labeling Act, 161-162
Federal Trade Commission (FTC)
Federal Fair Packaging and Labeling Act, 161-162
mail-order merchandise rules, 169-170
product labeling inquiries (Web pages), 164
Textile Fiber Productions Identification Act
Content Labeling Law, 162
Web site, 161
fee-for-service (indemnity) plans, 132-133
fees
accountants, 179
art and craft shows, 234
attorney, 175
contingent fees, 175
flat fees, 175
hourly fees, 175
tips on cutting attorneys' fees, 177
state corporation fees, 57-58
festivals, 229
fiber art
organizations, 379-380
suppliers, 381-382
trade publications, 380-381
fibers, labeling
Care Labeling Law, 162
Content Labeling Law, 162
Federal Fair Packaging and Labeling Act, 161-162
requirement inquiries (FTC Web pages), 164

files, signature, 333
finances
    accepting credit card payments, 145
    accounting, 136
        accrual method, 136
        cash method, 136
        payroll, 139
        setting up a system, 136-138
    banking concerns, 141
        account guidelines and special circumstances, 143-144
        bounced checks from customers, 144-145
        checking accounts, 142-143
    budgets, 149
        operating, 150-151
        start-up, 149-152
    income and expenses (profit and loss), 139-140
        cost-of-sales expenses, 139
        gross profit, 139
        income, 139
        miscellaneous income and expenses, 140
        net profit after taxes, 140
        net profit before taxes, 140
        operating expenses, 140
        owner's equity, 140
    key financial statements, 140
        balance sheets, 140
        cash flow analysis statements, 140-141
        income (P&L) statements, 140
financial management plans (business plans), 66-67
financial statements, 140
    balance sheets, 140
    cash flow analysis statements, 140-141
    income (P&L) statements, 140
fine arts and crafts, 21
fixed
    assets, 137
    costs, 215-216
Flammable Fabrics Act, 163
flat fees (attorney charges), 175
flea markets, 228
floral crafts
    suppliers, 371
    trade publications, 371
focus (business), refining, 20-21
follow-up sales, 269-270
Food and Drug Administration (FDA), food product safety
    gift baskets, 165
    resale and catering, 168-169

food
    containers
        lead testing, 161
    products (governmental regulations)
        gift baskets, 165
        resale and catering, 168-169
forecasters, fads and trends, 343
formulas, product pricing, 218-220
free offers, 222
freelance work
    designs
        books, 284-286
        consumer craft market, 283-286
        magazines, 284
        manufacturers, 286
    online resources, 207
    payment factors, 206
    research tips, 207
FTC (Federal Trade Commission)
    Federal Fair Packaging and Labeling Act, 161
    mail-order merchandise rules, 169-170
    product labeling inquiries (Web pages), 164
    Textile Fiber Productions Identification Act
        Content Labeling Law, 162
fur products, labeling requirement inquiries (FTC Web pages), 164

G

Gale's Directory of Associations, 41, 189
gateway access fees (merchant accounts), 156
General Information Services, 56
general
    ledgers, 137
    partnerships, 51-52, 56
        employer identification numbers (EINs), 56
gift basket making
    governmental food regulations, 165
    suppliers, 372
    trade publications, 372
    trade shows, 371-372
glass arts and crafts
    books, 374
    organizations, 372-373
    suppliers, 375

goals, 28-29, 32
    achieving, 14
    circumstantial flexibility, 33
    defining, 29-30
    quantifying, 30-31
    reviewing, 30
    short-term goal-setting, 31-32
Golden Rule of Exhibitors, 250-252
Good Manufacturing Practice Guidelines, 167
government regulations
    Celebrity Rights Act, 166
    Consumer Product Safety Act, 160-161
        lead testing for food or drink containers, 161
        paints and surface coatings, 161
        safety guidelines for making toys, 160
    food products
        gift baskets, 165
        resale and catering, 168-169
    Good Manufacturing Practice Guidelines
        cosmetics, 167
    home-based businesses, 107-108
        state business licenses, 108
    labeling
        aromatherapy products and herbal remedies, 168
        Care Labeling Law, 162
        Content Labeling Law, 162
        disclaimers, 170
        Federal Fair Packaging and Labeling Act, 161-162
        Flammable Fabrics Act, 163
        requirement inquiries (FTC Web pages), 164
        soap, 167-168
        State Bedding and Upholstered Furniture Laws, 163
        Wool Products Labeling Act, 162-163
    mail-order merchandise FTC Rules, 169-170
gross profit, 139
group events, planning, 265-268
Guide to Freelance Rates and Standard Practice, 207

H

handmade products
    current popular culture trends, 5-6
    identifying and filling market needs, 6-7

hang tags, suppliers' contact information, 360
hard goods, 154
health insurance, 132
  fee-for-service (indemnity) plans, 132-133
  managed care, 132
  small business provisions, 133
herbal remedies, 167
  Good Manufacturing Practice Guidelines, 167
  production and labeling regulations, 168
high-risk processors (merchant accounts), 154-156
home shows, 263-264
home-based businesses
  building codes, 105
  government regulations, 107-108
  licensing and permit requirements, 105-107
  popularity, 110
  safety issues, 108-109
    Occupational Safety and Health Act (OSHA), 109-110
  taxes, 119
    home-office storage deductions, 119-120
    IRS Publication 587, "Business Use of Your Home," 119
  zoning laws, 102
    Certificates of Occupancy, 104
    dealing with local building and zoning officials, 102-104
    obstacles, 104-105
horizontal presentation (retail merchandise), 301
hourly fees, attorneys, 175
household furnishings, labeling
  Care Labeling Law, 162
  Content Labeling Law, 162
  disclaimers, 170
  Federal Fair Packaging and Labeling Act, 161-162
  requirement inquiries (FTC Web pages), 164
  Wool Products Labeling Act, 162-163
how-to information, selling, 288
hyperlinks, 79

I

identities, business, 184
image-editing and design software packages, 77-78
  Adobe Software Products, 78
  Microsoft FrontPage 2000/PhotoDraw 2000 V.2, 78
  Microsoft Publisher 2000 Deluxe, 78
  Print Artist Grande Suite, 78
immerce, 153-154
income
  freelance work
    determination factors, 206
    online resources, 207
    research tips, 207
  hourly labor rates
    calculating, 203-205
income and expenses (profit and loss), 139-140
  cost-of-sales expenses, 139
  gross profit, 139
  income, 139
  miscellaneous income and expenses, 140
  net profit after taxes, 140
  net profit before taxes, 140
  operating expenses, 140
  owner's equity, 140
increased perceived values, 319
indemnity (fee-for-service) plans, 132-133
indirect costs, 215
  fixed costs, 215-216
  variable costs, 216
industrial design registration, 92-93
infringements, intellectual property rights, 95-96
ingredients, 167
Institute of Store Planners and Visual Merchandising and Store, The, *Stores and Retail Spaces 2*, 303
insurance, 126
  BOP (Business Owner's Policy) insurance programs, 131
  business income, 127-128
  Cause-of-Loss Form, 126-127
  health, 132
    fee-for-service (indemnity) plans, 132-133
    managed care, 132
    small business provisions, 133

liability, 128-129
  comprehensive general liability, 129-130
  products, 130-131
intellectual property, 86
  copyrights, 88-89
    copyright law, 88
    notice of copyright, 90
    owners' rights, 89
    proof of ownership, 89
    registering, 89-90
  industrial design registration, 92-93
  infringement issues, 95-96
  patents, 92
  plant breeders' rights, 93
  producing competitive products, 96-97
  protecting your rights, 94
  registering, 94
  trade name registration, 87-88
  trademarks, 91-92
  types, 86-87
Internet
  e-mail rules, 332-333
    signature files, 333
    spam versus permission-based e-mail, 333-334
  marketing
    domain names, 331-332
    keeping visitors at your site, 329-330
    strategies, 328-329
    Web site start-up, 325-328
    why people don't buy, 330-331
Internet Banking System, 155
inventory, 138
  categories, 138
  inventory control systems, 138-139
  turns
    retail sales, 294-295
invoices, pro-forma, 275
IRS (Internal Revenue Service)
  business deductions, 116, 120
    avoiding restrictions, 117
    business trip meals, 123
    capital expenses, 118
    criteria for deductibility, 117
    deductions for business expenses versus deductions for cost of goods sold, 118
    entertainment, 121-122
    equipment, 121
    hobby versus business distinctions, 116

home phones, 122-123
keeping records, 124
membership dues, 122
personal expenses, 119
vehicle usage, 120
home-based businesses, 119
home-office storage deductions, 119-120
obtaining forms, 123
Web site, 57

J

jewelry-making
organizations, 375
suppliers, 376
trade publications, 376
juried craft shows, 232

K–L

keystone method (retail pricing), 220-221
kits (corporate), 56

labels
aromatherapy products and herbal remedies, 168
disclaimers, 170
Federal Fair Packaging and Labeling Act, 161-162
Flammable Fabrics Act, 163
making required labels
supply sources, 164-165
requirement inquiries
FTC Web pages, 164
soap, 167-168
State Bedding and Upholstered Furniture Laws, 163
suppliers
contact information, 360
Textile Fiber Productions Identification Act
Care Labeling Law, 162
Content Labeling Law, 162
Wool Products Labeling Act, 162-163
Lamp Specialties, Inc., 370
laws
Celebrity Rights Act, 166
copyright, 88
food products
gift baskets, 165
resale and catering, 168-169
Good Manufacturing Practice Guidelines, 167

labeling
aromatherapy products and herbal remedies, 168
Care Labeling Law, 162
Content Labeling Law, 162
disclaimers, 170
Federal Fair Packaging and Labeling Act, 161-162
Flammable Fabrics Act, 163
requirement inquiries (FTC Web pages), 164
soap, 167-168
State Bedding and Upholstered Furniture Laws, 163
Wool Products Labeling Act, 162-163
safety
Consumer Product Safety Act, 160-161
zoning
home-based businesses, 102-104
lawyers. *See* attorneys
layout
art and craft show displays, 241-242
retail stores, 300
color effects, 300-301
merchandise arrangement, 301
traffic flow, 301
lead, Consumer Product Safety Act's (CPSA) requirements, 161
lead times, 187
leather crafts, suppliers, 376-377
legal assistance resources, 357-358
legal structures, businesses, 50
corporations, 52-58
partnerships, 51-53, 56-58
sole proprietorships, 50-51
liabilities, 138
liability insurance, 128-129
comprehensive general liability, 129-130
products, 130-131
licenses
home-based businesses requirements, 105-107
new product lines, 283
life choices, 14-15
compromise, 15
decision making, 14-15
life cycles, products, 343-344
lighting, art and craft show displays, 240
limited liability companies (LLCs). *See* LLCs
limited partnerships. *See* LLCs
liquid assets, 137

LLCs (limited liability companies), 51-52, 56
benefits over general partnerships, 53
employer identification numbers (EINs), 56
state regulations and fees, 57-58
versus corporations, 52-53
Lotus SmartSuite Millennium Edition, 75-76

M

M.Y.O.B. Premier 1.0 accounting software, 77
mail-order merchandise, FTC Rules, 169-170
make-it/take-it craft parties, 268-269
malls, craft, 253-254
benefits, 255
booth space monitoring, 257
contact information, 259-260
American Craft Malls, Inc., 259
Coomers, 259
Crafters Showcase, 259
Craftworks, 259
First Capital Craft Mall, 259
Handcrafters Barn, 259
Peddler's Village Craft Malls, 259
Quilted Bear, 260
contracts, 256
National Craft Association (NCA) Craft Mall Directory, 259
record systems, 257-258
selecting, 255-256
stocking and display setup programs, 255
tips for success, 256, 258
managed care systems, 132
manufacturers, freelance design work, 286
MAPs (Merchant Account Providers) fees, 156
margins, retail sales, 294
market research, 37-40
benefits, 38-39
computer utilizations, 81-82
data topics
customer information, 39
environmental factors, 40
marketplace competition, 39-40

primary, 40, 42, 44
  qualitative, 42-43
  quantitative, 42-44
process steps, 45, 47
  collecting data, 46
  defining marketing problems and opportunities, 45
  designing research instruments, 46
  developing objectives, budgets, and timetables, 45-46
  organizing and analyzing data, 47
  presenting and utilizing market research findings, 47
  selecting research types, methods, and techniques, 46
secondary, 40, 42
  sources, 41-42
types
  secondary, 41
market-based pricing, 217-218
marketing
  computer utilizations, 82
  e-mail rules, 332-333
    signature files, 333
    spam versus permission-based e-mail, 333-334
  keywords, 322
    content, 323
    patience, 323
    perseverance, 323-324
    plan, 322-323
  opportunities, 315, 317
    creating a market, 316-317
    off-hours marketing, 316
    self-promotion, 316
    word-of-mouth, 316
  plans, 67-68
  strategies
    attention-getting techniques, 308
    Business-Builder Marketing Approach, 317-322
    confident presentations, 313-314
    reaching your target market, 311-313
    silent sales partners, 308-311
  trade shows
    wholesale products, 272-273

materials logs, 215
meals, tax deductions, 123
membership dues, tax deductions, 122
Merchant Account Providers (MAPs) fees, 156
merchant accounts, 154-155
  costs, 156-157
    chargebacks, 156
    discount rates, 156
    gateway access fees, 156
    high-risk processors, 156
    MAP fees, 156
    monthly fees and minimums, 156
    setup and equipment fees, 156
    transaction fees, 156
  merchant brokers, 154
  microtransactions, 155
  phone-cash, 155
  telephone billing systems, 155
merchant brokers, 154
metal arts
  organizations, 377
  suppliers, 377-378
Microsoft FrontPage 2000/ PhotoDraw 2000 V.2 software, 78
Microsoft Money 2000 Business & Personal accounting software, 77
Microsoft Publisher 2000 Deluxe software, 78
microtransactions, 155
Midwest Art Fairs, 236
mileage rates, 120
minimum orders, 185-186, 275
mission statements
  business plans, 63
  developing, 21-22
molds, organizations, 378
monthly fees and minimums, merchant accounts, 156

N

names
  domain, 331-332
  selecting corporations, 55-56
  trade registration, 87-88
National Artcraft Co., 371
National Institute of American Doll Artists (NIADA), 370
National Mail Order Association, 358
National Trade and Professional Associations, 41, 189
national wholesale buying centers, 188

NCA (National Craft Association), 188, 191
necessary expenses, 117
"need to please," 209-210
needlework
  organizations, 379-380
  suppliers, 381-382
  trade publications, 380-381
needs, identifying and filling, 6-7
net profit
  after taxes, 140
  before taxes, 140
NIADA (National Institute of American Doll Artists), 370
no mass production, 95
numbers, sales tax, 114-115

O

occupancy, Certificates of Occupancy, 104
Occupational Safety and Health Act (OSHA)
  home-based businesses, 109
  Small Business Safety Management Series, 110
off-hours marketing, 316
Office 2000 Standard: Microsoft Office, 76
offshore companies, 58
open houses, 264-265
open-ended questions, 46
open-to-buy systems, 200-201
  buying tips, 201-202
  planning structure, 201
operating
  budgets, 150
    creating, 70
    reducing business costs, 151
  plans
    business plan descriptions, 67-68
ordering catalogs, wholesale buying, 184-185
ordinary expenses, 117
organizational phase, 12
organizations
  aromatherapy, toiletries, soaps, and personal care products, 361
  art, 364
  arts and crafts, 348-349
  beads, 365-366
  businesses, 352-353
  candle making, 366
  ceramics and pottery, 367
  decorative painting, 368-369

Gift Association of America (GAA), 303
glass arts and crafts, 372-373
Hobby Industry Association, 303
Insurance Information Institute, 129
jewelry-making, 375
metal arts, 377
molds and castings, 378
National Institute of American Doll Artists (NIADA), 370
National Writer's Union, 207
polymer clay, 378
rubber stamps, paper arts, and scrapbooks/memorybooks, 379
sewing, fiber art, and needlework arts, 379-380
Small Business Administration (SBA), 303
woodworking, 383
originality (product), 318-319
OSHA (Occupational Safety and Health Act)
  home-based businesses, 109
  Small Business Safety Management Series, 110
outdoor art and craft shows, 248
outsourcing services, 356
overhead, 215
  fixed costs, 215-216
  variable costs, 216
owner's equity, 140
owners' rights (copyrights), 89

P

paints, Consumer Product Safety Act's (CPSA) requirements, 161
paper arts
  organizations, 379
  suppliers, 379
  trade publications, 379
parties, make-it/take-it crafts, 268-269
partnerships
  agreements
    essential elements, 51
  employer identification numbers (EINs), criteria and steps for obtaining, 56
  general, 51-52, 56
  limited (LLCs), 51-52, 56
    benefits over general partnerships, 53
    state regulations and fees, 57-58
    versus corporations, 52-53

patents, 92
  books, 357
  research information, 357
payment methods, customers, 145
payroll
  accounting, 139
  services, 178
Peachtree 7.0 accounting software, 77
perceived values, 319
permission-based e-mail, 333-334
permits, home-based business requirements, 105-107
personal care products, 167
  aromatherapy products and herbal remedies, production, and labeling regulations, 168
  Good Manufacturing Practice Guidelines, 167
  organizations, 361
  publications, 362
  soap labeling, 167-168
  suppliers, 363
personal expenses, 119
personnel issues (business plans), 66
phone-cash, 155
photographs, arts and craft show applications, 233-234
planners, 11
planning
  group events, 265-268
  make-it/take-it craft parties, 268-269
plans
  business, 70
    advertising and public relations considerations, 71
    element descriptions, 63-69
    outline example, 62
    pricing and sales considerations, 70
    start-up capital determination, 70
  marketing, 322-323
  profit, 340-341
plant breeders' rights, 93
  obtaining, 93
  specific protections, 93
point-of-sale terminals, 155
policies, pricing, 213-214
  competitive pricing, 214
  cost pricing, 214
  value pricing, 213
polymer clay
  organizations, 378
  suppliers, 378

popular culture trends, 5-6
pottery
  organizations, 367
  suppliers, 367-368
preference checklists, 187-188
price comparisons, 221-222
price fixing, 217
pricing, 215
  cost determination, 216-217
  deceptive pricing, 221
    free offers, 222
    price comparisons, 221-222
  direct costs, 215
  indirect costs, 215
    fixed costs, 215-216
    variable costs, 216
  market-based pricing, 217-218
  policies, 213-214
    competitive pricing, 214
    cost pricing, 214
    value pricing, 213
  product formulas, 218-220
  real costs, 205-206
  retail, 220
    dollar markup method, 220-221
    keystone method, 220-221
  strategies, 211-213
  unit cost per item, 214-215
    materials logs, 215
    time logs, 214-215
primary research, 40, 42, 44
  qualitative, 42-43
  quantitative, 42-43
    mail surveys, 44
    personal surveys, 43
    telephone surveys, 44
Print Artist Grande Suite software, 78
pro-forma invoices, 275
productive phase, 12
products
  aromatherapy products and herbal remedies, production and labeling regulations, 168
  business plan descriptions, 64-65
  commercial use issues, 165
    Celebrity Rights Act, 166
    designer fabrics and logos, 166
  Consumer Product Safety Commission (CPSC), Consumer Product Safety Act, 160-161
  cosmetics, 167
    Good Manufacturing Practice Guidelines, 167
    soap labeling, 167-168

food
  gift baskets, 165
  governmental regulations, 165, 168-169
  resale and catering, 168-169
handmade
  current popular culture trends, 5-6
  identifying and filling market needs, 6-7
labeling
  aromatherapy products and herbal remedies, 168
  Care Labeling Law, 162
  Content Labeling Law, 162
  disclaimers, 170
  Federal Fair Packaging and Labeling Act, 161-162
  Flammable Fabrics Act, 163
  requirement inquiries (FTC Web pages), 164
  soap, 167-168
  State Bedding and Upholstered Furniture Laws, 163
  Wool Products Labeling Act, 162-163
life cycles, 343-344
originality, 318-319
personal care
  organizations, 361
  publications, 362
  suppliers, 363
pricing, 215
  cost determination, 216-217
  deceptive pricing, 221-222
  direct costs, 215
  formulas, 218-220
  indirect costs, 215-216
  market-based pricing, 217-218
  policies, 213-214
  real cost, 205-206
  retail, 220-221
  strategies, 211-213
  unit cost per item, 214-215
selling
  artisans' open houses, 264-265
  art and craft shows, 230-236, 239-252
  consignment, 260-261
  craft malls, 253-260
  follow-up sales, 269-270
  home shows, 263-264
  make-it/take-it craft parties, 268-269

planning group events, 265-268
  seasonal boutiques, 263-264
  wholesale, 271-278
products liability insurance, 130-131
professional help
  accountants, 177-178
    costs, 179
    types of services, 178
  attorneys, 172
    costs, 175, 177
    factors to consider, 173-174
    questions to ask prospective attorneys, 173
    research suggestions, 172
    situations suggested for legal consultation, 174-175
    working relationship factors, 176
  selecting appropriate professionals to meet your needs, 171-172
profit plans, 340-341
profit and loss, 139-140
  cost-of-sales expenses, 139
  gross profit, 139
  income, 139
  miscellaneous income and expenses, 140
  net profit after taxes, 140
  net profit before taxes, 140
  operating expenses, 140
  owner's equity, 140
  statements, 140
programs, stocking and display setup, 255
promotion
  art and craft show displays, 243
  retail stores, 301-302
proof of ownership (copyrights), 89
property (intellectual), 86
  copyrights, 88-90
  industrial design registration, 92-93
  infringement issues, 95-96
  patents, 92
  plant breeders' rights, 93
  producing competitive products, 96-97
  protecting your rights, 94
  registering, 94
  trade name registration, 87-88
  trademarks, 91-92
  types, 86-87

public accountants, 178
publications
  aromatherapy, toiletries, soaps, and personal care products, 362
  art, 364
  trade
    ABC Directory, The, 235
    Arts and Crafts Show Guide Magazine, 235
    Choices, 236
    Craft Master News, 236
    Festival Network Online, 236
    Mid-Atlantic Craft Show List, 236
    Midwest Art Fairs, 236
    National Craft Association, 236
    SAC News Monthly, 236
    Sunshine Artist Magazine, 236
    TSNN.com, 236
    Where It's at Magazine, 236
publishers, art and craft books, 349-350
publishing designs, 281-283

Q

qualifications, wholesale buying, 184
qualitative research, 42-43
quantitative research, 42-43
  mail surveys, 44
  personal surveys, 43
  telephone surveys, 44
QuickBooks Pro accounting software, 77
quizzes, discovering your passion, 15-16

R

rates
  freelance work
    determination factors, 206
    online resources, 207
    research tips, 207
  labor
    calculating hourly charges, 203-205
    real cost, 205-206
RBMCA (Revised Model Business Corporation Act), 57-58
real costs, 205-206
real-time processing, 155
records, business expenses, 124

regional wholesale buying centers, 188
registered agents, 57
registration
 copyrights, 89-90
 industrial design, 92-93
 intellectual property, 94
 trade names, 87-88
  corporate names, 87
 trademarks, 91-92
regulations (governmental)
 Celebrity Rights Act, 166
 Consumer Product Safety Act, 160
  lead testing for food or drink containers, 161
  paints and surface coatings, 161
  safety guidelines for making toys, 160
 food products
  gift baskets, 165
  resale and catering, 168-169
 FTC rules, 169-170
 Good Manufacturing Practice Guidelines
  cosmetics, 167
  home-based businesses, 107-108
 labeling
  aromatherapy products and herbal remedies, 168
  Care Labeling Law, 162
  Content Labeling Law, 162
  disclaimers, 170
  Federal Fair Packaging and Labeling Act, 161-162
  Flammable Fabrics Act, 163
  requirement inquiries (FTC Web pages), 164
  soap, 167-168
  State Bedding and Upholstered Furniture Laws, 163
  Wool Products Labeling Act, 162-163
reps (sales), wholesale products, 276-277
resale certificates, 114-115, 184
research (market), 37-40
 benefits, 38-39
 computer utilizations, 80-82
 data topics
  customer information, 39
  environmental factors, 40
  marketplace competition, 39-40

primary, 40, 42, 44
 qualitative, 42-43
 quantitative, 42-44
process steps, 45, 47
 collecting data, 46
 defining marketing problems and opportunities, 45
 designing research instruments, 46
 developing objectives, budgets, and timetables, 45-46
 organizing and analyzing data, 47
 presenting and utilizing market research findings, 47
 selecting research types, methods, and techniques, 46
secondary, 40-42
researching
 attorneys, 172
 start-up costs, 148-149
Revised Model Business Corporation Act (RBMCA), 57-58
ribbon suppliers, contact information, 360-361
Richards, Torrie, business story, 16-19
rights
 all, 286-287
 electronic, 286-287
rubber stamps
 organizations, 379
 suppliers, 379
 trade publications, 379

S

S corporations, 53
safety
 CPSC's guidelines
  lead testing for food or drink containers, 161
  paints and surface coatings, 161
  toys, 160
 food products
  governmental regulations, 165, 168-169
 home-based businesses, 108-109
  Occupational Safety and Health Act (OSHA), 109-110

show travel, 248-249
 vehicle, 249-250
salary
 freelance work
  determination factors, 206
  online resources, 207
  research tips, 207
 hourly labor rates
  calculating, 203-205
sales reps, wholesale products, 276-277
sales taxes
 resale certificates, 114-115
 sales tax numbers, 114-115
 tips, 115-116
scrapbooks
 organizations, 379
 suppliers, 379
 trade publications, 379
search engines, 80-81
seasonal boutiques, 263-264
secondary research sources, 40-42
 banks, real estate brokers, and insurance companies, 41
 books and business publications, 41
 Business Information Centers (BICs), 42
 Chambers of Commerce, 41
 college marketing departments, 41
 competitive businesses, 42
 federal government resources, 41
 libraries, 41
 magazines and newspapers, 41
 media representatives, 42
 regional planning organizations, 42
 trade associations, 41
 wholesalers and manufacturers, 41
self-assessments, 26
 entrepreneurial traits, 28
 personal strengths and weaknesses, 26-28
selling
 designs, 281-283
 how-to information, 288
 products
  artisans' open houses, 264-265
  arts and craft shows, 230-236, 239-252
  consignment, 260-261
  craft malls, 253-260
  follow-up sales, 269-270
  home shows, 263-264
  make-it/take-it craft parties, 268-269

planning group events, 265-268
seasonal boutiques, 263-264
wholesale, 271-278
selling out, 235
service (customer), 339-340
service businesses
"need to please," 209-210
pricing, 215
cost determination, 216-217
direct costs, 215
indirect costs, 215-216
market-based pricing, 217-218
policies, 213-214
strategies, 211-213
unit cost per item, 214-215
sewing
organizations, 379-380
suppliers, 381-382
trade publications, 380-381
shipping wholesale products
charges, 275-276
scheduling, 276
short-term goals, setting, 31-32
shows
art and craft
application process, 231-234
craft show checklist, 245-247
displays, 239-245
Exhibitors' Golden Rule, 250-252
locating, 235-236
selecting, 227-231
starting out, 234-235
survival tips, 247-250
home, 263-264
trade
wholesale buying, 188
wholesale marketing, 272-273
SIC (Standard Industrial Classification) code, 42
signature files, 333
signs, art and craft show displays, 241-242
silent sales partners, 308-311
slides, art and craft show applications, 233-234
soaps
organizations, 361
publications, 362
suppliers, 363
social trends, 342-343
soft goods, 154
software, 75

accounting packages, 76-77
DAC Easy, 77
M.Y.O.B. Premier 1.0, 77
Microsoft Money 2000 Business & Personal, 77
Peachtree 7.0, 77
QuickBooks Pro, 77
image-editing and design packages, 77-78
Adobe Software Products, 78
Microsoft FrontPage 2000/PhotoDraw 2000 V.2, 78
Microsoft Publisher 2000 Deluxe, 78
Print Artist Grande Suite, 78
Lotus SmartSuite Millennium Edition, 75-76
Office 2000 Standard: Microsoft Office, 76
WordPerfect Office 2000— Small Business Edition, 76
sole proprietorships, 50-51
sound, art and craft show displays, 240
spam, 333-334
Standard Industrial Classification (SIC) code, 42
start-up capital, determination factors, 70
start-up costs, 149-150
financing, 151-152
banks and credit unions, 152
friends and relatives, 152
personal savings, 151
venture capital firms, 152
researching, 148-149
starting out tips, 8-9, 12
assessing personal strengths and weaknesses, 26-28
entrepreneurial traits, 28
choosing the right business, 9-10, 19-20
defining your dream, 14
life choices, 14-15
quiz, 15-16
good reasons to start a business, 10-11
mission statements, 21-22
refining your business focus, 20-21
Richards, Torrie example, 16-19
strategy suggestions, 18-19

State Bedding and Upholstered Furniture Laws, 163
state business licenses, home-based businesses, 108
state corporation fees, 57-58
statements, financial, 140
balance sheets, 140
cash flow analysis statements, 140-141
income (P&L) statements, 140
statements of purpose. *See* mission statements
stocking and display setup programs, 255
storage deductions, home offices, 119-120
stores, retail, 293-294
advertising and promotion, 301-302
arts and crafts products, 297-298
employees, 296-297
inventory turns, 294-295
layout and design, 300-301
location selection, 296
margins, 294
profitability factors, 298-299
researching products, 299
resources, 303
technology advantages, 295-296
Stores and Retail Spaces 2 (Institute of Store Planners and Visual Merchandising and Store, The), 303
strategies
marketing, 315, 317
attention-getting techniques, 308
Business-Builder Marketing Approach, 317-322
confident presentations, 313-314
creating a market, 316-317
keywords, 322-324
off-hours marketing, 316
reaching your target market, 311-313
self-promotion, 316
silent sales partners, 308-311
Web sites, 325-332
word-of-mouth, 316
pricing, 211-213
structures, legal (businesses), 50
corporations, 52-58
partnerships, 51-53, 56-58
sole proprietorships, 50-51

studio tours, 264-265
success tips
   change challenges, 344
      diversification, 345
      expecting change, 344
      hidden opportunities,
         345-346
   comfort zone warnings,
      335-336
   creative thinking, 336-337
      brainstorming, 337-338
      competitive edge, 338-339
      customer service edge,
         339-340
   fads and trends, 341
      colors, 342-343
      differentiation descriptions,
         341-342
      forecasters, 343
      social trends, 342-343
   product life cycles, 343-344
   profit plans, 340-341
supplies
   art and craft show displays,
      244-246
   wholesale buying
      locating sources, 188-191
      minimum orders, 185-186
      shopping trade shows,
         192-193
      suppliers, 186-188
survival tips, arts and craft shows,
   247
   canopies (outdoor shows), 248
   travel safety, 248-249
   vehicle safety, 249-250

T

table covers, art and craft show
   displays, 243
table of contents (business plans),
   63, 69
target markets
   business plan descriptions, 65
   reaching, 311-313
tax havens, 58
taxes
   business deductions, 116, 120
      avoiding restrictions, 117
      business trip meals, 123
      capital expenses, 118
      cost of goods sold, 118
      criteria for deductibility,
         117
      entertainment, 121-122
      equipment, 121

hobby versus business dis-
      tinctions, 116
   home phones, 122-123
   IRS Publication 334, "Tax
      Guide for Small
      Businesses," 116
   keeping records, 124
   membership dues, 122
   personal expenses, 119
   vehicle usage, 120
corporate tax structures, 54-55
home-based businesses, 119
   home-office storage deduc-
      tions, 119-120
   IRS Publication 587,
      "Business Use of Your
      Home," 119
sales
   resale certificates, 114-115
   sales tax numbers, 114-115
   tips, 115-116
tax preparers, 178
technical compatibility, 155
telephone billing systems, 155
tents, 248
Textile Fiber Productions
   Identification Act
   Care Labeling Law, 162
   Content Labeling Law, 162
      requirement inquiries (FTC
         Web pages), 164
   Wool Products Labeling Act,
      162-163
textiles, labeling
   Care Labeling Law, 162
   Content Labeling Law, 162
   Federal Fair Packaging and
      Labeling Act, 161-162
   requirement inquiries (FTC
      Web pages), 164
time
   logging, 214-215
   maximizing, 207-209
toiletries
   organizations, 361
   publications, 362
   suppliers, 363
toys, CPSC's safety guidelines,
   160-161
trade associations, 41, 189-191
trade names, registration, 87-88
trade shows
   gift basket making, 371-372
   shopping tips, 192-193
   wholesale buying, 188
   wholesale marketing, 272-273
trademarks, 91
   books, 357
   criteria, 91

implications in corporate
      name selection, 55-56
   registration, 91-92
   research information, 357
   researching, General
      Information Services, 56
   searches, 91
traditional crafts, 21
traits, entrepreneurial success,
   11-12
   craftspeople, 11
   creative phase, 12
   organizational phase, 12
   planners, 11
   productive phase, 12
   self-assessment, 28
   visionaries, 11
transaction fees, merchant
   accounts, 156
travel safety, 248-249
trends
   colors, 342-343
   current popular culture, 5-6
   forecasters, 343
   identifying and filling needs,
      6-7
   social, 342-343
   versus fads, 341-342
turns (inventory), retail businesses, 294-295

U

U.S. Census Bureau Statistics, 41
"U.S. Industrial Outlook," 41
U.S. Patent and Trademark Office
   Web site, 56
U.S. Small Business
   Administration Web site, 114
unit cost per item, 214-215
   materials logs, 215
   time logs, 214-215
Urlich's Directory of Serials, 41

V

value pricing, 213
variable costs, 216
vehicle
   expenses, tax deductions,
      120-121
   safety, 249-250
venture capital firms, 152
vertical presentation (retail merchandise), 301
visionaries, 11

W

wages. *See* salary
wallets, electronic, 153
wedding gowns, labeling requirement inquiries (FTC Web pages), 164
White House Crafts Collection, 5
wholesale
  buying, 184
    locating sources, 188-191
    ordering catalogs, 184-185
    qualifications, 184
    shopping trade shows, 192-193
    suppliers, 186-188
    supplies, 185-186
  selling, 273-274
    mail tips, 278
    minimum order amounts, 275
    scheduling order shipments, 276
    selling direct, 277-278
    shipping charges, 275-276
    terms, 274-275
    timing, 271-272
    trade show marketing, 272-273
    utilizing sales reps, 276-277
woodworking
  organizations, 383
  suppliers, 383-384
  trade publications, 383
wool products, labeling
  Federal Fair Packaging and Labeling Act, 161-162
  Wool Products Labeling Act, 162-163
Wool Products Labeling Act, 162-163
WordPerfect Office 2000—Small Business Edition, 76
work area
  efficiency, 195-196
  planning, 196-198
    manufacturing tips, 198-200
workers' compensation, 128
World Wide Web. *See* Internet

X–Y

yarn products, labeling
  Care Labeling Law, 162
  Content Labeling Law, 162

Federal Fair Packaging and Labeling Act, 161-162
requirement inquiries (FTC Web pages), 164

Z

zoning laws, home-based businesses, 102
  Certificates of Occupancy, 104
  dealing with local building and zoning officials, 102-104
  obstacles, 104-105

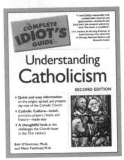

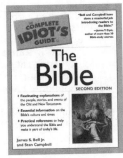

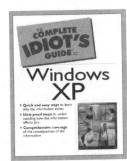